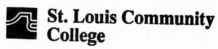

The Blackwell Encyclopedic Dictionary of International Management

About the Editors

Cary L. Cooper is Professor of Organizational Psychology at the Manchester School of Management (UMIST), UK. He has also been appointed Pro-Vice-Chancellor at the University of Manchester Institute of Science and Technology (UMIST). He is the author of over 80 books, has written over 250 scholarly articles and is editor of the *Journal of Organizational Behavior*. He is also the Founding President of the British Academy of Management.

Chris Argyris is James B. Conant Professor of Education and Organizational Behavior at the Graduate School of Business, Harvard University. He has written many books and received numerous awards, including the Irwin Award by the Academy of Management for lifetime contributions to the disciplines of management. Recently, the Chris Argyris Chair in Social Psychology of Organizations has been established at Yale University.

About the Volume Editor

John O'Connell holds the CV Starr Professorship in International Insurance and Risk Management at the American Graduate School of International Management (Thunderbird) in Arizona, USA. In his 25 years as a business professor O'Connell ha presented seminars and has consulted in Asia, Central America, Europe and throughout North America. A frequent contributor at international business meetings, he has also authored more than thirty articles in various academic and trade publications.

The Blackwell
Encyclopedic Dictionary of
International Management

Edited by John O'Connell

American Graduate School of International Management

Copyright© Blackwell Publishers Ltd, 1997
Editorial Organization© John O'Connell, 1997

First published 1997

Blackwell Publishers Inc.
238 Main Street
Cambridge, Massachusetts 02142, USA

Blackwell Publishers Ltd
108 Cowley Road
Oxford OX4 1JF
UK

Library of Congress Cataloging-in-Publication Data

The Blackwell encyclopedic dictionary of international management /
edited by John O'Connell
    p.   cm. – (Encyclopedia of management)
    Includes bibliographical references and index.
    ISBN 1-55786-924-3 (alk. paper)
    1. Industrial management–Dictionaries.   2. International business
    enterprises–Management–Dictionaries.   I. O'Connell, John.
    II. Series.
    HD30.15.B456   1996
    658.5'003—dc20   96-27366
                                          CIP

British Library Cataloguing in Publication Data
CIP catalogue record for this book is available from the British Library.

ISBN 1557869243

Typeset in 9½ on 11pt Ehrhardt by Page Brothers, Norwich
Printed in Great Britain by T. J. Press (Padstow) Ltd

This book is printed on acid-free paper

Contents

—— Preface ——

This book is comprised of practical, hands-on discussions of terms and concepts important to international managers. It provides a concise explanation of concepts and definitions of terms which frequently draw their attention. Each major term or concept is followed by a number of references from current literature to direct the reader to other writings if more in-depth knowledge is required. It is not merely a compilation of definitions, but also an explanation of terms and concepts which will many times include examples and real life applications. It is easy to read and practitioner oriented. You will use this book to discover the real impact of words/ideas used everyday in the realm of international management.

The subject matter of this book was developed by asking the question: "What information does an international manager require to enable him/her to successfully undertake the task of management in various locales and cultures?" In order to answer this question, one had to first determine why organizations sought to do business across borders. Was it merely the profit motive? Was it to increase market share and visibility? Was it to explore new and interesting possibilities for both personal and business growth? The realization that there were a large number of reasons for overseas activity brought about the need to determine what general topics, concepts and concerns were shared by managers regardless of the initial reason for them being involved in international endeavors. A review of literature and extensive interviewing took place to discover items in need of inclusion.

The initial list of major terms and concepts included: managing people, across-border money flows, trade terms and concepts, cultural differences, leadership differences, motivation and control in the international context, marketing, banking, compensation of expatriates, training and a number of other important areas. The list of terms and concepts associated with these topics extended far beyond the capability of a single volume to provide a reasonable review and discussion. The initial listing of specific terms and concepts was reviewed in order to determine which were the most commonly associated with the duties of one managing at the international level. This resulted in a list of approximately 1500 items selected for the current text.

Experts from all areas of international business/management were called upon to enter into more in-depth discussions of a number of topics. The reader will find these explanations throughout the volume. *The Encyclopedic Dictionary of International management* is intended to be a part of the international manager's library, not as a showpiece on the mantel, but as a tool to be used in the ongoing task of globalizing our thinking and understanding. I sincerely hope it lives up to its intention.

John O'Connell

List of Contributors

Max H. Bazerman
Northwestern University

David Bennett
Aston University

R. Ivan Blanco
Barry University, Florida

Norman E. Bowie
University of Minnesota

Michael Brocklehurst
Imperial College, London

Derek F. Channon
Imperial College, London

Jeffrey Cohen
Boston College

James A. Craft
University of Pittsburgh

Thomas G. Cummings
University of Southern California

Dale L. Davison
Thunderbird American Graduate School of International Management

Ismail Erturk
Manchester Business School

Jayne M. Godfrey
University of Melbourne

Llewellyn D. Howell
Thunderbird American Graduate School of International Management

Kent A. Jones
Babson College

Terry L. Leap
Clemson University

Mark E. Mendenhall
University of Tennessee

Michael H. Moffett
Thunderbird American Graduate School of International Management

Allen J. Morrison
Thunderbird American Graduate School of International Management

Nigel Nicholson
London Business School

John O'Connell
Thunderbird American Graduate School of International Management

Laurie Pant
Suffolk University

David A. Ricks
Thunderbird American Graduate School of International Management

David Sharp
University of Western Ontario

Caren Siehl
Thunderbird American Graduate School of International Management

Laura Westra
University of Windsor

David Yorke
Manchester School of Management

A

A/B   *see* AIRBILL

acceptance   It is very common to finance the purchase of imports or exports. This is generally accomplished through the issuance of a bill of exchange or a draft. It is also common for a third party (a bank for example) to guarantee the payment of the bill or draft. When this is done the bank "accepts" or guarantees payment by affixing its name to the front of the draft. The "acceptance" (guaranteed draft) is a negotiable instrument, that is it may be sold or otherwise transferred by the acceptor prior to its maturity date. An acceptance must have the signature or stamp of the acceptor and the date of the acceptance placed on the face of the instrument in order to be valid.

See also **Bill of exchange; Draft**

Bibliography

Johnson, H. (1993). *New global banker: What every U.S. bank must know to compete internationally.* Hinsdale, IL: Probus Publishing Company Inc.

Zodl, J. A. (1992). *Export–Import: Everything you and your company need to know to compete in world markets.* Cincinnati, OH: Betterway Books.

JOHN O'CONNELL

acceptance financing   A method of financing imports and exports through a short-term line of credit. The lending bank may include specific documentation to show evidence of title to the merchandise. The required documentation normally consists of either a warehouse receipt or a bill of lading.

Bibliography

Logue, D. E. (1995). *The WG&L handbook of international finance.* Cincinnati, OH: South-Western Publishing Company.

Zodl, J. A. (1992). *Export–Import: Everything you and your company need to know to compete in world markets.* Cincinnati, OH: Betterway Books.

JOHN O'CONNELL

accountability   The process of making management decision-makers responsible for their decisions. To identify persons making management decisions and developing a measurement standard to determine if decisions were correct. This is especially important in management where face-to-face contact between managers and home office personnel may be infrequent or nonexistent.

JOHN O'CONNELL

accounting differences   The differences that occur between nations with regard to accounting and reporting standards. The differences can be based upon social, cultural, legal, political, and economic factors. Social and cultural conditions can affect the way societies view secrecy, privacy, time, fate, and business, thus having a direct effect on what is reported in accounting statements. Legal requirements can vary widely from government to government, thus, accounting regulations vary as well. Political and economic conditions influence accounting differences the most as they tend to dictate what type of accounting is needed. For example, an unstable economy that is plagued with high inflation will need an accounting system that addresses the issue of inflation. There is a growing trend for harmonization of accounting standards and procedures in the global economy. Organizations such as the International Accounting Standards Committee (ISAAC), and the International Coordination Committee for the Accounting Profession (ICCAP) seek to harmonize accounting standards across borders.

Bibliography

Arpan, J. S. & Al Hashim, D. D. (1984). *International dimensions of accounting.* Boston, MA: Kent Publishing Company Inc.

JOHN O'CONNELL

accounting exposure   The risk of foreign exchange (currency) appreciation or depreciation which may alter the monetary values of accounting entries. Accounting exposure includes both translation risk and transaction risk. As an example, translation risk occurs when a parent organization must produce consolidated balance sheets for their multinational operations. In so doing, the parent company must translate the assets, liabilities, revenues, expenses, and income of their foreign operations into domestic currency terms. Transaction risk, occurs, on the other hand, when an organization is forced to pay for goods and services produced in another country. For example, a US computer manufacturer located in California would be required to pay a Japanese semiconductor manufacturer in Japanese yen, not in US dollars. The transaction, however, will need to be reported in US dollars on the US computer manufacturer's balance sheet. Changes in the value of foreign currency will affect the value of assets (translation) or the amount of foreign currency required to meet foreign obligations (transaction).

See also **Translation exposure**

Bibliography

Eiteman, D. K., Stonehill, A. J. & Moffett, M. H. (1992). *Multinational business finance.* 6th edn, Reading, MA: Addison-Wesley Publishing.

JOHN O'CONNELL

accounting system   *see* ACCOUNTING DIFFERENCES

acculturation   Acculturation is the process one goes through to become as comfortable as possible in another culture. Probably the most common method of acculturation is that of assimilating portions of the new culture to go along with those you already have. This does not involve giving up your own culture, but instead, adding those features of the new culture which allow you to function more effectively. There are also those people who attempt to avoid acculturation by separating themselves as much as possible from the local culture. They associate only with those persons of their own culture. This approach builds walls between cultures and is not suggested as an approach if intercultural understanding and dealings are intended.

Bibliography

Bird, A. & Dunbar, R. (1991). Getting the job done over there: Improving expatriate productivity. *National Productivity Review*, Spring, 145–56.
Mendenhall, M. & Oddou, G. (1985). The dimensions of expatriate acculturation: A review. *Academy of Management Review*, **10** (1), 39–47.

JOHN O'CONNELL

across-the-board tariff reductions   Tariffs may apply to literally hundreds or thousands of products or commodities imported and exported between countries. When countries reach a point in their international trade transactions in which a reduction in trade barriers is agreeable, working to reduce each individual tariff is time consuming and could be quite troublesome because of special interests in individual products. Instead of reviewing each tariff by itself, countries many times agree that it is time for agreements to reduce all tariffs by a specified amount (or in some cases to do away with tariffs for specific classes of goods or commodities). When these "across-the-board" agreements are reached, each country which is signatory to the agreement must abide by the arrangement. Across-the-board tariff reductions are also referred to as linear tariff reductions (inferring that each party moves in the same manner at the same time).

JOHN O'CONNELL

ad valorem duty   Ad valorem duties are taxes which are paid on imported items. The duty is expressed as a percentage amount of the value of goods which clear customs. Thus, if a 5% ad valorem duty was due on $50,000 worth of goods, the duty would amount to $2,500.

See also **Duty**

JOHN O'CONNELL

adaptability screening   The process of determining one's ability to deal with overseas assignments. Screening takes the form of testing (among other skills) the ability to deal with change; handle stress; make decisions without full knowledge; and be at ease in cultures which are entirely different than that of the person being tested. Screening can be an essential part of planning for the success of an expatriate.

Bibliography

Brown, R. (1987). How to choose the best expatriates. *Personnel Management*, June, 67.
Naumann, E. (1993). Organizational predictors of expatriate job satisfaction. *Journal of International Business Studies*, 61–4.

JOHN O'CONNELL

ADB   *see* ASIAN DEVELOPMENT BANK

address commission   *see* CARGO BROKER

admiralty court   A court having jurisdiction over matters covered by maritime law. The court deals with activities and breaches of law on seas or navigable waterways outside of a country's territorial waters. Each country normally assigns admiralty questions to a section of its legal system. For example, Federal District Courts in the United States and the Admiralty Division of the High Court of Justice in England decide admiralty matters.

JOHN O'CONNELL

admiralty law   *see* MARITIME LAW

ADR   *see*   ADVANCED   DETERMINATION RULING

ADR   *see*   ALTERNATIVE   DISPUTE   RESOLUTION

aduana   A Spanish word referring to a tax on goods brought into a country. It refers to a custom's duty.

JOHN O'CONNELL

advance against documents   This is a loan made by a bank or the buyer of goods to the seller of goods. An advance is commonly made on the basis of a sales contract or a bill of lading. This allows money to be obtained by the seller prior to delivery of the goods. The loan is paid back (or deducted from the buyer's amount due) upon delivery of the goods and presentation of proper documentation to allow the release of funds from the letter of credit or other payment instrument.

Bibliography

Zodl, J. A. (1992). *Export–Import: Everything you and your company need to know to compete in world markets*. Cincinnati, OH: Betterway Books.

JOHN O'CONNELL

advance import deposits   A refundable payment made to the appropriate government agency (commonly the central bank) to secure an import license. The deposit is returned to the importer within a short period of time after the import transaction takes place.

JOHN O'CONNELL

advanced determination ruling (ADR) An ADR allows a US company to secure an Internal Revenue Service opinion on pricing structures of goods purchased from foreign subsidiaries. An explanation is necessary to understand why an ADR may be a good idea. A United States company may elect to form a second company in an offshore location to act as a conduit for goods and materials purchased overseas. The reason for this would be to purchase all goods through the second company (which if properly formed will be in a country with much lower corporate income taxes) and then resell the goods to the parent organization. The intent of this arrangement is to allow the subsidiary to charge high prices (and pay low taxes on its profits) while the parent pays high prices for raw materials and deducts the high cost from parent company income. This process of establishing the price of goods is referred to as "transfer pricing." An advanced determination ruling is an application filed with the Internal Revenue Service of the United States to determine if the transfer pricing method used is valid. Many companies choose to undertake a determination before putting prices into affect. If the ruling goes against the company, adjustments must be made. If the ruling is favorable, the pricing structure may be used. Failure to secure a ruling ahead of time may place a company in jeopardy of IRS scrutiny along with fines and other payments associated with such scrutiny.

See also **Reinvoicing; Transfer price**

Bibliography

Grosse, R. & Kujawa, D. (1995). *International business: Theory and managerial applications*. 3rd edn, Boston, MA: Richard D. Irwin Inc.

JOHN O'CONNELL

advised letter of credit When an exporter's bank informs the exporter of the requirements to collect payment on a letter of credit, the exporter is said to be "advised." Thus, the term "advised letter of credit."

See also **Advising bank; Letter of credit**

JOHN O'CONNELL

advising bank Financing imports is more involved than financing the domestic purchase of goods. This is because two or more countries are involved and it is not always possible to use the importer's bank for all transfers of money. To get around some of the problems it has become the custom to use letters of credit (or other similar payment devices) issued by the importer's bank and transferred to the exporter's bank. Once the exporter's bank receives the letter of credit it informs ("advises") the exporter of its receipt and the terms of payment. Thus, the exporter's bank is sometimes referred to as the "advising" bank. In reality, any time a bank informs its customers of the receipt of a letter of credit or other payment document it is an "advising bank."

See also **Advised letter of credit; Issuing bank; Letter of credit**

Bibliography

Johnson, M. (1992). *Cultural guide to doing business in Europe*. 2nd edn, Boston, MA: Butterworth-Heinemann.

JOHN O'CONNELL

advisory capacity When conducting international operations it is not always possible to be in every location in which a signature or delivery or other activity is required. In cases in which a person (the principal) cannot be or elects not to be present, an agent is commonly appointed to represent that person's interests and act on his/her behalf. It is possible for an agent to have various degrees of authority to act on behalf of the principal. Full authority could be granted which allows the agent to change or otherwise abridge the terms of the contract or agreement without notifying the principal. Limited authority or "advisory capacity" gives the agent capacity to act on behalf of the principal but no authority to make or agree to changes without the expressed permission of the principal.

JOHN O'CONNELL

advocacy advertising Advertising which is aimed at supporting social or other causes. It has become very popular (and good business) for business organizations to support environmental causes; humane treatment of animals; human rights; safety; and other causes. Advocacy advertising builds goodwill amongst those members of the public who share the same concerns as the advertiser.

Bibliography

Clark, J. B. (1990). *Marketing today.* Englewood Cliffs, NJ: Prentice-Hall.

JOHN O'CONNELL

aesthetics   A culture's artistic views and attitudes. The views range from brightly colored artwork, dress and design to more muted tones; from primitive to contemporary; and from realism to impressionistic. The art of a culture tells much of that culture's development over time. Aesthetic values and other traditions and customs will help determine the types of clothing acceptable in the workplace, the color of office decor and sometimes even the location of an office.

JOHN O'CONNELL

AFDB   *see* AFRICAN DEVELOPMENT BANK

affective approach, to training   *see* EXPATRIATE TRAINING

affirmative action   This term describes government action intended to eventually equalize employment opportunities for all citizens of a particular country. From time to time this may require the favoring of certain categories of workers over others. In the United States, affirmative action came into effect with passage of the Civil Rights Act in 1964. Affirmative action required employers to favor women and minorities when hiring in order to overcome past decades of discriminatory hiring practices throughout the country.

See also **Equal opportunity; Pay equity**

Bibliography

Hayajneh, A. H., Haile, S. & Cunningham, B. (1994). The challenge of diverse work force in American organizations: Suggested techniques and competitive advantages. *Global Business Perspectives*, 1, 263–9.

JOHN O'CONNELL

affirmative dumping determination Dumping is an international trade term used to describe situations in which a country prices its exports at less than the same goods would be priced if sold domestically. Thus, the country is selling exports for less then it is offering the goods to its own people. The effect of "dumping" is to decrease the sales of domestically produced products in the importing country. Harm caused by dumping includes local companies losing profits or market share. In the United States, if a local company (or the government of the United States) feels that dumping is occurring, a request may be made to the International Trade Commission (ITC) for a ruling. If the ITC makes an "affirmative dumping determination," or in other words agrees that dumping is occurring, duties may be assessed against the importer of the goods. Duties have the effect of increasing the price of the goods on the final market, thereby defeating the attempt to dump goods in the United States.

Bibliography

Viner, J. (1991). *Dumping: A problem in international trade.* Caldwell, NJ: Augustus M. Kelley Publishers.

JOHN O'CONNELL

affreightment   *see*   CONTRACT   OF AFFREIGHTMENT

AFIDA   *see*   AGRICULTURAL   FOREIGN INVESTMENT DISCLOSURE ACT OF 1978

African Development Bank (ADB) A financial institution supported by member countries to promote economic development and trade in the region. The bank has 50 African country members and 25 members from outside the region, all of whom are interested in the further economic development of Africa. Loans are made to develop projects and industry in the area. Since many of the African nations are in the development stage, much of the bank's low interest funding goes to expand the infrastructure of the region (communications, transportation, agricultural base, and provision of utility services among others).

See also **Regional development banks**

Bibliography

Ludlow, N. H. (1988). *A practical guide to the development bank business: How to identify it, market to it, and win it*. Washington, D.C.: Development Bank Associates Inc.

JOHN O'CONNELL

AG Abbreviation for the German corporate form for large enterprises and company groups. The letters AG appear after the name of the corporation. AG stands for Aktiengesellschaft.

JOHN O'CONNELL

against all risks An insurance term describing coverage from all sources of loss except those which are specifically excluded or restricted in the contract. The list of exclusions and/or restrictions is normally much more extensive in land-based insurance contracts (e.g., buildings and personal property) than in marine insurance coverages (e.g., cargo coverage and hull policies). All-risk policies do not normally cover damage from all sources of loss. The term is often misleading to insureds.

JOHN O'CONNELL

Agency for International Development (AID) The Agency for International Development is an agency of the United States State Department. Its major function is to oversee the provision of economic assistance to foreign countries. The AID has ongoing, as well as emergency funding available for projects.

JOHN O'CONNELL

agreement corporation This is a United States term describing an organization which is established to conduct international banking activities. Also formally known as Edge Corporations (after the Edge Act which allowed their formation). An agreement corporation is a US bank branch or subsidiary of a US based corporation that is used mainly for international banking purposes. Agreement corporations have been allowed to operate since 1981 by US banking authorities as an answer to competition by foreign banking centers. These special corporations are exempt from normal banking and anti-trust legislation in regards to pricing and restrictive trade practices. This allows agreement corporations to be more creative and flexible in their activities than regular United States banks.

Bibliography

Johnson, H. (1993). *New global banker: What every U.S. bank must know to compete internationally*. Hinsdale, IL: Probus Publishing Company Inc.

JOHN O'CONNELL

Agreement on Customs Valuation Many imports are charged custom duties based upon the value of the goods imported. Under this system, the most important factor in arriving at the amount of duty, is the valuation placed on the import by a country's customs officials. The Agreement on Customs Valuation (also referred to as the Customs Valuation Code) set forth a standardized system for determining the value of imported goods. Instead of each country having its own system for determining values, the Agreement of Customs Valuation system is used for most of the world's imports. Standardization of this nature was and is the goal of the General Agreement on Tariffs and Trade (GATT). The valuation agreement came about as a result of the Tokyo Round of the GATT negotiations.

See also **General Agreement on Tariffs and Trade**

Bibliography

Simmonds, K. R. Musch, D. J. (eds) (1992). *Law and practice under the GATT and other trading agreements, North American Free Trade Agreements, United States–Canada Free Trade Agreements: Binational panel reviews and reports.* Dobbs Ferry, NY: Oceana Publications Inc.

JOHN O'CONNELL

Agricultural Foreign Investment Disclosure Act of 1978 (AFIDA)   In response to pressures of US agricultural interests, the United States Congress passed AFIDA as a method of determining the exact nature of foreign agricultural holdings in the country. The late 1970s saw an outcry over foreign investment and ownership of what many considered to be sacred US holdings or activities. AFIDA provided a means of keeping track of foreign investment in the agricultural area.

JOHN O'CONNELL

agunaldo (Mexico)   A bonus paid to employees of companies operating in Mexico. This "gift" is normally 2 to 4 weeks pay and is given to the employee during the Christmas holidays. Agunaldo is an example of a custom which impacts the profitability and operation of businesses in foreign countries. International managers must become aware of and honor such practices or face labor unrest in the foreign country and top management unrest in their home office.

JOHN O'CONNELL

AID   *see*   AGENCY   FOR   INTERNATIONAL DEVELOPMENT

air consignment note   *see* AIR WAYBILL

air freight   Cargo shipments made by aircraft. This is the most expensive form of shipment. It is also the most rapid.

JOHN O'CONNELL

air waybill (AWB)   When goods are shipped by air, the details of the shipping agreement are disclosed on what is referred to as an "air waybill." The information on the air waybill includes: the name of the owner of goods, the party to whom the goods are being shipped, the departure and destination points, the specific type of goods being shipped, and the value of the goods.

See also **House air waybill; Master air waybill**

Bibliography

Johnson, T. E. (1994). *Export–Import procedures and documentation.* New York: Amacom.

JOHN O'CONNELL

airbill (A/B)   When an air carrier receives goods for shipment a receipt for goods is provided. That receipt is referred to as an "airbill."

See also **Air waybill**

JOHN O'CONNELL

airport tax   When leaving some countries by air, a person is required to pay what is referred to as an "airport tax" or "departure tax." This fee is generally less than $20. It can be a surprise, however, especially to those travelers who have already converted all of their money to their home currency or spent all of the host country currency in their possession in anticipation of getting on the airplane.

JOHN O'CONNELL

alien   A person who is not a citizen of the country in which he/she lives. A "resident alien" has been given permission by the government of the host country to take up permanent residence. A resident alien is not granted citizenship. An "illegal alien" is a person who has not been given permission by the host government to live there.

JOHN O'CONNELL

alien corporation   In the United States, an alien corporation is one which is formed in a country other than the United States. Thus, a Japanese corporation doing business in the United States would be considered an "alien" corporation by the US. In other parts of the world, a corporation doing business in another country is referred to as a Foreign Corporation. Thus, the Japanese company doing business in a country other than the US would be called a foreign corporation.

See also **Foreign corporation**

JOHN O'CONNELL

alliances   When two or more entities agree to cooperate to achieve a goal or objective. Alliances have been forged between countries to deal with environmental problems, human rights, and other problems. Alliances are also common in the international business arena to promote the goals of cooperating businesses.

See also **Joint venture; Strategic alliance**

Bibliography

Michel, R. (1992). The do's and don'ts of strategic alliance. *Journal of Business Strategy*, 13, 50–3.

JOHN O'CONNELL

allowances   Expatriates often receive, as part of their compensation, additional funds for specific purposes to allow them to live more comfortably or to compensate them for inconveniences. Allowances could include: relocation costs; the expenses of home leave for the expatriate and his/her family; cost-of-living adjustments; educational costs for children; and other costs deemed important by the expatriate

and agreed to by the employer. Allowances can add a great deal to the cost of sending an employee on an overseas assignment.

See also **Compensation package**

Bibliography

Mendenhall, M., Punnett, B. & Ricks, D. (1995). *Global management*. Cambridge, MA: Blackwell Publishers.

JOHN O'CONNELL

all-risk clause   *see* AGAINST ALL RISKS

alongside   Cargo placed so it is capable of being loaded directly upon a ship. Cargo is placed "alongside" when it is on an adjacent dock, barge or other platform from which it may be transferred directly to the ship by the ship's tackle or other means (e.g., land-based cranes). The term is commonly used to assist in determining cargo pricing structure, the duration of responsibility on the part of the shipper, and delivery terms.

See also **Free alongside ship; INCOTERMS**

JOHN O'CONNELL

alternative dispute resolution (ADR)   International organizations often turn to alternative dispute resolution methods rather than attempt to settle disputes with a foreign entity under the laws of another country. Potential problems associated with having to take legal action in another country include: local laws which favor citizens of that country; completely different legal system which is unknown to the foreign company; and the potential for bad public relations associated with a foreign organization taking legal action against a fellow citizen. Alternative dispute resolution methods include arbitration, conciliation, and mediation. These methods are usually quicker and less costly than litigation. ADRs also do not result in decisions which are made public or which place fault. In the United States these benefits of ADRs are especially important. The use of alternative dispute resolution methods is very often included as a binding portion of international contracts (subject, of course, to the particular resolution technique being acceptable in the country in which the contract is drawn).

See also **Arbitration**

Bibliography

Litka, M. (1991). *International dimensions of the legal environment of business.* 2nd edn, Boston, MA: PWS-Kent Publishing Company.

JOHN O'CONNELL

American Accounting Association, International Section   The International Section of the American Accounting Association is comprised of a membership which is interested in making the tasks of accounting for international business transactions a simpler process. Rather than using individual country accounting procedures and standards, the International Section seeks to standardize accounting and auditing procedures on an international basis. Through membership of persons from other countries as well as members from US accounting firms and academics, the International Section is seeking to improve communication and cooperation throughout the world accounting profession.

JOHN O'CONNELL

American depository receipt (ADR)   Foreign companies commonly seek to raise capital in the United States. The registering of their securities with the US Securities and Exchange Commission, however, is a long and detailed process. Instead of trading their securities directly, many foreign firms deposit their securities with a US bank and receive in exchange an American depository receipt (ADR). An ADR is a negotiable instrument which can then be traded as if it were a US issued stock. ADRs still have to be registered with the Securities and Exchange Commission, but the registration process takes far less time than registering foreign securities.

Bibliography

Eiteman, D. K., Stonehill, A. J. & Moffett, M. H. (1992). *Multinational business finance.* 6th edn, Reading, MA: Addison-Wesley Publishing.

JOHN O'CONNELL

American depository share   Similar to an American depository receipt issued by a US bank, except that the "share" is issued by a securities firm.

See also **American depository receipt**

JOHN O'CONNELL

American Plan   When traveling on an "American Plan" all hotel, food and service charges are included in one package price. Generally, American Plan travel provides a meal for the traveler either from a preset menu (from which deviations are not normally allowed) or a buffet-style meal. Meal times are usually set by the hotel and travelers not eating during these time periods may have to pay for their own meal elsewhere. American Plan travel is good for those who seek some regimen and will abide by schedules, but for those seeking flexibility while traveling, American Plans may be too restrictive.

JOHN O'CONNELL

American style option   An agreement which allows the holder to buy or sell currency at a specified price any time prior to the expiration date of the option.

See also **European style option; Options**

JOHN O'CONNELL

AMF   *see* ARAB MONETARY FUND

AMU   *see* ARAB MAHGREB UNION

ANCOM   *see* ANDEAN COMMON MARKET

ANDEAN   *see* ANDEAN COMMON MARKET

Andean Common Market/Andean Pact (ANCOM) An economic agreement was forged in 1969 between several South American countries (Bolivia, Chile, Columbia, Equador, and Venezuela) to assist in reducing trade barriers and fostering the economic development of the members. (Chile dropped out of the pact a few years after its adoption.) The members eventually established the Andean Common Market in which trade restrictions between members have been reduced. The group continues in its efforts to reduce trade barriers, standardize rules regarding trade, and to support the economic development of the region. ANCOM members are also members of the Latin American Integration Association (LAIA), a larger group of countries seeking economic development and free trade in the entire region.

See also **Latin American Integration Association**

JOHN O'CONNELL

Andean Pact   *see* ANDEAN COMMON MARKET

antiboycott regulations It is against United States law for US firms to participate in or give support to boycotts of foreign organizations. It is illegal for United States firms to participate directly or to refuse to deal with firms who do not comply with a boycott.

See also **Boycott**

JOHN O'CONNELL

anti-diversion clause Sometimes the United States government issues restrictions on United States exports to certain countries. When this occurs certain categories of goods are identified as being those most likely to be illegally diverted to the restricted country. The

bills of lading or other transit documents of such products will display official wording that the export license of the exporter is not valid except for specified receivers of the goods. The official wording on the bill of lading or other transit documents is referred to as a destination control statement.

See also **Destination control statement**

Bibliography

Bowker, R. R. (1994). *Report on U.S. trade and investment barriers (1993): Problems of doing business with the U.S.* Chester, PA: Diane Publishing Company.

JOHN O'CONNELL

anti-dumping duty From time to time, products imported into a country have sales prices that are far below the exporter's local market price for such goods. This means the goods are sold for less in other countries than their market price in the exporter's home country. When this occurs production and distribution of similar domestic products of the importing country may be harmed. In order to protect local industry, taxes may be imposed on specific imports to drive their prices up, thereby allowing local industry to compete. This tax is sometimes referred to as an anti-dumping duty.

See also **Dumping; Duty**

Bibliography

Viner, J. (1991). *Dumping: A problem in international trade.* Caldwell, NJ: Augustus M. Kelley Publishers.

JOHN O'CONNELL

anti-dumping law Dumping, or the sale of goods in foreign markets at lower prices than in domestic markets, occurs for a number of reasons. For example, producers of goods in one country may find themselves with excess supply of products which cannot be absorbed into their domestic markets. Producers may attempt to sell these items in overseas markets at lower than they charge in home markets to reduce their inventories. An organization may also "dump" products on a foreign market in an attempt to quickly obtain new or increase an existing market share in a country. Regardless of the reasoning behind the practice of dumping, local competitors in the importing country are harmed by the practice. In response to past cases of dumping, governments of many countries have passed anti-dumping laws as well as becoming signatories to General Agreement on Tariffs and Trade's anti-dumping code. Additional taxes may be assessed on goods suspected of being dumped as well as other sanctions applied to countries participating in dumping activities.

Bibliography

Viner, J. (1991). *Dumping: A problem in international trade*. Caldwell, NJ: Augustus M. Kelley Publishers.

JOHN O'CONNELL

APO *see* ASIAN PRODUCTIVITY ORGANIZATION

appreciation (foreign currency)   Appreciation of currency and the potential profits for those who purchased currency before it increased in value has attracted a large number of investors and speculators who buy and sell various currencies throughout the world. Appreciation describes the increase in the value of a currency relative to other currencies. Increases in value can occur for a number of reasons related to a country's internal economic performance or government activity (for example increasing interest rates, or monetary authority action to increase currency value), or from the poor performance of another country's economy (low interest rates, low demand for the country's currency).

Bibliography

Miletello, F. C. & Davis, H. A. (1994). *Foreign exchange management*. Morristown, NJ: Financial Executives Research Foundation.

JOHN O'CONNELL

appropriate technology   The term used to describe which type of technology is suitable for a country. One of the major concerns of international organizations today is whether or not current technological advances – methods of doing business, up-to-date communications systems, robotics production, and others – can be used in developing nations. The use of advanced technologies requires an infrastructure which many nations do not possess. Also troubling is the cultural impact technological advancement sometimes carries with it. For example, will agribusiness approaches destroy the self-worth of farmers in developing nations leading to problems in the society? Is the appropriate technology for some countries one of a past era? If so, is that older technology still compatible with the technology presently used by multinationals? Answers to questions involving appropriate technology have implications both economically and socially for developing nations as well as the companies introducing the technology.

Bibliography

Dawson, L. M. (1987). Transferring industrial technologies to less developed countries. *Industrial Marketing and Management*, 16, 265–71.
Deans, P. C. & Kane, M. J. (1992). *International dimensions of information systems and technology*. 2nd edn, Boston, MA: PWS-Kent Publishing Company.

JOHN O'CONNELL

Arab Bank for Economic Development in Africa (ABEDA)   This is a regional development bank established by the Arab League to help meet the economic development needs of member countries. Member countries submit development projects to the bank for low cost funding.

Bibliography

Ludlow, N. H. (1988). *A practical guide to the development bank business: How to identify it, market to it, and win it*. Washington, D.C.: Development Bank Associates Inc.

JOHN O'CONNELL

Arab League   The League of Arab States (its official name) was established in 1945 as an association of Arab countries seeking cooperation in defending one another from outside forces and supporting the region's economic and social goals. Arab League membership includes: Algeria, Bahrain, Djibouti, Egypt, Iraq, Jordan, Kuwait, Lebanon, Libya, Mauritania, Morocco, Oman, Palestine, Qatar, Saudi Arabia, Somalia, Sudan, Syria, Tunisia, United Arab Emirates, and Yemen. The Arab League established and still supports the Arab Bank for Economic Development in Africa (ABEDA) and the Arab Monetary Fund (AMF).

See also **Arab Bank for Economic Development in Africa; Arab Monetary Fund**

JOHN O'CONNELL

Arab Mahgreb Union (AMU)   Founded in Marakesh, Morrocco in 1989, the Arab Mahgreb Union (also referred to as the Mahgreb Common Market) was formed to develop standardization of regulations regarding trade amongst its members and to begin to integrate the monetary systems thereby facilitating trade and commerce between member countries. Membership in the AMU includes: Algeria, Libya, Mauritania, Morocco, and Tunisia. The major goal of the AMU was to develop an integrated system of economies in North Africa. A direct result of the AMU was the development of the Mahgreb Economic Community with a scheduled beginning date of 1995.

JOHN O'CONNELL

Arab Monetary Fund (AMF)   Established in 1976 by the Arab League, the AMF provides financing for economic development in the region as well as fostering cooperation amongst its members. The AMF uses the Arab dinar as its unit of account. The Arab dinar is equal to one Special Drawing Right (SDR) of the International Monetary Fund.

See also **Arab League; International Monetary Fund**

JOHN O'CONNELL

arbitrage   Arbitrage is essentially following the old adage "buy low, sell high." Only in the case of arbitrage you buy low in one market and simultaneously sell high in another. For example, currency is traded in a number of markets throughout the world. Although the price of currency trades is generally very similar in all markets, sometimes a situation occurs in which the ask price (willingness to sell) in one market is less than the bid price (willingness to buy) in another market. Successful arbitrage could occur by purchasing in one market and simultaneously selling in the other market. (Technically this is referred to as "two point" or "locational" arbitrage. "Three point" or "triangular" arbitrage occurs where three currencies are traded against one another to arrive at a profit.) Arbitrage also takes place in the trading of other financial instruments or commodities.

Bibliography

Houthakker, H. S. & Williamson, P. J. (1994). *The economics of financial markets.* New York: Oxford University Press Inc.

Kenyon, A. (1990). *Currency risk and business management.* Cambridge, MA: Blackwell Publishers.

JOHN O'CONNELL

arbitrageur   In the world's financial markets there are persons who specialize in profiting from arbitrage transactions. Technically, they are referred to as "arbitrageurs."

See also **Arbitrage**

JOHN O'CONNELL

arbitration   Arbitration is one of the most common methods of alternate dispute resolution. Alternate dispute resolution is a method of settling legal questions without having to file lawsuits or otherwise use the litigation system of any given country. Arbitration is commonly called for in international contracts to avoid the cost and time commitment which is demanded by litigation. Litigation in a foreign country exposes an organization to a legal system which may favor local citizens. The legal system may also be totally unfamiliar to a foreign business-person, thereby placing this person at a distinct disadvantage when compared to local business people who have grown up with the system.

Arbitration involves a hearing before an impartial arbitrator. The arbitrator may be selected by the parties at odds or may have been agreed to in the original contract bringing the parties together. Depending upon the system under which the proceedings are heard, the arbitrator may be allowed to impose a compromise settlement or select between the positions presented by the parties in dispute. Decisions of the arbitrator are confidential and do not set precedent. Thus, a business desiring to settle a dispute in private and quickly would probably desire to use an alternate dispute resolution method such as arbitration. The United Nations convention on Arbitration established a number of rules and procedures which apply to the arbitration of international matters.

Bibliography

Litka, M. (1991). *International dimensions of the legal environment of business.* 2nd edn, Boston, MA: PWS-Kent Publishing Company.

JOHN O'CONNELL

arbitration agreements   An arbitration agreement specifies that if parties to a contract are in conflict, the arbitration process will be used to settle the dispute. Such agreements are common in international business contracts in order to avoid many of the problems associated with litigation. It is important that arbitration agreements specify the exact nature of the process to be used, the number of arbitrators, the country whose rules of arbitration are to be followed, and the language of the proceeding. If details of the arbitration process are not included in the contract then an arbitration organization should be specified. The International Chamber of Commerce has such a facility, as do many individual countries.

See also **Arbitration**

JOHN O'CONNELL

arbitration clause   *see* ARBITRATION AGREE-MENTS

area division structure   *see* GEOGRAPHIC STRUCTURE

arms-length pricing   Arms-length pricing refers to situations in which market forces establish the price of goods (i.e., no special relationship exists between buyer and seller). Thus, an organization purchasing under arms-length pricing would receive the best price negotiable. The price would tend to be similar for all buyers of similar nature. Arms-length concepts become a bit more important when one is dealing with "transfer prices" or "reinvoicing" activities. Transfer pricing or reinvoicing involve the buying and selling of goods between a parent company and its subsidiary. Such transactions many times come under the scrutiny of tax authorities. If other than arms-length pricing is used between parent and subsidiary it could have serious future income tax implications.

See also **Reinvoicing; Transfer price**

Bibliography

Eiteman, D. K., Stonehill, A. J. & Moffett, M. H. (1992). *Multinational business finance.* 6th edn, Reading, MA: Addison-Wesley Publishing.

JOHN O'CONNELL

ASEAN   *see* ASSOCIATION OF SOUTHEAST ASIAN NATIONS

Asia Currency Market   A major world currency market with activity centered in Singapore. The market began in 1968 when Singapore allowed foreign banks to offer dollar-denominated deposits while at the same time becoming active in the Eurocurrency Market. This provided a chance for Asian holders of dollars to keep them in Southeast Asia. The attraction to banks participating in the market was the large amount of dollars being held in the region, Singapore's low bank tax rate, and a regulatory climate which favored foreign branch bank operations. The market is open 24 hours a day with transactions taking place between the market and other markets and financial institutions throughout the world.

Bibliography

Miletello, F. C. & Davis, H. A. (1994). *Foreign exchange management*. Morristown, NJ: Financial Executives Research Foundation.

JOHN O'CONNELL

Asia dollar   This term describes dollar-denominated deposits which are held by Asian banks. Singapore is probably the most common place to find Asia dollar deposits.

See also **Asia Currency Market**

JOHN O'CONNELL

Asia Pacific Federation of Personnel Management Associations (APFPMA)   The Asia Federation is part of the larger World Federation of Personnel Management Associations. This group and the parent organization hold meetings and distribute publications of interest to persons having responsibilities in the area of human resources management. Membership places one in contact with many other parties having similar interests in the Asia/Pacific region.

JOHN O'CONNELL

Asian Development Bank (ADB)   This is one of the five regional development banks (also referred to as multilateral development banks), which are charged with responsibility for carrying out the economic development strategies of the United Nations Development Program (UNDP). The Asian Development Bank has 45 members (14 from outside of the region) and is located in Manila. Like other development banks, the ADB attempts to foster economic growth through funding of industrial, commercial, agricultural, and infrastructure projects of member countries. The Bank is owned by its member governments and is supported by government subscriptions as well as funds raised in international market transactions.

See also **Regional development banks; World Bank**

Bibliography

Ludlow, N. H. (1988). *A practical guide to the development bank business: How to identify it, market to it, and win it*. Washington, D.C.: Development Bank Associates Inc.
Scharf, T. & Shetty, M. C. (1973). *Dictionary of development banking: A compilation of terms in English, French, and German with definitions in English*. New York: Elsevier Science Publishing Co.

JOHN O'CONNELL

Asian Productivity Organization (APO)   This organization specializes in providing technical and managerial assistance to member nations in order to promote increased productivity and economic development of the region. The APO is located in Tokyo and has 14 members. Founded in 1971, the APO is geared toward regional economic development. The APO promotes sharing of management and technical assistance among member states.

JOHN O'CONNELL

assembly operations   A market entry strategy in which an organization sends parts for products to a foreign plant for final assembly. The products are then sold in the foreign market or exported to other countries. Assembly plants may allow a company to take advantage of low cost labor in the most labor intensive portion of production. There may also be lower duties and other taxes because unfinished products are imported instead of finished products. Assembly plants also allow a foreign manufacturer to meet host country requests for more domestic production while at the same time allowing the manufacturer to continue control over production by using its own subproducts as supplies and materials for the foreign assembly plant. A potential problem, especially with plants located to pacify foreign governments needs for domestic production, is that the foreign government may institute requirements on the amount of foreign parts which may be used in the host country. These requirements are referred to as domestic content requirements (DCRs).

See also **Domestic content requirements; Market entry strategies**

JOHN O'CONNELL

assignment (foreign) When an employee of an organization is sent to a country outside of his/her home country. The duration of assignments varies with the tasks the organization requires to be completed. Short-term assignments (less than six months) are probably trouble-shooting or specific task assignments requiring special expertise in an area of operations. Long-term assignments can run as long as five to seven years, whereas a two-to three-year assignment is more common. Regardless of the duration, the person to be sent overseas must be properly trained. The degree and type of training usually depend upon the tasks to be completed. The more complicated the task (thus, probable involvement of other employees) and the longer the duration, the more need for specialized language and cultural training.

See also **Expatriate; Expatriate training**

Bibliography

Mendenhall, M. E., Dunbar, E. & Oddou, Gary (1987). Expatriate selection, training, and career pathing: A review and critique. *Human Resource Management*, **26**, 331–45.

JOHN O'CONNELL

assignment completion Assignment completion occurs either when the expatriate's designated task or project is completed or the time period of the assignment expires. When an expatriate completes an assignment it generally means another move is in order. If the move is back to the home country there is a possibility that the employee and/or family members may suffer from reverse culture shock. The employee

has been out of contact with his/her own country's ways of doing things, current fads, educational changes, political changes, and probably also what has been going on in the company which sent the expatriate overseas in the first place. The expatriate has also probably assimilated much of the host country culture (some of which may not fit into the home country culture). It is extremely important to anticipate the return of an expatriate upon assignment completion (or sooner, considering how often expatriates fail in overseas assignments) and to provide guidance for the employee and any family members who were also overseas. Failure to plan may result in problems for the returnee which could likely hamper his/her continued success with the company.

See also **Assignment; Repatriation; Reverse culture shock**

Bibliography

Harris, J. E. (1989). Moving managers internationally: The care and feeding of expatriates. *Human Resources Planning*, **12**, 49–53.
Howard, C. G. (1991). *"Expatriate managers"* in *Proceedings of the International Academy of: Management and Marketing*. Washington, D.C.: Howard Publication – International Academy of Management.

JOHN O'CONNELL

assignment status The status of an expatriate on an overseas assignment refers to whether the expat's spouse or dependents travel overseas as well. There are really only two classes of status: (1) "Single Status" refers to an employee who is unaccompanied during the assignment. It doesn't matter if the expatriate is married or has children, if he/she goes on assignment alone it is considered single status. Before the days of political correctness, this was sometimes referred to as "bachelor" status. (2) "Married Status" refers to an employee who is accompanied on the assignment by his/her spouse or children. This is sometimes also referred to as "Family status." Assignment status is important because it determines in many companies the amount of compensation and other benefits one receives while on assignment. For example, if an employee had family status, provision for children's education is common; similarly, larger and different types of housing would be available for family status employees.

JOHN O'CONNELL

Association of Southeast Asian Nations (ASEAN)   This association's goals are to promote the economic and political well-being of its member nations. Membership in ASEAN is held by Brunei, Indonesia, Malaysia, the Philippines, Singapore, and Thailand. The original intent of the association was to develop member relationships so that all could act as a unified group, but because of the diversity between its members, the association has never fully attained its goals. The association is still active, however, in attempting to further develop the region.

JOHN O'CONNELL

assumed shelter cost   Shelter cost is the amount of money it takes to secure appropriate housing in a foreign country. "Assumed" shelter cost is an estimated amount which is used to determine the employee's housing allowance while on assignment. The employee is free to secure other housing if desired, but the housing allowance is normally all that is available from the company.

See also **Compensation package**

JOHN O'CONNELL

assured   This is the same as an "insured." This is the person or entity for whom the insurance contract provides coverage. It is extremely important to understand who is insured by a contract or money may be wasted in insuring parties who don't need to be, or coverage overlooked for a person or entity for which insurance was meant to provide coverage. This advice is especially important when securing coverage in foreign countries. Many times the types of coverage or the amounts an insured is used to are not available in all countries.

British insurers many times use the term assured. US insurers normally use the term insured.

JOHN O'CONNELL

assurex   The same as insurance company. British insurers also use this term. US insurers normally use the term insurance company or insurer. Most countries require an insured to purchase insurance locally unless coverage is not available on the local market. It is important to check laws outlining insurance requirements prior to securing coverage. Improperly placed insurance may be illegal and subject to fines or inability to collect insurance proceeds if a loss occurs.

JOHN O'CONNELL

at-post education   There are two definitions for this term: (1) Many families accompany employees sent on overseas assignments. One of the problems associated with taking children abroad is their education. At-post education means that educational facilities are available at the assignment location. Parents must carefully review the educational opportunities which exist at assignment locations to be certain their children are exposed to the appropriate level of educational opportunity. (2) Very few organizations offer an expatriate opportunities for continuing their cross-cultural training once overseas. At-post education is very important and should be offered by more organizations. At-post education allows the employee and family members to try out the new information related to the culture of the host country immediately. Prompt feedback adds greatly to a person's success and allows the expatriate to truly see if the new information actually assists in getting along in the new country. At-post education could also include additional language skills or other areas of interest.

Bibliography

Reynolds, C. (1986). "Compensation of overseas personnel" in *Handbook of Human Resource Administration*. 2nd edn, New York: McGraw-Hill.

JOHN O'CONNELL

ATA carnet ATA stands for Admission Temporaire or temporary admission. An ATA carnet allows certain types of property to be imported into and temporarily held in a country without payment of import duties. Property allowable under the ATA carnet includes product samples, advertising materials, professional equipment (for presentations, etc.) and promotional literature and items. An ATA carnet is valid for a one-year period. If property brought into a country under an ATA carnet is still in the country after a year, it becomes subject to duty payment.

See also **Carnet**

JOHN O'CONNELL

attaché A government official acting as an assistant to an ambassador or minister of a country. Attachés are stationed overseas (usually at embassies) and serve specific functions (e.g., commercial attachés deal with business interests of the home country; military attachés attend to military matters). Attachés can be of great assistance to home commercial interests seeking to expand operations to other countries.

See also **Consul**

JOHN O'CONNELL

autonomous duty Autonomous duties are levied as penalties against persons who attempt to circumvent customs restrictions or quotas. It is also applied to protect domestic industry against an unexpected increase in imports of specific types of products.

See also **Duty**

JOHN O'CONNELL

average This is an ocean marine insurance term describing a partial loss to a ship or its cargo. Depending upon the nature of coverage purchased partial losses may or may not be covered by the ocean marine insurance contract.

See also **General average**

JOHN O'CONNELL

avoidance strategies Avoidance is a risk management strategy which eliminates political risks for companies. Avoidance requires a company to stay out of those countries having political risk exposures which are above an acceptable level. The decision to avoid a country implicitly involves the company's willingness to give up any benefits which would have been derived from entering the country in the first place. Thus, political risk avoidance is essentially a cost/benefit analysis performed as part of the international management process. If a company is willing to give up potential profits, market share, and other benefits associated with operating in a foreign country in order to reduce its political risk position, then avoidance may be in order.

To entirely avoid political risks with respect to a given country, an organization cannot have any transactions or dependency upon any other companies within that same country (for example, raw materials suppliers). Government interference with a supplier could delay delivery of raw materials, increase prices, or make securing of materials impossible. Each government action affects the operations of all other companies which are dependent upon the supply of those raw materials.

See also **Political risk**

Bibliography

Coplin, W. D. & O'Leary, M. K. (1994). *The handbook of country and political risk analysis.* New York: Political Risk Services.
Yaprak, A. & Sheldon, K. T. (1984). Political risk management in multinational firms: An interrogative approach. *Management Decisions,*, 53–67.

JOHN O'CONNELL

away-from-post education Many parts of the world do not have formal educational facilities. If an expatriate is assigned to one of these locations, alternative arrangements to meet the educational needs of that employee's children must be found. One of the alternatives is to arrange for education away from the assignment location. Education facilities may be found in the nearest large city or there is an option of children attending boarding schools in yet another country. Children's education is important. Employers must seek out and inform employees of educational opportunities and alternatives whenever available.

Bibliography

Toyne, B. & Kuhne, R. J. (1983). The management of the international executive compensation and benefits process. *Journal of International Business Studies*, **14** (32), 37–50.

JOHN O'CONNELL

AWB   *see* AIR WAYBILL

B

bachelor status   When an employee goes to an international assignment location without being accompanied by his/her spouse the "status" of the employee is sometimes referred to as "bachelor" status. This may be important to an employee because bachelor status (now, frequently referred to as single status) is normally accompanied by a different set of compensation allowances than those provided to expatriates having family status.

See also **Assignment status**

JOHN O'CONNELL

back translation   When a document or communication is translated into another language, a back translation is often a good idea to assure that the original translation was correct. For example, a British manager was instructed to write a contract for a foreign partner's signature but the contract had to be in Japanese. The manager would normally write the contract in English and then have it translated to Japanese. In order to check on the validity of the initial translation, the Japanese contract should be "back translated" to English before being sent for signature. Problems associated with changed meanings or misinterpretation of intent will be minimized by such actions.

JOHN O'CONNELL

back-to-back letter of credit   A back-to-back letter of credit is a method of financing the export/import transaction. When an exporter requires some payment (to pay the exporter's suppliers, labor costs, etc.) prior to making goods for sale a back-to-back letter of credit may be required. An irrevocable letter of credit from the foreign buyer guarantees payment to the exporter, normally after delivery of the goods. If, however, the exporter causes a second irrevocable letter of credit to be issued in favor of his raw materials supplier (with the original letter acting as collateral) both the exporter and the supplier are guaranteed payment. When delivery of goods is made to the buyer, the bank honors both letters of credit paying off the supplier and remitting the remainder to the exporter. Without such financing, many export transactions would be impossible to complete.

See also **Letter of credit**

Bibliography

Johnson, T. E. (1994). *Export–Import procedures and documentation.* New York: Amacom.
Zodl, J. A. (1992). *Export–Import: Everything you and your company need to know to compete in world markets.* Cincinnati, OH: Betterway Books.

JOHN O'CONNELL

back-to-back loan   A back-to-back loan involves two parties in two different countries cooperating to reduce their overall cost of loans. In many instances, domestic borrowers receive favorable treatment over foreign borrowers with respect to interest rates. This is because local financial institutions generally have more knowledge of domestic companies than foreign companies and feel the risks are lower. A back-to-back loan takes advantage of each country's favoritism toward its domestic industries. For example, Company A and B are located in different countries. Company A's home currency is Yen and company B's home currency is the dollar. Both need to acquire the home currency of the other to conduct their international operations in each other's country. This is a situation in which a "back-to-back loan" may be beneficial to both companies. Company A can borrow its own currency (Yen) at home for a 7% annual rate and can borrow the foreign currency (dollar) at 8%. Company B can borrow its home currency (dollar) at 6% annual rate and the foreign currency (Yen) at 8% annually. If Company A borrows Yen at 7% and company B borrows dollars at 6% and then loan the funds to each other, both companies end up paying the lowest rates available. Company A pays 6% for dollars (instead of the 7% it was able to arrange itself) and Company B pays 7% for Yen (instead of the 8% it was able to arrange itself). This is an example of a successful back-to-back loan.

This sounds very simple and mathematically it is. The problem arises in finding other organizations who are willing to conduct such transactions. Many times back-to-back loans are arranged between parent companies and subsidiaries in order to assure (virtually) no added risk of loan repayment.

Bibliography

Logue, D. E. (ed) (1995). *The WG&L handbook of international finance.* Cincinnati, OH: South-Western Publishing Company.

JOHN O'CONNELL

balance sheet approach   When considering a compensation package for an expatriate, human resources managers often use a "balance sheet approach." This approach first ascertains the employee's current position with respect to income, benefits, taxes and other compensation and expenses (that is, a balance sheet of income and expenses is constructed). The current situation is then compared with the income, expenses, and taxes associated with the assignment location. Lower costs are credited and higher costs debited in an effort to make the compensation package for the home country and the host country relatively equal. That is, it may take more money or less in the host country to equal to the employee's current

standard of living. The balance sheet approach provides a reasonable method of determining if imbalances exist.

Bibliography

Pinney, D. L. (1982). Structuring an expatriate tax reimbursement program. *Personnel Administrator*, **27**, 19–25.
Reynolds, C. (1986). "Compensation of overseas personnel" in *Handbook of Human Resource Administration.* 2nd edn, New York: McGraw-Hill.

JOHN O'CONNELL

band   This term has two general meanings when viewed from an international standpoint: (1) When managing foreign exchange rates, it is the magnitude of change which is allowed before intervening measures are taken. (2) When viewing the Bank of England's measures to manage currency, the term "band" refers to the maturity dates of bills of exchange acquired by the bank. The higher the number of the "band" the longer the maturity date.

Editor's note: When reviewing the definition of any term it is very important to determine the context in which it is used. Context from an international standpoint includes the country in which the term is used or the nationality of the person communicating. The term "band" is a good example of contextual meanings.

JOHN O'CONNELL

Bank for International Settlements (BIS)
The BIS was founded in 1930 by an agreement signed by representatives from Belgium, France, Germany, Italy, and the United Kingdom. The purpose of the bank was to coordinate the activities of the central banks of the most highly industrialized nations.

The International Monetary Fund uses the bank to transfer its funds to other institutions. In addition to the original members, Canada, Japan, and the United States have become associated with the BIS.

Bibliography

Humphreys, N. K. (1993). *Historical dictionary of the International Monetary Fund.* Lanhau, Maryland: Scarecrow Press Inc.

JOHN O'CONNELL

Bank of Central African States (BCAS)
The BCAS was formed in 1955 by agreement between a number of central African nations. In its position as the central bank for members of the Central African Economic Community, the bank is the sole issuing body of currency and coins used by member countries. Member countries include: Cameroon, Central African Republic, Chad, Congo, and Gabon.

JOHN O'CONNELL

banker's acceptance Banker's acceptance is when a bank guarantees the payment of a bill of exchange or draft. It is very common to finance the purchase of imports or exports. This is generally accomplished through the issuance of a bill of exchange or a draft. It is also common for a third party (a bank for example) to guarantee the payment of the bill or draft. When this is done the bank "accepts" or guarantees payment by affixing its name to the front of the draft. The "acceptance" or "banker's acceptance" (guaranteed draft) is a negotiable instrument, that is it may be sold or otherwise transferred by the acceptor prior to its maturity date. An acceptance must have the signature or stamp of the acceptor and the date of the acceptance placed on the face of the instrument in order to be valid.

See also **Bill of exchange; Draft**

Bibliography

Eiteman, D. K., Stonehill, A. J. & Moffett, M. H. (1992). *Multinational business finance.* 6th edn, Reading, MA: Addison-Wesley Publishing.
Zodl, J. A. (1992). *Export–Import: Everything you and your company need to know to compete in world markets.* Cincinnati, OH: Betterway Books.

JOHN O'CONNELL

bareboat charter The chartering (renting/leasing) of a vessel in which the person or organization chartering the vessel pays a charter fee and all other costs of operating and maintaining the ship during the period of the charter. A bareboat charter can be used as a method of purchasing a ship under what is essentially a lease/purchase contract. If the intent of the vessel owner is to eventually transfer ownership of the vessel to the charterer, the rental/lease fee is sufficiently high that when the charter period is over, the vessel has been paid for.

JOHN O'CONNELL

bargaining The practice of negotiating the price of goods with shop owners. Generally this custom is carried out in small retail stores and is quite common in many countries. The intent of bargaining is to obtain a lower purchase price than is offered by the seller. Many shops in Mexico and India accept bargaining as a way of life. Be careful, however, because not all store owners may accept bargaining even if the practice is common in their country.

JOHN O'CONNELL

barriers Barriers are limitations on free trade which are usually imposed by governments. Barriers may also take the form of consumer demands or the nature of the economic development of a particular country. The nature of the barrier and its impact on a particular importer or exporter must be considered when selecting countries in which to conduct business operations. The following is a list of common types of barriers to free trade or other international business activities. The list is not exhaustive but does provide a feel for the types of barriers which exist.

1 Buy local campaigns – Many governments or other interest groups within a country attempt to use the patriotic feelings of consumers to encourage them to buy local items instead of imports. In some cases, rebates or tax incentives may be offered for local products which are not available to imports. Buy local campaigns by unions or

others have been very successful in increasing the demand for domestically-produced goods.

2 Custom's requirements – Time delays for custom's inspections, detailed paperwork, strict adherence to detailed standards for foreign products, quarantine requirements for certain goods or property, slow administrative processing, and other problems discourage exporters and importers. Delays and other requirements also add cost to the trade transaction, which is probably the most significant barrier to trade.

3 Discriminatory taxation – Foreign products may be taxed at higher rates than domestic products. The effect is to drive the price of imports higher than those of local products.

4 Domestic content requirements (DCR) – One method of increasing the domestic presence of foreign manufacturers is to require that goods produced in a country have a certain percentage of their value provided domestically. For example, assume a country or common market required at least 60% of the value of autos sold within its borders to be produced locally. Manufacturers would have to prove that for every $20,000 auto, local labor and locally produced parts made up at least $12,000 of that value. DCRs effectively prohibit a foreign auto manufacturer from establishing an assembly facility in another country and then importing all of the parts to construct an auto.

5 Duties – Taxes assessed against the value or numbers of products being imported into a country. (A duty could also apply to exports in some cases.) A duty raises the selling price of the products in the host country. Higher prices means fewer buyers and protection for local industry which may produce the same or similar products. There are a number of types of duties which may be used to achieve different outcomes.

6 Export quotas – Restrictions on the amount of specific goods which may be exported are common. If a country believes a specific product should remain in the domestic market (energy resources, for example) quotas on export may be established.

7 Infrastructure limitations – Lack of financial, transportation, or communication facilities is a barrier to modern trade activities. Although insufficient infrastructure levels are probably not a result of a government determined to discourage trade, insufficient infrastructure development may make efficient foreign operations impossible.

8 Import quotas – Restrictions on the amount of specific goods which can be imported into a country. In order to protect local industry government may institute controls to limit the numbers or values of goods imported. This allows local industry to develop and compete with imported items.

9 Labor laws – Labor laws which provide for large payments to employees upon dismissal or make it difficult to dismiss employees are also a barrier to the entry of a foreign company. Strict labor laws generally favor the employee and increase the costs to the employer.

10 Licensing requirements – In order to conduct import/export activities an import/export license must be secured from the appropriate governmental authority. Some countries make the task of securing a license quite simple while others have more arduous procedures to follow. Any additional paperwork, and regulations for special permits for special products or countries of origin, makes trade more difficult.

11 Local ownership requirements – These require a foreign company to be partially owned by local interests (many times a controlling interest of more than 50%). It discourages many investors because of the loss of control over the company's operations.

12 Past political risks – Prior government expropriation or confiscation of foreign company assets acts to increase the risk for investors thereby forming a barrier to their entering local markets.

13 Staffing restrictions – Foreign organizations may be required to limit the number of non-host country employees. The inability to bring expatriates into a country may affect the ability to properly manage a firm or to achieve the necessary level of skills to effectively operate the organization.

Barriers to free trade or other international business activity must be taken into consideration before the decision is made to enter a particular country. Barriers are not only those produced by government but also by unions, consumers, and the general level of economic development of a country.

See also **Duty**

Bibliography

Ashegian, P. & Ebrahimi, B. (1990). *International business.* Philadelphia, PA: HarperCollins.

Ball, D. A. & McCulloch, Jr., W. H. (1990). *International business: Introduction and essentials.* Homewood, IL: Irwin.

Bowker, R. R. (1994). *Report on U.S. trade and investment barriers (1993): Problems of doing business with the U.S.* Chester, PA: Diane Publishing Company.

Buchholz, R. A. (1991). Corporate responsibility and the good society: From economics to ecology. *Business Horizons*, **34**, 19–31.

Czinkota, M. R., Rivoli, P. & Ronkainen, I. A. (1989). *International business.* Chicago, IL: The Dryden Press.

Korth, C. (1985). *Barriers to international business.* Englewood Cliffs, NJ: Prentice-Hall.

Vernon, R. & Well, L. T. (1981). *Economic environment of international business.* 3rd edn, Englewood Cliffs, NJ: Prentice-Hall.

JOHN O'CONNELL

barter Bartering or the exchange of goods for other goods or services (instead of money) has been taking place for centuries in all parts of the world. Many believe that bartering is a process which takes place between local merchants and their customers. However, today's world of international trade has taken bartering from a simple transaction to an intricate method of arranging the transfer of goods from one multi-national company to another or between governments without full payment being made with currency. Barter agreements can overcome problems associated with currency inconvertibility as well as short-term deficiencies in a company's cash account.

See also **Countertrade**

JOHN O'CONNELL

base currency This is the currency in which a currency exchange rate is quoted. For example, if the US dollar is trading at 0.56 British pounds, the British pound is the base currency.

JOHN O'CONNELL

base salary An expatriate's base salary is the comparable salary for the same work and position as would be paid in the expatriate's home country. Adjustments are made to the base salary for expenses, inconveniences, and hardships encountered in the host country.

See also **Compensation package**

JOHN O'CONNELL

base workweek The "base workweek" is the number of days and hours an employee is expected to work in any given week. People who have worked in only one country many times do not realize the differences in what is expected of employees in different countries. A six-day workweek is common in many nations. The 40-hour workweek during five days is accepted in the United States (where four 9–10 hour days are also common, depending upon the employer). Many companies in Japan still adhere to an extremely long workday and workweek. It is very important that an expatriate manager be informed of local workweek customs in order to more effectively schedule his/her time as well as that of employees.

Bibliography

Howard, C. G. (1982). How best to integrate expatriate managers into the domestic organization. *Personnel Administrator*, July, 27–33.

JOHN O'CONNELL

basket of currencies A group of currencies used as the basis for valuing a single monetary unit. Groups of countries in many parts of the world are cooperating to promote their mutual economic interests. In some cases this results in the harmonizing and/or centralizing of monetary transactions between the countries. A standardized monetary unit is essential in order to achieve true economic integration. One of the problems associated with a centralized monetary system is: "Which of the countries' currency should be used as the standard for the group?" In order to avoid problems associated with nationalist sentiment toward one currency or another, some country groups have opted to develop a new currency unit. For example, the European Community developed the European Currency Unit or ECU. The ECU is valued by combining the weighted average of each member country's existing currency value. The member's currencies are referred to as a "basket of currencies." The basket of currencies which establish the value of the ECU is comprised of the national currency of each European Community member.

JOHN O'CONNELL

benchmarking This has become a highly fashionable "buzzword" in business, especially in the areas of operations management and strategic management. It denotes the identification of best practice in another organizational unit, followed by its analysis and adoption. An early example of the method being taken to an extreme was the Xerox Corporation's fightback against surgent Japanese competition in the copier market, where a wide range of business and operational processes were improved as a result of systematic benchmarking (for a case study report of the Xerox experience, *see* Jick, 1993). The car industry also contains numerous examples.

From an organizational behavior perspective it can be seen as a substitute for innovation, practised by "Analyzer" companies (*see* STRATEGIC TYPES) who seek to minimize first mover risks whilst reaping the benefits of excellence and competitiveness. Companies can benchmark their own best practice as well as that of others, and increasingly do so in the "soft" areas of human resources management through the use of employee attitude surveys and the like.

Usually, companies benchmark the practices of their best performing competitors, though commentators have pointed out the dangers of this, since bad practice or conservatism may predominate in a sector. It is said that

companies should benchmark *activities* not other companies, and may accrue the benefits of benchmarking most dramatically where the focus is on organizations quite dissimilar to themselves in type. This is more likely to lead to adoption and diffusion of new forms in a business (*see* INNOVATION ADOPTION; INNOVATION DIFFUSION), though inevitably raises issues of whether benchmarked practices are transferable and implementable. Other recommendations for effective benchmarking are that it should be creatively applied, rather than an exercise in mere imitation, and that it should be a continuous monitored activity, rather than a one-off effort at improvement (*see* CONTINUOUS IMPROVEMENT).

Bibliography

Jick, T. D. (1993). Managing change: Concepts and cases. Homewood, IL: Irwin..

NIGEL NICHOLSON

beneficiary A beneficiary is a party who receives the proceeds of an agreement to pay a stated sum. In international trade the agreement may be a letter of credit, a bill of exchange, or draft. In these trade documents the beneficiary is commonly an exporter waiting to be paid in return for delivery of goods. In insurance transactions the agreement is probably an insurance policy which states a beneficiary (as in a life insurance policy). In most life insurance policies the beneficiary can be almost anyone or anything (as allowed by law) listed by the policy owner.

JOHN O'CONNELL

benefit allowance An employee may receive additional payments from the employer with which to purchase insurance or other types of benefits. Expatriates also receive such payment although the benefits purchased may be different from those normally purchased in the home country. For example, education expenses for private schooling for children may seem appropriate benefit overseas, but left unfunded by the employer while in the home country.

See also **Compensation package**

JOHN O'CONNELL

Berne Convention for the Protection of Literary and Artistic Works (1886)   The Berne Convention is one of the oldest agreements dealing with copyright protection. Under the Berne Convention member countries offer each other the same protections as they would provide for their own citizen's copyrights. This is referred to as "national treatment." Copyrights protected by this agreement include those for the written word, music, and visual arts. Copyrights are afforded protection for the life of the author plus fifty years. Although the United States is not a signatory to the Berne Convention, US copyright laws also allow protection for the author's life plus fifty years.

Bibliography

Schultz, J. S. & Windsor, S. (1994). *International intellectual property protection for computer software: A research guide and annotated bibliography.* Littleton, CO: Fred B. Rothman & Company.
Seminsky, M. & Bryer, L. G. (eds) (1994). *The new role of intellectual property in commercial transactions.* New York: John Wiley & Sons.

JOHN O'CONNELL

Berne Union   *see* WORLD INTELLECTUAL PROPERTY ORGANIZATION

bid price   The bid price is what a buyer of a security is willing to pay. If there are parties willing to sell at that rate the bid price becomes the purchase price.

JOHN O'CONNELL

bilateral tax agreement   When two countries agree (for example, the United States and Great Britain) on a system to deal with a specific tax problem or question the agreement is referred to as a "bilateral tax agreement." For example, when employees are sent overseas they are generally subject to the income taxation laws of both the home and the host country. In an attempt to settle problems associated with double taxation, nations often enter into agreements outlining the procedures for handling taxation of income earned by a citizen of a foreign nation.

Bibliography

Mendenhall, M., Punnett, B. & Ricks, D. (1995). *Global management.* Cambridge, MA: Blackwell Publishers.
Reynolds, C. (1986). "Compensation of overseas personnel" in *Handbook of Human Resource Administration.* 2nd edn, New York: McGraw-Hill.

JOHN O'CONNELL

bilateral trade   Any interchange of goods or services between two nations is referred to as bilateral trade. Bilateral trade is normally controlled by agreements between the two countries. However, if both countries are also members of other associations of countries (EC, NAFTA, etc.) trade between the two would be governed by the association rules as well.

JOHN O'CONNELL

bilateral treaty   A treaty which has been officially accepted by the governments of two countries. The treaty binds only the signatories to the agreement. Cooperative treaties related to trade, movement of people, military concerns, and many other areas, are in effect between countries throughout the world.

JOHN O'CONNELL

bill of entry   A written statement specifying the type of goods being shipped and their values. The shipper of the goods is responsible for the provision of this statement. Many countries require the filing of a bill of entry prior to allowing goods to clear customs.

JOHN O'CONNELL

bill of exchange   Documents which instruct a specific party (usually a bank) to pay their holder a certain amount of money upon their presentation. A bill of exchange is a common method of providing for payment in international trade transactions. The bill of exchange may also specify that other documents be present (e.g., bill of lading) in order to complete payment. In the United States a bill of exchange is referred to as a "draft."

Bibliography

Grosse, R. & Kujawa, D. (1995). *International business: Theory and managerial applications*. 3rd edn, Boston, MA: Richard D. Irwin Inc.

JOHN O'CONNELL

bill of lading   A transportation document which provides the following: evidence that a contract has been entered into to transport goods; a statement establishing title to goods being shipped; and a receipt for the carriage of goods. A bill of lading is usually a negotiable document. This means that title to goods being shipped may be transferred during shipment. Title is transferred by assigning the bill of lading to another party. There are a number of different kinds of bills of lading. The following lists those encountered the most often.

1 Air waybill (AWB) – The name given to a bill of lading when goods are shipped by air. The bill provides details of the shipping agreement. The information on the air waybill includes: the name of the owner of goods, the party to whom the goods are being shipped, the departure and destination points, the specific type of goods being shipped, and the value of the goods.
2 Clean bill of lading – A bill of lading issued by a carrier for goods which were received in good condition. A clean bill of lading provides proof that up until the time goods were transferred to the carrier, no damage had occurred. This assists in placing responsibility if in fact goods are eventually delivered in other than undamaged condition.
3 Combined transport bill of lading – A combined transport bill of lading allows

goods to be shipped over more than one method of transportation (ship, rail, truck) without the need for separate bills of lading.
4 Dirty bill of lading – When goods are received in damaged condition for shipment on a vessel, the master of the ship will note the damage on the bill of lading. A bill of lading with such a notation is referred to as a "dirty" bill of lading. If goods were received in good condition the bill of lading would be a clean bill of lading.
5 Foul bill of lading – A bill of lading for goods which were received by the carrier in damaged condition. A notation on the bill indicates the existence of damage.
6 Inland bill of lading – The name given to a bill of lading when goods are shipped over land by truck or rail. Many times several bills will have to be prepared when goods are transported by different types of carriers (inland, ocean, etc.).
7 Negotiable bill of lading – A negotiable bill of lading allows transfer of ownership of goods while the goods are in transit. The holder of the bill must then pay for the goods upon arrival at the final destination as well as provide all other documentation specified in the bill of lading.
8 Ocean bill of lading – A bill of lading used when goods are consigned to an international transportation company for shipment to a foreign country. The ocean bill provides details of the shipping transaction as well as of the goods, buyers, sellers, etc.
9 On-board bill of lading – When cargo is placed on board a ship for transportation, an on-board bill of lading is given to the exporter when the ship leaves port. The bill provides a list of goods loaded by the carrier. An on-board bill is used as proof of shipment and is many times part of the documentation required for the exporter to be paid.
10 On-deck bill of lading – When cargo is placed on the deck of a ship for delivery, an on-deck bill of lading is given to the exporter when the ship leaves port. The bill provides a list of goods loaded on the deck of the ship. An on-deck bill is used as proof of shipment and is many times part of the documentation required for the exporter to be paid. On-deck transit is more

dangerous than if cargo is carried in the hold of a ship. Insurance and financing for such transit may be more difficult to obtain or may be more costly.

11 Order bill of lading – This type of bill of lading is a negotiable instrument. That is, it may be used to transfer title to goods being shipped to another party. The transfer may occur at any time during the transit process simply by conveying the order bill to another party. This form of bill of lading was previously referred to as a "uniform bill of lading."

12 Straight bill of lading – This type of bill of lading is a nonnegotiable (meaning that it cannot be used to automatically transfer title to goods by simply transferring the bill to another party) instrument used to establish the details of shipment of goods. The bill specifies the party to whom the goods are to be delivered as well as other information. Presentation of the bill will release cargo to the holder.

13 Through bill of lading – When shipment of cargo must stop at a port enroute special documents are necessary to avoid duties and other costs. A through bill of lading is used to designate cargo which is passing through a port to its final destination.

14 Uniform bill of lading – A bill of lading which meets the requirements of the United States Federal Bill of Lading Act of 1915.

See also **House air waybill; Master air waybill**

Bibliography

Ashegian, P. & Ebrahimi, B. (1990). *International business.* Philadelphia, PA: HarperCollins.

Ball, D. A. & McCulloch, Jr., W. H. (1990). *International business: Introduction and essentials.* Homewood, IL: Irwin.

Czinkota, M. R., Rivoli, P. & Ronkainen, I. A. (1989). *International business.* Chicago, IL: The Dryden Press.

Daniels, J. D. & Radebaugh, L. E. (1994). *International business: Environments and operations.* 7th edn, Reading, MA: Addison-Wesley Publishing.

Johnson, T. E. (1994). *Export–Import procedures and documentation.* New York: Amacom.

United States Customs Service (1994). *A basic guide to importing.* Lincolnwood, IL: NTC Publishing Group.

Zodl, J. A. (1992). *Export–Import: Everything you and your company need to know to compete in world markets.* Cincinnati, OH: Betterway Books.

JOHN O'CONNELL

birdyback An informal term describing containerized cargo shipped by air.

JOHN O'CONNELL

BIS *see* BANK FOR INTERNATIONAL SETTLEMENTS

black market A black market is a market in which illegal goods and services are bought and sold. If a person wants to buy or sell a good or service which is barred or made illegal by the government the transaction would take place in an illegal or "black" market. Black market sales of goods occurs quite often in countries suffering shortages of goods or where government action restricts the types or sources of goods which can be sold domestically. If a demand exists for such goods, a black market will probably develop. Black market transactions are generally discouraged by governments, which institute criminal sanctions against those who buy or sell black market goods or services.

See also **Gray market**

JOHN O'CONNELL

black money Black money is money obtained through illegal means. Black money is normally subject to confiscation under the laws of most nations. Many countries also make assets purchased with illegally obtained money (homes, cars, real estate, etc.) also subject to confiscation. A common example of black money is funds generated from illegal activities of international crime syndicates.

See also **Dirty money**

JOHN O'CONNELL

bloc   *see* TRADING BLOC

blocked account   A blocked account is an account in a financial institution from which funds cannot be withdrawn without the permission of appropriate governmental authorities. Accounts may be blocked by law enforcement departments in cases of illegal activity by the account holder; by governments in cases of war or political problems with other countries, (the US blocked – "froze" – the accounts of Iraq after Iraq's invasion of Kuwait in the early 1990s); or by the courts as a source of funds to settle disputes or in cases of bankruptcy of the account holder.

JOHN O'CONNELL

blocked currency   The government of a country "blocks" a currency by restricting its flow out of the country. Currency flow may be restricted for a number of reasons. Some reasons are: to assure at least some of the profits from foreign ventures remain in the country; to reduce the drain of hard currencies from the country; or to punish another country by restricting the rights of its citizens or industries from having local operations. Blocking may apply to all transfers of a currency or selectively (e.g., for a certain percentage of a foreign company's local profits or dividend payments).

JOHN O'CONNELL

body language   One of the types of communication which must be mastered by international managers is that of body language. Body language is nonverbal communication, which in some cultures "speaks much more loudly than words." Body language includes: eye movements, expressions, gestures, folding of arms, head movements, tone of voice (not what is said, but how), and other motions or movements made by a person. Few western managers know that the culture of Japan teaches that one should bow their head out of humility or as a sign of respect. Lack of eye-to-eye contact is sometimes interpreted by westerners as a sign of hiding something or disrespect. Training in nonverbal communication is extremely important for managers who deal with people from other cultures or employees who may become expatriates for a company.

See also **Cross-cultural training**

Bibliography

Kuroda, Y. & Suzuki, T. (1991). A comparative analysis of the Arab culture: Arabic, English, and Japanese language and values. *International Association of Middle Eastern Studies*,

Landis, D. & Brislin, R. (1983). *Handbook on intercultural training*. New York: Pergamon Press.

JOHN O'CONNELL

bonded storage   Bonded storage is used for the temporary storage of goods. While goods are stored in bonded warehouse facilities, duties and other taxes are not normally payable. When the merchandise is released from the warehouse, taxes are due. Imported goods may be temporarily stored in such facilities while packaging takes place or while awaiting payment of import duties. Bonded storage is also used for the warehousing of items which must age or cure prior to being sold (alcoholic beverages for example). Some alcoholic beverages may remain in storage for years in the aging process. Taxes payable (which many times make up a large part of the sales price) are deferred until goods are released from the bonded warehouse.

JOHN O'CONNELL

bonded warehouse   *see* BONDED STORAGE

bonus system   A bonus system involves a payment by a government to domestic producers of goods to encourage the increased production of those goods. The General Agreement of Trade and Tariffs (GATT) forbids governments from subsidizing products to make their prices lower than foreign competitors. Such subsidies are referred to as illegal bounties. A bonus system is very similar to an illegal bounty in that the government offers home producers incentives (lower taxes, etc.) to produce more goods. A bonus payment is legal if used to offset increased local production costs due to high-cost raw materials which must be imported to make the product. In reality any bonus gives local producers an advantage because local products can be sold at lower prices thereby discouraging the importation of goods.

JOHN O'CONNELL

bounty One of the ways a government can build its export markets is to subsidize local producers to allow the offering of exports at a lower cost than competitor countries. Subsidies can take many forms (outright grants or payments; tax holidays, etc.) but regardless of the form, such payments are treated as "bounties" and are an illegal part of international trade. Although developing countries may find some exemptions to illegal bounty regulations (in order to speed the development process), other nations are forbidden from making such payments under the General Agreement on Tariffs and Trade (GATT).

See also **General Agreement on Tariffs and Trade**

Bibliography

Simmonds, K. R. & Musch, D. J. (eds) (1992). *Law and practice under the GATT and other trading agreements, North American Free Trade Agreements, United States–Canada Free Trade Agreements: Binational panel reviews and reports.* Dobbs Ferry, NY: Oceana Publications Inc.

JOHN O'CONNELL

boycott A boycott is a concerted effort to reduce purchases of particular products. Boycotts may also apply to purchases from specific manufacturers, or all purchases from a specific country. Boycotts have been implemented by one country against another because of human rights violations, environmental concerns, or for many other reasons. Boycotts have been implemented by special interest groups against manufacturers because the labeling or name of the product was interpreted as being against a religious belief; because the company was from another country; even because a product logo or trademark was thought by some to represent a satanic symbol. Whatever the reason, a well organized boycott of a product or country's goods can have a devastating impact on sales. Efforts should be made to determine if the wording, symbols used, or references in advertising or packaging have any special cultural meaning. Failure to identify people, causes, or cultures who might be offended by one's product, its packaging, or advertising materials may lead to a totally unexpected boycott of goods.

Bibliography

Cateora, P. R. (1993). *International marketing.* 5th edn, Homewood, IL: Irwin.

JOHN O'CONNELL

brand extension Using the name of a well-known parent company or a successful product line to introduce additional products. Brand extension is normally a good marketing plan. However, in international business it could lead to unexpected results. An organization cannot take for granted that its name and advertising programs will be as effective in foreign countries as they are at home. Differences in the meaning of words or symbols could be fatal for an organization. In order to combat potential problems some organizations actually change the name of their international products or companies to mask the fact that they are "American" or "French" in areas where public acceptance of the home country is poor. Before adding to a product line through brand extension it is best to research questions related to negative feelings associated with a type of product, its design or name. As long as the company name, advertising, packaging, etc. are not viewed in a negative manner, brand extension is an effective method of introducing new products.

Bibliography

Buzzell, R. D., Quelch, J. A. & Bartlett, C. A. (1995). *Global marketing management: Cases and readings.* Reading, MA: Addison-Wesley.

Kaynak, E. & Ghauri, P. N. (eds). (1994). *Euro-marketing: Effective strategies for international trade and export*. Binghamton, NY: Haworth Press Inc.

JOHN O'CONNELL

brand piracy This is the unauthorized and therefore illegal use of a brand name or product which has trademark, patent, or copyright protection. It is a form of property right theft which is common in many countries of the world. "Rolex" watches may be purchased in many parts of Southeast Asia for $29.95 or in New York City for $50.00. Louis Vuitton handbags are sold in many parts of the world for 10% of their cost in Louis Vuitton stores. Of course these watches and handbags are copies of the original with pirated brand names and designs. Copies of original designs using well-known brand names are often referred to as knock-offs. Knock-offs of well-known brands of watches, clothing, handbags, and other products account for billions of dollars in lost revenues each year for the legal producers of the products. International producers of items subject to brand pirating must carefully research protections provided by countries in which they trade.

See also **Intellectual property**

Bibliography

Cateora, P. R. (1993). *International marketing*. 5th edn, Homewood, IL: Irwin.
International Intellectual Property Alliance Staff (1992). *Copyright piracy in Latin America: Trade losses due to piracy and the adequacy of copyright protection in 16 Central and South American countries*. Washington, D.C.: International Intellectual Property Alliance.

JOHN O'CONNELL

break-bulk When cargo is of insufficient size to fill a container it is broken into smaller lots (boxes, drums, etc.) and then placed in the ship's hold. This is referred to as a break-bulk shipment. Break-bulk shipments are common when shipping small amounts of goods overseas.

JOHN O'CONNELL

Bretton Woods Conference This 1944 conference was one of the most important ever held with respect to international monetary history. The conference established the gold standard for currency valuation. Although the linking of gold to currency values was notable, that standard was abolished at another conference in Washington D.C. in 1971 (now referred to as the Smithsonian Agreement after the location of the conference). The important and lasting achievement of the Bretton Woods Conference was the establishing of the International Monetary Fund and the International Bank for Reconstruction and Development (the World Bank) which exist today to foster international trade and development. Bretton Woods was the beginning and even though all of its ideas were not to survive, the conference did bring nations together to plan for freedom of trade and economic development on a worldwide scale.

See also **International Monetary Fund; World Bank**

Bibliography

Humphreys, N. K. (1993). *Historical dictionary of the International Monetary Fund*. Lanhau, Maryland: Scarecrow Press Inc.
Salda, A. C. (1992). *The International Monetary Fund: A selected bibliography*. New Brunswick, NJ: Transaction Publishers.

JOHN O'CONNELL

bribery The seeking to influence a decision (most commonly of a public official) through the giving of favors, gifts, or money directly to the official or to others on his/her behalf. Bribery of a public official is illegal in virtually all countries. Both the official and the person presenting the bribe are subject to criminal action if found guilty of the act. A problem exists, however, as to what the exact nature of bribery is and when (if ever) it is legal to make payments to officials or others to obtain preferential treatment. Some countries have attempted to outline legal versus illegal activities in their antibribery legislation (*see* FOREIGN CORRUPT PRACTICES ACT for the United States' approach). Generally, if a payment or gift is given in order to influence the decision of a public official, the payment is a bribe and is illegal.

Bribery or questionable payments are known by many names throughout the world. The following is a partial list of terms used in various languages. Note that the terms used below are not all illegal activities in their home country:

Language	term	meaning
Arabic:	baksheesh	"gratuity"
French:	pot-de-vin	"jug of wine"
	or pourboire	"tip"
German:	nutzliche abgabe	"useful contribution"
	or Schmiergeld	"grease money"
Italian:	bustarella	"little envelope"
	or baccone	"little bite"
Japanese:	kuroi kiri	"black mist"
Persian:	bakshish	"tip"
Spanish:	el soborno	"payoff"
	or la Mordida	"the bite" (Mexico)
Yiddish:	schmir	"smear" or "grease"

English: Bribery, pay offs, payola, lure, bait, compensation, lubrication, grease payments, and others.

Bibliography

Bowie, N. E. (1990). "Business ethics and cultural relativism" in P. Madsen and J. M. Shafritz (eds) *Essentials of Business Ethics.* New York: Meridian.

Coye, R. (1986). Individual values and business ethics. *Journal of Business Ethics,* **5** (1), 45–9.

D'Andrale, K. (1985). Bribery. *Journal of Business Ethics,* **4,** 239–48.

Johnson, H. L. (1985). Bribery in international markets: Diagnosis, clarification, and remedy. *Journal of Business Ethics,* May, 447–55.

Lane, W. H. & Simpson, D. G. (1984). Bribery in international business: Whose problem is it?. *Journal of Business Ethics,* February, 35–42.

Tong, H. (1982). What American business managers should know and do about international bribery. *Baylor Business Studies,* November, 7–18.

JOHN O'CONNELL

British Export Credits Department   A government department charged with the responsibility for encouraging the export of British goods. The department provides money for export financing for such goods. Without the provision of export financing many exporters would have to sell goods on a cash before delivery basis in order to avoid credit risks. This method of selling usually decreases the demand for goods from importers who want the goods in their possession before payment is made. An alternative for an exporter is to sell goods in small lots in order to decrease the credit risk. Again this is not the most efficient method of selling or transporting goods. Local financing of export sales is necessary and is contributed to in Great Britain by the British Exports Credits Department.

JOHN O'CONNELL

broker   A person acting on behalf of another in order to carry out a transaction. Many times buyers and/or sellers are unable to carry out certain transactions themselves. When this occurs it is common to hire a broker to act as a representative. Brokers are experts in the transactions in which their assistance is required and can save a great deal of time and effort for their clients. Brokers may act on behalf of buyers, sellers, or may even buy for their own account (take ownership themselves) hoping to profit from resale at a later time. Brokers acting for their own account are also referred to as market makers or dealers.

JOHN O'CONNELL

buffer stock   A country's "own" supply of a commodity. When a country's supply of a commodity is too high the price for that commodity decreases. If forced to place all of the commodity on the market, the country's farmers, etc., would suffer because of lower world prices. International commodity agreements recognize this problem by allowing countries to purchase excess commodities and place them in a reserve (buffer stock) until prices increase to allow a profit on these goods. The international community carefully monitors buffer stocks to assure that government purchase is not used as an illegal subsidy instead of being used only to stabilize the market when demand is low and supply of commodities is high.

JOHN O'CONNELL

built-in export department   One of the methods of handling international trade activities is to form a department within the company to deal with exports. This allows personnel to begin to become familiar with international transactions and to better control the flow of goods, as well as to internalize this function.

JOHN O'CONNELL

bulk cargo   Cargo which does not lend itself to containerization or storage in boxes or drums is referred to as bulk cargo. Bulk cargo is usually loaded into or onto the ship in raw form. Such cargo usually consists of grain, coal, unrefined ore, raw timber, and similar commodities. Containerization of such cargo would dramatically increase the shipping cost, with little or no resulting benefit to either the exporter or the importer.

JOHN O'CONNELL

bulk carrier   A specially designed ship to carry bulk cargoes. Cargo such as coal and grain are loaded by means of conveyer belts, shoots lowered from grain elevators, or other mechanical means. It is possible to section off a ship in order to carry more than one type of bulk cargo (e.g., different grades of fuel oil).

JOHN O'CONNELL

Bureau of Export Administration (BXA/ BEA)   A United States Department of Commerce agency with responsibility for carrying out the country's export policy. The agency also issues export licenses and keeps track of businesses and individuals who have violated US export rules.

JOHN O'CONNELL

business visitor visa   *see* COMMERCIAL VISA; VISA

bustarella   An Italian term for bribery which means "little envelope."

See also **Bribery**

JOHN O'CONNELL

buy national   Government or private promotion to encourage citizens to buy products manufactured locally. Many times union groups or other special interest groups will embark on advertising campaigns suggesting that it is the patriotic duty of citizens to buy local products instead of imported items. Such campaigns are aimed at the protection of a country's jobs and industries from outside competition. In some cases manufacturers and governments may offer rebates, discounts, or other incentives to purchase local goods instead of imports.

JOHN O'CONNELL

buy-back agreements   An agreement between an importer of capital goods and the exporter of those goods to accept payment in the form of the finished product of the importer. For example, a machine manufacturer sells machinery to a textile company in another country. The machinery manufacturer agrees to accept payment for the machines in the form of finished textile goods produced by the buyer. The textile goods are then disposed of by the machine manufacturer. This is a form of countertrade.

See also **Countertrade**

Bibliography

Zodl, J. A. (1992). *Export–Import: Everything you and your company need to know to compete in world markets.* Cincinnati, OH: Betterway Books.

JOHN O'CONNELL

buying agent   When a company does not have employees stationed overseas to purchase goods, a buying agent may be employed to represent the company. Buying agents know the foreign market for goods and how to negotiate in foreign markets. They can be of great assistance in completing foreign transactions. The authority of the agent should be carefully spelled out in the contract between the agent and the company to make certain the company's interests are appropriately represented.

JOHN O'CONNELL

C

cable rates Occasionally, foreign exchange transactions are made by cable transfer. When this occurs the transfer is instantaneous. The rate a bank charges for this type of transaction is slightly higher than the normal rate because the money merely passes through the bank rather than being held for any period of time.

JOHN O'CONNELL

CACM *see* CENTRAL AMERICAN COMMON MARKET

CAD *see* CASH AGAINST DOCUMENTS

camp status Employees are many times assigned to overseas locations which provide a very different standard of living than they are used to. In those places where common amenities are unavailable (grocery stores, electricity, communications, etc.) companies may actually provide employees with a camp or compound in which to live. The compound not only provides for the basic (and sometimes not so basic) needs of employees, but also offers an additional degree of security if necessary.

JOHN O'CONNELL

Canadian International Development Agency (CIDA) A Canadian government agency with responsibility for assisting Canadian

organizations to enter less developed country markets. Grants, loans, technical assistance, and investment assistance is provided by the agency.

JOHN O'CONNELL

CAP *see* COMMON AGRICULTURAL POLICY

capital movements code An agreement between members of the Organization for Economic Cooperation and Development (OECD) in which they agreed to refrain from restricting the flow of direct investment capital between member countries. Although in specific instances signatories to the agreement can impose limited restrictions on foreign investment for specific industries deemed susceptible to foreign takeover, direct investment normally remains unhampered.

JOHN O'CONNELL

capitalism An economic system which, for the most part, allows the market system to determine production and pricing of goods and services, allows private ownership of property and means of production, and free entry into most markets. Individual initiative is promoted and rewarded. During the late 1980s many countries have moved from communist, government-controlled economies toward capitalism and free markets. The move has been slow and sometimes difficult but as time passes more and more governments are leaning toward privatizing many activities and promoting individual/group private ventures.

JOHN O'CONNELL

captive insurance company An insurance company formed for the specific purpose of insuring its owners. In the 1970s captive insurance companies became popular as a means for large organizations to guarantee themselves a market for necessary insurance while at the same time gaining some degree of control over the operations of the insurer itself. Early in the captive movement it was possible to deduct from one's business income taxes the premiums paid to a captive. However, changes in tax law severely limited an organization's ability to deduct premiums paid to a captive except for those actually used to pay losses and other insurer expenses or to purchase reinsurance. The use of captives, however, continued to grow mainly because of the failure of the insurance market to offer consistent coverage at reasonable rates.

Bibliography

Rejda, G. E. (1995). *Principles of risk management and insurance*. 5th edn, New York: HarperCollins.

JOHN O'CONNELL

cargo broker A person who acts as a middleman between cargo owners and shipowners. By locating ships for hire, the cargo broker earns a commission. The commission is also referred to as an "address commission." Cargo brokers play an important role in international trade, especially when one considers the inexperience of many cargo owners in terms of transporting goods overseas.

JOHN O'CONNELL

cargo insurance Insurance covering goods being shipped by sea. Although it is possible to specify sources of loss which are covered it is far more common to issue such insurance on an "all-risk" basis (i.e., all sources of loss are covered unless they are specifically excluded or

restricted). Common exclusions include war, delay in shipment, negligent packing, wear and tear, and others. An infrequent shipper of goods may purchase a marine policy for a single shipment, whereas a frequent shipper of goods would probably benefit from an "open cargo" policy. The open cargo policy allows shipments throughout the policy period (commonly one year), with automatic coverage being applied to each shipment. The shipper normally pays a deposit premium at the beginning of the year (based upon an estimate of insured amounts being shipped) and then settles with the insurer for the actual additional or return premium at the end of the policy period.

JOHN O'CONNELL

Caribbean Common Market *see* CARIBBEAN ECONOMIC COMMUNITY

Caribbean Development Bank (CDB) This development bank was begun in 1969 by Caribbean nations seeking to further the economic development of the area. Like other development banks, the CDB concentrates on projects to build infrastructure and increase agricultural production. Member countries include those located in the Caribbean as well as others interested in promoting the economic development of Caribbean nations. Members include: Antigua, the Bahamas, Barbados, Belize, the British Virgin Islands, Canada, the Cayman Islands, Colombia, Dominica, Grenada, Guyana, Jamaica, Montserrat, St. Kitts, Trinidad and Tobago, the Turks and Caicos Islands, the United Kingdom, and Venezuela.

Bibliography

Ludlow, N. H. (1988). *A practical guide to the development bank business: How to identify it, market to it, and win it*. Washington, D.C.: Development Bank Associates Inc.

JOHN O'CONNELL

Caribbean Economic Community (CARICOM) The Caribbean Economic Community was founded in 1973 to promote the economic development of its member nations. Along with economic development, CARICOM is committed to establishing true free trade amongst members as well as forming a monetary union by the year 2000. Members have common import duties aimed at developing local industry and agricultural pursuits. Members of the Caribbean Economic Community are the English-speaking countries of the Caribbean: Antigua, the Bahamas, Barbuda, Barbados, Belize, Dominica, Grenada, Guyana, Jamaica, Montserrat, St. Kitts and Nevis, St. Lucia, St. Vincent, the Grenadines, and Trinidad and Tobago.

Bibliography

Winham, G. R. (1992). *The evolution of international trade agreements.* Toronto, Ontario: University of Toronto Press.

JOHN O'CONNELL

CARICOM *see* CARIBBEAN COMMON MARKET; CARIBBEAN ECONOMIC COMMUNITY

carnet When goods enter a country all duties and taxes must normally be paid. There are, however, situations in which duties do not have to be paid. One such situation exists when goods are brought into a country to serve as sales samples, for professional purposes, or if the goods are on the way to another country. In these situations, temporary entry to the country is usually under the "carnet" system. A carnet is a set of vouchers issued by International Chambers of Commerce or other business associations which are accepted by customs officials as proof that the goods are not for resale in the country. Carnets are usually good for one year. If the goods have not been transported out of the country by that time, duties will be payable. There are three major types of carnets:

1 ATA carnet – ATA stands for Admission Temporaire or temporary admission. An ATA carnet allows certain types of property to be imported into and temporarily held in a country without payment of import duties. Property allowable under the ATA carnet includes product samples, advertising materials, professional equipment (for presenta-

tions, etc.), and promotional literature and items. An ATA carnet is valid for a one-year period. If property brought into a country under an ATA carnet is still in the country after a year, it becomes subject to duty payment.

2 ECS carnet – This is a very specific use of carnet. ECS stands for Echantillon Carnet Sample. The ECS carnet is used specifically for trade samples or other commercial samples (not imports, just samples). Under the ECS carnet literally all entry requirements are nullified. Thus no duties are payable on commercial or sales samples. The ECS carnet is usually good for up to one year.

3 TIR carnet – TIR refers to the French words, Transport International Routier, which translates into International Road Transport. This type of carnet is used for goods which are passing through a country on the way to another country. As long as the goods are not unloaded and reloaded in the country the carnet allows goods to pass without customs duties or customs inspection (of course when the goods reach the final country destination all customs inspections and duties for the final country apply).

Bibliography

Johnson, T. E. (1994). *Export–Import procedures and documentation.* New York: Amacom.
Zodl, J. A. (1992). *Export–Import: Everything you and your company need to know to compete in world markets.* Cincinnati, OH: Betterway Books.

JOHN O'CONNELL

carriage and insurance paid to (CIP) Under this trading term the seller is responsible for the cost of inland freight in the export country; the cost of loading the vessel; the cost of ocean or air freight; and securing and paying for export insurance. The buyer is responsible for unloading the vessel; import duties and costs; and inland freight in the buyer's country. Title to goods and risk passes from the seller to the buyer when the goods reach the first carrier. The seller is responsible for securing the export license and the buyer the import license.

Bibliography

International Chamber of Commerce (ICC) (1990). *Incoterms 1990*. New York, NY: ICC Publishing Corp.

JOHN O'CONNELL

carriage paid to (CPT)   Under this trading term the seller is obligated to pay the transportation charges of the goods to a specified location. All responsibilities for the goods (loss, damage, and possible cost increases) is transferred to the buyer when they reach the first carrier. Under this term the seller is responsible for any inland freight charges in the export country; loading of the vessel; and the cost of ocean or air freight. The buyer is then responsible for export insurance; unloading the vessel; import duties and costs; and any inland freight costs in the buyer's country. Title to the goods passes upon delivery to the first carrier (if several carriers are involved). The seller is responsible for securing the export license and the buyer the import license.

Bibliography

International Chamber of Commerce (ICC) (1990). *Incoterms 1990*. New York, NY: ICC Publishing Corp.

JOHN O'CONNELL

carrier's lien   The right of the provider of transportation to attach or hold the property being shipped as collateral until such time the transportation costs are paid. The holding of property may be the best recourse a carrier has to assure prompt payment of transportation costs.

JOHN O'CONNELL

cartel   When individuals, organizations, or countries form a group in order to regulate the supply and therefore the price of a commodity, the group is referred to as a "cartel." Although cartels are illegal in some countries, international business has produced a number of cartels. Probably the most notable cartel is the Organi-

zation of Petroleum Exporting Countries (OPEC). OPEC has been in the news for years because of its attempts to restrict production of oil among member countries, thereby supporting the world price. OPEC members include: Algeria, Gabon, Indonesia, Iran, Iraq, Kuwait, Libya, Nigeria, Qatar, Saudi Arabia, the United Arab Emirates, and Venezuela.

Bibliography

Czinkota, M. R., Rivoli, P. & Ronkainen, I. A. (1989). *International business*. Chicago, IL: The Dryden Press.

JOHN O'CONNELL

cash against documents (CAD)   A buyer pays cash to an intermediary (e.g., a commission house) in exchange for title documents (e.g., bill of lading) to goods. Title is transferred to the buyer through the exchange of cash for documents.

JOHN O'CONNELL

cash before delivery   *see* CASH IN ADVANCE

cash in advance (CIA)   This payment term requires the buyer to provide payment prior to the shipment of goods. CIA is usually used for small purchases, special orders, or when a product has been modified for the buyer. CIA terms are used sparingly because the buyer of goods generally wants to have delivery (to himself/herself or a designated place) before paying for goods.

JOHN O'CONNELL

cash management   One of the most important tasks of international finance associated with a multinational enterprise (MNE) is cash management. Cash management is essentially knowing what the cash needs are throughout the MNE; what the sources of cash are (parent and subsidiary operations, investment returns, borrowing, etc.), how to effectively access cash when needed, and how to most effectively use available cash when not needed in company operations. One of the problems with multinational operations is that delays or restrictions are often encountered when attempting to move cash out of certain countries. Also the cost of moving cash between countries will normally involve fees and/or expenses not encountered with domestic cash movements. One of the challenges of international cash management is to get cash to where it is needed, when it is needed, with the fewest movements (therefore, the lowest transfer costs).

See also **Coordination center; Multilateral netting**

Bibliography

Celi, L. J. & Rutizer, B. (1991). *Global cash management.* 1st edn, New York: Harper Business (HarperCollins).

Eiteman, D. K., Stonehill, A. J. & Moffett, M. H. (1992). *Multinational business finance.* 6th edn, Reading, MA: Addison-Wesley Publishing.

Kuhlmann, A. R., Mathis, F. J. & Mills, J. (1991). *First steps in treasury management: Prime cash.* 2nd edn, Toronto, Canada: Treasury Management Association of Canada.

JOHN O'CONNELL

cash with order (CWO)   A payment term which specifies that the purchaser of goods must pay in full when the order is placed. This term is used when purchasers have shown themselves to be less than credit worthy, for purchasers unknown to the seller, and for goods which are made to order for a buyer.

JOHN O'CONNELL

CBD   *see* cash before delivery

CCC   *see* COMMODITY CREDIT CORPORATION

CDB   *see* CARIBBEAN DEVELOPMENT BANK

Center for International Briefing   A training center in Great Britain which is one of the few places in the world known for its training of executives and their families in cross-cultural education. The center is also known as Farnham Castle.

JOHN O'CONNELL

Central American Common Market (CACM)   The CACM was created in 1960 to foster economic development and cooperation between member nations. CACM manages the Central American Clearing House which handles central bank transactions of member countries. Member countries are: Costa Rica, El Salvador, Guatemala, and Nicaragua. It is the intent of member nations that the CACM be the first step to a true trade area to be known as the Economic and Social Community of Central America.

Bibliography

Winham, G. R. (1992). *The evolution of international trade agreements.* Toronto, Ontario: University of Toronto Press.

JOHN O'CONNELL

Central American Development Bank of Economic Integration (BCEI)   The central bank of the Central American Common Market. Common market members include: Costa Rica, El Salvador, Guatemala, Honduras, and Nicaragua.

Bibliography

Ludlow, N. H. (1988). *A practical guide to the development bank business: How to identify it, market to it, and win it.* Washington, D.C.: Development Bank Associates Inc.

JOHN O'CONNELL

centralized management   A company that holds all decision-making authority and control processes in the hands of a few managers in the home office is considered to have a highly centralized management system. When authority and control is transferred to others in the company, the company is said to be "decentralizing" its management. One of the major issues for multinational business operations is the degree of home office control which is exerted over foreign operations.

Before determining the degree of centralized control a number of questions must be answered by the parent company. A brief review of those questions follow. In their book *Global Management*, authors Mendenhall, Punnett, and Ricks discuss seven areas which must be reviewed when considering the degree of centralization of a multinational organization:

1 Type of industry – If the industry of the parent company and the subsidiary can achieve economies of scale through standardization of product or process or if the product produced or service provided must be standardized to assure uniformity and consistency, moves toward centralization are normally called for.

2 Nature of the subsidiary – Can the subsidiary be adapted to the methods used by the parent or do local production requirements and/or regulations dictate that the process must be different? If the subsidiary is a manufacturer of products which are the same as those produced by the parent, centralization success is enhanced.

3 Functional areas – Functional areas of an organization (finance, accounting, etc.) are rather simple to centralize as long as the information required by the host countries is capable of being produced by the central functional area. If not, even functional areas may have to be decentralized.

4 Parent company philosophy – This refers to the basic corporate feelings concerning centralization of control. Some organizations believe strongly that controls must be centralized whereas others approach management of subsidiaries with a *laissez faire* attitude. Truly global firms tend to be centralized, whereas multidomestic firms tend to be decentralized.

5 Parent company confidence in subsidiary's management – The more competent the management of the subsidiary, the less likely a parent company will decide to centralize operations. However, if the parent lacks confidence or has little knowledge of subsidiary manager's abilities, the tendency would be toward centralization.

6 Cultural similarity – Using cultural similarity alone one could make a case both for and against centralization of control. If, for example, the parent and the subsidiary are similar, top management may determine that the subsidiary could function alone because it will be run in the same manner as the parent. Conversely, similarity of cultures may also lead to centralization because there is likely to be more acceptance of parent company control because management at all levels has similar values and attitudes about how to run a business.

The same dichotomy exists if cultures are very different. For example, very different cultures may make some parent company management fearful that the subsidiary will be managed in an inferior manner. This would lead to centralized control. A different parent company facing the same scenario could elect to decentralize because the cultural differences are too great to be managed externally.

7 Firm-specific advantages – The strengths of the parent company and the subsidiary must be reviewed to determine whether individual areas of management should be centralized, while others are decentralized. If research and development is the major strength of the parent company, that function will most likely be centralized. If local promotion and advertising is a strength of the subsidiary, that function may remain decentralized.

The seven factors mentioned by Mendenhall, Punnett, and Ricks are certainly not exhaustive (other factors could include: local regulation, proximity to final markets, or demands of providers of raw materials or national interests of the host country) but they do point out the importance of making a centralization decision only after considerable time is taken to determine what is best for each subsidiary. The common reason "Because that's how we've always done it" is not viable in the international setting.

Bibliography

Adler, N. J. (1991). *International dimensions of organizational behavior*. 2nd edn, Belmont, CA: Wadsworth Inc.

Austin, J. E. (1990). *Managing in developing countries: Strategic analysis and operating techniques.* New York: Free Press.

Daniels, J. D., Pitts, R. A. & Tretter, M. J. (1985). Organizing for dual strategies of product diversity and international expansion. *Strategic Management Journal,* 6, 223–37.

Herbert, T. T. (1984). Strategy and multinational organization structure: An interorganizational relationships perspective. *Academy of Management Review,* **19** (2), 259–71.

Higgins, J. M. & Vincze, J. W. (1993). *Strategic management and organizational policy.* New York: CBS College Publishing.

Hodgetts, R. H. & Luthans, F. (1994). *International management.* 2nd edn, New York: McGraw-Hill Inc.

Mendenhall, M., Punnett, B. & Ricks, D. (1995).. *Global management.* Cambridge, MA: Blackwell Publishers.

Rosenzweig, P. M. & Singh, J. V. (1991). Organizational environments and the multinational enterprise. *The Academy of Management Review,* 16, 340–61.

JOHN O'CONNELL

certificate of health   When exporting goods which are meant for human consumption or for use in medical care of humans, all countries require that certification of the product's purity be provided. The certification document is generally required to be certified by appropriate officials of the exporting country. The intent of health certification is to reduce the chances of importing contaminated goods which may cause disease or introduce pests into a country.

Bibliography

Johnson, T. E. (1994). *Export–Import procedures and documentation.* New York: Amacom.

United States Customs Service (1994). *A basic guide to importing.* Lincolnwood, IL: NTC Publishing Group.

JOHN O'CONNELL

certificate of inspection   This trade document certifies that goods were in good condition immediately prior to shipment. This document provides the seller with proof that undamaged goods were delivered for shipment. It can then be inferred that any damage was caused during the shipping process. Pinpointing the portion of transit in which damage occurred may play an important part in determining responsibility for damage and potential insurance payments.

Bibliography

Johnson, T. E. (1994). *Export–Import procedures and documentation.* New York: Amacom.

United States Customs Service (1994). *A basic guide to importing.* Lincolnwood, IL: NTC Publishing Group.

JOHN O'CONNELL

certificate of manufacturing   This document is given by the manufacturer to a bank or some other party which has issued a letter of credit. It certifies that the manufacturing process has been completed and the goods are ready for the buyer. The certificate allows the seller to be paid. The certificate is also known as a manufacturing certificate.

Bibliography

Johnson, T. E. (1994). *Export–Import procedures and documentation.* New York: Amacom.

United States Customs Service (1994). *A basic guide to importing.* Lincolnwood, IL: NTC Publishing Group.

JOHN O'CONNELL

certificate of origin   Some countries impose tariffs on certain goods from certain countries. In order to determine which imported goods are subject to tariffs, a country may require a document certifying the country of origin of the goods. The certificate allows a country to properly assess applicable tariffs or to release goods in a shorter period of time if no duties are payable.

Bibliography

Johnson, T. E. (1994). *Export–Import procedures and documentation.* New York: Amacom.

United States Customs Service (1994). *A basic guide to importing.* Lincolnwood, IL: NTC Publishing Group.

JOHN O'CONNELL

CFR   *see* COST AND FREIGHT

CHAPS   *see* CLEARING HOUSE AUTOMATED PAYMENT SYSTEM

CHIPS   *see* CLEARING HOUSE INTERBANK PAYMENT SYSTEM

CIA   *see* CASH IN ADVANCE

CIF   *see* COST, INSURANCE AND FREIGHT

CIP   *see* CARRIAGE AND INSURANCE PAID TO

circular letter of credit   A circular letter of credit is also referred to as a "traveler's letter of credit" or "traveler's credit." This document is used to provide payments to a person who will be traveling in a foreign country. The person holding the letter of credit presents it to a bank specified in the letter and is able to withdraw funds up to the limit established by the letter.

See also **Letter of credit**

JOHN O'CONNELL

civil law   This system of law depends upon a written body of laws to determine the outcome of legal disputes. Unlike common law, which relies upon past decisions, civil law is linked to the codes and statutes in force in a particular country. This means that as one moves from country to country (assuming all have civil law systems) the legal interpretation of an action or a contract will vary. When organizations seek to become multinational, they should also seek expert assistance in reviewing the various codes and statutes which demand their compliance. Civil law systems exist in most of Europe, Latin America, some African countries, and Japan.

See also   **Common law system; Legal system**

Bibliography

Litka, M. (1991). *International dimensions of the legal environment of business.* 2nd edn, Boston, MA: PWS-Kent Publishing Company.

JOHN O'CONNELL

clean bill of lading   A bill of lading issued by a carrier for goods which were received in good condition. A clean bill of lading provides proof that up until the time goods were transferred to the carrier, no damage had occurred. This assists in placing responsibility if in fact goods are eventually delivered in other than undamaged condition.

JOHN O'CONNELL

clean collection   When only a financial document needs to be presented to a bank in order to make payment to the exporter this is referred to as a "clean collection." Although the term clean collection was replaced by the term "clean remittance" by the International Chamber of Commerce, many people still use the old term, "clean collection."

JOHN O'CONNELL

clean remittance   An alternate term for clean collection.

See also **Clean collection**

JOHN O'CONNELL

clearing account barter   This is an agreement under which two companies (each in different countries) contract with one another to exchange their goods over a period of time. Actually, a type of countertrade.

See also **Compensatory trade**

JOHN O'CONNELL

clearing house automated payment system (CHAPS)   The Chaps system is responsible for processing interbank transactions involving accounts denominated in British pounds sterling. Both domestic and foreign banks are serviced through the system, which is located in London.

JOHN O'CONNELL

clearing house interbank payment system (CHIPS)   The CHIPS system is responsible for processing hundreds of billions of dollars of international transactions each day. CHIPS is a US-based clearing-house for processing Eurocurrency, foreign exchange, and other interbank transactions involving dollar-denominated accounts. The clearing house is operated by the New York Clearing House Association and clears accounts of both US Banks and branches or subsidiaries of foreign banks with dollar-denominated accounts.

JOHN O'CONNELL

closed economy   This type of economy attempts to require that all economic transactions be carried out within a given country. Such systems have long been associated with communist countries, but are becoming fewer and far less important with the passage of time. Even those countries espousing stringent support for communistic forms of government are moving toward internationalization of their economies by increasing foreign trade. China is an example of a formerly closed economy which has become more open to international commerce.

JOHN O'CONNELL

code law   A system of law based upon the interpretation of teachings included in a religious text. For example, Muslim Law is a code law based upon the Koran. Because of its deep religious roots, code law is sometimes referred to as "revealed" law, or being sent from the scriptures. For international businesses from common or civil law countries, code law is probably the most difficult of all to understand. Since the basis of code law is a religious text, those not familiar with the writing may be at a great disadvantage in seeking decisions under its rules.

Bibliography

Litka, M. (1991). *International dimensions of the legal environment of business.* 2nd edn, Boston, MA: PWS-Kent Publishing Company.

JOHN O'CONNELL

code of liberalization of capital movements   *see* CAPITAL MOVEMENTS CODE

codetermination   This is a very important concept in relation to who is responsible for determining the strategic goals and objectives as well as the direction of activity of an organization. In most countries, this would be the board of directors (of course, serving at the discretion of the stockholders). Under codetermination, employees of the organization have the right to assist in the basic strategic decisions affecting the firm. In Germany, codetermination means that an employee of an organization "must" be placed on that organization's board of directors. Thus, the direction of the organization is partially determined by the employees as well as the owners of the firm (i.e., "codetermination"). The European Community has agreed to adhere to laws requiring employee input on decisions affecting the strategic plans of an EC company. Strategic planning is thought to be so important that mandating that one of the most affected parties (employees) be included in the planning process was made a part of the EC's "Community Charter of the Fundamental Rights of Workers". Although board membership of employees has been a practice for many years for some organizations, many companies still feel that employees do not have the right to participate in a company's strategic decision-making process. If these companies begin operations in the EC, the strategic management process will have to change.

Bibliography

Rugman, A. M. & Hodgetts, R. M. (1995). *International management: A strategic management approach.* New York: McGraw-Hill Inc.

JOHN O'CONNELL

COFACE COFACE is the French government agency responsible for providing export credit insurance for French companies. With the assistance of this agency French exporters are able to secure financing for their activities which might not otherwise be available. COFACE stands for Compagnie Française d'Assurances pour le Commerce Extérieure.

JOHN O'CONNELL

COFC When a container is carried by rail it may be referred to as COFC or container on flatcar.

See also **Container**

JOHN O'CONNELL

collaborative strategies *see* ENTRY STRATEGIES

collection papers Collection involves the payment by an importer for goods sold by an exporter. Collection papers are the documents specified in the sales contract which must be provided to the buyer (or the buyer's bank) in order for payment to be made.

JOHN O'CONNELL

combination export manager (CEM) Combination export managers are in the business of purchasing goods from a number of companies and then combining those goods to either meet existing orders or to place on the export market. Many times manufacturers of goods do not produce sufficient quantities to take advantage of the most efficient modes of transportation or discounts for shipment of large lots. A CEM can take advantage of such efficiencies and/or discounts by combining the production of many companies. Although CEMs do occasionally work on a commission basis for manufacturers, they more commonly buy and sell as a separate entity involved in the export business. It is very common for CEMs to specialize in particular goods or industries. In this way they become familiar to both producers and buyers of particular goods.

Bibliography

Daniels, J. D. & Radebaugh, L. E. (1994). *International business: Environments and operations.* 7th edn, Reading, MA: Addison-Wesley Publishing.

JOHN O'CONNELL

combined transport bill of lading A combined transport bill of lading allows goods to be shipped over more than one method of transportation (ship, rail, truck) without the need for separate bills of lading.

JOHN O'CONNELL

combined transport operator (CTO) While most carriers of goods operate only one mode of transportation, a number of carriers combine two or more (air, sea, land). Carriers shipping under more than one mode of transportation are referred to as combined transport operators.

JOHN O'CONNELL

commercial attaché A government representative sent to a foreign country as part of a country's formal diplomatic staff with an assignment to promote the importation of home country products and services to the host country. Assistance to home country exporters in the form of local information on markets, regulations, and contacts is provided. Persons in these positions can be of enormous assistance in beginning trade activities with other countries.

JOHN O'CONNELL

commercial invoice   A commercial invoice is a document which is used to provide details of an international trade transaction. Information normally required includes the following: buyer and seller names, types of property, value of goods, origin and destination points, and parties accepting delivery of goods.

JOHN O'CONNELL

commercial risk   When a business begins it faces the risks that the economic conditions it hoped would be present will change, causing the business to suffer losses or less profit or growth then originally expected. This risk is referred to as the "business risk." The new venture also faces the possibility that persons or firms purchasing goods or services on credit will not or cannot pay their debts. This is referred to as the "credit risk". When one combines the business and credit risks the result is the "commercial risk" a business faces.

A business operating in a single economy cannot do much to affect the business risk. Most businesses are so small as to have very little financial impact on an entire economy. Thus, businesses spread their risk by moving into international activities. It is a fair bet that when one economy is down another will be on the upswing. Credit risk can be managed by instituting credit controls and management techniques from the outset of a business. Good credit management is one of the keys to successful business operations.

Bibliography

Bishop, P. & Dixon, D. (1992). *Foreign exchange handbook: Managing risk and opportunity in global currency markets.* New York: McGraw-Hill Inc.

Eiteman, D. K., Stonehill, A. J. & Moffett, M. H. (1992). *Multinational business finance.* 6th edn, Reading, MA: Addison-Wesley Publishing.

Rosenzweig, P. M. & Singh, J. V. (1991). Organizational environments and the multinational enterprise. *The Academy of Management Review,* 16, 340–61.

JOHN O'CONNELL

commercial visa   A commercial visa is issued to business travelers who are visiting a country on a temporary basis. Usually a business traveler is not allowed to be paid a salary by a company in the host country (local salary earners are usually not eligible for a commercial visa, although exceptions are made). Commercial visa holder activities are also stated in each country's immigration laws. Common activities which are allowed are: attend business conferences or conventions; conduct sales meetings; negotiate business contracts; purchase goods for export; as well as other specifically allowed business activities. Other categories of business visitors may be eligible for special visa status. The party seeking special status must check with a consulate or the immigration authorities of the proposed host country.

See also **Visa**

JOHN O'CONNELL

commission agent   It is common for companies involved in foreign trade to work through representatives or agents who sell goods on behalf of the companies. These agents usually work for a percentage of the goods sold (a commission). In many countries these agents are referred to as manufacturer's representatives. Commission agents usually specialize in certain types of products or industrial output in order to build their relationships with both buyers and sellers. In order to monitor their activities, commission agents are required by many countries to be registered and bonded.

JOHN O'CONNELL

commodity   It is important to recognize that the term commodity does not mean the same thing in all contexts. A commodity is commonly broadly defined in international trade to include anything which is traded or purchased, other than a service. This broad definition includes both manufactured goods as well as grains, oil, livestock, and other agricultural or extractive goods. In financial markets commodities refer to grains, livestock, metals, etc. but not general manufactured goods. Agreements between countries related to commodity trade may be very specific (listing the items agreed upon) or broad-based (with little definition). The context in which the term is used will determine its meaning. Failure to know the context may result in misunderstandings.

JOHN O'CONNELL

commodity cartel *see* INTERNATIONAL COMMODITY GROUP

Commodity Credit Corporation (CCC) The Commodity Credit Corporation is a United States Department of Agriculture agency. The purpose of the agency is to assist in keeping US agricultural production stable and profitable while at the same time meeting the needs of the country. The CCC provides price supports and other subsidies to agricultural entities. Whenever possible, the agency also encourages the export of US agricultural goods.

See also **Common Agricultural Policy**

JOHN O'CONNELL

Common Agricultural Policy (CAP) Common agricultural policy is created when a group of countries agree to cooperate to standardize their agricultural policies for the benefit of the signatories of the agreement. Common markets are good examples of groups of countries which often have common agricultural policies. These policies usually are aimed at improving the status of farmers by stabilizing prices, providing price supports when necessary, and seeking to further develop agricultural production and distribution in the area. The European Community is one of the best examples of a common market providing a Common Agricultural Policy for its member countries.

See also **Commodity Credit Corporation**

Bibliography

Ashegian, P. & Ebrahimi, B. (1990). *International business*. Philadelphia, PA: HarperCollins.

Winham, G. R. (1992). *The evolution of international trade agreements*. Toronto, Ontario: University of Toronto Press.

JOHN O'CONNELL

Common External Tariff (CAT/CXT) This is the set of tariffs established by the members of a common market or free-trade area to apply to goods imported from outside the member countries. Common external tariffs reflect the protectionist needs of all of the trade area's members. Thus, if one country's industry was threatened by imports from outside the trade area, high tariffs would apply to those products in "all" member countries. The tariffs do not apply "between" members, just to outsiders. A high tariff would make the member country's goods more competitive which would not only keep its domestic demand but increase the demand from other member countries.

JOHN O'CONNELL

common law system Under this system of law each situation is subject to review based upon the precedents established through prior court rulings and from custom of the country. Although not restricted to them, common law is found mainly in the English-speaking countries. Matters of law and dispute are dealt with by the system employing a judge and jury. Contract interpretation under common law is many times more liberal than under other systems. Thus, the terminology used in contractual agreements must be precise and clearly express the intent of the parties.

See also **Legal system**

Bibliography

Litka, M. (1991). *International dimensions of the legal environment of business*. 2nd edn, Boston, MA: PWS-Kent Publishing Company.

JOHN O'CONNELL

common market A common market is a geographic region in which the countries agree to cooperate with one another to further their joint economic interests. Within the boundaries of the common market, countries strive to reduce and eventually do away with barriers to free trade. Major goals of common markets are the elimination of duties, customs delays, and other barriers to the free flow of goods, services and people between the member countries. Tariff systems may be established to protect common market countries as a whole from foreign competition. Common markets also address the standardization of currency, product standards, and coordinated fiscal policy to make the market work as if it was one nation instead of many. Many common markets exist around the world. Probably the most well known is the European Community, which has progressed nearer the goal of true freedom of movement and trade then any other common market.

See also **European Community**

Bibliography

Springer, B. (1992). *The social dimension of 1992: Europe faces a new EC.* New York: Greenwood Press.
Winham, G. R. (1992). *The evolution of international trade agreements.* Toronto, Ontario: University of Toronto Press.

JOHN O'CONNELL

communication   The ability to transmit information in such a way that the intent of the communication is received by the appropriate person. Communication is not merely writing letters, sending a fax, or even face-to-face conversations. Writing or speaking are merely means of communication. Great skill is required to formulate information in a way which is understandable to others. Even greater skill is required when communications flow between countries or cultures. Not only must a person communicate his/her own thoughts and feelings but the communication may be in a different language or to persons with very different educational abilities, and will also be received by persons of different beliefs, values, and attitudes. Education in proper communication is essential for managerial success. Such education must include communications with diverse work groups and cultures.

See also **Cross-cultural communication**

Bibliography

Francis, J. N. (1991). When in Rome? The affects of cultural adaptations on the intercultural business negotiations. *Journal of International Business Studies,* 22 (3), 403–28.
Johnson, M. (1992). *Cultural guide to doing business in Europe.* 2nd edn, Boston, MA: Butterworth-Heinemann.
McLaughlin, M. L., Cody, M. J. & Read, S. (1992). *Explaining one's self to others: Reason-giving in a social context.* Hillsdale, NJ: Lawrence Erlbaum Associates.

JOHN O'CONNELL

Compagnie Française d'Assurances pour le Commerce Extérieure   *see* COFACE

comparative cost advantage   When a country is able to supply one or more of the resources to produce a product at lower prices than other countries, it has a comparative cost advantage. Mexico, for example, has a comparative cost advantage in terms of labor expense when compared to its northern neighbors and the rest of the industrialized nations of the world. Many of the industrialized nations are capitalizing on Mexico's low wages by building and operating plants on the Mexican border. This helps both the Mexican people and the companies seeking lower costs. The cost advantage could be in any of the resources necessary for production: labor, energy, raw materials, or other areas. One of the problems with comparative cost advantages is that they are transient. That is, as Mexico's economy develops and more companies seek low labor costs, demand will push costs higher. It is also possible that as citizens of Mexico see the money being made by foreign companies, demands will be made to make their wage system equal to that of the home countries of the visiting organizations.

There is another aspect of comparative cost advantage that carries with it a great deal of concern. Comparative cost advantage is also present when the cost of complying with regulations governing an organization's actions are extremely high in the home country whereas those regulations do not exist (or the cost of compliance is far less) in a host country (*see* REGULATORY COST ADVANTAGE). Current examples of regulatory cost advantage give rise to some serious ethical and/or legal questions. For example: "Do companies locate in countries because laws are less stringent than in the company's home country?"; "Does evidence indicate that companies have left countries because of what they consider an oppressive legal system (for example from the United States because of its high cost of litigation; uncertainty; and high liability insurance costs)?"; "Do companies locate in developing countries to avoid strict pollution liability regulations and responsibility?"; or "Are high levels of taxation for social insurance and pension plans driving companies to other countries?" Questions such as these are common. The answer to each is probably "yes." One must remember, though, that monetary rewards for taking advantage of regulatory cost advantages are probably only temporary as environmental legislation sweeps the globe and countries realize the long-term effects of their legal systems. Whether to take advantage of cost advantages may actually be more of an ethical decision on the part of a company instead of a financial one.

Bibliography

Davis, K. & Blomstrom, R. L. (1975). *Business and society: Environment and responsibility*. 3rd edn, New York: McGraw-Hill.

JOHN O'CONNELL

compensation package (expatriate) The total of various types of compensation which are paid to an expatriate. The package can include the employee's base salary, plus differentials for housing; home leave; children's education; auto allowance; and other benefits. The package compensates the expatriate for work performed as well as the inconvenience of moving and working overseas. Compensation packages may include a number of different categories of payments or benefits. A list of common categories of pay or other compensation provides an idea of the variety of costs or expenses which may be incurred by an expatriate

as well as the immense cost frequently associated with sending an employee overseas. The following list is arranged alphabetically with the terms commonly used in international human relations management. Some terms are narrowly defined, while others are quite broad and overlap with others on the list.

1 Base salary – An expatriate's base salary is the comparable salary for the same work and position as would be paid in the expatriate's home country. Adjustments are made to the base salary for expenses, inconveniences, and hardships encountered in the host country.

2 Benefit allowance – An employee may receive additional payments from the employer with which to purchase insurance or other types of benefits. Expatriates also receive such payment although the benefits purchased may be different from those normally obtained in the home country. For example, education expenses for private schooling for children may seem appropriate benefit overseas, but left unfunded by the employer while in the home country.

3 Completion allowance – Sometimes referred to as a completion bonus, this payment is offered an employee as incentive to stay the full time period of the assignment. An employee may encounter situations of such inconvenience, hardship or danger, that employers have difficulty with employees requesting early departure from assignments. The completion allowance is a reward which is offered to the employee, but is actually paid at the end of the normal assignment period (or at other times if agreed upon between employer and employee).

4 Cost of living allowance – An additional amount of compensation paid to an employee on foreign assignment. The allowance permits the employee to maintain the same standard of living in the host country as was normal in the home country. The allowance includes funds for increased costs of food, transportation, housing, and other goods and services. The problem which arises many times, however, is that the quality or quantity of goods and services normally available is not the same as in the

home country. For example, the cost of housing in Japan is far greater than in the United States. A housing allowance would be given to make up for the cost difference, but housing in Japan is normally quite small when compared to the United States and can be quite inconvenient for US citizens.

5 Danger pay – Employees may be placed in danger when they are transferred to certain countries because of political unrest, actions of terrorists, active war or insurrection, or public reaction to citizens of specific foreign countries. Some companies will compensate their employees at higher levels when the job places them in extraordinarily high danger. "Danger" pay is given to employees from the time they enter the dangerous country or region until the time they leave. Danger pay may also be referred to as hazardous duty pay.

6 Education allowance – When a person is accompanied by family members on an overseas assignment special arrangements can be made for the children's education. Differences exist in educational facilities and programs throughout the world. To exactly match the needs of a child in two different countries may be difficult. An education allowance provides funds which may be used to provide special education opportunities or enroll a student in private school. In this way the child's educational progress will be affected as little as possible by the move to a foreign country.

7 Enroute expenses – Travel expenses between the home country and the assignment location are referred to as "enroute" expenses. Enroute expenses include: airfare and other transportation expense; meals; hotel costs; tips and other incidental expenses. Enroute expenses can be very high and should be reimbursed (or better yet, paid in advance) by the employer.

8 Expatriate differential – Companies many times pay (or make available as a benefit) an extra amount of compensation to expatriates to make up for the inconvenience and extra problems associated with living outside of one's own country. The differential makes up for higher housing costs; education for children; leasing an automobile or other costs. The differential ceases to be paid

when the expatriate returns to the home country. Sometimes this causes problems with living standards because often the same amount of money purchases so much more overseas than in the employee's home country. The expatriate literally suffers a reduced standard of living when returning to the home country.

9 Fringe benefits – Items of indirect compensation provided to employees. Fringe benefits include: insurance (life, health, disability, dental, legal services, and others are available); company-sponsored education programs; scholarship programs for employee's children; vacation time; employer paid or subsidized lunches; company car; sick leave; retirement programs; and many others depending upon the country of employment and the agreement with the employer. Fringe benefits are provided for a number of reasons including the following: (a) incentives for persons to begin and continue employment, (b) to increase morale, (c) due to local customs, (d) union agreements. Many fringe benefits also receive favored tax treatment for both the employer and the employee. For example, in the United States employer paid insurance premiums are generally not taxed as income (subject to some specific exceptions) to employees and are deducted as a business expense by the employer. Fringe benefits which are not taxable or taxable at a lower rate for employees (e.g., employer paid life insurance in the United States) are referred to by some people as "perqs" or "perquisite."

10 Furnishing allowance – An amount of money made available to an expatriate to furnish the apartment or home selected in the host country.

11 Hardship allowance – An organization sending employees overseas may offer additional pay for the inconvenience or because the location of overseas employment is considered less than desirable. Such pay is often referred to as a "hardship allowance."

12 Home leave – An expatriate (including family) is often given paid leave each year to return to his/her home country. Normally all expenses of the trip home are paid by the company. Home leaves were devel-

oped to allow expatriates and their families to maintain ties with relatives, friends, and others. This eases problems commonly associated with the transition to and from the foreign location.

13 Housing allowance – A common benefit provided to expatriates. Housing allowances are provided in several forms: additional salary to help pay housing costs; provision of employer-owned housing in the foreign country; and reimbursement (or paid directly to the landlord) of the actual cost of housing incurred by the expatriate.

14 Living allowance – An additional amount of compensation to account for additional costs of living in an expatriate's host country versus the home country. Examples of costs of living which are commonly higher in other countries are: food, housing, transportation, and services. If the expatriate would normally take advantage of goods and services while in the home country, a living allowance is normally provided for those same goods and services in a host country. This is an important consideration for an employee considering an overseas assignment. It is also important to recognize that the degree or quality of goods or services may also vary and must be taken into consideration as well.

15 Overbase compensation – Base salaries between the home country and the host country are usually equalized for an expatriate. That is the pay in the host country would be the same for the same job in the home country. Adjustments in the form of higher pay to offset inconveniences, dangers not occurring in the home country, or longer periods of work (as are expected in some countries) are referred to as "overbase" compensation.

16 Relocation allowance – A payment given to employees to cover the cost of moving themselves, family, and personal possessions to the site of a foreign assignment. The costs of relocating employees may be quite high depending upon the assignment location.

17 Rest and relaxation leave (R&R) – When an expatriate employee is assigned to a location which is exceptionally inconvenient compared to the employee's home country (some Middle Eastern oil-field locations, for example) companies often pay for a week or two-week excursion away from the location to rest and relax. R&R allows employees to reacclimatize themselves in order to avoid burnout.

18 Settling-in allowance – Moving to another country normally takes a considerable amount of time and effort before all of one's personal property and family is settled in a new home. It is common for expatriates to take a minimal amount of personal property when first assigned and live in temporary quarters until suitable permanent accommodation can be found. This is generally a good idea because an expatriate does not always know the nature of the accommodation and cannot make rational decisions about what property to bring, what amount is appropriate, and what will fit into the new living situation. A settling-in-allowance is an amount of money given to an expatriate for temporary quarters, storage expenses in the new country, and other expenses (known and unknown) likely to be associated with the initial move to a new country.

19 Travel time – As part of the compensation package, most companies allow an expatriate a specified number of days to travel to their assignment country. Full pay and specified expenses are paid during this period of time.

It is also very important when comparing average housing, food, or transportation costs between the home and host countries, to not only consider the cost differential but also the qualitative differences. For example, the average middle manager in the United States may have housing costs of $2,000 per month, whereas the Japan assignment will have average housing costs of $5,000 per month. What is often overlooked is that the United States housing is a detached home having 3,000 square feet of area, whereas the Japanese home is an apartment having 1,200 feet of living space. Qualitative differences are important and cannot be made up for with additional compensation alone.

Bibliography

Bird, A. & Dunbar, R. (1991). Getting the job done over there: Improving expatriate productivity. *National Productivity Review*, Spring, 145–56.

Black, J. S. & Gregerson, H. B. (1991). When Yankee comes home: Factors relating to expatriate and spouse repatriation adjustment. *Journal of International Business Studies*, **22 (4)**, 471–94.

Business International Corporation (1982). *World executive compensation and human resource planning*. New York: Business International Corporation.

Feldman, D. C. & Thomas, D. C. (1992). Career management issues facing expatriates. *Journal of International Business Studies*, **23 (2)**, 271–94.

Feldman, D. C. & Thompson, H. B. (1993). Expropriation, repatriation, and domestic geographical relocation: An empirical investigation of adjustment to new job assignments. *Journal of International Business Studies*, **24 (3)**, 507–30.

Harris, J. E. (1989). Moving managers internationally: The care and feeding of expatriates. *Human Resources Planning*, **12**, 49–53.

Harvey, M. (1985). The executive family: An overlooked variable in international assignments. *Journal of International Business Studies*, Columbia Journal of World Business, 785–800.

Pulatie, D. (1985). How do you ensure success of managers going abroad. *Training and Development Journal*, December, 22–4.

Reynolds, C. (1986). "Compensation of overseas personnel" in *Handbook of Human Resource Administration*. 2nd edn, New York: McGraw-Hill.

Toyne, B. & Kuhne, R. J. (1983). The management of the international executive compensation and benefits process. *Journal of International Business Studies*, **14 (32)**, 37–50.

JOHN O'CONNELL

compensation trade   When an importer and an exporter agree to exchange specified goods as payment to each other for those goods. The exchange does not have to occur at the same time. This is a form of countertrade.

See also **Countertrade**

Bibliography

Zodl, J. A. (1992). *Export–Import: Everything you and your company need to know to compete in world markets*. Cincinnati, OH: Betterway Books.

JOHN O'CONNELL

compensatory duty   A reduction in tax for one commodity in exchange for increased taxes on others. A country may reduce duties on some imports from a particular country to offset higher duties being paid on other commodities. It is possible that higher duty items are more subject to public scrutiny and thus require the duty to remain high. To provide some break to a country's trading partner, duties on other items may be relaxed.

See also **Concessional duty; Duty**

JOHN O'CONNELL

compensatory trade   An arrangement in which partial or total payment for imports is made in the form of goods or services rather than money. Compensatory trade is another name for Countertrade. There are a large number of compensatory arrangements ranging from informal barter between willing buyers and sellers to different types of contractual agreements between governments or business organizations.

See also **Countertrade**

JOHN O'CONNELL

completion allowance   Sometimes referred to as a completion bonus, this payment is offered (and paid when the duration of an overseas assignment is completed) to an employee as incentive to stay the full time period of the assignment. An employee may encounter situations of such inconvenience, hardship or danger, that employers have difficulty with employees requesting early departure from assignments. The completion allowance is a reward which is offered to the employee, but is actually paid at the end of the normal assignment period (or at other times if agreed upon between employer and employee).

See also **Compensation package**

JOHN O'CONNELL

compound duty   A tax placed on imported items, the amount of which is based upon two types of duties: a percentage of the value of the goods (called an "ad valorem" duty) and a specific tax per unit (called a "specific duty") of the goods (weight, numbers). The sum of these customs taxes is referred to as a compound duty. An example will assist in understanding: Country A assesses a compound duty on imports of car batteries. The duty consists of 10% of the value plus $1.00 per battery. A shipment of 100 batteries valued at $2,000 would be assessed at a $300 compound duty (10% of $2,000 + $1.00 x 100 = $300).

Bibliography

Nexia International Staff (1994). *International handbook of corporate and personal taxes.* New York: Chapman & Hall.

JOHN O'CONNELL

comprehensive export credit insurance coverage   This insurance provides coverage for losses (above those normally expected in the course of business) caused by a buyer failing to make payment due to political and commercial risks. Political risks are those associated with acts of government, whereas commercial risk includes insolvency of a buyer or other economic reasons for nonpayment. Another type of loss commonly covered by the broader forms of this coverage is if a foreign buyer cannot convert currency in order to make payment to the insured. Coverage is generally very broad, but one cannot rely on the name of an insurance contract (e.g., "comprehensive") to imply coverage. Each contract must be carefully reviewed in making a purchase decision.

See also **Political risk; Political risk insurance**

JOHN O'CONNELL

concessional duty   A duty between trading partners which is very low. Concessional duties are also applied by industrialized nations to developing nations in order to promote developing country economic growth.

See also **Duty**

JOHN O'CONNELL

concessional financing   International economic development depends in part upon the willingness of industrialized countries to subsidize some of the development efforts of less developed countries (LDCs). One of the ways of accomplishing subsidization of development is to offer loans to LDCs on terms normally not available under usual financing conditions. Concessional loans are provided at far lower than market rates for such countries, for longer terms, and with conditions which allow grace periods for payments. Concessional financing is part of the responsibilities normally given to development agencies of various industrialized countries and to local and regional development banks. Loans are commonly given for infrastructure projects and agricultural development leading to more self-sufficiency for the LDC.

Bibliography

Ludlow, N. H. (1988). *A practical guide to the development bank business: How to identify it, market to it, and win it.* Washington, D.C.: Development Bank Associates Inc.
Scharf, T. & Shetty, M. C. (1973). *Dictionary of development banking: A compilation of terms in English, French, and German with definitions in English.* New York: Elsevier Science Publishing Co.

JOHN O'CONNELL

confirmed letter of credit   This is a letter of credit guaranteed by the exporter's bank. This type of letter of credit poses the least risk for the exporter of goods. A bank in the exporter's own country guarantees payment even if the importer, or the importer's bank, fails to remit funds to the exporter's bank. Normally, the exporter's bank requires the importer's bank to deposit funds before the goods are shipped, in order to guarantee payment. Upon presentation of the letter of credit and compliance with all terms of the letter, payment is made to the exporter. If payment is not made by the importer or the importer's bank, the exporter's bank will make payment by virtue of its confirming or guaranteeing the letter of credit.

See also **Letter of credit**

Bibliography

Johnson, T. E. (1994). *Export–Import procedures and documentation*. New York: Amacom.

JOHN O'CONNELL

confiscation   This is one of the major political risks faced by multinational enterprises. Confiscation is the taking of private property by a government without any offer of compensation. Governments which confiscate privately-owned property of foreign organizations or individuals usually use the excuse that the foreign firm was exploiting the host country or that relations between the governments are too strained to allow any representative of the foreign country to continue in business. Political risk insurance may be purchased to protect against confiscation of property.

See also **Political risk; Political risk insurance**

Bibliography

Coplin, W. D. & O'Leary, M. K. (1994). *The handbook of country and political risk analysis*. New York: Political Risk Services.

Howell, L. D. (1994). The political sociology of foreign investment and trade: Testing risk models for adequacy of protection. *AGSIM Faculty Publication*, No. 94–05.

JOHN O'CONNELL

consign   To consign is to place goods into the hands of another party. In international trade that other party is normally a carrier who is to deliver the goods to a specified destination and party. A bill of lading or other transit or sales document usually specifies the name of the owner and purchaser of goods, as well as the carrier involved.

JOHN O'CONNELL

consignee   A consignee is the party to whom goods are sent. In international trade the consignee is usually the buyer or importer of goods, although it could also be an agent who then sells goods on behalf of the owner.

Consignees do not take title to goods until they are sold and the purchase price paid to the owner or consignor.

JOHN O'CONNELL

consignment   Consignment is a process through which an owner of goods (consignor) transfers them to an agent (consignee) who is then responsible for selling the goods to others. In international trade, consignment is actually a method of financing import transactions. The exporter of goods (consignor) transfers goods to an importer (consignee) who then sells the goods. When the goods are sold the proceeds are divided between the agent (a commission for selling the goods) and the exporter (the balance of the amount paid).

JOHN O'CONNELL

consignor   A consignor is the owner of goods which are transferred to another party (the consignee) for future sale. Title to goods normally remains with the consignor until goods are sold. The consignee receives a commission from the sales and the consignor receives the balance of the sales price.

JOHN O'CONNELL

consolidation   The combination of goods into a single shipment. A producer of goods will often not have sufficient quantity to take advantage of the lowest transportation rates (full carload or full container). Reduced costs might be achieved if producers could coordinate the shipping of goods so that the combined amount shipped is eligible for lower rates. The combining of goods from several producers is referred to as "consolidation." The process of consolidation could take place through agreements between producers and also through specialists called freight forwarders or freight consolidators.

JOHN O'CONNELL

consul   A consul is a person sent to a foreign country by a government to represent the personal and business interests of citizens of the home country. In this capacity, a consul often is involved in answering questions regarding business opportunities in the host country in the hopes of fostering increased imports. Consuls are very important contacts in foreign countries because of their knowledge of commercial regulations as well as the business needs of the host country. Consuls will also address questions regarding home country citizen's rights as well as assisting with travel papers, etc. needed by citizens of the home country. Consuls are often referred to as "attachés."

JOHN O'CONNELL

consul general A government official stationed in a major commercial center outside of his own country. A consul general is in charge of other consuls located in other offices in that same country.

See also **Consul**

JOHN O'CONNELL

consular declaration A written description of exports being shipped to another country. The description is made by a consul representing the importing country. A more detailed description of the entire export transaction is included in a consular invoice.

See also **Consular invoice**

JOHN O'CONNELL

consular invoice An official statement outlining the details of an export transaction. The invoice is created prior to the export's movement to another country by a consul representing the importing country. The invoice includes: the type of property, the property value, the origin of the property, the destination, and the method of transport. Consular invoices are required in many transactions. They allow a country to keep concise records of imports as well as to make certain that what is sent is what was described in the invoice.

Bibliography

Johnson, T. E. (1994). *Export–Import procedures and documentation.* New York: Amacom.

Zodl, J. A. (1992). *Export–Import: Everything you and your company need to know to compete in world markets.* Cincinnati, OH: Betterway Books.

JOHN O'CONNELL

consularization Consularization is the process of stamping documents or translations with the official seal of an embassy or consulate of a country. Many times documents must have an official government seal to be accepted as valid. Documents which are commonly stamped are college records of persons seeking to continue school overseas, birth certificates, translated contracts, and other personal records.

JOHN O'CONNELL

consulate A government office located in a foreign country with responsibility for acting on behalf of the business interests of the home country. It is a very important contact point for domestic business seeking to expand internationally.

JOHN O'CONNELL

container A specially designed metal box used to ship goods without the necessity of unloading each of the items in the box each time the container is moved from one transportation mode to another. Specially designed, water-tight, metal containers are used for shipping over the seas. Many times the same container is shipped by rail, truck, and ship without the necessity of unpacking. Containers capable of being transferred between different types of transportation systems are called "intermodal containers." When a container is carried by rail it is often referred to as container-on-flatcar or COFC.

JOHN O'CONNELL

container ship A ship which is specially designed and outfitted to carry containers. This type of ship has become the major method of transporting finished goods by water.

JOHN O'CONNELL

containerization The process of placing goods in containers for shipment.

See also **Container**

JOHN O'CONNELL

contraband Contraband describes goods which are forbidden by a government to be held in the country, produced, exported, or imported. Probably the most widespread type of contraband in today's world are illegal, narcotic drugs. Different countries have different laws pertaining to what constitutes contraband and the penalties associated with possessing such goods in that country. In many countries pornographic material is considered to be contraband, while in others it is not. Possession of alcohol will cause a person problems in some countries while in others the laws are more forgiving. Possession of a small amount of illegal, narcotic drugs is punishable by death in Malaysia and by a jail term in the United Kingdom.

It is very important for persons traveling to other countries to be aware of the local laws and the penalties for breaking those laws. The same awareness must be exhibited by international organizations in their training of employees to be assigned overseas or even when going on short business trips. Failure to inform employees of additional dangers (different laws concerning contraband) may make an employer partially responsible for problems which result for both the employee and the organization. Expatriate family members must also be made aware of the rules of the host country.

Bibliography

Sarachek, B. (1994). *International business law: A guide for executives with case examples.* Pennington, NY: Darwin Press Inc.
Torbiorn, J. (1982). *Living abroad.* New York: John Wiley.

JOHN O'CONNELL

contract frustration A British term for contract repudiation or the default on the payment of a contractual obligation on the part of a foreign government.

See also **Contract repudiation; Political risk**

JOHN O'CONNELL

contract manufacturing A method of entering a foreign market in which a company uses manufacturers in foreign countries to make (or assemble) their product and distribute it through the foreign manufacturer's existing marketing channels. Thus, entry to the country is achieved with the assistance of local companies using proven marketing channels. Although the cost of this type of method is usually a substantial portion of the product revenues, it allows a company to test the market for its goods and become more familiar with doing business overseas.

See also **Market entry strategies**

Bibliography

Deresky, Helen (1994). *International management.* 1st edn, New York: HarperCollins.

JOHN O'CONNELL

contract of affreightment When goods are to be transported over water, a vessel operator must agree to provide sufficient space on a vessel (ship, barge, etc.) at a specific point in time. A contract of affreightment is a contract between the owner of goods and the vessel operator. The contract details the terms of the transport agreement.

JOHN O'CONNELL

contract of carriage An agreement between an owner of goods and a carrier which leads to the transportation of goods. The contract generally includes all of the details of the transit transaction (destination, type of goods, values, cost of shipping, responsibilities for damaged goods, etc.).

JOHN O'CONNELL

contract repudiation From time to time a contractor will enter into a contract with a foreign government only to find that the contract cannot be fulfilled. This may be because the government terminates the contract without showing cause, refuses to pay for delivered goods, cancels the contractor's license to operate, or otherwise causes cancellation of the contract. Contracts with private buyers are subject to the same set of circumstances, although legal remedies may be available which are lacking when dealing directly with government contracts. Although most contracts are fulfilled without problem, a sufficient number are not honored to support the growth of a specific type of insurance to protect against contract repudiation.

See also **Political risk; Political risk insurance**

JOHN O'CONNELL

contract repudiation coverage   This type of political risk insurance provides coverage for noncompliance with contracts by a foreign government. An insured doing business with a foreign government faces the risk that the government will not comply with the contract thereby causing loss to the insured. For example, a building construction contractor expects to be paid when the building is completed, but may not if the government terminates the contract or makes it impossible for the contractor to complete the project on schedule thereby forcing a default. Insurance against contract repudiation commonly provides coverage for: unilateral government termination of a contract without cause; nonpayment by a government for service or other contracts; license termination which forces the company to default; embargoes which make completion impossible; and other government actions as outlined in each policy. Some insurers will also offer coverage for war risk.

See also **Political risk; Political risk insurance**

Bibliography

Coplin, W. D. & O'Leary, M. K. (1994). *The handbook of country and political risk analysis.* New York: Political Risk Services.

JOHN O'CONNELL

convention   In international business, the term convention usually refers to an agreement made between countries. Thus, the "Convention on the Prevention of Marine Pollution by Dumping of Wastes and Other Matter" is an "agreement" which forbids the dumping of pollutants into the sea from a ship or an aircraft. The United Nations refers to most of its major agreements as conventions.

JOHN O'CONNELL

conversion   *see* FOREIGN EXCHANGE

convertibility   The ability to exchange one currency for another. In international business the convertibility of currency cannot be taken for granted. Some countries will not allow conversion of certain currencies, while others may institute restrictions "after" a foreign organization has begun operations. Insurance is available against two convertibility problems: (1) a currently convertible currency becoming inconvertible or (2) long administrative delays in allowing convertibility.

See also **Inconvertibility of currency coverage; Political risk insurance**

Bibliography

Eiteman, D. K., Stonehill, A. J. & Moffett, M. H. (1992). *Multinational business finance.* 6th edn, Reading, MA: Addison-Wesley Publishing.

JOHN O'CONNELL

convertible currencies   Currencies which may be easily exchanged for other currencies are considered "convertible."

See also **Convertibility**

JOHN O'CONNELL

cooperation agreement   When there is a need in one country for resources in order to produce products and the availability of those resources in another country a cooperation agreement may be in order. For example, country A needs electrical power to produce clothing and country B has excess electrical power but needs clothing. An agreement is made for country B to supply power in return for future payment in clothing that country A is then able to produce.

See also **Barter**

JOHN O'CONNELL

cooperative exchange agreements   One of the most important agreements which must be carried out between members of a common market or other regional economic development association. Cooperative exchange agreements attempt to reduce and eventually remove restrictions to currency exchanges; for example, between a common market's member countries. Freedom from government imposed restrictions or barriers will normally lend more stability to all of the currencies of member nations. This in turn will promote additional trade within the market as well as increased cooperation amongst member nations. Through the European Monetary System the European Community has progressed along the lines of cooperative exchange agreements. If EC plans become reality, EC member countries will eventually have a single currency.

Bibliography

Winham, G. R. (1992). *The evolution of international trade agreements.* Toronto, Ontario: University of Toronto Press.

JOHN O'CONNELL

coordination center   A financial clearing house to handle the needs of an organization. A coordination center is usually located in a tax haven or other site which offers low operating costs and favorable tax regulations. The center is a centralized finance and planning unit with responsibility for handling financial transactions of a region or worldwide operations of the company; providing a central location for all administrative processes of the company (accounting, information systems, insurance and self-insurance administration, and other administrative activities); and the planning function related to all of its activities.

Bibliography

Celi, L. J. & Rutizer, B. (1991). *Global cash management.* 1st edn, New York: Harper Business (HarperCollins).

JOHN O'CONNELL

copyright   Protection for written or artistic work given by a government for a specific period of time. Items subject to copyright are literary works, works of art, musical scores, stories or words to a song; labels; and other written works. It is very common for citizens of some countries to use copyrighted works without authorization from the copyright holder. The unauthorized use is commonly referred to as pirating or copying and is illegal in most countries of the world. Pirating of copyrighted works costs copyright holders billions of dollars in lost revenues each year. Any holder of a copyright should strongly consider protecting that right in as many countries as possible. Several international agreements have been reached which protect copyrights and other intellectual property rights (this term also includes patents and other rights as well).

See also **Berne Convention for the Protection of Literary and Artistic Works; Universal copyright convention**

JOHN O'CONNELL

corporate culture   Corporate culture is defined as the set of common values, attitudes, and behaviors which are perceived as being those of the organization. As with other cultures, corporate culture is taught to employees both explicitly and by example. Corporate values and attitudes include: ethical standards, flexibility of management, creativity of employees, concern for public welfare, and the need for compliance with the law. It is expressed in a number of ways: the facilities of an organization (showplaces of modern construction or traditional office structures); the way employees dress (formally or informally); availability of management (open door or three-week appointments?). Organizations generally attempt to hire those individuals which fit well into their corporate culture. This virtually guarantees the continuance of the culture.

International organizations sometimes run into problems when they attempt to extend their corporate culture to overseas operations. Conflict may occur between the corporate culture and that of the host country culture. Companies which have carried out international operations over extended periods of time, generally begin to see their corporate culture become more cosmopolitan.

Bibliography

Deal, T. E. & Kennedy, A. A. (1982). *Corporate cultures.* Reading, MA: Addison-Wesley Publishing.

Hofstede, G. (1980). *Culture's consequences: International differences in work-related values.* Beverly Hills, CA: Sage Publications.

JOHN O'CONNELL

cost and freight – named port of destination (CFR) When this trade term is used the seller is responsible for all inland costs and freight charges in the seller's country; cost of loading vessels and for ocean or air freight charges necessary to bring goods to a specified port of destination. The buyer is responsible for arranging and purchasing export insurance; import duties; and inland freight charges in the buyer's country. Title of the goods passes when the goods cross the rail of the ship while being loaded for shipment to the buyer. The seller is responsible for securing the export license and the buyer the import license.

Bibliography

International Chamber of Commerce (ICC) (1990). *Incoterms 1990.* New York, NY: ICC Publishing Corp.

JOHN O'CONNELL

cost differential *see* COST OF LIVING ALLOWANCE

cost, insurance and freight (CIF) This trade term describes a situation in which the seller is responsible for inland freight charges in the seller's country; cost of loading the vessel; all ocean/air freight charges; and the securing and cost of export insurance. The buyer is responsible for unloading the vessel; import duties; and inland freight charges in the buyers country. Title of the goods transfers when the goods cross the ship's rail in the initial loading for export. The seller has the responsibility for securing the export license and the buyer the import license.

Bibliography

International Chamber of Commerce (ICC) (1990). *Incoterms 1990.* New York, NY: ICC Publishing Corp.

JOHN O'CONNELL

cost of living allowance An additional amount of compensation paid to an employee on foreign assignment. The allowance permits the employee to maintain the same standard of living in the host country as was normal in the home country. The allowance includes funds for increased costs of food, transportation, housing, and other goods and services. The problem which arises many times, however, is that the quality or quantity of goods and services normally available is not the same as in the home country. For example the cost of housing in Japan is far greater than in United States. A housing allowance would be given to make up for the cost difference, but housing in Japan is normally quite small when compared to the United States and is often quite inconvenient for US citizens.

See also **Compensation package**

Bibliography

Golding, J. (1993). *Working abroad: Essential financial planning for expatriates and their employers.* Plymouth: International Venture Handbooks.

JOHN O'CONNELL

counterfeit *see* PIRACY

counterpurchase agreements   Two purchase contracts are agreed to by buyer and seller. Buyer agrees to purchase goods or services at a specified price (contract number one). Seller agrees to purchase a certain value of goods from buyer over a given period of time (contract number two). Contract number one is not valid unless contract number two is accepted and signed. Thus all or part of the sales price of the original goods or services is paid for with other goods or services.

See also **Countertrade**

JOHN O'CONNELL

countertrade   An arrangement in which partial or total payment for imports is made in the form of goods or services rather than money. Countertrade is also sometimes referred to as Compensatory Trade. There are a large number of countertrade arrangements ranging from informal barter between willing buyers and sellers to a number of different types of contractual agreements between governments or business organizations.

Countertrade takes place for a number of reasons. There may be little or no currency available, unstable governments make currency difficult to exchange, or currency restrictions may be in effect. In these situations a number of countertrade scenarios may be appropriate. The following is a list of some of the more common types of countertrade.

1 Buy back – An agreement between an exporter of capital goods (for example, processing equipment to be used by the buyer to produce a finished product) to accept future payment for those goods in the form of the finished product of the buyer.
2 Compensation trade – When an importer and an exporter agree to exchange specified goods as payment to each other for those goods. The exchange does not have to occur at the same time.
3 Cooperation agreements – When there is a need in one country for certain resources in order to produce products and there is availability of those resources in another country a cooperation agreement may be in order. For example, country A needs electrical power to produce clothing and country B has excess electrical power but needs clothing. An agreement is made for country B to supply power in return for future payment in clothing that country A is then able to produce.
4 Counterpurchase agreements – Two purchase contracts are agreed to by buyer and seller. The buyer agrees to purchase goods or services at a specified price (contract number one). The seller agrees to purchase a certain value of goods from the buyer over a certain period of time (contract number two). Contract number one is not valid unless contract number two is accepted and signed. Thus all or part of the sales price of the original goods or services is paid for with other goods or services.
5 Offset trade – When an importer pays an exporter with goods or services.
6 Switch trade – A situation in which an importer is contractually bound to complete the purchase of goods from an exporter. The importer for some reason cannot fulfill its contract and instead "switches" the contract to another importer who then fulfills the remaining portion of the contract. Switching many times involves several importers who may pay in currency or in goods. Exporters allow switching to occur in order to complete the countertrade transaction.

The above are all examples of trade in which countertrade plays a role in an international trade transaction. Countertrade is an important facet of world commerce and should be considered by companies seeking to do business with organizations or governments of countries in which appropriate currency is blocked or in short supply. Countertrade may also be a way of turning what otherwise may be a bad loan or unpaid transaction into something of potential value.

Bibliography

Czinkota, M. R., Rivoli, P. & Ronkainen, I. A. (1989). *International business.* Chicago, IL: The Dryden Press.

Eiteman, D. K., Stonehill, A. J. & Moffett, M. H. (1992). *Multinational business finance.* 6th edn, Reading, MA: Addison-Wesley Publishing.

Grosse, R. & Kujawa, D. (1995). *International business: Theory and managerial applications.* 3rd edn, Boston, MA: Richard D. Irwin Inc.

Rugman, A. M. & Hodgetts, R. M. (1995). *International management: A strategic management approach.* New York: McGraw-Hill Inc.

JOHN O'CONNELL

countervailing duty (CVD) When a foreign government provides subsidies for the production of goods, those goods can be exported at low sale prices. In an attempt to offset the impact of exporting country subsidies, importing countries often attach a special duty to counter the low import price (thus, the name countervailing duty). The CVD raises the price of the import thereby reducing the competitive effects of the export country's original government subsidy.

JOHN O'CONNELL

country of origin This term can refer to two different things: (1) In international trade, the country of origin refers to the place where production originally took place. Country of origin is important because different rules may apply to imports from different countries. For example, goods from one country may be banned because of political problems between countries or different amounts of import duty may apply to goods from different countries. Country of origin normally must be prominently displayed on the goods themselves as well as on the shipping papers (*see* MARKING); (2) The country which an expatriate comes from is also referred to as the country of origin. After the assignment is completed it is also the country to which the expatriate is expected to return.

JOHN O'CONNELL

country risk The financial risk associated with conducting a transaction with or in a country with weak or unstable economic, political, or social systems. The degree of country risk is not subject to exact measurement, but instead must be inferred through the evaluation of a number of factors. These factors include:

1 Economic stability – The degree to which the performance of the country's economy is positive and can be expected to remain so. Factors associated with economic stability include inflation rates, balance of payments, public debt, private debt, stability of monetary system, interest rates, currency values, industrial base, reliance of foreign investment or imports, and others.

2 Political stability – Stability of the current government, wars, rebellions, strong opposing parties, terrorism, strong labor unions, type of government, relations with neighboring countries, and others.

3 Social stability – Level of education, religious affiliations, legal system, class systems, poverty level, strong culture, and others.

Country risk adds to the overall degree of risk associated with doing business in a foreign country. Most companies today review, in some manner, the degree of country risk before they become committed to interaction with a given country.

See also **Political risk**

Bibliography

Cosset, J. & Roy, J. (1991). The determinants of country risk ratings. *Journal of International Business Studies,* **22** (1), 135–42.

Doz, Y. L. & Prahalad, C. K. (1980). How MNCs cope with host government intervention. *Harvard Business Review,* March–April, 150.

Gregory, A. (1989). "Political risk management" in A. Rugman (ed.), *International Business in Canada.* 310–29. Scarborough, Ontario: Prentice-Hall, Canada.

Kennedy, C. R. Jr. (1991). *Managing the international business environment: Cases in political and country risk.* Englewood Cliffs, NJ: Prentice-Hall.

Kenyon, A. (1990). *Currency risk and business management.* Cambridge, MA: Blackwell Publishers.

Rogers, J. (1986). *Global risk assessments: Issues, concepts, and applications.* Riverside, CA: Global Risk Assessments.

JOHN O'CONNELL

country risk assessment   An attempt to evaluate the extensiveness of economic, political, and social risks associated with a particular country or region of the world. Risk assessment allows management to estimate the potential impact of country risk on their activities in the country. The greater the country risk, the greater the return that should be expected from an investment or loan. The factors associated with country risk are very similar to those associated with what is referred to as "political risk." This is because many of the contributing factors to country risk result in government action to resolve problems. Political risk is the impact of government action on an organization's assets and its ability to continue operations. A detailed discussion of risk assessment is under the heading of "Political risk assessment."

Bibliography

Coplin, W. D. & O'Leary, M. K. (1994). *The handbook of country and political risk analysis.* New York: Political Risk Services.
Cosset, J. & Roy, J. (1991). The determinants of country risk ratings. *Journal of International Business Studies*, **22** (1), 135–42.
Howell, L. D. (1994). The political sociology of foreign investment and trade: Testing risk models for adequacy of protection. *AGSIM Faculty Publication*, No. 94–05,

JOHN O'CONNELL

country similarity theory   The conduct of trade is dependent upon there being a supply of goods and services and a corresponding demand for those (or similar) goods and services. The country similarity theory states that countries having the most similarities with one another (degree of industrialization; per capita incomes; savings habits; communications and transportation systems; degree of technology; language; etc.) will be the most likely to trade with one another. This rather logical theory is based upon the premise that similar countries will be interested in similar goods and services. Not a devastatingly scientific theory, but one which at least points to specific countries as being good candidates for a company's first foray into international trade.

JOHN O'CONNELL

court of arbitration   One of the major problems associated with international transactions is knowing what to do if a dispute arises between companies from different countries. Many companies attempt to reduce the time and expense related to this type of problem by agreeing ahead of time that disputes will be handled through arbitration. The major source of arbitration assistance internationally is the International Chamber of Commerce (ICC). The ICC established the International Court of Arbitration, which acts as the decision-making body in arbitration matters. The court hears matters which are voluntarily placed in front of it by parties in dispute. The parties must agree before they begin their business relationship to abide by the decisions of the arbitration process specified in their contract. Access to the court may be achieved by contacting the International Chamber of Commerce. The court itself is located in Paris.

See also **Arbitration; International Chamber of Commerce**

Bibliography

Litka, M. (1991). *International dimensions of the legal environment of business.* 2nd edn, Boston, MA: PWS-Kent Publishing Company.

JOHN O'CONNELL

Court of Justice   *see* EUROPEAN COURT OF JUSTICE

CPT   *see* CARRIAGE PAID TO

crédit mixte   A French term meaning that the financing provided for an export transaction comes from two sources: normal bank lines of credit and from government assistance funds.

JOHN O'CONNELL

credit protocol   This is an agreement between credit-granting agencies in two countries to each provide credit to importers from the other country. When a company is involved with numerous import transactions it is time consuming and sometimes costly to arrange for the transfer of currency for each separate transaction. A simpler way of financing purchases in another country is for the trade financing agencies of both countries to agree that the company in country A can use the credit available from the agency in country B to finance its purchases. This allows the company to arrange for financing in the foreign country rather than in its own country – a much simpler process. The agreement between credit-granting agencies is essentially a guarantee of the private company's borrowings from the foreign credit-granting agency.

JOHN O'CONNELL

credit risk insurance   Insurance which protects against a borrower defaulting on a debt to the insured. International trade is commonly carried out with some form of credit being advanced by the exporter to the importer. Credit insurance reimburses the exporter if the importer fails to pay for the ordered goods. International credit insurance resembles credit insurance secured for an exporter's domestic credit risk. That is, the price of insurance generally is dependent upon the insured's credit policies, amounts outstanding, and past credit history. This type of insurance is underwritten very differently from other insurances. With credit risk insurance the insured's financial condition, financial management, and credit policies provide the basis for pricing and issuing the insurance contract.

Bibliography

Eiteman, D. K., Stonehill, A. J. & Moffett, M. H. (1992). *Multinational business finance.* 6th edn, Reading, MA: Addison-Wesley Publishing.

JOHN O'CONNELL

creeping expropriation   Expropriation involves government action to seize the assets of a foreign entity. Expropriation infers a quick action by government. Creeping expropriation, on the other hand, involves the gradual removal of property rights from a foreign entity. Creeping expropriation could take many forms: gradual increases in tax rates on profits which eventually make a business unprofitable to operate; instituting ever-increasing barriers to removing profits or dividends from the country; gradually increasing property tax rates for foreign companies; changing the percentage of ownership which must be held locally; as well as many other actions. Creeping expropriation takes place over the long run and is generally not subject to political risk insurance compensation.

See also **Political risk**

Bibliography

Coplin, W. D. & O'Leary, M. K. (1994). *The handbook of country and political risk analysis.* New York: Political Risk Services.
Gregory, A. (1989). "Political risk management" in A. Rugman (ed.), *International Business in Canada.* 310–29. Scarborough, Ontario: Prentice-Hall, Canada.

JOHN O'CONNELL

cross-cultural communication   Communication between cultures is one of the greatest challenges facing an international manager. Not only does the manager face the normal problems of creating a concise and clear communication, but the communication must be accomplished in the context of another culture. The following discussion reviews a number of areas which must be considered in order to conduct successful cross-cultural communication.

1 The medium of communication – The "medium" is the method by which a message is sent. Mediums of communication include writing (notes, E-mail, annual statements, letters, etc.), speaking (telephone, videotape, public address system, face-to-face conversation, etc.), body language (eye contact, motions of the hands and arms, head down or looking straight ahead, etc.), tone of voice (high anxious tone, soft, aggressive and loud), depicting a message in pictures (directions for use, signs, etc.), or any combination of mediums. A very important aspect of cross-cultural commu-

nications is knowledge of which medium is acceptable for different situations. For example, is a note sufficient to convey a message or do the formalities of a culture require a face-to-face meeting. Sending a note may be taken as a rude approach from someone who does not want to face the person receiving the message. On the other hand, a face-to-face meeting when a simple note would convey the same message may place more importance on the communication than intended by the sender. The medium used depends on a number of factors including: large or small audience; how quickly the message must be sent; distance of communication (across the room or to another country); intent of message (good news or downsizing of the organization); legal considerations (contracts, hiring/firing); simple or complex message; message content needed in future; and the availability of various communications media.

2 The information intended versus the information received – People normally feel that communication is successful when the person receiving the message does not have any questions or does not express any concern over the message's content. If the sender delved further into the reasons that no questions were asked or concerns expressed he/she may find one or more of the following had occurred: the receiver did not understand the message sufficiently to respond in any manner; the receiver felt the message content was irrelevant and chose to ignore it; the message was unimportant and did not affect the receiver; or any number of other misinterpretations which occur during the process we call "communication." When developing information to be included in a communication the sender must take into consideration the audience (education level, cultural values, need for direction as well as acceptance of direction from superiors, etc.). The challenge in cross-cultural communication is to make certain that the message is received in the way intended. This requires a great deal of understanding on the part of the sender of the receiver's cultural background and current situation. Failure to have knowledge of the parties who receive messages will virtually assure miscommuni-

cation. The message will be either too intricate, too simple, or irrelevant to some or all of those to whom it is transmitted. The result will be that the message is not understood (too intricate), people feel talked down to (too simple), or the message is not taken seriously (felt to be irrelevant).

3 Timing of communications – Determining the appropriate time for communicating certain ideas is extremely important for successful cross-cultural communications. Some cultures desire to discuss work only at work and leave the rest of the time for family and friends. Japanese managers may allow themselves to have fun after work but rarely on the job. Social occasions are just that in many countries, whereas in the United States social occasions are commonly the site of business contacts. The first time one meets a Middle Eastern business person is not the time to get right to business discussions, relationship-building and trust are important precursors to business activity. Even important communications must be relayed at the appropriate time or their import may be overshadowed by the ill timing of the message.

4 Who communicates – One of the problems international managers have is that they are unfamiliar with communication patterns in different cultures. Cultures in which relationship building is important may not allow a business discussion to take place between the company president and an unknown representative from another company. Instead a lower level manager or representative will act as a go-between. The importance of a message will often dictate who the communicator will be. For example, when Johnson and Johnson had a problem with Tylenol which had been tampered with, the head of the company appeared on television. This showed the importance of the message to the consuming public. If a middle manager had made the recall announcement its impact would not have been as great.

When communicating across cultures it is important to know the expectations of all parties to the communication. Expectations as to the proper wording, timing, place of communication, sender of the message, and appropriate medium of communication. If the timing, wording, sender or receiver, medium, or any of a number of other important considerations is inappropriate, the communication has a good chance of failing.

Bibliography

Black, J. S. & Mendenhall, M. (1993). Resolving conflicts with Japanese: Mission impossible?. *Sloan Management Review*, Spring, 83.

Brislin, R. W. (1981). *Cross-cultural encounters.* New York: Pergamon Press.

Evans, W. A., Sculli, D. & Yau, W. S. L. (1987). Cross-cultural factors in the identification of managerial potential. *Journal of General Management*, 13 (1), 52–7.

Francis, J. N. (1991). When in Rome? The affects of cultural adaptations on the intercultural business negotiations. *Journal of International Business Studies*, 22 (3), 403–28.

Hayes, J. & Allison, C. W. (1988). Cultural differences in the learning styles of managers. *Management International Review*, 28 (3), 75–80.

Moran, R. (1988). *Venturing abroad in Asia: Complete business traveller's guide to cultural differences in eleven Asian countries.* New York: McGraw-Hill Book Co.

Moran, R. T. (1994). *NAFTA: Managing the cultural differences.* Houston, TX: Gulf Publishing Company.

Terpstra, V. & David, K. (1985). *The cultural environment of international business.* Dallas, TX: South-Western Publishing.

JOHN O'CONNELL

cross-cultural training   Cross-cultural training is designed to help people become more aware of the differences between cultures throughout the world. An understanding of the differences makes employees more sensitive to the values, wants, and needs of others. Such an awareness can make management more effective and employees more productive in jobs located either in other countries or involving contacts with other countries. Friction associated with work force diversity may also be reduced through cross-cultural training.

Cross-cultural training is commonly carried out in the following ways: (1) lectures by persons familiar with different cultures; (2) awareness training in which employees are exposed to the values and behaviors found in a particular culture; (3) experiential training through field trips, role playing, or country visits; (4) attribution training to assist in developing an understanding of why people act or do things in the way they do; (5) behavior modification training to allow employees to understand the reward and punishment systems in another country.

See also **Expatriate training**

Bibliography

Alkhafaji, A. F. (1990). *International management challenge.* Acton, MA: Copley.

Evans, W. A., Sculli, D. & Yau, W. S. L. (1987). Cross-cultural factors in the identification of managerial potential. *Journal of General Management*, 13 (1), 52–7.

Ferraro, G. P. (1990). *The cultural dimension of international business.* Englewood Cliffs, NJ: Prentice-Hall.

Kuroda, Y. & Suzuki, T. (1991). A comparative analysis of the Arab culture: Arabic, English, and Japanese language and values. *International Association of Middle Eastern Studies,*

Landis, D. & Brislin, R. (1983). *Handbook on intercultural training.* New York: Pergamon Press.

Mendenhall, M. E., Dunbar, E. & Oddou, Gary (1987). Expatriate selection, training, and career pathing: A review and critique. *Human Resource Management*, 26, 331–45.

Pulatie, D. (1985). How do you ensure success of managers going abroad. *Training and Development Journal*, December, 22–4.

Ronen, S. & Tung, R. L. (1981). Selection and training of personnel for overseas assignments. *Columbia Journal of World Business*, Spring, 68–78.

JOHN O'CONNELL

cross licensing   Situations exist in which different companies are working on similar research and development projects at the same time. One company makes advances in one area and the other in a second area. By joining effort and sharing discoveries and technology, both companies could move forward more quickly then either could alone. This synergistic approach (resulting in mutual benefit) could be accomplished by a cross-licensing arrangement. Under cross-licensing each company gives the other permission to use patented or copyrighted technology, processes, or inventions. Cross-licensing achieves two things: (1) gains for both companies are increased through the dual use of intellectual property rights; and (2) both companies still protect their property rights because the only party able to use them is the company designated in the cross-licensing agreement.

Bibliography

Deresky, Helen (1994). *International management.* 1st edn, New York: HarperCollins.

Seminsky, M. & Bryer, L. G. (eds) (1994). *The new role of intellectual property in commercial transactions.* New York: John Wiley & Sons.

JOHN O'CONNELL

cross rate of exchange   When seeking to compare the relative value of a number of different currencies it is common to compare all currencies to a single base. For example, when seeking to compare French francs, British pounds, and Japanese yen the simplest way may be to compare them all to the United States dollar. This provides a good measure of their comparable value. The determination of an exchange rate between two or more currencies by using a third currency's exchange rate as a base develops what is referred to as a "cross rate of exchange."

JOHN O'CONNELL

CTO   *see* COMBINED TRANSPORT OPERATOR

cultural adaptation   The process through which a person becomes able to function successfully in another culture. Failure to adapt is the major reason expatriates find themselves unable to complete overseas assignments. Generally people are chosen for overseas assignment for their technical ability or other skills related to the tasks required of them by the employer. Thus, it is typically not the inability to do a task which causes failure, it is the inability to adapt to the new cultural environment.

See also **Environment, cultural**

Bibliography

Briody, E. K. & Chrisman, J. B. (1991). Cultural adaptation on overseas assignments. *Human Organization,* **50** (3), 264–82.

David, K. (1991). *"Field research" in the cultural environment of international business.* Cincinnatti, OH: South-Western.

Francis, J. N. (1991). When in Rome? The affects of cultural adaptations on the intercultural business negotiations. *Journal of International Business Studies,* **22** (3), 403–28.

Howard, C. G. (1982). How best to integrate expatriate managers into the domestic organization. *Personnel Administrator,* July, 27–33.

Johnson, M. (1992). *Cultural guide to doing business in Europe.* 2nd edn, Boston, MA: Butterworth-Heinemann.

Watson, W. E., Kumar, K., Subramanian, R. & Nonis, S. A. (1990). Differences in decision making regarding risk between culturally diverse and culturally homogeneous groups.. *IAMM Proceeding,* **1**, 130–2.

JOHN O'CONNELL

cultural adoption   Many employees who are sent overseas not only learn to work and live within a new culture but actually take on some of the culture's values, etc. as their own. For example, some employees sent to Asia take on the local religion and values in place of those of their original culture. Although cultural adoption is not necessarily good or bad, care must be taken by the employee to determine the impact of such changes upon returning to the home country. Employees who adopt important cultural attributes of their host country may not desire to come home when the time comes. The new location has in fact become their home.

See also **Cultural adaptation**

JOHN O'CONNELL

cultural assimilation   This is the process through which a person not only is aware of the differences and nuances of a new culture, but also is able to incorporate these differences into daily work and private lives. This does not mean the employee gives up home country values or attitudes, but instead takes the position that both cultures can coexist with one another. A simple home country example will show how this works in a diverse work force. An employee works his way up in the organization from yard worker to middle management. The employee is able to easily converse with yard workers and top management on their terms. Two separate cultures exist between workers and top management, but this manager has learned to coexist in each without making judgments about which is better or worse or good or bad. Cultural assimilation does much the same thing for expatriates.

Bibliography

Glover, M. K. (1990). Do's and taboos: Cultural aspects of international business. *Business America*, **August**, 2–6.

JOHN O'CONNELL

cultural borrowing   When a person is placed into another culture some of the culture's attributes may take the place of some attitudes, values or ways of doing things that person learned in his/her home culture. A person coming home from an overseas assignment may very well exhibit not only the values, etc. of his/her original culture but also some of those of the new culture. The person has borrowed items or beliefs from the new culture. Generally, upon return to the home culture, borrowed beliefs slowly become extinguished.

See also **Cultural adoption**

Bibliography

Black, J. S. & Gregerson, H. B. (1991). When Yankee comes home: Factors relating to expatriate and spouse repatriation adjustment. *Journal of International Business Studies*, **22 (4)**, 471–94.
Moran, R. T. (1989). Coping with re-entry shock. *AGSIM Faculty Publication*, No. **89–05**,
Napier, N. K. & Peterson, R. B. (1990). Expatriate re-entry: What do repatriates have to say?. *Human Resource Planning*, **14**, 19–28.

JOHN O'CONNELL

cultural diversity   The existence of different cultures between countries; in different parts of the same country; or within a single organiza-

tion. Multinational organizations as well as many purely domestic organizations are faced with cultural diversity every day. Diversity may be displayed in the variety of social and ethnic backgrounds of workers or the variety of customers one serves. Learning to live and work in a culturally diverse world requires education and the ability to accept others as they are.

See also **Cross-cultural training; Cultural variables**

Bibliography

Ajiferuke, M. & Boddewyn, J. (1970). Culture and other explanatory variables in comparative management studies. *Academy of Management Journal*, **13**, 153–63.
Anderson, L. R. (1983). Management of the mixed-cultural work group. *Organizational Behavior and Human Performance*, **31**, 303–30.
Cox, T., Lobel, S. A. & McLeod, P. L. (1991). Effects of ethnic group cultural differences on cooperative and competitive behavior on a group task. *Academy of Management*, **4**, 827–47.
Evans, W. A., Sculli, D. & Yau, W. S. L. (1987). Cross-cultural factors in the identification of managerial potential. *Journal of General Management*, **13 (1)**, 52–7.
Hofstede, G. (1980). *Culture's consequences: International differences in work-related values*. Beverly Hills, CA: Sage Publications.

JOHN O'CONNELL

cultural empathy   The word "empathy" means a sharing of feelings. Cultural empathy means that a person has an awareness and understanding of the cultural attributes of a given society and how they differ from his/her own culture. One who is empathetic will tend to be more accepting of differences rather than seeing them as good/bad or right or wrong. This will lead to a better acceptance of the empathetic person into the new cultural setting.

See also **Cultural sensitivity**

Bibliography

Ajiferuke, M. & Boddewyn, J. (1970). Culture and other explanatory variables in comparative management studies. *Academy of Management Journal*, **13**, 153–63.

Ferraro, G. P. (1990). *The cultural dimension of international business*. Englewood Cliffs, NJ: Prentice-Hall.

Kuroda, Y. & Suzuki, T. (1991). A comparative analysis of the Arab culture: Arabic, English, and Japanese language and values. *International Association of Middle Eastern Studies*.

JOHN O'CONNELL

cultural factors   *see* CULTURAL VARIABLES

cultural insensitivity   The inability of a person to accept or to become aware of cultural differences. Insensitivity leads to miscommunication, increased stress for all parties involved, and an increased risk of unsuccessful business outcomes.

See also **Cultural sensitivity**

JOHN O'CONNELL

cultural literacy   Cultural literacy is the expert knowledge of both surface and core cultural values, norms, mores, traditions, and operating procedures of a culture. Empirical research in the field shows that expatriates serving in expatriate assignment must increase their cultural literacy in order to be successful in these assignments.

Cultural literacy involves more than knowing, for example, when and how to bow in Japan when greeting a client. An expatriate who is culturally literate understands why that tradition exists, and understands the deeper core cultural values to which that tradition is linked. When expatriates do not possess high levels of cultural literacy they naturally operate from their personal views regarding what is and what is not appropriate behavior across various life situations in the foreign culture. One's personal views are obviously only workable as guides to behavior in one's culture of birth. Thus, applying personal views as guides to one's behavior while overseas invariably leads expatri-

ates into troubling, embarrassing, and sometimes dangerous incidents in the foreign culture.

Cultural literacy enables an expatriate to understand the reasons behind the behavior he or she encounters overseas, and this understanding enables the expatriate to avoid stereotyping, racial prejudice, and other forms of inappropriate behavior while living and working in a foreign culture. Living and working in a foreign culture requires the expatriate to learn a new mental framework, one that can guide the expatriate in choosing culturally correct behaviors in the foreign culture. The acquisition of cultural literacy requires significant amounts of effort by the expatriate. Companies often try to assist in this task by offering cross-cultural training programs and other types of training.

Bibliography

Black, J. S., Gregersen, H. B. & Mendenhall, M. (1992).. *Global Assignments: Successfully Expatriating and Repatriating International Managers*, San Francisco: Jossey-Bass.

Black, J. S. & Mendenhall, M. (1990). A practical but theory-based framework for selecting cross-cultural training methods. *Human Resource Management*, **28**, 511–39.

Black, J. S., Mendenhall, M. & Oddou, G. (1991). Toward a comprehensive model of international adjustment: an integration of multiple theoretical perspectives. *Academy of Management Review*, **16**, 291–317.

Mendenhall, M. & Oddou, G. (1985). The dimensions of expatriate acculturation: a review. *Academy of Management Review*, **10**, 39–47.

Oddou, G. & Mendenhall, M. (1984). Person perception in cross-cultural settings: a review of cross-cultural and related literature. *International Journal of Intercultural Relations*, **8**, 77–96.

MARK E. MENDENHALL

cultural maps   A cultural map groups countries (cultures) based upon their similarity to one another. Cultural maps were developed by Geert Hofstede as a method of comparing cultures along what he referred to as value dimensions. A cultural map essentially shows how cultures of different countries are similar and how they are different along four dimensions: (1) Individualism – the tendency to look out for yourself first and the employer and society next. (2) Masculinity – aggressiveness, assertiveness, and inability to think of the good of others. (3) Power distance – the acceptance of an unequal distribution of power between employees of an organization; the acceptance of the right of others to command. (4) Uncertainty avoidance – the degree of acceptance of uncertain situations; the willingness to make decisions; to be flexible. Charts (cultural maps) are developed by showing the degree to which a country exhibits each of the dimensions. Countries tend to cluster when their value dimensions are similar.

The implications of cultural maps in the international business setting are very important. If one agrees with the precept that interactions between parties (trade agreements, contracts, etc.) who are similar are more likely to be successful then if the parties are dissimilar, cultural maps may allow an organization to better choose international partners based upon similar cultural attributes. Maps can also be of assistance even if countries are not close together on various attributes, because a manager will have an idea of the "differences" which do exist. This allows training and other preparation to occur to deal with those differences more successfully. The idea of a cultural map is not the source of all answers, but it is a valuable tool for use by international organizations.

See also **Value dimensions**

Bibliography

Elashmawi, F. & Harris, P. R. (1993). *Multicultural management: New skills for global success*. Houston, Texas: Gulf Publishing Company.
Ferraro, G. P. (1990). *The cultural dimension of international business*. Englewood Cliffs, NJ: Prentice-Hall.
Hofstede, G. (1980). *Culture's consequences: International differences in work-related values*. Beverly Hills, CA: Sage Publications.

JOHN O'CONNELL

cultural noise Cultural noise refers to impediments to successful communication between people of different cultures. Sources of cultural noise include differences in: language (e.g., same words have different meanings); values (e.g.,

importance of being on time or setting work schedule times in a culture); nonverbal cues (e.g., interpretation of body language); and many others. Persons involved in international communication (or domestic, if communication involves other cultures) should be aware of any barriers which may affect the message from being interpreted in the way the sender intended. This requires special understanding of the communication process and the various sources of cultural noise which may impede that process.

See also **Communication; Cross-cultural communication**

Bibliography

Moran, R. (1988). *Venturing abroad in Asia: Complete business traveller's guide to cultural differences in eleven Asian countries*. New York: McGraw-Hill Book Co.

JOHN O'CONNELL

cultural norms Cultural norms are standards of conduct or acceptable behavior in any given culture. The way people communicate (adding gestures versus just speaking); the way they eat (fork in right hand if from United States and left hand if from Europe); how close one stands when communicating to another (distant in the United States, close in Latin America); equality of men and women (strive for equality in many countries; not an issue in other countries); the work ethic (commitment to employer versus individual creativity); and many other situations are influenced by the norms of a society or culture. An expatriate or other person living overseas should be aware of the normative behaviors of the host country prior to taking up residence.

See also **Cultural variables; Expatriate training; Value dimensions**

Bibliography

Howard, C. G. (1982). How best to integrate expatriate managers into the domestic organization. *Personnel Administrator*, July, 27–33.

JOHN O'CONNELL

cultural orientation   *see* CROSS-CULTURAL TRAINING; EXPATRIATE TRAINING

cultural profiles   A description of a country (culture) based upon its acceptance or adherence to specific cultural variables. Cultural profiles are used to compare countries and cultures based upon preselected dimensions.

See also **Cultural variables; Value dimensions**

JOHN O'CONNELL

cultural relativism   Cultural relativism refers to the proposition that what is right or wrong, good or bad, justifiable or not, depends upon the culture in which it occurs. Two examples illustrate cultural relativism: drinking alcoholic beverages is not bad or wrong in Great Britain or Ireland but is wrong (and punishable by authorities) in Middle Eastern countries; bribery is illegal under the laws of the United States, but is an accepted business practice in many countries.

It is difficult to dispute the above part of the cultural relativism proposition (that major differences exist between cultures/countries between what is considered good/bad; moral/immoral; etc). However, problems of ethics and even law may occur if one takes cultural relativism to its extreme and believes the following; "Therefore, in order to get along in another country/culture, it is acceptable to act in the same manner as those from that country/culture." As an example of potential problems, such a feeling would allow a United States organization (when in another country which lacked strict antibribery laws) to bribe public officials, even though bribery is illegal under the US Foreign Corrupt Practices Act. Cultural relativism may be an appropriate part of the decision-making process in some instances, but its application must be tempered by common sense and a respect for the laws of both the host and home country.

Bibliography

Bowie, N. E. (1990). "Business ethics and cultural relativism" in P. Madsen and J. M. Shafritz (eds) *Essentials of Business Ethics.* New York: Meridian.

JOHN O'CONNELL

cultural sensitivity   An awareness of the differences between cultures and how these differences affect ways in which others work and live. It is the acceptance of differences, rather than a feeling that one way of doing things is either right or wrong. A culturally sensitive person is open to other ways of doing things and cares about adapting to differences rather than changing others to fit a model of "how one is supposed to act or believe."

See also **Cross-cultural training; Cultural insensitivity; Expatriate training**

Bibliography

Black, J. S. & Mendenhall, M. (1993). Resolving conflicts with Japanese: Mission impossible?. *Sloan Management Review*, Spring, 83.
Glover, M. K. (1990). Do's and taboos: Cultural aspects of international business. *Business America*, August, 2–6.
Ricks, D. A. (1983). *Big business blunders: Mistakes in multinational marketing.* Homewood, IL: Dow Jones-Irwin.

JOHN O'CONNELL

cultural value dimensions (Hofstede's)   *see* VALUE DIMENSIONS

cultural variables   The factors which are evaluated in determining the extent and nature of cultural differences. The following set of variables were described by Harris and Moran in their interesting book *Managing Cultural Differences.* Each variable is important to an international manager because it may be the source of a particular work behavior or attitude with which the manager is unfamiliar.

Harris and Moran's cultural variables are presented below (in alphabetical order, not order of importance):

1 Associations – This variable addresses the various groups with which an individual may be associated. Groups are of many types: fraternal, religious, business, professional, trade, union, advocacy (e.g., environmental), political, and many others. Each group may have an impact on an employee in terms of ethical issues, work habits, priorities, loyalties, and other important factors which may affect job performance. The exact nature of the impact depends upon the employee, the group, and the country/culture being reviewed.

2 Economy – General economic factors also contribute to the way people conduct themselves on the job. The type of economy (capitalist, high government control, low government control, public versus private ownership, etc.) affects areas such as incentive systems, availability of goods and services, a worker's feelings about achievement, and loyalty to an employer.

3 Education – The types and amounts of educational opportunities offered in a country provide a reasonable measure of the availability of trained employees as well as the needs for further training to meet the needs of employers. Educational levels may dictate hiring practices (host country nationals versus expatriates) as well as the types and levels of company training programs to be offered.

4 Health – Of growing importance is the general health of people in a country. Healthy employees tend to be more productive and happier then those suffering ill health. The quality and availability of the health-care system in a country will affect the services, etc. which may have to be provided by a company. Social health-care versus private health-care has great implications for employee expectations about what the company should provide in benefits. In some countries employers are actively involved in promoting the good health of employees and their families, while in other countries employers do not become involved.

5 Kinship – The family and its importance in the life of an employee is another cultural variable which may affect employees. The trend toward family unit size is decreasing in some countries and holding stable in others. Large families are common in some countries, while smaller ones seem more acceptable in others. Family units consisting of only immediate family (parents and children) exist in many parts of the world whereas extended family units (grandparents, parents, children, and other family members) are common elsewhere. The responsibilities placed upon a family in terms of time commitments and income needs have real implications for employers.

6 Politics – The political system found in a particular country impacts both employees and the employer. If the system is democratic, employees will probably be more democratic and flexible in their attitudes. Controlled political systems (communistic, dictatorial) may decrease creativity, company loyalty, and the work ethic as well as other characteristics normally thought to be important to managers. Politics may dictate the sources of raw materials for a company, the sources of labor, the type of distribution system used, and the general activities related to commerce.

7 Recreation – This variable describes the role of leisure time in the life of a worker and his/her family. In some countries leisure time is an important and sought-after goal. Company benefits in these countries include long vacations, personal days off, provision of company-sponsored recreation activities, and on site workout and sports facilities. None of these benefits exist in some countries. In other countries, the employer is a part of the employee's leisure time as well and the employee's family literally becomes a part of the bigger company family. A country's/culture's need for leisure or free time and what the employee normally does with this time has important implications for a manager.

8 Religion – In certain countries religion is the most important cultural variable related not only to the workplace but also to the daily lives of the people (Middle Eastern countries). In other countries the impact is much more difficult to perceive or measure (United States, Australia). Religious teach-

ings guide the everyday work and other activities of many workers around the world. These must be taken into consideration by managers when dealing with many factors such as employee workweek, hours of work, religious holidays, values of the company.

Bibliography

Deresky, Helen (1994). *International management.* 1st edn, New York: HarperCollins.

England, G. E. (1978). Managers and their values systems: A five-country comparative study. *Columbia Journal of Business*, Summer, 35–44.

Graham, J. L. (1985). The influence of culture on business negotiations. *Journal of International Business Studies*, 16 (1), 81–96.

Harris, P. R. & Moran, R. T. (1987). *Managing cultural differences.* 2nd edn, Houston, Texas: Gulf Publishing.

Kelley, L., Whatley, A. & Worthley, R. (1987). Assessing the affects of culture on managerial attitudes: A three-culture test. *Journal of International Business Studies*, Summer, 17–31.

Mead, Richard (1994). *International management: Cross cultural dimensions.* Cambridge, MA: Blackwell Publishers.

Webber, R. (1969). *Culture and management, text and readings in comparative management.* Homewood, IL: Irwin.

JOHN O'CONNELL

culture A culture is defined as the way a given people think, behave, feel, and react to circumstances. Cultural attributes are learned from family and friends, handed down from generation to generation, transferred through religious beliefs and teachings, taught through the application of value systems, and are observed through the customs of a nation or people. A culture is not defined by geographic boundaries (even though persons within a geographic region may be similar from a cultural basis) but instead by the value system, norms, and reward systems associated with various groups of people. Culture is shared by those who are a part of it and passed on to others in the future.

See also **Cultural variables; Value dimensions**

JOHN O'CONNELL

culture shock Frustration, confusion, fear, apprehension, and even disorientation because of differences between a person's own culture and the culture in which he/she is currently working or living. Expatriates many times suffer from culture shock. A person who does not know how to behave in personal or business activities in another culture may feel (and actually be) left out of activities and discussions. The expatriate may be perceived as being uncaring about the concerns and values of others.

Culture shock can lead to dissatisfaction and anxiety on the part of the employee. An employee (and family members as well) must be properly oriented to the new culture to reduce the impact of culture shock. Without this cultural integration the chances of expatriate failure are dramatically increased.

See also **Cross-cultural training; Expatriate training**

Bibliography

Briody, E. K. & Chrisman, J. B. (1991). Cultural adaptation on overseas assignments. *Human Organization*, 50 (3), 264–82.

Hofstede, G. (1980). *Culture's consequences: International differences in work-related values.* Beverly Hills, CA: Sage Publications.

Moran, R. T. (1989). Coping with re-entry shock. *AGSIM Faculty Publication*, No. 89–05,

Oberg, K. (1960). Culture shocks: Adjusting to new cultural environments. *Practical Anthropology*, July–Aug 1960, 177–82.

JOHN O'CONNELL

currency depreciation A decrease in the value of a currency with respect to the value of other currencies. When this occurs, that currency will purchase less on the international market and import costs will increase. An organization holding a currency that depreciates or is a creditor of anyone paying in that currency will show a decline in asset value.

JOHN O'CONNELL

currency devaluation *see* DEVALUATION

currency diversification A person or company desiring to reduce the currency risk (fluctuations, devaluation) may decide to conduct operations in a number of different currencies. The theory is that decreases in value of one currency may be offset by increases in others. Reducing risk through investment diversification and product diversification are aspects of the same diversification strategy.

JOHN O'CONNELL

currency futures market *see* FUTURES

currency hedge *see* FOREIGN EXCHANGE RISK MANAGEMENT

currency inconvertibility A government may restrict the right of foreign firms to repatriate (send home) profits to their home country. Thus, all profits remain in the foreign country. If an organization does not have other operations in that country, or the owners do not have residence there this may cause great hardship. Inconvertibility may arise because of the passage of new laws or because of administrative slowdown. Administrative slowdown refers to situations in which the government bureaucracy in a foreign country slows (either intentionally or not intentionally) the process to convert currency to such a point that it becomes a financial burden to foreign-owned companies. Insurance is available for both causes of currency inconvertibility.

See also **Political risk; Political risk insurance**

JOHN O'CONNELL

currency option A currency option allows a person to buy or sell currency at a fixed price for a specified period of time. Persons purchasing options are usually seeking to hedge a previous commitment of currency or to profit if the exchange rate moves in the "right" direction for their investment.

See also **Foreign exchange risk management**

Bibliography

Peters, C. C. & Gitlin, A. W. (eds) (1993). *Strategic currency investing: Trading and investing in the foreign exchange markets.* Hinsdale, IL: Probus Publishing Company Inc.

JOHN O'CONNELL

customhouse broker Importers often feel that their tasks are complete when arrangements have been made to pay for and take delivery of imported items. However, another obstacle may lie in the path of the successful completion of the transaction: the customs authority of a country. Obtaining custom's approval to bring goods into a country (clearing customs) is not always a simple task. Appropriate papers must accompany imports and all requirements of the importing country must be met. Privately-owned and operated consultants called customhouse brokers are ready to assist importers in clearing goods through customs. All necessary papers will be obtained, clearances, certificates (country of origin, health, etc.) and the documents will be checked by the broker in order to speed the customs clearing process. For this service they charge a fee. Customhouse brokers are licensed by the appropriate government agency. These people generally know how to get goods cleared quickly and are usually worth the expenditure.

JOHN O'CONNELL

customs agencies The government agency responsible for enforcing regulations applicable to the importation and exportation of goods from a country. In this capacity, customs agents inspect property, classify as to type of good or commodity, determine if any special regulations apply to the property, assess applicable duties or other charges, and eventually clear (or in some cases refuse admittance to or confiscate) property. Customs authorities are usually charged with reducing the incidence of smuggling of legal property as well as the entrance of illegal property into a country.

Bibliography

Albaum, Gerald, Strandskov, Jesper, Duerr, Edwin & Dowd, Lawrence (1994). *International marketing and export management*. 2nd edn, Wokingham: Addison-Wesley.

Zodl, J. A. (1992). *Export–Import: Everything you and your company need to know to compete in world markets*. Cincinnati, OH: Betterway Books.

JOHN O'CONNELL

customs broker   *see* CUSTOMHOUSE BROKER

customs classification   Imports are classified in order to keep records of the amounts and values of goods brought into a country. Classifications are also made to determine which tariffs (if any) or other duties apply. Goods are also checked to ascertain whether they are restricted or banned from entry to a country.

JOHN O'CONNELL

customs clearing agent   *see* CUSTOMHOUSE BROKER

customs clearing time   The time it takes for customs officials of a country to make inspections and process the paperwork necessary to allow goods to enter a country. The time period varies depending upon the type of property and the country into which it is imported.

JOHN O'CONNELL

customs declaration   A form presented to customs inspectors at the point of entry as a verification of the types and values of property which are brought into a country by travelers. Most people who have traveled internationally have filled out a customs declaration form.

JOHN O'CONNELL

customs invoice   A document sometimes required by customs authorities in order to allow imports to enter a country. A customs invoice must be completed on the form specified by the country. The invoice includes information which the country desires but which is not found on the ordinary commercial invoice.

See also **Entry documents**

Bibliography

Johnson, T. E. (1994). *Export–Import procedures and documentation*. New York: Amacom.

JOHN O'CONNELL

customs valuation   The value of goods as set by the customs authorities of a country. The value normally should be near the price of the goods noted on the customs declaration form plus any adjustments allowed under customs regulations of a country. In the United States, an importer can dispute the value assigned by inspectors, up to and including a hearing in front of the US Customs Court.

JOHN O'CONNELL

customs valuation code   *see* AGREEMENT ON CUSTOMS VALUATION

CVD   *see* COUNTERVAILING DUTY

— D —

D/A *see* DOCUMENTS AGAINST ACCEPTANCE

DAC *see* DEVELOPMENT ASSISTANCE COMMITTEE

DAF *see* DELIVERED AT FRONTIER

danger pay Employees may be placed in danger when they are transferred to certain countries because of political unrest, actions of terrorists, active war or insurrection, or public reaction to citizens of specific foreign countries. Some companies will compensate their employees at higher levels when the job places them in extraordinarily high danger. "Danger" pay is given to employees from the time they enter the dangerous country or region until the time they leave. Danger pay may also be referred to as hazardous duty pay.

See also **Compensation package**

JOHN O'CONNELL

date draft A draft which expires in a specified number of days after its issuance, even if not yet presented for payment.

See also **Draft**

JOHN O'CONNELL

dating systems The way the calendar date is expressed in numbers is different in various countries. For example: 4/7/95 either means April 7, 1995 in the United States or July 4, 1995 in Great Britain. The difference lies in the ordering of the day, month, and year. Although this may seem to be a minor inconvenience, think about the United States manufacturer with a contract to produce goods for a European purchaser as of 4/12/95. The US manufacturer is ready for delivery on April 12, 1995 but the European purchaser is not ready to take delivery until December 4, 1995. To avoid problems with numerical dating always abbreviate the month when dating international correspondence. Thus, July 12, 1995 becomes either JUL/12/95 or 12/JUL/95. Either way it is clear that the month is July and the day is the 12th.

JOHN O'CONNELL

DCR *see* DOMESTIC CONTENT REQUIREMENTS

DDP *see* DELIVERED DUTY PAID

DDU *see* DELIVERED DUTY UNPAID

de facto protectionism Countries often pass legislation to restrict the flow of certain imports. These protectionist activities comprise statutory moves toward protecting local goods manufacturers and distributors. Even without statutes or formal regulations countries can still protect what they see as their national interests. De facto protectionism may take the form of delays in clearing imported goods, setting standards for imports which are difficult to meet, or making it difficult to secure import licenses. All of these activities are examples of protectionist actions even though such actions are not backed by formal government action.

Bibliography

Bowker, R. R. (1994). *Report on U.S. trade and investment barriers (1993): Problems of doing business with the U.S.* Chester, PA: Diane Publishing Company.

Korth, C. (1985). *Barriers to international business.* Englewood Cliffs, NJ: Prentice-Hall.

JOHN O'CONNELL

debt rating   The level of credit-worthiness of an organization. An organization's debt rating will affect its ability to secure funds and the cost of those funds.

See also **International debt rating**

JOHN O'CONNELL

decentralized management   The degree to which control of functions or operations is vested in a multinational company's foreign subsidiaries. The more decision making and control is left to the subsidiary the more decentralized the management. For examples of factors to review to decide whether management should be centralized or decentralized (*see* CENTRALIZED MANAGEMENT).

Bibliography

Phillips, N. (1992). *Managing international teams.* London, England: Pitman Publishing.

Punnett, B. J. & Ricks, D. (1992). *International business.* Boston, MA: PWS-Kent.

JOHN O'CONNELL

deconsolidation   *see* BREAK-BULK

delivered at frontier – named place (DAF)
A trading term under which the seller's responsibilities for goods ceases when the goods are delivered at the frontier (border, but before customs border) of the country named in the contract. This term is generally used for land transportation by rail or truck.

Bibliography

International Chamber of Commerce (ICC) (1990). *Incoterms 1990.* New York, NY: ICC Publishing Corp.

JOHN O'CONNELL

delivered duty paid – named place of destination (DDP)   This trade term describes the situation in which the seller of goods has the greatest amount of responsibility. The seller is responsible for: inland freight in the seller's country; vessel loading costs; water/air freight charges; costs of unloading the vessel; import duties; and inland freight charges in the buyer's country. If the named place of destination is the buyer's loading dock, the seller is responsible for all costs to that point. The buyer bears no responsibility until the goods are delivered to the named destination. Title transfers on the dock of the place of destination. The seller is responsible for securing the export and the import license.

Bibliography

International Chamber of Commerce (ICC) (1990). *Incoterms 1990.* New York, NY: ICC Publishing Corp.

JOHN O'CONNELL

delivered duty unpaid – named place of destination (DDU)   Under this trading term the seller makes goods available at a specified location in the buyer's country. The seller is responsible for the cost of inland freight in the seller's country; cost of loading the vessel; ocean/air freight costs; securing and paying for export insurance; the cost of unloading the vessel and the cost of inland transportation in the buyer's country to the specified point of destination. The buyer is responsible for import duties. Title to the goods transfers at the specified point of destination. The seller is responsible for securing the export license and the buyer the import license.

Bibliography

International Chamber of Commerce (ICC) (1990). *Incoterms 1990.* New York, NY: ICC Publishing Corp.

JOHN O'CONNELL

delivered ex quay duty paid – named port of destination (DEQ – duty paid) This trade term requires the seller to deliver goods to the buyer at the quay (wharf) at a specified port. The seller is responsible for inland freight charges in the export country; the cost of loading the vessel; all costs of ocean/air freight; securing and paying for export insurance; the cost of unloading the vessel; and import duties. The buyer is responsible for paying inland freight in the buyer's country. Title to goods transfers when goods reach the dock in the importer's country. The seller is responsible for securing the export license and the import license.

Bibliography

International Chamber of Commerce (ICC) (1990). *Incoterms 1990.* New York, NY: ICC Publishing Corp.

JOHN O'CONNELL

delivered ex quay duty unpaid – named port of destination (DEQ – duty unpaid) This trade term requires the seller to provide for land transportation in the seller's country; load the goods on the vessel/aircraft; obtain and pay for export insurance; and unload the goods from the ship at the port of destination. The buyer is responsible for import duties and any inland freight charges in the buyer's country. Title to goods transfers when goods reach the dock in the importer's country. The seller is responsible for securing the export license and the buyer the import license.

Bibliography

International Chamber of Commerce (ICC) (1990). *Incoterms 1990.* New York, NY: ICC Publishing Corp.

JOHN O'CONNELL

delivered ex ship – named port of destination (DES) This trade term requires the seller to make goods available to the buyer while on the ship at the specified point of destination. The seller is responsible for any inland freight charges in the seller's country; costs of loading the goods onto the vessel; cost of ocean/air freight; and securing and paying for export insurance. The buyer is responsible for costs of unloading the goods from the vessel; import duties; and any inland freight charges in the buyer's country. Title to the goods transfers while the goods are still on board the ship in the import country's port. The seller is responsible for securing the export license and the buyer the import license.

Bibliography

International Chamber of Commerce (ICC) (1990). *Incoterms 1990.* New York, NY: ICC Publishing Corp.

JOHN O'CONNELL

delivery risk Risk associated with fears of a buyer that parts or repairs will not be available for machinery or equipment purchased overseas. Delivery risk is the uncertainty concerning delays in delivery of parts, lack of guarantees that parts will be available in the future, or interference with deliveries because of labor unrest or government action in a foreign country.

JOHN O'CONNELL

demurrage A penalty imposed upon a charterer (one who rents or leases) if the vessel is not returned to the owner on time. Situations arise when a ship is not promptly unloaded at the destination port. This could be due to a large number of ships awaiting unloading or for other reasons. The charter for the vessel provides a period in which to unload the ship and also for any required layovers. If the actual unloading time or the layovers are in excess of that provided for in the charter, a penalty may be assessed. This penalty is referred to as demurrage. Demurrage can also be charged by other forms of carriers (e.g., a railroad) for delays in the loading/unloading.

JOHN O'CONNELL

denationalization The process of transferring ownership and operational control from government to private ownership.

See also **Privatization**

JOHN O'CONNELL

dependent visa *see* VISA

depreciation With respect to currency exchange rates depreciation refers to the fall in value of one currency relative to other currencies. The fall in value could be due to a nation devaluing its currency or other imbalances between countries.

See also **Devaluation**

JOHN O'CONNELL

DEQ – duty paid *see* DELIVERED EX QUAY – DUTY PAID

DEQ – duty unpaid *see* DELIVERED EX QUAY – DUTY UNPAID

DES *see* DELIVERED EX SHIP

destination control statement This United States document is used to discourage exporters or others from transferring goods bound for a given location to another location which is not authorized by the US government. For example, if electronic goods were not able to be exported to a given country, a destination control statement may be issued for shipments of electronic

goods out of the US. The statement would be attached to all transportation papers (bills of lading, etc.) clearly indicating the party and the country to which the goods must be shipped. No deviation from the listed location is allowed.

Bibliography

United States Customs Service (1994). *A basic guide to importing*. Lincolnwood, IL: NTC Publishing Group.

Zodl, J. A. (1992). *Export–Import: Everything you and your company need to know to compete in world markets*. Cincinnati, OH: Betterway Books.

JOHN O'CONNELL

devaluation When a currency declines in value relative to other currencies. Although the process of devaluation may take place over a long period of time, the term devaluation is usually associated with a government action which dramatically reduces currency values as of a specific time.

JOHN O'CONNELL

Development Assistance Committee (DAC) The Organization for Economic Cooperation and Development (OECD) established the Development Assistance Committee to oversee development assistance activities of OECD members. The purpose of the Committee is to avoid duplication of effort in order to make the OECD activities as efficient as possible.

JOHN O'CONNELL

development banks Banks which are established by a government or governments to enhance the economic development of a certain country, geographic region, or the entire world. In addition to assisting member countries, development banks also make loans available to less developed countries (LDCs) at subsidized rates.

See also **Regional development banks; World Bank**

Bibliography

Ludlow, N. H. (1988). *A practical guide to the development bank business: How to identify it, market to it, and win it.* Washington, D.C.: Development Bank Associates Inc.

JOHN O'CONNELL

Development Center of the Organization for Economic Cooperation and Development   The Center was begun by members of the Organization for Economic Cooperation and Development in 1961. The purpose of the Center is to gather and disseminate information and ideas pertaining to economic development. By using the experience of the membership of the OECD, the Center produces information which is provided to developing nations to assist in their further development.

See also **Organization for Economic Cooperation and Development**

JOHN O'CONNELL

differential duty   A duty based upon the status of trading partners. Those countries seen as the most advantageous partners generally receive lower duties than partners whose trade status is not as high.

See also **Duty**

JOHN O'CONNELL

diplomat   In the international political arena a diplomat is an official representative of a government who carries out relations with foreign governments. The highest ranking diplomat is an ambassador.

JOHN O'CONNELL

diplomatic agent   Under international law a diplomatic agent is any person given responsibility and authority to act on behalf of a nation in its relations with other nations. Diplomatic agents carry out negotiations between countries, conduct the transaction of business requiring official recognition, and generally deal with all other official governmental interactions with other nations.

JOHN O'CONNELL

direct exchange rate   When an exchange rate between two currencies is stated in terms of one of the currencies (e.g., one British sterling pound is equal to $1.56 US dollars). This is referred to as a direct exchange rate.

JOHN O'CONNELL

direct importing   Direct importing exists when the only parties to the transaction are the importer who arranges the purchase of goods from an exporter and the exporter who sells the goods. No intermediaries (freight forwarders, customhouse brokers, etc.) are involved with the transaction. Direct importing requires a great deal of knowledge of the import transaction and its various requirements as well as a good deal of faith in the exporter.

Bibliography

United States Customs Service (1994). *A basic guide to importing.* Lincolnwood, IL: NTC Publishing Group.

JOHN O'CONNELL

direct marketing   When goods are sold directly to the consumer without passing through the hands of wholesalers or retailers. Direct marketing can take the form of telephone sales, mail order sales, door-to-door sales, and sales obtained through responses to television advertising which refers customers to the manufacturer of goods. In some countries direct sales are extremely popular. Amway, Avon, and Mary Kay have international reputations in the direct sales arena.

Assuming that all local laws are followed, direct marketing may be a way of testing a foreign market before taking the plunge into full overseas operations. In fact, it may be found that in some organizations, direct marketing efforts can take the place of some current international activities with little or no reduction in the bottom line.

Bibliography

Albaum, Gerald, Strandskov, Jesper, Duerr, Edwin & Dowd, Lawrence (1994). *International marketing and export management*. 2nd edn, Wokingham: Addison-Wesley.
Cateora, P. R. (1993). *International marketing*. 5th edn, Homewood, IL: Irwin.

JOHN O'CONNELL

direct selling   *see* DIRECT MARKETING

dirty bill of lading   When goods are received in damaged condition for shipment on a vessel, the master of the ship will note the damage on the bill of lading. A bill of lading with such a notation is referred to as a "dirty" bill of lading. If goods were received in good condition the bill of lading would be a clean bill of lading.

JOHN O'CONNELL

dirty float   When currency is allowed to seek its own level of value based upon market condition, the currency is said to float. When a government attempts to control the direction and magnitude of currency fluctuation the float is described as "dirty float."

JOHN O'CONNELL

dirty money   Earnings from illegal activities are referred to as dirty money. The nomenclature of crime is such that we even distinguish between how dirty the money is. "Black" money is received from actual illegal activities such as drug smuggling. "Gray" money is received from business deals which may not be illegal, but are certainly suspicious. The suspicions are that if anyone checked, the deal might be illegal. Dealing in dirty money is an illegal act in most countries.

JOHN O'CONNELL

DISC   *see* DOMESTIC INTERNATIONAL SALES CORPORATION

discriminatory taxation   Charging higher tax rates to foreign companies than for domestic companies. This type of protectionist action is not as common as it has been in the past but it still exists in many countries. The system of taxation in a foreign country must be considered when determining the method by which a company will enter that country. For example, if a local company is charged lower tax rates than a foreign-owned company, a local joint venture may be in order.

See also **Barriers; Political risk**

JOHN O'CONNELL

distributor   A distributor is an intermediary who acts on behalf of others to distribute goods. Distributors are very common in international trade. Instead of attempting to directly enter foreign markets (normally a very time-consuming and expensive proposition) an exporter may instead enter into a relationship with an importer to become a "distributor" for the exporter. A distributor does more than just import goods. A distributor also packages or repackages if necessary, advertises the goods, distributes them, and may even provide service after the sale. For all of this activity the distributor usually retains a portion of the sales and is commonly granted exclusive rights to distribute the product in a specified region. Hiring a distributor to handle goods in a foreign country is one of the simpler methods of entering a foreign market.

Bibliography

Cateora, P. R. (1993). *International marketing*. 5th edn, Homewood, IL: Irwin.

JOHN O'CONNELL

diversification strategy   In a domestic market, diversification usually means to broaden a product line so that the company is not overly reliant on a single product. In international business, diversification also applies to product lines, but it can also apply to geographic expansion. A company may diversify its activities in terms of the number of countries within which it sells products. Thus, no single country becomes the one that makes or breaks the firm. Geographic diversification also has an interesting impact on currency risk. The more diverse the operations of a company the less likely it will suffer dramatic losses due to currency devaluation in a single country. The company now deals in many currencies, which theoretically spreads its risks, thereby smoothing currency fluctuations.

Bibliography

Albaum, Gerald, Strandskov, Jesper, Duerr, Edwin & Dowd, Lawrence (1994). *International marketing and export management.* 2nd edn, Wokingham: Addison-Wesley.
Majaro, S. (1977). *Marketing: A strategic approach to world markets.* London: George Allen and Unwin.

JOHN O'CONNELL

dock receipt   A receipt issued in conjunction with the ocean carriage of goods. When cargo is received at the carrier's location, the carrier issues a dock receipt signifying its arrival. The receipt is then used to complete the Bill of Lading.

See also **Bill of lading**

JOHN O'CONNELL

documentary collection   When an exporter transfers goods to an importer in another country, the importer must provide certain documents (e.g., bill of lading, export declaration, etc.) to the import country's customs authority in order to take possession of the goods. Under a documentary collection, a bank representing the exporter has possession of the documents needed to release goods. Upon presentation of payment from the importer, the bank transfers the documents and the importer gains title and possession of the imported goods. Documentary collection may be of two types: documents against payment (D/P) and documents against acceptance (D/A).

See also **Documents against acceptance; Documents against payment; Entry documents**

Bibliography

Zodl, J. A. (1992). *Export–Import: Everything you and your company need to know to compete in world markets.* Cincinnati, OH: Betterway Books.

JOHN O'CONNELL

documentary credit   The formal name for a letter of credit.

See also **Documentary letter of credit**

JOHN O'CONNELL

documentary draft   A documentary draft is a type of bill of exchange. Documentary drafts are used in international commerce as payment instruments for exports. A draft is merely an instruction to a bank to pay a certain amount of money to a specific person. A documentary draft requires the person seeking to be paid (usually the exporter) to present documents related to the sale of goods. Documents could include a bill of lading; shipping papers; and others as stated in the draft.

See also **Bill of exchange**

JOHN O'CONNELL

documentary letter of credit   This is the formal name for a letter of credit. A seller under a letter of credit is paid by a bank upon presentation of the shipping papers and other documents specified in the letter of credit. Unless it is irrevocable, a letter of credit does not guarantee that the credit might not be revoked by the bank prior to presentation of the documents. Specific types of letters of credit are available to provide additional assurances to the seller that payment will be made upon presentation of the proper documents.

See also **Letter of credit**

JOHN O'CONNELL

documents *see* ENTRY DOCUMENTS

documents against acceptance (D/A) It is very common for an exporter to provide for a bank to transfer title documents to the buyer. The exporter generally requires the bank to hold title until receipt of bill of exchange or other payment from the buyer. Once the conditions are met and the payment is accepted by the bank the title documents are released to the buyer.

JOHN O'CONNELL

documents against payment (D/P) An exporter may require a buyer to wait for the transfer of title to exported goods until the buyer's draft has been paid or presented for payment. Under documents against payment method, the bank must hold the title documents until the draft is cashed or presented for cashing. Thus no money changes hands until all documents are in order and the draft is actually presented for cashing.

JOHN O'CONNELL

domestic content requirements (DCR) One method of increasing the domestic presence of foreign manufacturers is to require that goods produced in a country have a certain percentage of their value provided domestically. For example, assume a country or common market required at least 60% of the value of autos sold within its borders to be produced locally. Manufacturers would have to prove that for every $20,000 auto, local labor and locally-produced parts made up at least $12,000 of that value. DCRs effectively prohibit a foreign auto-manufacturer from establishing an assembly facility in another country and then importing all of the parts to construct an auto. As such, DCRs are a barrier to free trade.

See also **Barriers**

JOHN O'CONNELL

Domestic International Sales Corporation (DISC) A DISC is a United States corporation which has at least 95% of its profits and 95% of its equipment values associated with export activities. If a US corporation qualifies as a DISC it can secure export loans from the US Treasury at lower than market rates. The purpose of legislation creating DISCs was to assist in the growth and development of US export companies.

JOHN O'CONNELL

double taxation One of the problems sometimes encountered by employees sent on overseas assignments is the income tax implications of working in one country, but being a citizen of another country. Since most tax systems base their assessment on the total income of a person, it is possible that the expatriate will be requested to pay taxes in the host country and in the home country "based upon the same income." Countries which commonly have foreign workers employed within their borders often have tax agreements with other countries to assure that taxes are only paid once. Persons employed overseas must carefully determine their tax status in each country in which they work or live. If tax laws do assess more taxes than would have been collected in the home country, the compensation package for the overseas worker is often adjusted to reduce the burden.

See also **Compensation package**

Bibliography

Nexia International Staff (1994). *International handbook of corporate and personal taxes*. New York: Chapman & Hall.

JOHN O'CONNELL

draft A draft is technically a type of bill of exchange. Drafts are commonly used to pay for exports. The actual details of payment (timing, documents necessary, etc.) are included in the wording of the draft itself. The person securing a draft (usually the seller or exporter of goods) is referred to as the "drawer." The party responsible for paying the draft (usually a bank) is referred to as the "drawee." The drawee is instructed to remit the amount of the draft when the details of the transaction (as outlined in the draft) have been completed.

See also **Bill of exchange**

Bibliography

Albaum, Gerald, Strandskov, Jesper, Duerr, Edwin & Dowd, Lawrence (1994). *International marketing and export management.* 2nd edn, Wokingham: Addison-Wesley.

JOHN O'CONNELL

drawback When used in reference to importing goods to the United States, drawback is the refunding of duties paid by US importers of goods. Duties may be refunded only under specific circumstances. Circumstances in which refunds may be made include: merchandise returned to the exporter as unfit; merchandise not ordered by the importer (if returned to the exporter); and goods which are processed in some manner and then re-exported. Importers seeking to receive drawback payments must apply to the US customs authorities within a specified period of time after the goods were originally imported.

Bibliography

Serko, D. (1991). *Import practice: Customs and international trade law.* New York: Practicing Law Institute.
United States Customs Service (1994). *A basic guide to importing.* Lincolnwood, IL: NTC Publishing Group.
Zodl, J. A. (1992). *Export–Import: Everything you and your company need to know to compete in world markets.* Cincinnati, OH: Betterway Books.

JOHN O'CONNELL

drawee In export financing, the person or entity responsible for paying a bill of exchange or draft. Usually, the importer's bank is designated as the drawee on behalf of the importer.

See also **Bill of exchange**

JOHN O'CONNELL

drawer In export financing, the person or entity who receives the proceeds of a bill of exchange or draft. Usually, the buyer or importer of goods (drawee) causes a draft to be drawn in the favor of the seller or exporter (drawer).

See also **Bill of exchange**

JOHN O'CONNELL

drop-lock floating-rate note An interesting combination of a bank loan and a bond (usually found only in international finance). The float-rate note portion is a standard variable rate loan in which interest payments are set by the market. The drop-lock portion is a guarantee built into the loan that if interest rates fall to a certain point the loan will be replaced with long-term bonds carrying the lower interest charge as a fixed rate. The loan is a floating-rate instrument unless the interest rate drops. The rate is then locked by replacing the loan with fixed-rate bonds.

Bibliography

Eiteman, D. K., Stonehill, A. J. & Moffett, M. H. (1992). *Multinational business finance.* 6th edn, Reading, MA: Addison-Wesley Publishing.

JOHN O'CONNELL

dual currency bond A bond issued in one currency, but redeemable in another currency. Until maturity, interest payments on the bond are made in the issuing currency. The intent of structuring such a bond is to take advantage of low interest rates associated with one of the stronger currencies, yet at maturity redeem the bond in the home country's currency.

JOHN O'CONNELL

dumping According to the traditional definition, dumping is the practice of price discrimination in international trade, in which the exporter charges a lower price for a specific product in the export market than in his home market. International trade law, as embodied in the General Agreement on Tariffs and Trade

(GATT) article VI, recognizes two additional definitions of dumping, which can be applied if the exporter's home price is deemed inappropriate as a basis for comparison:

(1) charging a lower price for a product in one export market than in another export market; and
(2) charging a price that does not cover the cost of production, including a "reasonable" addition for selling cost and profit.

US international trade law generalizes the definition of dumping as the sale of an imported product at "less than fair value" according to the applicable basis of price comparison. According to GATT rules, if an investigation finds that dumping has taken place and "injures" a domestic industry (see below), the importing country can impose an antidumping duty in the amount of the difference between the export price and the "fair value" price.

Viner (1923) was the first to offer a systematic investigation of dumping. For the purposes of economic analysis, the central questions focus on the motivation for and welfare effects of dumping. If an exporting firm with price-making power has the ability to isolate markets with differing price elasticities of demand, for example, simple profit-maximizing behavior motivates a systematic pricing policy of dumping as an international form of third-degree price discrimination ("persistent" dumping, in Viner's terms). Typically, factors such as transportation cost or import restrictions in the exporter's home country, as well as an international market structure restricting competition, contribute to the exporter's ability to price discriminate. In addition, temporary surpluses may lead to "sporadic" dumping and third-party consignment sales may lead pricing differentials that can be characterized as "inadvertent" dumping. In these scenarios, dumping generally improves consumer welfare in the importing country while decreasing the welfare of import-competing producers, with a net gain to the importing country as long as competition itself is not significantly reduced.

The main focus of anti-dumping laws, however, is the fear of predatory dumping (*see* PREDATORY DUMPING), which is presumably motivated by a strategy by the exporter of undercutting prices of domestic producers in the targeted export market in order to drive them out of business and monopolize the market, thus decreasing total welfare in the importing country. Typically, such a strategy would require pricing below the marginal cost of production, which differs significantly from that of simple price discrimination. In addition, the "cost of production" definition of dumping, described above, may merely reflect the loss-minimizing practice of equating marginal revenue and marginal cost and then setting price below average total cost but above the shutdown point of the firm (*see* AVERAGE VARIABLE COSTS) when the firm's demand curve lies below its average total cost curve. In short, dumping may merely reflect traditional profit-maximizing/loss-minimizing behavior by firms in international markets that does not involve predatory motives.

Although the conditions for a successful predatory strategy are difficult to fulfill (see Boltuck and Litan, 1991, chapter 1), antidumping laws are driven principally by the fear of predatory dumping, whether or not there is evidence that the exporter is capable of pursuing such a strategy. According to GATT rules, in order to impose antidumping duties an antidumping investigation must establish:

(1) that dumping has taken place and
(2) that the dumping causes or threatens "material" injury to a domestic industry.

Bibliography

Boltuck, R. & Litan, R. E. (1991). *Down in the Dumps: Administration of the Unfair Trade Laws*. Washington: Brookings Institution.
Viner, J. (1923). *Dumping: A Problem in International Trade*. New York: Augustus M. Kelley.

KENT A. JONES

duty A tax on goods imported into (or exported from) a country. The purpose of a duty is to increase the price of goods to make domestic goods more competitive or to raise tax revenues for a government. Duties may also be used to punish exporters or countries for unfair trade practices. There are a number of different types of duties which may be applied to imports or exports. A list of different types of duties follows.

1 Ad valorem duty – Ad valorem duties are taxes which are paid on imported items. The duty is expressed as a percentage amount of the value of goods which clear customs. Thus, if a 10% ad valorem duty was due on $50,000 worth of goods, the duty would amount to $5,000.

2 Anti-dumping duty – From time to time, products imported into a country have sales prices which are far below the exporter's local market for such goods. This means the goods are sold for less in other countries than their market price in the exporter's home country. When this occurs production and distribution of similar domestic products of the importing country may be harmed. In order to protect local industry, taxes may be imposed on specific imports to drive their prices up, thereby allowing local industry to compete. This tax is sometimes referred to as an anti-dumping duty (*see* DUMPING).

3 Autonomous duty – Autonomous duties are levied as penalties against persons who attempt to circumvent customs restrictions or quotas. It is also applied to protect domestic industry against an unexpected increase in imports of specific types of products.

4 Compensatory duty – A reduction in tax for one commodity in exchange for increased taxes on others. A country may reduce duties on some imports from a particular country to offset higher duties being paid on other commodities. It is possible that higher duty items are more subject to public scrutiny and thus require the duty to remain high. To provide some break to a country's trading partner duties on other items may be relaxed.

5 Concessional duty – A duty between trading partners which is very low. Concessional duties are also applied by industrialized nations to developing nations in order to promote developing country economic growth.

6 Countervailing duty (CVD) – When a foreign government provides subsidies for the production of goods, those goods can be exported at low sales prices. In an attempt to offset the impact of exporting country subsidies, importing countries often attach a special duty to counter the low import price (thus, the name countervailing duty). The CVD raises the price of the import thereby reducing the competitive effects of the export country's original government subsidy.

7 Differential duty – A duty based upon the status of trading partners. Those countries seen as the most advantageous partners generally receive lower duties then partners whose trade status is not as high.

8 Exclusionary duty – This duty is aimed directly at stopping the importation of certain items or punishing a country for unfair trade practices. The suggested US 100% duty on Japanese luxury automobiles in 1995 is an example of an exclusionary duty imposed to punish Japan for what the US felt were unfair trade practices.

9 Marking duty – "Marking" is the indication of imports as to the country of origin. If improper marking occurs an additional duty is applied as a penalty.

10 Penalty duty – Any duty which is additional to regular duties. Penalty duties are imposed to add additional costs on an exporter/importer for not complying with fair trade practices or the customs laws of a country. Penalty duties include "marking" duties, "exclusionary" duties, "anti-dumping" duties, and "retaliatory" duties.

11 Preferential duty – When a country offers favored treatment to another country it often does so by reducing duties on products imported from that country. Such duties are referred to as preferential duties.

12 Prohibitive duty – A duty designed to stop the flow of imports of specific goods. Prohibitive duties may be arranged so as to apply at a low rate for a specified number or value of goods and then at a much higher or prohibitive rate for additional numbers of imports.

13 Protective duty – A tax placed on imported goods to carry out protectionist activities of a government. Taxes increase the cost of imports to consumers thereby reducing their demand. Properly applied duties will increase the development of local industry, as well as protect it from foreign competition.

14 Retaliatory duty – A penalty duty (in addition to other duties) imposed by a

country to punish another country for unfair trade practices. President Clinton's 1995 threat to increase United States duties to 100% on imported Japanese luxury cars is in retaliation for Japan's closed markets with respect to most imports.

15 Specific duty – A tax levied on imports. The amount of duty is specified as an amount per unit of weight or unit of other measurement. For example, $1.00 per item imported or $1.00 per pound or hundred weight.

16 Unilateral duty – A duty imposed by executive order to punish a country for unfair trade practices. It may also be used to reduce the flow of specific types of imports. Unilateral duties are temporary, lasting until the trade problem has been resolved.

Bibliography

Albaum, Gerald, Strandskov, Jesper, Duerr, Edwin & Dowd, Lawrence (1994). *International marketing and export management.* 2nd edn, Wokingham: Addison-Wesley.

Czinkota, M. R., Rivoli, P. & Ronkainen, I. A. (1989). *International Business.* Chicago, IL: The Dryden Press.

Daniels, J. D. & Radebaugh, L. E. (1994). *International business: Environments and operations.* 7th edn, Reading, MA: Addison-Wesley Publishing.

Grosse, R. & Kujawa, D. (1995). *International business: Theory and managerial applications.* 3rd edn, Boston, MA: Richard D. Irwin Inc.

Johnson, T. E. (1994). *Export–Import procedures and documentation.* New York: Amacom.

Rugman, A. M. & Hodgetts, R. M. (1995). *International management: A strategic management approach.* New York: McGraw-Hill Inc.

Taoka, G. M. & Beeman, D. R. (1991). *International business.* New York: Harper Collins.

Toyne, B & Walters, Peter, G. P. (1993). *Global marketing management.* Boston: Allyn and Bacon.

Zodl, J. A. (1992). *Export–Import: Everything you and your company need to know to compete in world markets.* Cincinnati, OH: Betterway Books.

JOHN O'CONNELL

duty remission   When goods are imported duties are commonly paid. Duties add to the cost of the goods. If goods are to be combined into other products and then re-exported the government may allow import duties to be refunded. The refunding of a duty essentially lowers the cost of goods for the importer making it more likely that additional goods will be imported and then re-exported. This increase in export activity is the ultimate goal of duty remission.

JOHN O'CONNELL

E

EBRD *see* EUROPEAN BANK FOR RECON-
STRUCTION AND DEVELOPMENT

EC *see* EUROPEAN COMMUNITY

economic exposure   The foreign exchange
risk associated with doing business in other
countries. The total economic exposure is the
extent to which the overall present value of an
organization may be impacted by fluctuating
exchange rates. The selling of products, obtaining of raw materials or subproducts, and other
activities expose a business to economic exposure. The value of currency may rise or fall
before, during, or after a transaction takes place.
Parties to import/export transactions or businesses doing business in other countries are
therefore exposed to losses related to deteriorat-
ing currency values while awaiting payment for
goods already delivered or those currently being
delivered.

Bibliography

Miletello, F. C. & Davis, H. A. (1994). *Foreign
exchange management*. Morristown, NJ: Financial
Executives Research Foundation.
Weigand, R. (1983). International investments:
Weighing the incentives. *Harvard Business Review*,
July–August, 146–52.

JOHN O'CONNELL

economic integration   Economic integration
is the final step in cooperation between countries
to establish freedom of movement of goods,
services, and people. True economic integration
would mean the following to member nations: no
barriers to trade or flow of goods; free flow of
capital and financial resources; and freedom of
people to move within the borders of the
association of countries. A common monetary
system and policy is essential for viable economic
integration. In 1995 there is as yet no group of
countries which has achieved true economic
integration. Perhaps the European Community
comes as close as any, but there are still barriers
which are gradually being eroded. One of the
major problems associated with economic integration is that individual countries must be
willing to give up some of their national power
and control in favor of what some call a
"supranational agency" (an organization with
authority over a group of nations). The
European Community is an example of a
common market organization which has
assumed a degree of supranational authority.

See also **Supranational agencies**

Bibliography

Springer, B. (1992). *The social dimension of 1992:
Europe faces a new EC*. New York: Greenwood
Press.
Winham, G. R. (1992). *The evolution of international
trade agreements*. Toronto, Ontario: University of
Toronto Press.

JOHN O'CONNELL

economic union   Economic unions are agreements between countries to coordinate and guide
the economic development and activities of the
member countries. Economic unions are often
referred to as trading blocs or common markets.
In order for an economic union to be successful,

national borders between member countries must be open to free trade and free movement of capital, people, and other resources. Movement must be made toward standardizing monetary systems between countries or possibly introducing a single monetary system. Examples of economic unions in various stages of development include: the European Economic Community, the North American Free Trade Association, Latin American Integration Association, Economic Community of West African States, and the Association of Southeast Asian Nations.

Bibliography

Springer, B. (1992). *The social dimension of 1992: Europe faces a new EC.* New York: Greenwood Press.

Winham, G. R. (1992). *The evolution of international trade agreements.* Toronto, Ontario: University of Toronto Press.

JOHN O'CONNELL

ECS carnet An ECS carnet allows the importer of sales or trade samples to delay or avoid payment of import duties on these samples. This is a very specific use carnet. ECS stands for Echantillon Carnet Sample. The ECS carnet is used specifically for trade samples or other commercial samples (not imports, just samples). Under the ECS carnet literally all entry requirements are nullified. Thus no duties are payable on commercial or sales samples. The ECS carnet is usually good for up to one year.

See also **Carnet**

JOHN O'CONNELL

edge corporation This is a United States term describing a US organization established to conduct international banking activities. Also formally known as an Agreement Corporation. An edge corporation is a US bank branch or subsidiary of a US-based corporation that is used mainly for international banking purposes. Edge corporations have been allowed to operate since 1981 by US banking authorities as a response to competition from foreign banking

centers. These special corporations are exempt from normal banking and anti-trust legislation with regard to pricing and restrictive trade practices. This allows edge corporations to be more creative and flexible in their activities than regular US banks.

Bibliography

Eiteman, D. K., Stonehill, A. J. & Moffett, M. H. (1992). *Multinational business finance.* 6th edn, Reading, MA: Addison-Wesley Publishing.

JOHN O'CONNELL

education allowance When a person is accompanied by family members on an overseas assignment special arrangements are often made for the children's education. Differences exist in educational facilities and programs throughout the world. To match exactly the needs of a child in two different countries may be difficult. An education allowance provides funds which may be used to provide special education opportunities or enroll a student in a private school. In this way the child's educational progress will be affected as little as possible by the move to a foreign country.

See also **Compensation package**

JOHN O'CONNELL

EEC   *see* EUROPEAN COMMUNITY

EFTA   *see* EUROPEAN FREE TRADE ASSOCIATION

EIB   *see* EUROPEAN INVESTMENT BANK

embargo   To embargo is to prohibit or forbid the movement of certain or all goods to a certain country or countries. One of the most recent embargoes was that placed against Iraq after its invasion of Kuwait in the early 1990s. As of the writing of this book (mid-1995) much of that embargo is still in place. As with the United

Nations' sanctioned embargo of Iraq, most embargoes are implemented in times of war or to attempt to force political change other than by military force. Embargoes are difficult to implement and even more difficult to enforce over long periods of time. Embargoes not only harm the country to which they are imposed, but also all of the international exporters and support organizations who were involved with export of goods and services to that country.

Bibliography

Korth, C. (1985). *Barriers to international business.* Englewood Cliffs, NJ: Prentice-Hall.

JOHN O'CONNELL

embassy An official diplomatic delegation of a nation which represents that country's interests in a foreign country. An embassy is the highest level of diplomatic representation and is located in the capital city of a foreign country. Embassy activities are managed by an ambassador who is designated an official representative by the highest government officials of his/her country. In this capacity the ambassador is responsible for carrying out all diplomatic activity between the home and host country.

JOHN O'CONNELL

EMC *see* EXPORT MANAGEMENT COMPANY

employee categories A multinational company may employ workers from a number of different countries. Employees are often classified by their country of origin. The implications associated with hiring persons from each category will be discussed after detailing each of the most common employee categories.

Multinational firms that operate in a number of countries may select employees from a variety of sources: a company may hire parent country nationals (PCNs – who are defined as persons from the home country of the organization) to fill positions at overseas locations. When PCNs are sent overseas they are referred to as expatriates. The use of expatriates, however, is often restricted by the host country government.

ment. Host countries place limits on numbers of expatriates or make it difficult, administratively, to secure proper work papers. A multinational using expatriates may also find itself with a system of management which becomes extremely expensive and difficult to perpetuate (*see* ETHNOCENTRISM; EXPATRIATE).

A multinational firm may also hire Host Country Nationals (HCNs) to staff its overseas operations. Host country nationals, who know the local culture and monetary system, will not have problems fitting into the society, and will not have the culture shock and other problems commonly associated with expatriate employees. Hiring host country nationals will also meet host government leanings toward keeping the benefits from multinational companies within its borders. Problems may arise, however, in that there may be few host country nationals who have the experience necessary to be productive in a new organization. Lack of local educational opportunities or similar industries in the host country poses a real problem for multinationals. Often multinational companies will be forced to overstaff in order to meet local demands while at the same time providing overall supervision through the use of expatriates. Generally, as time passes and local workers gain experience, overstaffing problems disappear (*see* HOST COUNTRY NATIONALS; POLYCENTRIC APPROACH TO HIRING).

A multinational firm could also hire persons from outside either the home or host country. For example, a French firm with a subsidiary in Brazil may transfer a British manager to work in Brazil. This is an example of using a Third-Country National (TCN) to fulfill employment needs. Although the person chosen may be the best from a management or skill point of view, the TCN may suffer from the same problems as any other expatriate and the company may run afoul of host government wishes (*see* GEOCENTRISM; THIRD-COUNTRY NATIONAL).

The hiring of employees for overseas operations is an extremely important task. Not only do employees need to have the technical abilities to carry out their jobs, but also the cultural knowledge to successfully live in a different country. Employee selection also may be affected by host country governments seeking to provide local benefits.

Bibliography

Brown, R. (1987). How to choose the best expatriates. *Personnel Management*, **June**, 67.

Hays, R. D. (1974). Expatriate selection: Insuring success and avoiding failure. *Journal of International Business Studies*, **5**, 25–37.

Ronen, S. & Tung, R. L. (1981). Selection and training of personnel for overseas assignments. *Columbia Journal of World Business*, Spring, 68–78.

Tung, R. L. (1984). "Strategic management of human resources in the multinational enterprise," in *Human Resource Management*. New York: John Wiley & Sons.

JOHN O'CONNELL

employment agreement *see* EMPLOYMENT CONTRACT

employment contract Employment contracts are common in international business. An employment contract details the conditions of employment including: salary, benefits, overseas allowances, vacation or other release time, days and hours of work, confidentiality of information, severance pay, etc. Although not required in many companies, employment contracts should be considered when benefits, living conditions, allowances, etc. differ from those provided to domestic employees. A common cause of such differences is an overseas assignment.

Employment contracts could also be a part of the collective bargaining process in which union or other groups of employees enter into formal contracts to provide labor or other services.

Bibliography

Business International Corporation (1982). *World executive compensation and human resource planning*. New York: Business International Corporation.

JOHN O'CONNELL

EMS *see* EUROPEAN MONETARY SYSTEM

enroute expenses Travel expenses between the home country and the assignment location are referred to as "enroute" expenses. Enroute expenses include: airfare and other transportation expense, meals, hotel costs, tips, and other incidental expenses. Enroute expenses can be very high and should be reimbursed (or better yet, paid in advance) by the employer.

See also **Compensation package**

JOHN O'CONNELL

entering foreign markets *see* MARKET ENTRY STRATEGIES

Enterprise for the Americas Initiative (EAI) The Enterprise for The Americas Initiative is a long-run plan to unify North and South American countries into a hemispheric trading group. The North American Free Trade Agreement is the latest step in linking the Americas into a powerful trading bloc. In order to be successful the industrialized nations of the area must commit vast resources to further the development of many Latin American countries. The goal of the EAI is very ambitious, but recent achievements in the area of trade agreements as well as movement toward more political and economic stability in Central and South America provide added hope for its success.

JOHN O'CONNELL

entrepôt trade Entrepôt is a French word meaning a place to store goods on a temporary basis for redistribution. Entrepôt trade takes place when goods are brought to a warehouse where they are prepared for re-exporting. Preparation may include packaging or repackaging; consolidation or being held for auction in preparation for re-exporting. Major centers for entrepôt trade are Hong Kong, Rotterdam, and Singapore. These ports (ocean and air) provide easy access to other modes of transportation for redistribution or transshipment of goods.

JOHN O'CONNELL

entry documents When goods are imported into a country they first must pass through customs for inspection, application of duties, and formal review of documents required for entry. If entry documents are not made available or are incomplete, goods will not normally be allowed to enter. Entry documents which may be required include:

1 Commercial invoice – A commercial invoice is a document which is used to provide details of an international trade transaction. Information normally required includes: buyer and seller's names, types of property, value of goods, origin and destination points, and parties accepting delivery of goods.

2 Pro forma invoice – Sometimes the commercial invoice associated with an export/import transaction is not available when goods are ready to enter a country. The US customs authorities allow the importer to substitute a pro forma invoice until the original commercial invoice can be presented.

3 Customs invoice – Some countries require a customs invoice. A customs invoice must be completed on the form specified by the country. The invoice includes information which the country desires to know but which is not found on the ordinary commercial invoice.

4 Entry manifest or customs manifest – Some countries require that a specific form, referred to as an entry or customs manifest, be provided. The manifest acts as documentation of the release of the goods.

5 Proof of right of entry (bill of lading or evidence of title or possession) – Documents used to prove ownership or legal possession of goods are needed in order to allow their entry. In other words, proof that the goods are being brought to a country by a party who has the legal right to seek entry for those goods.

6 Packing list – Generally a shipper will prepare a form that lists the types and quantities of goods being shipped. The list is used by the shipper and the receiver of goods to verify receipt of goods. This list may also be required by some customs authorities.

7 Certificate of origin – Some countries impose tariffs on certain goods from certain countries. In order to determine which imported goods are subject to tariffs, a country may require a document certifying the country of origin of the goods. The certificate allows a country to properly assess applicable tariffs or to release goods in a shorter period of time if no duties are payable.

8 Certificate of health – When exporting goods which are meant for human consumption or for use in medical care of humans, all countries require that certification of the product's purity be provided. The document is generally required to be certified by appropriate officials of the exporting country. The intent of health certification is to reduce the chances of importing contaminated goods which may cause disease or introduce pests into a country.

9 Surety bond – Customs authorities often require importers to post a bond to guarantee payment of duties or other assessments. If duties and costs are not paid the customs authority may apply to the surety for payment under the bond.

10 Phytosanitary inspection certificate – A phytosanitary inspection certificate is an official government statement from the exporting country that exports of plants, animals, meat, and other commodities have been inspected and are free from disease or insects which might damage the health or agriculture of the importing country.

11 Miscellaneous documents – Customs authorities also may request special documents associated with certain types of property or for imports from certain countries.

Importers and exporters should seek assistance from the customs authorities of each country before entering into import/export contracts. This will allow the identification of documents required to complete the transaction.

Bibliography

Albaum, Gerald, Strandskov, Jesper, Duerr, Edwin & Dowd, Lawrence (1994). *International marketing and export management.* 2nd edn, Wokingham: Addison-Wesley.

Deresky, Helen (1994). *International management.* 1st edn, New York: HarperCollins.

International Chamber of Commerce (ICC) (1990). *Incoterms 1990*. New York, NY: ICC Publishing Corp.

Johnson, T. E. (1994). *Export–Import procedures and documentation*. New York: Amacom.

United States Customs Service (1994). *A basic guide to importing*. Lincolnwood, IL: NTC Publishing Group.

Zodl, J. A. (1992). *Export–Import: Everything you and your company need to know to compete in world markets*. Cincinnati, OH: Betterway Books.

JOHN O'CONNELL

entry strategies   *see* MARKET ENTRY STRATEGIES

environment and environmental ethics
In the sense intended by "Environmental Ethics" (EE), "environment" refers specifically to the natural world of which humans are a part. It includes landscapes which function according to evolutionary natural processes. But, since human kind has substantially altered many natural systems, the "environment" also includes areas manipulated for the human use, including landscapes where agriculture, agroforestry, and cities are located.

EE appears at first to be a species of applied ethics, like business ethics or bioethics, applying ethics to the problems of human interaction with the environment. Unlike those disciplines, however, EE goes beyond the appropriate application of familiar doctrines to a certain species of practical problems: it requires that we extend or transcend our accepted moral doctrines because it forces us to rethink the boundaries of the morally considerable. Whatever our moral persuasion, we must go beyond the "anthropocentric" paradigm (that is, the position that only humans are morally considerable and that they are at the "center" of our moral reasoning), to establish who or what might possess moral standing (Van DeVeer, 1986). EE is broader, more inclusive than other practical ethics; hence it is, in some sense, a *new* ethic, addressing as it does totally new problems in many areas (Callicott, 1984; D. Scherer, 1990; L. Westra, 1994).

EE requires us to confront problems that cannot be easily resolved if we cling to pure anthropocentrism; they may remain intractable even if ours is a "weak" anthropocentrism, that is, one which admits environmental values beyond those of economic exploitation of nature (Norton, 1991). Thus the first question raised by EE, is where do we draw the boundaries of the moral community? Is sentience necessary for the inclusion of non-human animals (Singer, 1993)? Or should we consider all individual organisms equally, because of their individual teleology, their unique desire to realize themselves, which supports their intrinsic worth (Taylor, 1986)? And what of natural "wholes" such as ecosystems (Rolston, 1988; Leopold, 1969; Westra, 1994a)? Many philosophers argue that *all* these entities are valuable, hence merit inclusion in the moral community, whereas others draw the line at sentience only, or limit themselves to individual rights (Regan, 1983).

The approach we choose will dictate how we respond to the many environmental problems we encounter, problems of pollution, resource depletion, animal exploitation, waste disposal, population explosion, and erosion and depletion of soils; problems involving the air we breathe, the sun that warms the earth, the water and land we need to survive, and biotic impoverishment of habitats, loss of species, climate changes – all of which affect our life-support systems. Aside from the moral considerability question, other novel aspects of environmental problems predicate the need for a new ethic. All actions in regard to the environment can now be defined as "upstream/downstream," as all our activities have unprecedented effects through the future (in time) and globally (in space). Nothing we do, given our increasing technological powers, can be viewed as yielding limited, spatially circumscribed consequences. Thus our actions now require new social constraints, as "traditionally broad concepts of liberty," are no longer appropriate (Scherer, 1990).

Further, our environmental moral conflicts are no longer limited to disagreements about external constraints, or conflicts about group preferences. Internal conflicts are also unavoidable: we *know* that not all our preferences and choices are acceptable, as our very lifestyle has been called into question. Each one of us must thus resolve the internal conflicts between "consumer" and "citizen," learning to modify and restrain the former, while emphasizing the latter and our commitment to our community and to life on earth (Sagoff, 1989). A new understanding of what it means to be moral, and an ecological ethics which is "deep" rather than "shallow" (Naess, 1992), is required, and a changed lifestyle, based on reproductive and consumerist restraint, a changed diet, and new intellectual or spiritual goals.

EE is a relatively new field, but several conflicting approaches are already discussed in the literature. I alluded earlier to the anthropocentric/non-anthropocentric dichotomy. Some argue that to view purely human concerns as central is nothing but "speciesism" (that is, a position that is based inappropriately on the "superior" value of our species over others), whereas others respond that only humans can be moral or even appreciate or discuss questions of value, hence the moral view must be human. Another conflict is that between individualists and holists. Some ask whether individual animals or plants have value or even rights. Others argue that wholes such as species, ecosystems, the land, or the biosphere might represent the most appropriate locus of value instead (Rolston, 1988; Leopold, 1969; Westra, 1994a). Yet another debate centers on the role of science such as biology or ecology in environmental ethics.

Those who accept a holistic ethics tend to allow the scientific "is," uncertain and incomplete though it is, to provide the limits appropriate to the moral "ought" which dictates environmentally good actions (Rolston, 1988). Others prefer not to tie EE to the methodological difficulties and the predictive uncertainties of a young, science-like ecology, with its many approaches and varied scalar perspectives (Shrader-Frechette & McCoy, 1993).

In essence, EE is basic to social, political, and economic policy-making, and represents one of the major considerations required of business operations. Nowhere can the power and the reach of business have a deadlier impact on human and non-human life than through its interaction with the environment. By the same token, it is in the environmental realm that large corporate bodies, particularly multinationals, can make the greatest contribution to the public good, if their operation is seriously guided by an ecologically sound environmental ethics.

Examples of destructive business behavior are unfortunately more frequent and better know than their opposite actions. Bhopal and Exxon Valdez are names everyone has heard, whereas efforts like the funding of buffer zones sustainability next to Amisconde's Man-in-the-Biosphere project in Costa Rica, by MacDonald's Corporation, has never made front-page news (Lacher & Cesca, 1995). Another environmental problem connected with some business operations is only now being clearly recognized in all its implications, although it has a long and nefarious history: that of "environmental racism." Both "risky business" operations and hazardous-waste disposal facilities tend to permit economic considerations *only* to guide their siting policies, and thus most often choose poor areas where house and land values are lower. Hence they tend to choose existing "brownfields," already present in and around areas inhabited primarily by persons of color (Bullard, 1994; Westra & Wenz, 1995).

When business practices are hazardous to human beings, through their environmental impact, corporations may simply respond by appealing to traditional moral theories to evaluate their activities. For instance, utilitarian doctrines will dictate that the "good" of the many should represent the proper goal of moral agents; and, provided that the "good" is defined and understood in communitarian terms, rather than as aggregate preferences or purely as economic benefits, this approach may work, at least in a limited manner. Deontological emphasis on respect for human rights, if it is based on Kant's doctrine of the absolute value of life, would not permit that human health and life be risked, no matter what other benefits might accrue to any of the parties involved. Finally, Rawlsian "fairness" might serve (a) to limit unjust burdens imposed on some stakeholders in the interest of business development or profit; and (b) to curtail the exploitation of the weakest and most powerless, and thus perhaps to attack "environmental racism" from another direction.

In fact, many of the consequences of their operations can be made environmentally sound, simply through a consideration of their possible effect on human beings (thus remaining within the ambit of traditional moral theory, for instance the harm principle). Business should monitor closely their products, their processes, and their practices, in regard to both their internal and their external stakeholders, in order not to impose unacceptable risks, often unknown by those exposed to such risks and uncompensated (Westra, 1994b).

But there are other, more far-reaching problems (e.g., questions of siting location or waste disposal), where guidelines reaching beyond present, existing human stakeholders, to the non-human environment, may provide a more inclusive perspective. In general, it is hard to quantify, specify, or defend in a court of law, hazards to human health which may take years to develop. But both non-human animals and the ecosystem habitat we share with other creatures, may already be affected, in a demonstrable, non-controversial way. It is in these cases that ethics that demand respect for the environment as such might be more effective from the moral standpoint and that of public policy. The same attitude may be found increasingly in new regulations and laws. For instance, land-use cases which might have been treated as a "taking" in earlier times, now may be dealt with under the heading of "police powers," to prevent owners' business choices and to protect some endangered and fragile ecosystems, such as wetland, for future generations, when all may depend on these ecosystems' "services."

At the international level, biodiversity treaties, or the ozone protocol, also indicate a trend to universal regulation, and away from the need to demonstrate harm to a specific individual before restraints may be instituted.

After all, even the Endangered Species Act demands the protection of *habitats*, in order to ensure their goals in regard to some species. Finally, even major economic players such as the World Bank, have also changed their practices to emphasize the importance of environmental impact, which is now the major consideration in their lending policies (Goodland & Daly, 1995).

Bibliography

Bullard, R. (1994). *Dumping in Dixie*. Boulder, Colo.: Westview Press.

Callicott, J. F. (1984). "Non-Anthropocentric Value Theory and Environmental Ethics," . *American Philosophy Quarterly*, 21.

Goodland, R., and Daly, H. (1995). "Environmental Sustainability: Universal and Non-negotiable," in Perspectives on Implementing Ecological Integrity, L. Westra and J. Lemons (eds.). Dordrecht, The Netherlands: Kluwer Academic Publishers.

Lacher, T., and Cesca, R. (1995). "Ethical Obligations of Multinational Corporations to the Global Environment: MacDonald's and Conservation," in . *Perspectives on Implementing Ecological Integrity*, L. Westra and J. Lemons (eds.). Dordrecht, The Netherlands: Kluwer Academic Publishers.

Leopold, A. (1949). *A Sand County Almanac and Sketches Here and There*. New York: Oxford University Press.

Norton, B. (1991). *Toward Unity Among Environmentalists*. New York: Oxford University Press.

Regan, T. (1983). *The Case for Animal Rights*. Berkeley, Calif.: University of California Press.

Rolston, H. (1988). *Environmental Ethics*. Philadelphia: Temple University Press.

Sagoff, M. (1989). *The Economy of the Earth*. Cambridge, Mass.: Cambridge University Press.

Scherer, D. (ed.). (1990). *Upstream/Downstream: Issues in Environmental Ethics*. Philadelphia: Temple University Press.

Shrader-Frechette, K., and McCoy, E. (1993). *Method in Ecology*. Cambridge: Cambridge University Press.

Singer, P. (1993). *Practical Ethics*. 2nd edn. New York: Cambridge University Press.

Taylor, P. (1986). *Respect for Nature*. Princeton: Princeton University Press.

Westra, L. (1994a). *An Environmental Proposal for Ethics: The Principle of Integrity*. Lanham, Md.: Rowman Littlefield.

Westra, L. (1994b). "Corporate Responsibility and Hazardous Products," . *Business Ethics Quarterly*, Vol. 4, No. 1, pp. 97-110.

Westra, L., and Wenz, P. (eds) (1995) *The Faces of Environmental Racism: Confronting the Global Equity Issue*. Lanham, Md.: Rowman Littlefield.

LAURA WESTRA

environment, cultural   *see* CULTURAL DIVERSITY

environmental analysis   *see* ENVIRONMENTAL SCANNING

environmental orientation This is part of the training process for employees who expect to be assigned to overseas locations. In addition to the cultural aspects of the new country, employees must also be familiar with the political scene, language, monetary system, transportation and communications systems, and other aspects of the living "environment." Knowledge of these items will decrease inconvenience and stress for the new expatriate.

See also **Expatriate training**

JOHN O'CONNELL

environmental scanning Environmental scanning is the process of examining the marketing environment, usually with the intention of identifying trends and developments in the environment which may require marketing strategies or tactics to be adjusted. The complexity, volatility, and potential strategic significance of environmental developments are becoming more apparent to many organizations and there is increasing attention to using information and communication technologies to cope with the rapidly growing volume of data concerning environmental developments. For example, there are now many commercially available marketing information systems (MkIS) and executive information systems (EIS) which claim to offer environmental scanning services. On closer examination, however, these systems often only scan those aspects of the environment at which they are "directed" (through programming) by the systems designers and managers involved and so they risk perpetuating and legitimizing the very perceptual prejudices which they are meant to correct. Computer systems do, of course, provide a valuable aid to coping with the sheer diversity and volume of environmental data, both in terms of scanning and in terms of analysis and manipulation, but there is no substitute for the human characteristics of alertness, curiosity, and openness-to-innovation which are essential in turning environmental "scanning" into environmental "understanding."

Bibliography

Brownlie, D. (1994). Environmental scanning. In M. J. Baker (Ed.),. *The marketing book*, 3rd e d n , 139–92, London: Heinemann.
Calori, R. (1989). Designing a business scanning system. *Long Range Planning*, **22**, (113) Feb. 69–82.

DAVID YORKE

EPC *see* EUROPEAN PATENT CONVENTION

equal opportunity United States government action intended to offer equal access to employment opportunities for all citizens. In the beginning, equal opportunity regulations applied only to women and minorities, but have been expanded to include handicapped persons, and others. The reason for equal opportunity regulation is not only to correct what the government felt was unfair treatment in the past but also to stop further discrimination from occurring to other groups of people. Any organization coming to a country with equal opportunity laws must strictly comply with these laws. Severe penalties apply to any organization found to be in noncompliance.

See also **Affirmative action; Pay equity**

JOHN O'CONNELL

equivalence of advantages *see* RECIPROCITY

equivalent treatment When two countries agree to treat goods imported from each other as if they were local goods (i.e., the same laws and regulations which apply to local goods are applied to imported goods). Thus, imported items from countries which are part of the agreement are treated as if they were local goods when applying taxes, product standards, etc. This type of agreement is also referred to as national treatment, a reciprocal agreement, or reciprocity.

See also **Reciprocity**

JOHN O'CONNELL

escape clause With respect to international trade agreements between countries, an escape clause gives the ability to a country to temporarily suspend portions of the agreement if domestic industries become seriously threatened by imports. The escape clause essentially allows a country the option of reviewing its trade agreements if import strategies are not working to the mutual benefit of agreeing countries. Unforeseen increases in, or local demand, for imports of a certain industry could cause irreparable harm to local production. Escape clauses are supported by the General Agreement on Tariffs and Trade (GATT) as a method of beginning the alteration of trade agreements should the need arise.

Bibliography

Mautner-Markhof, F. (1989). *Processes of international negotiations.* Boulder, CO: Westview Press.

Simmonds, K. R. & Musch, D. J. (eds) (1992). *Law and practice under the GATT and other trading agreements, North American Free Trade Agreements, United States–Canada Free Trade Agreements: Binational panel reviews and reports.* Dobbs Ferry, NY: Oceana Publications Inc.

JOHN O'CONNELL

ethnocentric approach to hiring If one is ethnocentric in hiring practices, employees of a multinational company who are from the home country will be given preference. This could be because of lack of knowledge of foreign employee's qualifications for positions or due to bias against workers from outside the home country. Ethnocentric hiring fills all important positions with employees from the home country. This reduces potential for advancement for all other employees. This method of staffing foreign operations is extremely expensive. It also disregards the need to develop management talent in host countries. Ethnocentric hiring may lead to host countries instituting regulations to restrict the number of expatriates coming to the country.

See also **Staffing**

Bibliography

Edstron, A. & Lorange, P. (1984). Matching strategy and human resources in multinational corporations. *Journal of International Business Studies,* **15** (2), 125–37.

Heller, J. E. (1980). Criteria for selecting an international manager. *Personnel,* May–June, 47–55.

Martinez, Z. L. & Ricks, D. A. (1989). Multinational parent companies' influence over human resource decisions of affiliates: U.S. forms in Mexico. *Journal of International Business Studies,* **20** (3), 465–87.

JOHN O'CONNELL

ethnocentrism This is a feeling that one's own attitudes, values, and ways of thinking are the best. An ethnocentric person would feel that different attitudes, values, norms, etc. commonly found in other cultures, are not as good as his/her own ways of thinking or acting. This approach to other cultures is the least likely to be successful in terms of a person adapting to or being assimilated into that culture.

JOHN O'CONNELL

Europe 1992 The phrase "Europe 1992" was an expression of the proposed economic unification of the European Community (EC). The date was the target for the various agreements between countries of the EC to go into full effect. Although by 1995 much progress had been made toward complete economic integration, much more has to be done. Member countries still have some trade restrictions, political problems between governments are slowing progress, and integration seems to be hampered by less than glowing economic performance.

See also **European Community**

Bibliography

Springer, B. (1992). *The social dimension of 1992: Europe faces a new EC.* New York: Greenwood Press.

JOHN O'CONNELL

European Bank for Reconstruction and Development (EBRD) A bank, established in 1991, for the purpose of promoting free enterprise in the former communist nations of eastern Europe. The bank's interests include providing venture capital for industry, assisting firms with privatization of former governmental operations, and assisting in solving the many environmental problems facing eastern Europe.

Bibliography

Ludlow, N. H. (1988). *A practical guide to the development bank business: How to identify it, market to it, and win it.* Washington, D.C.: Development Bank Associates Inc.

JOHN O'CONNELL

European Central Bank (ECB) One of the conditions which must be met in order to achieve complete economic integration of the European Community is that a single monetary system be developed under the care of a single central bank. The European Central Bank is a proposal, not a reality. Planners suggest the Bank will be functional by the year 2000.

JOHN O'CONNELL

European Commission The European Commission is a supranational body (a separate entity whose policies span a number of countries) created by the European Community (EC) to suggest and initiate regulations affecting all EC nations. The commission is comprised of a representative from each EC nation (two each from France, Germany, Great Britain, Italy, and Spain). The commission attempts to see that the implementation of EC directives (policies agreed to by members) is accomplished. The commission also has the power to rule on mergers of companies which may affect competition and the distribution of goods (mainly drugs and food) which may be unfit for consumption. The Commission is the implementation body of the European Community.

See also **European Community**

Bibliography

Yannopoulos, G. N. (1988). *Customs unions and trade conflicts: The second enlargement of the European Community.* London: Routledge.

JOHN O'CONNELL

European Community (EC) The European Community (EC) is the name given to a group of European nations who have entered into agreements intended to lead to complete economic integration in the future. The EC is composed of: Belgium, Denmark, France, Germany (now reunified Germany), Greece, Ireland, Italy, Luxembourg, the Netherlands, Portugal, Spain, and the UK. Several other countries are seeking membership at this time. The EC has succeeded in reducing most barriers to trade and movement of goods, services, and people between member countries. Originally referred to as the European Economic Community (EEC), the greatest movement towards integration came in 1992 when the majority of intercountry agreements were scheduled to take effect. This was some 35 years after the EEC was first conceived under the Treaty of Rome (1957). The EC is governed by four major councils or divisions.

1 European Commission – The European Commission is a supranational body (a separate entity whose policies span a number of countries) created by the European Community (EC) to suggest and initiate regulations affecting all EC nations. The commission is comprised of a representative from each EC nation (two each from France, Germany, Great Britain, Italy, and Spain). The commission attempts to see that the implementation of EC directives (policies agreed to by members) is accomplished. The commission also has the power to rule on mergers of companies which may affect competition and the distribution of goods (mainly drugs and food) which may be unfit for consumption. The Commission is the implementation body of the European Community.

2 The European Council of Ministers – The Council of Ministers is the highest formal governing body of the European Community. The Council is comprised of repre-

sentatives of member countries and has responsibility for final action on policies proposed by the European Commission. The Council has the right to amend or reject policies sent for its review.

3 The European Court of Justice – The European Court of Justice is charged with responsibility over interpretation of European Community (EC) agreements and the settlement of disputes between member countries and all others seeking EC-wide opinions. The opinions handed down by the court are binding on all EC members.

4 The European Parliament – The European Parliament provides advice to the European Council and European Commission as to suggested policies. The Parliament has no formal power to accept or reject or change policies, thus its advice may be taken or discarded as the Council and Commission see fit. The Parliament is, however, the closest an EC division gets to a democratically empowered body. Its members are elected by the member countries and, theoretically, serve to promote the best interests of the EC as a whole.

Bibliography

Deresky, Helen (1994). *International management.* 1st edn, New York: HarperCollins.

Eiteman, D. K., Stonehill, A. J. & Moffett, M. H. (1992). *Multinational business finance.* 6th edn, Reading, MA: Addison-Wesley Publishing.

Grosse, R. & Kujawa, D. (1995). *International business: Theory and managerial applications.* 3rd edn, Boston, MA: Richard D. Irwin Inc.

Hodgetts, R. H. & Luthans, F. (1994). *International management.* 2nd edn, New York: McGraw-Hill Inc.

Punnett, B. J. & Ricks, D. (1992). *International business.* Boston, MA: PWS-Kent.

Springer, B. (1992). *The social dimension of 1992: Europe faces a new EC.* New York: Greenwood Press.

Toyne, B & Walters, Peter, G. P. (1993). *Global marketing management.* Boston: Allyn and Bacon.

JOHN O'CONNELL

European company   In line with economic integration efforts, the European Community (EC) has established a procedure for forming "European Companies." A European company is similar to other companies except that it is capitalized in European currency units (ECUs) and must comply with the rules set forth by the EC. Until legal integration occurs, European companies must comply with many of the laws of the specific country in which the company is registered. Although registered in a specific country, an EC company is an accepted legal entity in all EC member countries.

See also **European Community**

JOHN O'CONNELL

European Council   The European Council is comprised of the heads of government of European Community member countries. The European Council provides a platform to discuss policy differences and problems of implementing integration. Because of the high level governmental participation in the Council its negotiations lead to suggestions which are generally agreed to by the European Commission and the Council of Ministers.

See also **European Community**

JOHN O'CONNELL

European Council of Ministers   The Council of Ministers is the highest formal governing body of the European Community. The Council is comprised of representatives of member countries and has responsibility for final action on policies proposed by the European Commission. The Council has the right to amend or reject policies sent for its review.

See also **European Commission; European Community**

JOHN O'CONNELL

European Court of Justice   The European Court of Justice is charged with responsibility over interpretation of European Community (EC) agreements and the settlement of disputes between member countries and all others seeking EC-wide opinions. The opinions handed down by the court are binding on all EC members.

See also **European Community**

JOHN O'CONNELL

European Currency Unit (ECU) The European Currency Unit (ECU) is the currency or unit of account of the European Monetary System. It is the first step toward a true national currency for the EC. Currently (1996) the ECU is seeing limited use, but its popularity is growing (especially in the private financing area). The value of the ECU is based upon a weighted average of the values of all EC member country currencies. The weighting is associated with the economic size of each country. Thus a currency from a country with a very large economy has more of an impact on ECU value than does the currency from a smaller country.

Bibliography

Daniels, J. D. & Radebaugh, L. E. (1994). *International business: Environments and operations.* 7th edn, Reading, MA: Addison-Wesley Publishing.
Eiteman, D. K., Stonehill, A. J. & Moffett, M. H. (1992). *Multinational business finance.* 6th edn, Reading, MA: Addison-Wesley Publishing.

JOHN O'CONNELL

European Economic Area (EEA) The EEA is a planned expansion of the free trade area of Europe. European Economic Area membership includes the countries making up the European Free Trade Association (EFTA) and those comprising the European Community (EC). A number of EFTA nations have already moved toward becoming members of the EC, but the joining of members from both organizations was not yet complete in 1996. If accomplished, the EEA will form a common market throughout Europe, thereby enhancing its power as a trading bloc.

JOHN O'CONNELL

European Free Trade Association (EFTA) EFTA is a free trade area comprised of a number of European nations. The association sought to reduce or do away with trade barriers between member countries in an expedited manner. Many members of EFTA have already gained, or are in the process of gaining, membership in the European Community. It is felt that EFTA will eventually merge with the EC as EFTA membership dwindles and EC successes continue.

JOHN O'CONNELL

European Investment Bank (EIB) The European Investment Bank is the long-term lending facility of the European Community. The bank provides loans to member countries mainly in the area of infrastructure development (communications, transportation, energy production) as well as for industrial development. The bank also provides loans to less developed countries when the interests of its member countries are being served.

JOHN O'CONNELL

European Monetary System (EMS) The European Monetary System was established by the European Community (EC) to provide a standard system under which barriers to free flow of capital would be eliminated. If true economic integration was to be achieved individual country rules and regulations would have to give way to the EC-wide, standardized regulations. The Monetary System developed the European Currency Unit (ECU) as its official monetary unit. A standardized system of determining and stabilizing exchange rates between member countries was introduced. The European Monetary Cooperation Fund was established to lend support to member countries with short-term balance of payments problems. Although not all of the actions of the EMS have been successful it continues to play an important role towards the eventual complete economic integration of the EC.

See also **European Community**

JOHN O'CONNELL

European Parliament The European Parliament provides advice to the European Council and European Commission as to suggested policies. The Parliament has no formal power to accept or reject or change policies, thus its advice may be taken or discarded as the Council and Commission see fit. The Parliament is, however, the closest an EC division gets to a democratically empowered body. Its members are elected by the member countries and, theoretically, serve to promote the best interests of the EC as a whole.

See also **European Community**

JOHN O'CONNELL

European Patent Convention (EPC) The EPC is an agreement to establish a system in which a single patent (the European Patent) could be obtained and would be legal and enforceable, under the same set of regulations, in all European nations. Today a party seeking to register a patent must apply to the European Patent Office in Munich, Germany. Here the application is reviewed and if approved, a patent is awarded. Under the agreement process, the patent eventually becomes an individual patent in each of the EC nations. Only one application to one agency is required.

JOHN O'CONNELL

European Telecommunications Standards Institute (ETSI) The institute was established to research, advise, and assist the European Community in standardizing the specifications for communications equipment within the EC. As with other products, communications equipment specifications were not standardized between countries before the advent of the EC. Full economic integration will be assisted by continued efforts toward specifications which apply to "all" EC members. The ETSI is only one of a number of research efforts and agreements to harmonize standards throughout the EC.

Bibliography

Sandholtz, W. (1992). *High-tech Europe: The politics of international cooperation*. Berkeley, CA: University of California Press.

JOHN O'CONNELL

European style option A European style option gives the holder the right to buy or sell a stated amount of currency at a specified price. The option can only be used on the expiration date of the option.

See also **American style option; Options**

JOHN O'CONNELL

evaluation of international managers *see* PERFORMANCE EVALUATION

evolution of global organization This is the growth path commonly exhibited by organizations as they move from domestic to international operations, and then on to becoming a global organization.

In their article, "Developing Leaders for the Global Enterprise," authors Rhinesmith, Williams, Ehlen, and Maxwell postulate that businesses go through four stages of development as they begin to enter and are finally absorbed into international trade or other international activity. Each stage is more complex than its predecessor. The stages are:

Domestic enterprise – An organization operating only within the boundaries of a single country. All activities and resources used in its operations are derived from the local economy.
Exporter – As an organization finds success locally it may extend its product distribution to include other countries. Generally this is accomplished by entering into agreements with parties in other countries who act as distributors or purchasers of the organization's goods or services. The exporter organization has little knowledge of (and probably sees little need to know about) international trade, political events, econom-

ics, or cultural differences between countries. As exports increase, however, the need to know becomes more important and evident to the organization's management.

International or multinational organization – The organization has grown to the point that its personnel and facilities are forced outside of its home country. Failure to move will result in the organization becoming unable to take advantage of economies or efficiencies available in other parts of the world. The organization also realizes that it must become more a part of the actual world in which its products or services are being distributed. Although the organization may work through joint-venture partners or other agreements, it still maintains control over its operations. Local activities or facilities may be independent but still respond to home office strategic plans and goals.

Global enterprise – This organization is a natural evolution of the continued growth and expansion of the international organization. There is no place in the world which is not a potential market, source of a partner, or a facilities location. Efficiency and competition become the driving force instead of a linkage to any particular country or culture.

Bibliography

Daniels, J. D. & Radebaugh, L. H. (1993). *International dimensions of contemporary business*. Boston, MA: PWS-Kent Publishing.
Hodgetts, R. H. & Luthans, F. (1994). *International management*. 2nd edn, New York: McGraw-Hill Inc.
Phatak, A. V. (1989). *International dimensions of management*. 2nd edn, Boston, MA: PWS-Kent Publishing.
Rugman, A. M. & Hodgetts, R. M. (1995). *International management: A strategic management approach*. New York: McGraw-Hill Inc.
Walter, I. & Murray, T. (1988). *Handbook of international management: International corporate planning*. New York: John Wiley.

JOHN O'CONNELL

exchange controls When a government seeks to interfere with the market forces which establish the value of a currency, the government normally establishes what are referred to as "exchange controls." Exchange controls attempt to regulate either the supply of foreign exchange or the parties to which foreign exchange is allocated. Restrictions on the convertibility of currency or limitations on the amounts of currency which may be taken from a country are examples of exchange controls. Although use of exchange controls is currently (1996) in disfavor, some countries still apply controls in attempts to solve balance of payments problems. Controls, however, cause additional problems because foreign exchange is what is used to purchase imports. Thus, import transactions will also be affected if exchange controls are instituted.

Bibliography

Ellsworth, P. T. (1990). *The international economy*. New York: Harper & Row.

JOHN O'CONNELL

exchange exposures Exchange exposures are the ways an organization can suffer losses due to changes in the rates of exchange between currencies. The exposure essentially is due to the fact that payables, receivables, or investments denominated in other currencies may change in value over time. There are two categories of business activity that expose a business to losses due to fluctuations in exchange rates.

1 Transaction exposure – This exposure arises when a business enters into transactions in which foreign currency payments are expected to be made "to" the business at some time in the future or in which foreign currency payments are to be made "by" the business at some time in the future. As time passes currency values may change. If foreign currency values fall, the business will be paid in lower value currency. If foreign currency values increase, the company will have to use more of its domestic currency to purchase foreign currency with which to pay debt.

2 Translation exposure – Translation exposure is an accounting measure. If an organization has assets valued in a foreign currency, it faces the possibility that the

currency will fall in value. If this occurs, the decrease in value "translates" into reduced value of business assets.

Bibliography

Eiteman, D. K., Stonehill, A. J. & Moffett, M. H. (1992). *Multinational business finance.* 6th edn, Reading, MA: Addison-Wesley Publishing.

JOHN O'CONNELL

exchange permit   In countries having foreign exchange controls, persons seeking to convert currency must make application to the monetary authority. If the application is approved an "exchange permit" is issued.

JOHN O'CONNELL

exchange rate   An exchange rate is the cost of a currency expressed in another currency. For example: if 1 British pound sterling may be exchanged for $1.64 in United States dollars the exchange rate is $1.64 US/1 pound sterling.

JOHN O'CONNELL

exchange risk   *see* EXCHANGE EXPOSURES

exchange risk management   *see* FOREIGN EXCHANGE RISK MANAGEMENT

exchange spread   This term describes the difference between the price being offered for a currency (bid price) by a buyer and the price being requested for a currency (ask price) by a seller.

JOHN O'CONNELL

exclusionary duty   This duty is aimed directly at stopping the importation of certain items or punishing a country for unfair trade practices. The suggested US 100% duty on Japanese luxury automobiles in 1995 is an example of an exclusionary duty imposed to punish Japan for what the US felt were unfair trade practices.

See also **Duty; Unfair trade**

JOHN O'CONNELL

exclusive agent   This term describes the relationship between a principal (e.g., a manufacturing company) and an agent (e.g., a manufacturer's representative) in which the principal grants the agent exclusive rights (e.g., to sell a particular product in a particular country or region). Thus, the exclusive agent is the only party who can represent the manufacturer in selling products in a specific geographic region. Anyone seeking the product will have to work through the exclusive agent. In return for the grant of exclusivity, the agent usually agrees to some minimum level of representation and performance.

Bibliography

Clark, J. B. (1990). *Marketing today.* Englewood Cliffs, NJ: Prentice-Hall.

JOHN O'CONNELL

ex dock   A pre-1990 trading term which requires the seller of goods to make goods available at the seller's dock. The buyer takes responsibility for all costs and activities related to the goods from that point forward. Under 1990 INCOTERMS the specification "ex works" (EXW) would be used to specify delivery at the seller's location.

See also **Ex works; INCOTERMS**

Bibliography

International Chamber of Commerce (ICC) (1990). *Incoterms 1990.* New York, NY: ICC Publishing Corp.

JOHN O'CONNELL

ex factory   A pre-1990 trading term which requires the seller of goods to make goods available at the seller's factory. The buyer takes responsibility for all costs and activities related to the goods from that point forward. Under the 1990 INCOTERMS the specification "EX WORKS" (EXW) would be used to specify delivery at the seller's location.

See also **Ex works; INCOTERMS**

Bibliography

International Chamber of Commerce (ICC) (1990). *Incoterms 1990*. New York, NY: ICC Publishing Corp.

JOHN O'CONNELL

exim bank   *see* EXPORT–IMPORT BANK

exit visa   Exit visas are often required of commercial visa-holders who have been permitted to work in a foreign country. The exit visa allows immigration authorities to keep track of work-permit holders as well as verifying that all local income and other taxes which may be due are paid before the commercial visitor is allowed to leave the country.

See also **Visa**

JOHN O'CONNELL

expat   *see* EXPATRIATE

expatriate   An expatriate is a person who was transferred to a foreign country by his/her employer. It is common for multinational companies to send home country nationals to represent the company overseas. While in the host country and away from their home country, these employees are referred to as expatriates. Expatriates also include employees from outside of the home country who are transferred to a third country.

See also **Expatriate training; Selection of expatriates**

Bibliography

Bird, A. & Dunbar, R. (1991). Getting the job done over there: Improving expatriate productivity. *National Productivity Review*, Spring, 145–56.

Howard, C. G. (1991). "Expatriate managers," in *Proceedings of the International Academy of: Management and Marketing*. Washington, D.C.: Howard Publication – International Academy of Management.

Kobrin, S. J. (1988). Expatriate reduction and strategic control in American multinational corporations. *Human Resource Management*, **27** (1), 63–75.

Mendenhall, M. & Oddou, G. (1985). The dimensions of expatriate acculturation: A review. *Academy of Management Review*, **10** (1), 39–47.

Napier, N. K. & Peterson, R. B. (1990). Expatriate reentry: What do repatriates have to say?. *Human Resource Planning*, **14**, 19–28.

JOHN O'CONNELL

expatriate allowance   *see* EXPATRIATE DIFFERENTIAL

expatriate assignment   An expatriate assignment is a job transfer that takes the employee to a workplace that is outside the country in which he or she is a citizen. There are differences between an expatriate assignment and other job assignments of an international nature. Expatriate assignments are longer in duration than other types of international assignments (e.g. business trips), and require the employee to move his or her entire household to the foreign location. Thus, in an expatriate assignment, the employee's home base of business operations is in the foreign country.

Expatriate assignments offer unique challenges to expatriate employees. Virtually all expatriates run into situations where the home office wants them to do one thing, while local situations dictate that another thing should be done instead. For example, in Japan, local conditions dictate that market-share growth should be the main criterion of a subsidiary's performance, while the home office may force the subsidiary managers into focusing on quarterly profits as the main criterion of organizational performance.

The expatriate assignment requires expatriate managers to face a number of complex issues that their domestic counterparts either do not face, or face with less intensity. Examples of such issues are the integration of large international acquisitions, understanding the meaning of performance and accountability in a globally integrated system of product flows, building and managing a worldwide logistics capability, developing multiple country-specific corporate strategies, managing products and services around the world with differing competitive dynamics in each market, forming and managing collaborative agreements (OEM contracts, licensing, joint ventures), balancing the need for global integration while simultaneously responding to local demands, and managing a multicultural workforce within foreign environments.

Expatriates usually find an expatriate assignment to be one of the biggest challenges of their entire career. Increasingly, firms are investing in cross-cultural training programs to prepare expatriates to operate successfully in their expatriate assignment. Additionally, most companies offer a variety of support systems to employees as part of the expatriate assignment. One of the principal barriers to cross-cultural adjustment is the lack of a way for expatriates – especially non-working spouses of employees – to become members of a social network. Many firms offer programs of one sort or another that are geared to helping expatriates to develop friendships with other expatriates and host-nationals, and to provide support with the day-to-day realities of living in a foreign culture (housing, schooling, transportation, shopping, and so forth) (*see* EXPATRIATE SUPPORT SYSTEM).

Expatriate assignments are much more costly than simply hiring local nationals to work in foreign subsidiary; however, there are advantages to using expatriates over local nationals. Expatriates know how the parent company operates and can pass on this knowledge to local employees. By working overseas they learn how foreign markets operate, and how foreign consumers and clients react to the products or services the company offers. Also, they gain skills in cross-cultural management and develop a global perspective. Expatriate assignments, then, can be a powerful strategic tool in developing global business skills within the senior ranks of a firm's management.

Bibliography

Black, J. S., Gregersen, H. B. & Mendenhall, M. (1992).. *Global Assignments: Successfully Expatriating and Repatriating International Managers*, San Francisco: Jossey-Bass.

Black, J. S., Mendenhall, M. & Oddou, G. (1991). Toward a comprehensive model of international adjustment: an integration of multiple theoretical perspectives. *Academy of Management Review*, **16**, 291–317.

Mendenhall, M., Punnett, B. J. & Ricks, D. (1995).. *Global Management*, Cambridge, MA: Blackwell Publishers.

Prahalad, C. K. (1990). Globalization: the intellectual and managerial challenges. *Human Resource Management*, **29**, 27–37.

MARK E. MENDENHALL

expatriate differential Companies often pay (or make available as a benefit) an extra amount of compensation to expatriates to make up for the inconvenience and extra problems associated with living outside of an individual's home country. The differential makes up for higher housing costs; education for children; leasing an automobile; or other costs. The differential ceases to be paid when the expatriate returns to the home country. Sometimes this causes problems with living standards because often the same amount of money purchases so much more overseas than in the employee's home country. The expatriate literally suffers a reduced standard of living when returning to the home country.

Bibliography

Golding, J. (1993). *Working abroad: Essential financial planning for expatriates and their employers*. Plymouth: International Venture Handbooks.

Harris, J. E. (1989). Moving managers internationally: The care and feeding of expatriates. *Human Resources Planning*, **12**, 49–53.

JOHN O'CONNELL

expatriate premium   *see* EXPATRIATE ALLOWANCE

expatriate selection *see* SELECTION OF EXPATRIATES

expatriate support system The expatriate support system (ESS) is a set of programs developed by a company to develop and promote multicultural skills among employees who must travel abroad on long-term assignments. The system's effectiveness is measured by its ability to smooth out an employee's transition from the USA (or any other country) to a different country's cultural environment. The system may not eliminate all the pains created by this cultural transition, but it should reduce them to a minimum. The most effective ESS is that which allows employees to become open-minded, to learn how to adapt to a new environment, and even enjoy the cultural transition as a valuable learning experience. The support system should also address the needs of the employee's spouse and children traveling with him or her.

An ESS includes all or any combination of the following: educational programs to develop employees' multicultural skills; a mentorship or buddy program in the foreign country to help employees during the first weeks abroad; short travel programs to the country of destination prior to the actual assignment to help the employee get acquainted with the country; supplying employees with information about schools, churches, recreational activities, native meals, transportation systems, driver's license, health care, and many other aspects of the new country. It must include programs to ease employees' re-entry to the USA (or home country), to help them cope with the fact that they are now different and that being different is fine. This component should also involve other employees who must interact with a returning colleague. As employees accept the new cultural diversity paradigm and learn how to cope with it, the ESS should be deactivated.

R. IVAN BLANCO

expatriate training Providing employees going on foreign assignment with the knowledge and techniques necessary to be successful on their assignments. Training may take place both prior to and after the actual assignment transfer has been made. The types and extensiveness of training should be based upon both the duration and the importance of the foreign assignment. It is logical that an employee sent overseas for 60 days would need different types of training than an employee sent overseas for three years. An employee sent to do a specific job within an organization facility in another country needs different training than the employee sent to develop new markets or to negotiate contracts with foreign partners or governments. Differences in what is expected of employees must be factored into the duration and type of training offered to each employee. Failure to properly train expatriates will almost assure their failure to either complete the foreign assignment or to meet employer expectations in cases where the full assignment period has been achieved.

Training an expatriate's family members to recognize the problems and inconveniences of foreign assignment is also extremely important. Family members face the same problems as the expatriate in terms of language differences; cultural adaptation; living condition changes; and other possible sources of problems. What many people do not realize, however, is that the expatriate still has the organization as a base from which to work (fellow employees, familiar products, communication with home office, etc.) whereas family members may be virtually uprooted with few if any ties with their former home. A sound expatriate training program includes the training of family members as well as the employee.

Expatriate training is commonly divided into three approaches:

Information giving approach – This is the most widespread of all of the approaches. Unfortunately, many companies offer only this approach. Included in this approach is information about the new country's culture, geography, living conditions, life-styles, and language. Commonly used methods to provide this type of training include: seminars, films, audio tapes, books and brochures. This approach offers information only, without the chance to apply the new information or to test its assimilation by the students.

Affective approach – This approach attempts to apply training in a more experiential manner. Real examples of problems are set forth for discussion: role-playing activities take place; stress reduction and change management techniques are taught. This type of training prepares the expatriate on a more realistic and practical level. Affective approaches seek to allow the individual to become more self-confident; what is being taught will actually increase his/her ability to carry out the assignment more effectively.

Immersion Approach – This approach seeks to place the employee in as similar a condition as the activity actually taking place in the foreign country. Immersion may include visits to the new country to allow the employee to explore and learn on a first-hand basis. Immersion training involves extensive simulation of common problem situations in which the employee can learn without being exposed to failure while actually on the overseas assignment. The approach seeks to teach the employee to be sensitive to other cultures and act accordingly. This approach is normally very time consuming and expensive. It relies on a low student to instructor ratio and a substantial commitment of resources by the organization.

All of the approaches are focused upon allowing the employee to overcome problems associated with overseas assignments. It may even be necessary to use one or more of these approaches when sending an employee to a different part of the same country.

Bibliography

Hays, R. D. (1974). Expatriate selection: Insuring success and avoiding failure. *Journal of International Business Studies*, 5, 25–37.

Mendenhall, M. E., Dunbar, E. & Oddou, Gary (1987). Expatriate selection, training, and career pathing: A review and critique. *Human Resource Management*, 26, 331–45.

Ronen, S. & Tung, R. L. (1981). Selection and training of personnel for overseas assignments. *Columbia Journal of World Business*, Spring, 68–78.

Torbiorn, J. (1982). *Living abroad*. New York: John Wiley.

JOHN O'CONNELL

export agent A party who assists in moving goods between buyers and sellers, but never takes title to the goods himself. This is an extremely important function in international trade. It is carried out by a large number of specialists in a variety of areas. Agents locate and bring together products, manufacturers, markets, buyers, and sellers of goods. The agent could work on behalf of either the seller (exporter) or buyer (importer). The following list consists of agents with a variety of responsibilities. A particular type of agent listed may be just another name for one of the other categories. They are still listed and briefly identified because the alternate name may not be known by the international businessperson. Common types of export agents include:

1 Broker – A broker is a person who brings together a buyer and a seller. An export broker brings together exporters and importers for a fee. A broker generally does not have any further involvement in the trade transaction (although some brokers can and do provide additional services).

2 Buying agent – When a company does not have employees stationed overseas to purchase goods, a buying agent may be employed to represent the company. Buying agents know the foreign market for goods and how to negotiate in foreign markets. They can be of great assistance in completing foreign transactions. The authority of the agent should be carefully spelled out in the contract between the agent and the company to make certain the company's interests are appropriately represented.

3 Cargo broker – A person who acts as a middle-man between cargo owners and shipowners. By locating ships for hire, the cargo broker earns a commission. The commission is often referred to as an "address commission." Cargo brokers play an important role in international trade, especially when one considers the inexperience of many cargo owners in terms of transporting goods overseas.

4 Combination export manager (CEM) – Combination export managers are in the business of purchasing goods from a number of companies and then combining those goods to meet existing orders or to

place on the export market. Often manufacturers of goods do not produce sufficient quantities to take advantage of the most efficient modes of transportation or discounts for shipment of large lots. A CEM can take advantage of such efficiencies and/or discounts by combining the production of many companies. Although CEMs do occasionally work on a commission basis for manufacturers, they more commonly buy and sell as a separate entity involved in the export business. It is very common for CEMs to specialize in particular goods or industries. In this way they become familiar to both producers and buyers of particular goods.

5 Commission agent – It is common for companies involved in foreign trade to work through representatives or agents who sell goods on behalf of the companies. These agents usually work for a percentage of the goods sold (a commission). In many countries these people are referred to as manufacturers' representatives. Commission agents usually specialize in certain types of products or industrial output in order to build their relationships with both buyers and sellers. In order to monitor their activities, commission agents are required by many countries to be registered and bonded.

6 Confirming house – A United Kingdom trade intermediary who performs financing and other functions for exporters. The confirming house, unlike other export agents, actually finances exports by allowing the exporter to be paid from its funds when the exports are shipped. The confirming house also usually handles the contracts for both the seller and buyer and may arrange transportation if necessary.

7 Customhouse broker – Importers often feel that their tasks are complete when arrangements have been made to pay for and take delivery of imported items. However, another obstacle may lie in the path of the successful completion of the transaction: the customs authority of a country. Obtaining custom's approval to bring goods into a country (clearing customs) is not always a simple task. Appropriate papers must accompany imports and all requirements of

the importing country must be met. Privately-owned and operated consultants called customhouse brokers are ready to assist importers in clearing goods through customs. All necessary papers will be obtained, clearances, certificates (country of origin, health, etc.) and the documents will be checked by the broker in order to speed the customs clearing process. For this service they charge a fee. Customhouse brokers are licensed by the appropriate government agency. These people generally know how to get goods cleared quickly and are usually worth the expenditure.

8 Distributor – A distributor is an intermediary who acts on behalf of others to distribute goods. Distributors are very common in international trade. Instead of attempting to directly enter foreign markets (normally a very time-consuming and expensive proposition) an exporter may instead enter into a relationship with an importer to become a "distributor" for the exporter. A distributor does more than just import goods. A distributor also packages or repackages if necessary, advertises the goods, distributes them, and may even provide service after the sale. For all of this activity the distributor usually retains a portion of the sales and is commonly granted exclusive rights to distribute the product in a specified region. Hiring a distributor to handle goods in a foreign country is one of the simpler methods of entering a foreign market.

9 Exclusive agent – This term describes the relationship between a principal (e.g., a manufacturing company) and an agent (e.g., a manufacturer's representative) in which the principal grants the agent exclusive rights (e.g., to sell a particular product in a particular country or region). Thus, the exclusive agent is the only party who can represent the manufacturer in selling products in a specific geographic region. Anyone seeking the product will have to work through the exclusive agent. In return for the grant of exclusivity, the agent usually agrees to some minimum level of representation and performance.

10 Export broker – A broker is a person who brings together a buyer and a seller. An export broker brings together exporters and

importers for a fee. A broker generally does not have any further involvement in the trade transaction (although some brokers can and do provide additional services).

11 Export commission house – An export commission house is an agent of the buyer of goods. Export commission houses are located in the country which produces the exports. As an agent for the export buyer, the export commission house seeks out manufacturers of products requested by importers. The commission house handles the majority of the transaction thereby relieving both the exporter and the importer from a great deal of work. Commission houses are compensated through commissions paid by the buyer of goods.

12 Export trading company (ETC) – An export trading company is an organization established for the purpose of facilitating the export of goods and services. The company's ownership may be domestic, foreign, or any combination of the two. Its clients are producers of goods, importers of all types, governments of different countries, all of whom are interested in exporting or importing items.

13 Freight forwarder – A freight forwarder is a trade intermediary who arranges for the transportation of goods. Freight forwarders can also offer additional services to exporters and importers because of the expertise they gain in dealing with the trade transaction.

14 Import broker – Many persons who are involved in exporting activities do not have the knowledge or contacts to successfully conduct trade activities. An import broker is hired by exporters to locate buyers (importers) for the exporter's goods. Typically, the import broker receives a commission for services rendered.

15 Intermerchant – An intermerchant works for exporters and importers to solve problems with converting soft currencies to hard currencies. Some currencies are more readily convertible than others. The so called "hard" currencies are regularly traded and generally pose no problems in the exchange process. "Soft" currencies, however, are often difficult to exchange. An intermerchant is a person specializing in solving problems associated with hard and

soft currency exchange. The intermerchant makes necessary arrangements for paying for goods sold between countries with hard currencies and those with soft currencies.

16 Manufacturer's export agent – This trade intermediary acts on behalf of producers who desire to offer goods for export. The agent, who finds buyers for the producer's goods, does not purchase for his own account and is paid strictly on a commission basis.

17 Resident buyer – This intermediary represents foreign buyers of locally produced goods. Most resident buyers are employees of the foreign firms they represent. Resident buyers look to establish long-term relationships with producers of goods by handling all of the details of purchase, shipping, and delivery to the foreign buyer.

18 Resident buying agents – Most organizations conducting international trade do not use their own employees to either buy or sell goods in various countries. The differences between business practices, language, and cultural problems usually make employee arrangements difficult at best. Instead of using employees, organizations may turn to intermediaries in each country to secure goods needed by the organization in its home country (or other country of production). Intermediaries who purchase goods for a foreign company (to be shipped to that foreign company) are referred to as "resident buying agents."

19 Resident selling agents – Most international enterprises do not have actual production taking place in each of the countries. They also normally do not have their own employees in each country because the costs would be prohibitive for all but the largest of organizations. It is very common under these circumstances to use the services of an intermediary to sell a company's goods in overseas markets. Intermediaries who act on behalf of an organization to sell its products in a given country are referred to as "resident selling agents."

20 Wholesaler/distributor – Wholesalers/distributors purchase large quantities of goods from suppliers and resell them on international markets. Often individual importers do not have the ability to secure certain

products from overseas suppliers or they find that suppliers will sell only in container lots or other large bulk quantities. The inability to secure small amounts of goods at fair prices has led to the development of wholesale international traders and distributors. Wholesale international traders purchase large quantities of goods from suppliers, break them into smaller lots, and resell the goods to others. By working through the international wholesaler/distributor the smaller business may have access to a larger number of goods than would otherwise be (economically) available.

Bibliography

Czinkota, M. R., Rivoli, P. & Ronkainen, I. A. (1989). *International Business*. Chicago, IL: The Dryden Press.

Grosse, C. U. & Grosse, R. E. (1988). *Case studies in international business*. Englewood Cliffs, NJ: Prentice Hall.

Johnson, T. E. (1994). *Export–Import procedures and documentation*. New York: Amacom.

Maruca, R. F. (1994). The right way to go global: An interview with whirlpool CEO David Whitman. *Harvard Business Review*, March–April, 134–45.

Zodl, J. A. (1992). *Export–Import: Everything you and your company need to know to compete in world markets*. Cincinnati, OH: Betterway Books.

JOHN O'CONNELL

Export and Import Bank of Japan (EIBJ)   This is an important financial institution with respect to the development of Japanese export trade as well as a source of funding for development banks for various economic development projects. The EIBJ supports exports by providing loans to the buyers of Japanese goods as well as to Japanese manufacturers of goods in order to generate increased supplies for export.

Bibliography

Ludlow, N. H. (1988). *A practical guide to the development bank business: How to identify it, market to it, and win it*. Washington, D.C.: Development Bank Associates Inc.

JOHN O'CONNELL

export barriers   *see* BARRIERS

export broker   A broker is a person who brings together a buyer and a seller. An export broker brings together exporters and importers for a fee. A broker generally does not have any further involvement in the trade transaction (although some brokers can and do provide additional services).

See also **Export agent**

JOHN O'CONNELL

export commission house   An export commission house is an agent of the buyer of goods. Export commission houses are located in the country which produces the exports. As an agent for the export buyer, the export commission house seeks out manufacturers of products requested by importers. The commission house handles the majority of the transaction thereby relieving both the exporter and the importer from a great deal of work. Commission houses are compensated through commissions paid by the buyer of goods.

Bibliography

United States Customs Service (1994). *A basic guide to importing*. Lincolnwood, IL: NTC Publishing Group.

JOHN O'CONNELL

export contact list   One of the difficulties of successfully entering into international trade activities is developing the contacts (buyers, persons providing advice, etc.) to assist in the start-up phase of exporting. The United States International Trade Administration (ITA) offers mailing lists of foreign firms and government agencies that may be interested in various US products. Lists are available by contacting the ITA.

Bibliography

Johnson, T. E. (1994). *Export–Import procedures and documentation*. New York: Amacom.

JOHN O'CONNELL

export credit   Two meanings are attached to this term, one for a buyer of goods and one for a seller. Export credit to a purchaser of goods comes in the form of loans or other financing mechanisms to purchase exports. Export credit to a seller of exports comes in the form of loans or other financing provided to domestic producers of goods in order to increase the availability of goods for export purposes. Export credits of both kinds can be found through export development agencies or banks in various countries.

Bibliography

Zodl, J. A. (1992). *Export–Import: Everything you and your company need to know to compete in world markets.* Cincinnati, OH: Betterway Books.

JOHN O'CONNELL

Export Credit Guarantees Department (ECGD)   The ECGD is a United Kingdom government department established to promote exports of UK goods. The ECGD promotes trade by providing subsidization for bank loans to UK exporters, as well as other financial guarantees for exporters. The ECGD also offers insurance on UK foreign investments.

JOHN O'CONNELL

export documents   The types of documents necessary for exporting goods depends upon the nature of the goods and the countries from which the goods are shipped and the country of destination. The documents are essentially the same as those required for entry into various countries.

See also **Entry documents**

Bibliography

International Chamber of Commerce (ICC) (1990). *Incoterms 1990.* New York, NY: ICC Publishing Corp.
Johnson, T. E. (1994). *Export–Import procedures and documentation.* New York: Amacom.

United States Customs Service (1994). *A basic guide to importing.* Lincolnwood, IL: NTC Publishing Group.

JOHN O'CONNELL

export duty   Governments of developing nations sometimes feel the need to tax items being exported from their countries. These taxes are referred to as export duties. Reasons for the taxes include a need for revenues by the government or a need for the goods to remain inside the country with the tax acting as incentive to keep goods within the national borders.

JOHN O'CONNELL

export financing   There are a number of methods of paying for goods and services imported from other countries. The methods are relatively common and are much the same as those used in the financing of other goods and services. Eight common methods are reviewed below.

1 Acceptance financing – A method of financing imports and exports through a short-term line of credit. The lending bank may include specific documentation requirements to show evidence of title to the merchandise. The required documentation normally consists of either a warehouse receipt or a bill of lading.

2 Collection – Collection involves the payment by an importer for goods sold by an exporter. Collection papers are the documents specified in the sales contract which must be provided to the buyer (or the buyer's bank) in order for payment to be made.

3 Consignment – Consignment is a process through which an owner of goods (consignor) transfers them to an agent (consignee) who is then responsible for selling the goods to others. In international trade, consignment is actually a method of financing import transactions. The exporter of goods (consignor) transfers goods to an importer (consignee) who then sells the goods. When the goods are sold the

proceeds are divided between the agent (a commission for selling the goods) and the exporter (the balance of the amount paid).

4 Documentary credit – This is the formal name for a letter of credit. A seller under a letter of credit is paid by a bank upon presentation of the shipping papers and other documents specified in the letter of credit. Unless it is irrevocable, a letter of credit does not guarantee that the credit might not be revoked by the bank prior to presentation of the documents. Specific types of letters of credit are available to provide additional assurances to the seller that payment will be made upon presentation of the proper documents (see LETTER OF CREDIT).

5 Factoring foreign accounts receivable – With regard to financing a company's operations, factoring refers to the use of accounts receivable as a source of borrowed funds or as an asset to be sold to others. Banks will often grant credit based upon the value of the accounts receivable of a company. As the receivables are collected the bank is repaid.

6 Foreign accounts receivable purchases – Factoring is also accomplished by parties who purchase the foreign receivables of an exporter at a discount. The company receives immediate payment and the factor receives payments from the debtors.

7 Open account – A method of arranging payment for exports which provides a stated number of days in which the importer must make payment. Open accounts are normally used only when the importer is well known to the exporter.

8 Payment in advance – When an exporter has no dealings with an importer or those dealings were less than satisfactory, payment in advance may be required. Payment in advance may also be required when the order is for specially designed or custom-made goods which no other importer could use.

Bibliography

Bowker, R. R. (1993). *International handbook of financial reporting*. London: Chapman & Hall.
Johnson, T. E. (1994). *Export–Import procedures and documentation*. New York: Amacom.
United States Customs Service (1994). *A basic guide to importing*. Lincolnwood, IL: NTC Publishing Group.
Zodl, J. A. (1992). *Export–Import: Everything you and your company need to know to compete in world markets*. Cincinnati, OH: Betterway Books.

JOHN O'CONNELL

export insurance Export insurance is coverage purchased by the exporter to protect against the failure of the foreign purchaser to pay for goods order and delivered. Failure to pay may be because of an action of the government (political risk) or a failure of the business (commercial risk – a buyer's inability or refusal to pay). Insurance is available for both the commercial risk and political risk.

See also **Political risk**

Bibliography

Rejda, G. E. (1995). *Principles of risk management and insurance*. 5th edn, New York: HarperCollins.

JOHN O'CONNELL

export license An export license (or permit) allows an exporter to transport goods to locations outside of a country. The license is secured from the appropriate government agency in the country of export. Export licenses allow the government to keep track of the types, amounts, and destinations of exports from a country. It is very important to check the requirements of each country as differences exist. There are three categories of export licenses:

1 General license – Although referred to as a license, a general license is actually a broad government statement allowing goods to be exported. Thus, exporters have "license" to send goods abroad.

2 Individually validated licenses (IVL) – Certain type of goods (armaments, super technology, etc.) or shipments to certain countries may require prior governmental approval. Government approval is shown by the issuance of a license to the specific exporter which allows specified goods to be

exported to a stated destination. Additional documents are usually required for the issuance of IVLs, as well as during the export process itself. Exact documentation needs will be provided by the appropriate government department.

3 Special licenses – A special license may be required for the export of services, to supply goods on a continuing basis for a specified project, or other situations outlined by the governmental unit responsible for export control and record keeping.

Bibliography

United States Customs Service (1994). *A basic guide to importing*. Lincolnwood, IL: NTC Publishing Group.

Johnson, T. E. (1994). *Export–Import procedures and documentation*. New York: Amacom.

JOHN O'CONNELL

export management company (EMC)   Export management companies provide services to local companies seeking to export goods. Services vary from acting as the agent of the exporter, to arranging sales, to purchasing the goods in the name of the EMC for reselling. More commonly, however, an EMC acts as an external export department for companies who are new to exporting and do not have the in-house expertise to carry out the entire export transaction. Hiring a specialized company to perform export related activities is often the least time-consuming way to enter the export market. EMCs may be compensated on a commission, fee, or other basis as agreed under contract with the exporter.

JOHN O'CONNELL

export permit   *see* EXPORT LICENSE

export quotas   Controls placed on the quantity of a particular type of export. Quantitative restrictions may be imposed to ration the export of goods necessary in the home economy or to limit the amount of specific goods going to a particular destination.

JOHN O'CONNELL

export restraints   *see* EXPORT QUOTAS

export sales subsidiary   An export sales subsidiary essentially removes the export function from the parent company and places the function in a separate wholly-owned subsidiary. The export subsidiary purchases goods from the parent company, then resells and exports the goods. Subsidiaries perform much the same function as an export department except that the subsidiary usually has better (and simpler) access to export financing, is able to add products from outside the parent company in order to round out its product line, and is able to segregate costs and expenses more effectively than an internal department.

Bibliography

Griffin, J. (1994). *International sales and the middleman: Managing your agents and distributors*. London: Mercury

JOHN O'CONNELL

export structures   *see* MARKET ENTRY STRATEGIES

export subsidies   Government payments or services to promote exports of domestic goods. Such payments or services act to reduce the cost of production of goods for producers. This in turn allows goods to be exported at lower costs, thereby enhancing their competitive position. Government subsidies of export goods is banned by the General Agreement on Tariffs and Trade (GATT) but subsidies still occur under the guise of various assistance programs. Less developed countries may be able to secure an exemption from GATT's subsidy ban in order to develop their economies more quickly.

Bibliography

Simmonds, K. R. (ed.) (1991). *Law and practice under the GATT and other trading agreements: The Association of South-East Asian Nations (ASEAN)*. Dobbs Ferry, NY: Oceana Publications Inc.

JOHN O'CONNELL

export tariff *see* EXPORT DUTY

export trading company (ETC) There are two distinct definitions of this term: (1) An export trading company is an organization established for the purpose of facilitating the export of goods and services. The company's ownership may be domestic, foreign, or any combination of the two. Its clients are producers of goods, importers of all types, governments of different countries, all of whom are interested in exporting or importing items. (2) A specially recognized (Under the Export Trading Act of 1982) company organized for the purpose of exporting United States goods and services. ETCs are eligible for special business and financial assistance through government and private sources and are exempt from many of the provisions of US antitrust laws (because their operations involve mainly foreign transfer of goods).

JOHN O'CONNELL

Export–Import Bank (EXIM) The Export–Import Bank is a United States government agency providing financial services related to international transactions. Services provided by the EXIM Bank include: furnishing development loans and financial guarantees to foreign countries and large organizations seeking to undertake development projects in other nations; various guarantees and insurance programs for political risk exposures; credit guarantees for foreign trade financing through commercial banks; and discounted loans to banks to assist banks in offering loans to US exporters.

See also **Political risk**

JOHN O'CONNELL

exporting This is one of the simplest methods of foreign market entry. The product is exported to a buyer who then distributes it to the foreign market. Market entry of the product is achieved without considerable investment of either time or capital. The key to exporting is knowing the components of the export transaction very well. If knowledge is not present there are a number of export agents available to assist the exporter of products.

See also **Export agent; Market entry strategies**

Bibliography

Hampton, D. R., Summer, C. E. & Weber, R. A. (1987). *Organizational behavior and the practice of management*. Glenview, IL: Scott, Foresman.

JOHN O'CONNELL

exposure Exposure describes the extent to which an organization's financial condition is affected by various factors. Factors include: fluctuations in exchange rates, market price changes during the export transaction, government action causing political risk, and others.

JOHN O'CONNELL

exposure risks *see* COMMERCIAL RISK; COUNTRY RISK; EXCHANGE RISK; POLITICAL RISK

expropriation This form of political risk involves a government seizing a foreign organization's property. Compensation is not guaranteed. If forthcoming, compensation after expropriation may be delayed and be in amounts far less than the actual value of the assets taken. Expropriation in one form or another has taken place in most industrialized and developing nations.

See also **Political risk**

Bibliography

Morgan, L. L. (1977). *The case for the multinational corporation*. New York: Praeger.

JOHN O'CONNELL

ex quay *see* DELIVERED EX QUAY

ex ship   *see* DELIVERED EX SHIP

extra-territorial application of employment law   The application of equal employment opportunity (EEO) laws such as Title VII of the 1964 Civil Rights Act, the Age Discrimination in Employment Act (ADEA), and the Americans with Disabilities Act (ADA) in multinational enterprises (MNEs) has generated a degree of uncertainty. Foreign employers doing business in the United States must generally abide by US EEO law (*Sumitomo Shoji America* v. *Avigliano*, 28 FEP Cases 1753, 1982; *MacNamara* v. *Korean Airlines*, 48 FEP Cases 980, 1988). The US Supreme Court ruled in *Boureslan* v. *Aramco*, 55 FEP Cases 449 (1991) that Title VII did not apply to American citizens working abroad for American employers. This ruling was overturned by the Civil Rights Act of 1991. Section 701 of Title VII now provides language similar to that contained in the ADEA and the ADA. Thus, US citizens working in foreign countries for US companies are protected from various types of employment discrimination based on race, sex, religion, national origin, color, age, and disability status. There is an exemption if compliance with Title VII or the ADA would cause the employer to violate the law of a foreign country where the employee is working. Section 702 of Title VII also states that the law "shall not apply to an employer with respect to aliens outside of any State" (Bureau of National Affairs, 1991).

Bibliography

Bureau of National Affairs (1991).. *Fair Employment Practices*, Washington, DC: Bureau of National Affairs.

TERRY L. LEAP

EXW   *see* EX WORKS

ex works (named place) (EXW)   A trading term expressing the seller's obligation to make goods available to the buyer at the seller's location. Under ex works terms the seller is not responsible for anything except making the goods available to the buyer at the seller's location. The buyer is responsible for: inland freight charges in the seller's country; costs of loading the vessel/air carrier; ocean or air freight charges; securing and paying for export insurance; unloading the vessel at its destination; import duties; and any inland freight charges in the buyer's country.

Bibliography

International Chamber of Commerce (ICC) (1990). *Incoterms 1990*. New York, NY: ICC Publishing Corp.

JOHN O'CONNELL

F

facilitating intermediary In international trade a facilitating intermediary is someone who assists in expediting the trade transaction, but who does not take possession of the goods being moved. Examples of facilitating intermediaries are banks, various agents or brokers who bring together buyers and sellers, insurance companies, and others.

JOHN O'CONNELL

factor In general a factor is someone who carries out business activities. It is also a person or entity that sells or transfers property for a commission. In accounts receivable financing a factor is an entity that finances trade by purchasing the foreign accounts receivables of an exporter. Since collection of receivables entails some risk, receivables are purchased at a discount to cover the additional risk taken on by the factor. In some countries (e.g., Great Britain) a factor is an export intermediary charged with selling the exporter's goods or services. The factor actually takes title and possession of goods for resale to foreign markets in the factor's own name.

JOHN O'CONNELL

factor mobility This term, when applied to the factors of production (capital, labor, and materials), is the degree to which those factors are allowed to move freely between countries. The intent of economic integration is to allow factors of production to move freely between countries.

JOHN O'CONNELL

factoring With regard to financing a company's operations, factoring refers to the use of accounts receivables as a source of borrowed funds or as an asset to be sold to others. Banks will often grant credit based upon the value of the accounts receivables of a company. As the receivables are collected the bank is repaid (in theory). Factoring is also accomplished by parties who purchase the foreign receivables of an exporter at a discount. The company receives immediate payment and the factor receives payments from the debtors.

Bibliography

Arpan, J. S. & Al Hashim, D. D. (1984). *International dimensions of accounting*. Boston, MA: Kent Publishing Company Inc.

JOHN O'CONNELL

failure rates Although not a pleasant task, determining the rate of failure of employees assigned to overseas positions is important to an organization. Records can show the trends over time as well as offering comparisons with other companies. If the human relations department keeps such records along with the reasons for failure, programs may be instituted to increase expatriate success. For example, if a common reason for failure is language unfamiliarity, intensive language education could be instituted for all future expatriates.

See also **Expatriate; Expatriate training**

Bibliography

Black, J. S. (1988). Work role transitions: A study of American expatriate managers in Japan. *Journal of International Business Studies*, **19** (2), 277–94.

JOHN O'CONNELL

family status When an employee is sent on an overseas assignment and is accompanied by his/her spouse and/or children, the employee has a "family" assignment status. Assignment status is one of the determining factors of the numbers and types of compensation allowances and benefits available to the employee.

See also **Assignment status**

JOHN O'CONNELL

FAS *see* FREE ALONGSIDE SHIP

FASB 52 This is an important accounting standard in the United States with regard to foreign financial transactions. The Financial Accounting Standards Board statement 52 explains how foreign exchange transactions must be accounted for on the books of US organizations. A tax expert is strongly recommended when dealing with foreign currency transaction accounting. Many countries have similar standards related to transactions in foreign currency.

Bibliography

Ferris, K. R. (1993). *Financial accounting and corporate reporting: A casebook*. 3rd edn, Homewood, IL: Irwin.

JOHN O'CONNELL

FCA *see* FREE CARRIER

FCIA *see* FOREIGN CREDIT INSURANCE ASSOCIATION

FCPA *see* FOREIGN CORRUPT PRACTICES ACT

field experience This term has two common meanings: (1) A training method in which an individual is exposed to cultural and other differences found in a new country by actually traveling to and living in the country. The purpose of this type of training is to place the future expatriate in the environment in which he/she is expected to function. This will give information to both the employee and the employer as to the potential success of the move. (2) Actual job experience in the field. Many people are hired on the basis of their field experience (e.g., actual sales positions held for a potential sales manager; or work on an oil rig for a potential oil company manager) because of the understanding it gives them of the basic functions of the business. College professors are many times criticized by their students for their lack of "real world" or field experience.

JOHN O'CONNELL

financial infrastructure The internal monetary and financial system of a country. The infrastructure is comprised of the major financial institutions: banks, financial organizations, and insurance companies.

JOHN O'CONNELL

financial repatriation and multinational firms The return on any investment, whether a stock, bond, or construction of a manufacturing facility, is determined by the cash flows returned over time. Multinational firms must, in order to pursue the maximization of stockholder wealth, return cash flows from foreign affiliates to the parent in order to ultimately justify the investment. The way in which cash flows are repatriated to the parent firm will have, however, a significant impact on the profitability of the foreign affiliate, the parent, and the tax liabilities of both. A number of recent cases of multinational firms earning substantial returns on their foreign affiliates, but not via dividend distributions, has raised the level of concern of host- and home-country governments over the repatriation policies and decisions of their multinationals. This article provides some preliminary evidence on a national basis of the methods employed by U.S.-based firms in the repatriation of earnings from foreign affiliates.

Repatriation of Earnings Versus Foreign Income

The *repatriation of earnings* is distinctly different from what is often termed *foreign income*. The U.S. Department of Commerce (the primary source of data for this analysis) defines *foreign income* as the total of distributed earnings (dividends paid to the U.S.-based firm), reinvested earnings (retained earnings of the foreign affiliate of the U.S.-based firm), and net interest income from the foreign affiliate. (The use of the terms *parent* and *affiliate* is a little troublesome in the following analysis, given the data collected by the U.S. Department of Commerce. The cash flows reported to the Department of Commerce are for foreign firms which a U.S.-based firm (incorporated within the United States) holds a 10 per cent or greater voting equity interest. The U.S. firm, therefore, may not be a true *parent* (holding controlling or exclusive interest), but simply a major equity holder.) Both distributed earnings and net interest are net of withholding taxes by the host-country government. *Repatriated earnings*, which we wish to distinctly differentiate from *foreign income*, occur in four major forms:

1. *Distributed earnings or dividends.* Dividends, or distributed earnings, are profits from foreign affiliate operations arising from either current period or prior period earnings, including capital gains/losses, which are paid to the owners of the affiliate (either foreign or domestic). (Unless otherwise noted, we refer here to the *net payment* resulting from the series of cash flows between affiliate and parent. It is not unusual for payments to be made both to the parent from the affiliate, and to the affiliate from the parent – interest payments, for example.)
2. *Royalties and license fees.* Fees paid for the use, sale, or purchase of intangible property, such as technological techniques, patents, brand names, and so forth.

3. *Net interest.* Interest paid by the foreign affiliate resulting from credit extended by the parent to the foreign affiliate for its capitalization and on-going funding needs, as well as interest payments on capital leases.
4. *Distributed charges.* Charges imposed by the parent on the foreign affiliate for services provided. This category includes allocated expenses (allocated expenses or reimbursements for management, professional, technical, or other services that normally would be included in "other income" in the income statement of the provider of the service), rentals for the use of tangible property (rentals for operating leases of one year or less and net rent on operating leases of more than one year; net rent is equivalent to the total lease payment less the return of capital (depreciation) component), and film and television tape rentals.

A potential fifth method of repatriating earnings is in the form of *intra-firm debt*. Whereas net interest payments implicitly measure the return on intra-firm debt, the ability to restructure the repayment schedule on principal does allow the individual multinational firm significant discretion. However, the U.S. Department of Commerce data does not consider this a repatriation of earnings, and we will omit this potential form of repatriation for the purposes of this article. (The subject is an important one. Many U.S.-based multinational firms have in the past made loans from their foreign affiliates to the U.S. parent with no interest charges and no debt maturity stated. The U.S. tax authorities have subsequently reclassified these financial structures as dividends for all intents and tax purposes.)

The distinction between *foreign income* and *repatriation of earnings* recognizes that distributed earnings (dividends) represent a distribution of part of foreign income, whereas the other three primary conduits of cash flow are charges or rents for services or technologies or capital used by foreign affiliates and are deducted on determining foreign income. All of these cash flows are separate from the business risk of the foreign affiliate – i.e., determined and fixed by contract – whereas dividend distributions are normally a function of foreign income available to be distributed.

Table 1   Comparison of foreign income and repatriation of earnings: foreign affiliates of U.S.-based firms, 1993 (millions of U.S. dollars)

Income of foreign affiliate				*Repatriation of earnings from foreign affiliate*
	Net receipt ($)	*With tax*	*Net remittance* ($)	
Gross earnings including capital gains				
Less royalties and license fees	14,926	(746)	14,179	(1) Royalties and license fees from affiliate
Less distributed charges	4,908	(-0-)	4,908	(2) Distributed charges from affiliate
Earnings before interest and taxes				
Less interest	1,398	(169)	1,229	(3) Interest earnings from affiliate
Earnings before taxes				
Less corporate taxes				
Earnings after tax	56,117			
Reinvested	29,565			
Distributed (dividends)	26,552	(947)	25,605	(4) Net distributed earnings from affiliate (dividends)
Income = earnings before capital gains plus capital gains income plus net interest after withholding taxes less withholding taxes on distributed earnings = 56,117 + 1,398 – 169 – 947 = $56,399				Sum of four = total repatriated earnings = 14,179 + 4,908 + 1,229 + 25,605 = $45,921

Notes

1. Data abstracted from "U.S. direct investment abroad: reconciliation with international transactions accounts," Table 2, U.S. direct investment abroad: detail for historical-cost position and balance of payments flows, *Survey of Current Business*, U.S. Department of Commerce, August 1994, p. 128.
2. All values are net cash inflows received by U.S-based firms; receipts from foreign affiliates less payments to foreign affiliates.
3. All cash flows repatriated to the United States are net of withholding taxes. Withholding tax rates for royalties, interest, and dividends are normally determined by bilateral tax treaty. Currently, there are no withholding taxes on charges to foreign affiliates by host country governments.
4. A foreign affiliate may owe interest, royalties, and other payments to un-affiliated firms (other than the U.S.-based firm which may or may not be its parent). This analysis focuses on those cash flows due the U.S.-based firm alone.

Recent Repatriation Amounts and Trends

Table 1 provides a methodological comparison of *foreign income* and *repatriation of earnings* to U.S.-based firms from foreign affiliates, as well as empirical estimates of total net cash flows for U.S.-based firms in 1993. As shown, the relationship between income and repatriation is a loose one, with three of the four cash flows of repatriation – royalties, charges, and net interest – acting as costs within the income statement of the foreign affiliate. The value of foreign income itself includes both reinvested earnings and distributed earnings, whereas repatriation's total value is largely determined by the dividend distribution decision by/for the foreign affiliate.

Table 2 provides an overview of repatriation from foreign affiliates for the 1989–93 period. The first and foremost observation is the relative growth of royalties as a proportion of

Table 2 Repatriated earnings of U.S.-based firms from all foreign affiliates, 1989–1993 (millions of U.S. dollars, percentage of total repatriation)

Cash flow	1989	1990	1991	1992	1993
Royalties and license fees	$9,158	$12,381	$12,970	$14,284	$14,179
	(18%)	(22%)	(25%)	(27%)	(31%)
Charges for services	4,341	4,460	4,434	4,880	4,908
	(8%)	(8%)	(9%)	(9%)	(11%)
Net interest received	57	1,663	1,045	1,004	1,229
	(0%)	(3%)	(2%)	(2%)	(3%)
Distributions (dividends)	37,793	37,123	32,716	33,081	25,605
	(74%)	(67%)	(64%)	(62%)	(56%)
Total repatriation	$51,349	$55,632	$51,165	$53,249	$45,921
Foreign income	$52,628	$57,150	$50,687	$48,561	$56,399

Source: Data abstracted from "U.S. direct investment abroad: reconciliation with international transaction accounts," *Survey of Current Business*, U.S. Department of Commerce, annually.

total repatriated funds, rising from 18 per cent to 31 per cent, while dividends dropped precipitously from 74 per cent in 1989 to about 56 per cent in 1993. A second point is that total repatriated cash flows – in nominal dollars – remained relatively constant over this period, approximately $50 billion per year. It is fairly clear, however, that dividends are in recent periods increasingly less dominant as the method employed for the repatriation of cash flows from the foreign affiliates of U.S.-based firms.

Dividends – the distributed profits of foreign affiliates – are, of course, the most obvious and historically the largest in terms of repatriation. Dividends are, however, an increasingly smaller proportion of total earnings repatriated to U.S.-resident firms. Although total repatriated earnings and total foreign income are of a very similar magnitude over this period, the distinction is significant. For example, in both 1991 and 1992, total repatriated earnings exceeded the total amount of foreign income for that year by all foreign affiliates of U.S.-based multinational firms. It appears that, even in this most recent period, there are changing patterns of earnings remittance by U.S. multinationals.

Summary

Multinational firms must continually balance the needs of their shareholders for current income, and the needs of their foreign affiliates for profitability and reinvestment, with the complexities of international taxation, currency risk, and country risk. The method by which U.S.-based multinational firms repatriate their profits has been changing in recent years. It appears that for the present, a number of alternative repatriation methods such as royalties and license fees may continue to grow as conduits for the repatriation of foreign earnings.

MICHAEL H. MOFFETT
and DALE L. DAVISON

FIRP *see* FOREIGN INCOME INFORMATION RETURNS PROGRAM

first world country   First world countries are those that are highly industrialized, have high per capita incomes in relation to most other countries, high levels of education, and other economic and social attributes one might expect from nations such as Australia, Canada, Germany, Great Britain, France (in fact virtually all of western Europe), Japan, the United States, and a few other countries. These countries are also referred to as the highly industrialized countries.

JOHN O'CONNELL

fiscal clearance   In order to exit a host country, an expatriate or other foreign resident may have to submit a document verifying that all local income taxes have been paid. This is referred to as a fiscal clearance document. If tax debts have not been satisfied, exit will usually be denied.

JOHN O'CONNELL

fixed exchange rate systems   Fixed exchange rates are the result of government action which allows for no variation between currencies to occur. Fixing of exchange rates requires agreements between countries to "peg" or link the value of their currency to some common commodity or other value. For example, if currencies are linked to the value of gold, even though gold may rise or fall in value, the relative value of each currency (the exchange rate) remains unchanged.

See also **Floating exchange rate**

JOHN O'CONNELL

flag   When used in reference to the operation of vessels, the term "flag" means the country in which the vessel is registered.

JOHN O'CONNELL

flag of convenience   Vessels are often "flagged" or registered in countries other than that in which they are owned. Although country of registry sometimes appears to be an insignificant point, it can be very important for a number of reasons. Different countries treat shipping interests differently with respect to taxation. Flagging in one country versus another could save considerable amounts in tax payments. Some countries have restrictions as to how many foreign sailors may be used to staff ships, while other countries do not have such regulations. A ship owner may desire to flag a ship in a country allowing less expensive, foreign staffing of ships. Neither of these reasons for registering a ship outside of the home country is particularly notable as long as the shipowner assures competent staffing takes place. Another area, however, deserves some attention. Not all countries which register vessels have the same degree of safety and inspection requirements for vessels or their crew. Before chartering, shipping, or traveling on vessels of foreign registry it is best to determine the standards used to register the vessel. Most of the industrialized nations have registry requirements which are very strict. That is one of the reasons for the flight to other foreign registries. The registry practices of some countries may provide minimal standards for safety.

Bibliography

Zodl, J. A. (1992). *Export–Import: Everything you and your company need to know to compete in world markets.* Cincinnati, OH: Betterway Books.

JOHN O'CONNELL

floating exchange rate   When the exchange rate between currencies is determined by market forces, it is said to be subject to a "floating exchange rate." Floating rates are allowed to fluctuate in terms of their relationship to other currencies.

JOHN O'CONNELL

FO   *see* FREE OUT

FOA   *see* FOOD AND AGRICULTURE ORGANIZATION; FREE ON AIR

FOB   *see* FREE ON BOARD

Food and Agriculture Organization (FAO)
One of the United Nation's most ambitious programs seeks to end hunger in all nations of the world. In order for this to occur, food production must be increased and distribution channels developed to move food where it is needed. The Food and Agricultural Organization is an agency of the United Nations whose sole responsibility is to move toward the achievement of the "end hunger" goal. In this capacity the FAO coordinates world agricultural development and sponsors research programs related to improving agricultural output and distribution.

JOHN O'CONNELL

FOR   (pre-1990 trading term) *see* FREE ON RAIL; INCOTERMS

force majeure   In legal terms, a force majeure is an act of a superior power or one which is irresistible (unable to be controlled). Such acts include natural disasters (floods, earthquakes, hurricanes, tornadoes, tsunamis, etc.) or acts of persons or nations (bankruptcies or wars, etc.). The importance of this term becomes apparent when applied to contractual relationships. A force majeure clause excuses a party to a contract from complying with its terms if the noncompliance was caused by factors outside of that parties' control. Not all contracts have force majeure clauses but such clauses are common in foreign trade and transit contracts.

JOHN O'CONNELL

forecasting political risk   "Political risk" is the term that is used in describing the possibility that political or social actions or characteristics in a host country will negatively affect a foreign investment. Specifically, they could affect the business such that investors will lose income, capital plant, or equipment, in part or in entirety, or simply have a reduced profit margin. The best

approach to understanding the concept of political risk and the role and methods of forecasting is to examine exactly what is at risk and what risk means in applied business terms. The critical questions are as follows: What exactly constitutes a loss that is political or social in its origins and not commercial? How is risk or probability of that loss calculated? How is that probability projected into the future (a forecast) so that it can be applied in a practical business context?

The U.S. government's Overseas Private Investment Corporation (OPIC) pays claims for losses by American companies occurring from four causes that are defined as resulting from political sources: these are (1) expropriation, (2) inconvertibility, (3) war damage, and (4) civil strife damage. Expropriation is an act of government. Inconvertibility is also the result of a governmental decision. War and civil strife damage are the results of either government decisions (including the military leadership) or responses to those government decisions by opponents.

The Multilateral Investment Guarantee Agency (MIGA) of the World Bank and private insurers such as AIG also cover, under political risk insurance, breach of contract for political reasons. The latter include such matters as unilateral termination of a contract by a government, government regulations that prevent execution of a contract, embargoes by other governments, war circumstances that result in contract repudiation, and other similar causes. Politically motivated strikes, corruption, and government interference in personnel policy are among other sources of loss for foreign investors that can be considered to be "socio-political."

Losses with political or social origins come in many other forms than those routinely covered by OPIC, MIGA, or private insurers such as AIG. For example, *Political Turmoil* is a response to government actions and decisions, and is probably not even directed at the business that might suffer through disruption; *Equity Restrictions* would be a government decision or a decision by a segment of the government, such as a ministry; *Personnel/Procurement Interference* occurs in many political systems; *Taxation Discrimination*, directed at particular companies or particular nationalities, is the result of a decision of someone in government and may reflect social issues or prejudices; *Repatriation Restrictions, Exchange Controls, Tariff Imposition, Nontariff Barrier Imposition,* and *Fiscal/Monetary Expansion,* all of which may affect businesses negatively, are the result of government decisions. *Labor Cost Expansion* may result indirectly from government decisions. *Payment delays* and *bureaucratic sluggishness* may be a function of government policy or simply government inefficiency, but both have to do with the way in which the government operates.

Many businesses lose profits through politically motivated *strikes.* Others find a drain through *corruption,* which may be a significant problem because of government tolerance or by virtue of social acceptance. In many countries, corruption has simply gotten out of hand and the government is unable to control it (a comment on the state of the government) or is unwilling to control it (having to do with the ideology or the ethics of the government). *Kidnapping* of executives for political reasons (including raising money for dissident political groups) is very common in some of the major emerging markets. There are many means by which companies suffer detrimental consequences that have their sources in the actions of the government or the nature of the society represented by that government.

A forecast links the act resulting in loss (e.g., civil strife damage) to the causes of the act (e.g., an ethnic dispute dissolving into open conflict) or predictors of the cause. Based on historical memory, an argument is made that the presence of ethnic tension has a good probability of resulting in civil strife. The existence of an attribute is followed by an event a certain percentage of the time. This question can be tested empirically (i.e., is there a correlation between ethnic tension and losses to foreign businesses?) if appropriate data are available.

Forecasting has taken four basic forms in the models that have been in recent use. For a variety of reasons, all are linear projections with multiple indicators from which the forecasts are made. Type I is a correlation from current attributes of countries. A list of attributes that are deemed significant correlates of future trouble are scored to create an index (score) that should project to an equivalent level of danger (and loss) to the firm. The attributes are

seen in the present; losses are expected to follow in time.

An example of a Type I forecast is that provided in a 1986 article in *The Economist.* In the article a list of factors was presented that were described as economic, political, and social; and a scheme was provided for weighting their individual impacts and relative roles (measures of "risk" contribution). An additive method was offered for combining the risk scores and ranking them in such a way as to advise the reader of useful directions to take in investment. An index of risk was created, based on 100 points. Of those 100, 33 were attributed to economic factors, 50 to politics, and 17 to "society." For the political risk portion of the index, *The Economist* chose six political variables and four social variables: *bad neighbors* (3 negative points), *authoritarianism* (7 points), *staleness* (5 points), *illegitimacy* (9 points), *generals in power* (6 points), *war/armed insurrection* (20 points), *urbanization pace* (3 points), *Islamic fundamentalism* (4 points), *corruption* (6 points), and *ethnic tension* (4 points).

Type II forecasts are those that ask experts to project the attributes out into the future. If this approach were applied in the case of *The Economist,* the question to the expert would be "What will the level of ethnic tension be five years from now in country X?" rather than "What is the level of ethnic tension now?" That having been done, there would be no time-lag between the attribute and the problem for the business. The Business Environment Risk Intelligence (BERI) Political Risk Index is an example of a Type II forecast. Like the 1986 ratings in *The Economist,* the BERI Index is based on scores assigned to ten "political" variables by experts; and, also similarly, the BERI PRI is clearly identified as being "sociopolitical." The ten variables are divided into three categories: "internal causes of political riskl," "external causes of political risk," and "symptoms of political risk."

The "internal causes" are:

(1) fractionalization of the political spectrum and the power of these factions;

(2) fractionalization by language, ethnic and/or religious groups and the power of these factions;

(3) restrictive (coercive) measures required to retain power;

(4) mentality, including xenophobia, national-ism, corruption, nepotism, and willingness to compromise;

(5) social conditions, including population density and wealth distribution;

(6) organization and strength of forces for a radical left government.

The "external causes" are:

(7) dependence on and/or importance to a hostile major power;

(8) negative influences of regional political force.

Two "symptoms of political risk" are:

(9) societal conflict involving demonstrations, strikes, and street violence;

(10) instability as perceived by nonconstitu-tional changes, assassinations, and guerrilla wars.

Type III forecasting is to project the losses or the actions which account for the losses themselves out into the future. For example, it is easy to understand how a war going on today could be damaging infrastructure necessary for successful business activity. But will there be a war going on five years from now, or – a more difficult question – will there be bureaucratic inefficiency five years or ten years from now? As difficult as this type of projection might be, it does skip the intervening stage of trying to project first to whether there will be ethnic tension five years from now and then whether that ethnic tension will result in civil strife that could damage physical plant five years from now. An example of the Type III forecast also comes from BERI in its Operations Risk Index (ORI). In Operations Risk, the analyst assesses the likely occurrence, five years hence, of *nationalization, bureaucratic delays, currency convertibility, enforceability of contracts, avail-ability of communications and transportation infrastructures*, and *availability of capable local management and partners*. Several of these are precisely the actions against which OPIC, MIGA, and AIG insure.

Type IV provides a distinct approach. In this method, future governments are projected by the analyst (stage 1), and then the behaviors of those governments toward businesses are simi-larly projected (stage 2). The only current example of Type IV forecasting is that of Political Risk Services (PRS) and their use of the PRINCE model.

Ordinarily, the PRS experts forecast the three most likely governments (or "regimes") to be in power 18 months or five years from the present, and then predict how they will behave toward businesses at that time. The behavior variables employed in the PRS analysis represent a different stage than those used by *The Economist* and BERI PRI. While the former examine societal and system attributes, PRS – with one exception – examine direct government actions or economic functions. It is thus somewhat like the BERI Operations Risk Index except that PRS adds the dimension of the combined effect of likely governments at the future points. If three potential governments have likelihoods of 60 per cent, 30 per cent, and 10 per cent, each of their possible behaviors are included in the forecast at the level of their likelihood of being in a position to carry out that behavior. These PRS action variables include *Equity Restrictions, Personnel/Procurement Interference, Taxation Discrimination, Repatriation Restrictions, Exchange Control Imposition, Tariff Imposition, Nontariff Barrier Imposition, Payment Delays, Fiscal/Monetary Expansion*, and *Labor Cost Expansion*.

Each of the types of forecast listed above has its advantages and disadvantages. Some are better than others in their forecasting ability. Some are more digestible by users than others, while sometimes also being less capable. What should be known is that there are reasonably sophisticated models within each category, that the use of appropriate models can aid businesses in avoiding or managing risk, and – most importantly – that the use of any of these forecasting techniques will assist the firm in identifying risks to businesses in an increasingly complex and dangerous political environment.

Bibliography

Anonymous (1986). Countries in trouble. *The Economist*, December 20, 25–8.

Brewer, T. L. (1985). Politics, risks, and international business. In T. L. Brewer (Ed.) *Political risks in international business: New directions for research, management, and public policy*. (pp. 3–12). New York: Praeger.

Coplin, W. D. & O'Leary, M. K. (1983). *Introduction to political risk analysis, learning packages in the policy sciences.* Policy Studies Associates.

Coplin, W. D. & O'Leary, M. K. (1976).. *Everyman's PRINCE: A guide to understanding your political problems,* (rev. edn). North Scituate, MA: Duxbury.

Howell, L. D. (1986). Area specialists and expert data: The human factor in political risk analysis. In J. Rogers (Ed.),. *Global risk assessments,* (pp. 47), book 2, Riverside, CA: GRA, Inc.

Howell, L. D. (1992). Political risk and political loss for foreign investment. *The International Executive,* **34,** (6), 485–98.

Howell, L. D. (1994). An introduction to country and political risk analysis. In Coplin, W. D. & O'Leary, M. K. (eds),. *The handbook of country and political risk analysis,* (pp. 3–9). East Syracuse, NY: Political Risk Services.

Howell, L. D. & Chaddick, B. (1994). Models of political risk for foreign investment and trade: An assessment of three approaches.. *Columbia Journal of World Business,* Winter, 70–90.

Wagner, D. (1990). Why political risk insurance will grow in the 1990s. *Risk Management,* October, 34–9.

LLEWELLYN D. HOWELL

foreign affiliate   When an organization in one country owns or controls an organization in another country, the second organization is referred to as a foreign affiliate.

JOHN O'CONNELL

foreign assignment   International organizations generally require some employees to assume positions outside of their home country. Any position which requires an employee to live in another country to carry out his/her work-related duties is considered a foreign assignment. Foreign assignments are usually for a matter of months or years. Thus, the occasional business trip does not usually fall into the foreign assignment category in most organizations.

See also **Assignment**

Bibliography

Brislin, R. W. (1981). *Cross-cultural encounters.* New York: Pergamon Press.

JOHN O'CONNELL

foreign bills   *see* BILL OF EXCHANGE

foreign branch   One of the ways of conducting business in another country is to establish a foreign branch office. An organization, with foreign branches, has its own employees in the branch offices to represent the company at the local level in foreign countries. Foreign branches are often staffed by local employees (host country nationals) as well as expatriates from any other of the company's locations.

See also **Expatriate**

Bibliography

Kelley, L., Whatley, A. & Worthley, R. (1987). Assessing the affects of culture on managerial attitudes: A three-culture test. *Journal of International Business Studies,* Summer, 17–31.

JOHN O'CONNELL

foreign corporation   In most countries (with the major exception being the United States) a foreign corporation is one which is formed in another country. Thus, a Korean company doing business in Mexico is considered a foreign corporation by Mexico. In the United States, however, the term "foreign corporation" refers to a corporation formed in a different "state" of the United States. Thus, a Delaware corporation doing business in California is considered a foreign corporation. The United States reserves the term "alien corporation" for a company formed outside of the country.

See also **Alien corporation**

JOHN O'CONNELL

Foreign Corrupt Practices Act (FCPA)   A United States law (1977) which prohibits a US company from making payments to foreign government officials to influence those officials to make decisions beneficial to the company. The FCPA is essentially a United States law against bribing foreign officials to act on behalf of a US company. Under the act, no bribe, contribution, transfer of funds, or other payment can be made to or on behalf of a foreign government official for the purpose of benefiting a US company. US firms doing business overseas are required to keep detailed records of expenditures related to overseas activities and make those records available to the Securities and Exchange Commission and/or The United States Department of Justice.

Bibliography

Cash, M. M. (1988). *Strategic intervention in organizations: Resolving ethical dilemmas in corporations.* Newbury Park, CA: Sage.
Gillespie, K. (1987). Middle East response to the U.S. Foreign Corrupt Practices Act. *California Management Review*, Summer, 9–30.
U.S. Congress (1977). Foreign Corrupt Practices Act of 1977. *The United States Code of Congressional and Administrative News*, 95th Congress, First Session 1977, Vol. 1, 91 stat., Public Law 95–213 1494–500.
Wood, D. J. (1994). *Business and society.* 2nd edn, New York: HarperCollins.

JOHN O'CONNELL

foreign credit insurance *see* CREDIT RISK INSURANCE

Foreign Credit Insurance Association (FCIA) One of the risks of entering into foreign trade transactions is that the buyer of goods will not pay for them. Although a similar risk exists with domestic sales, foreign sales are particularly risky for several reasons. Foreign buyers are sometimes thousands of miles away, making normal credit worthiness checks are difficult if not impossible to accomplish; foreign payments may be withheld because of a foreign government's actions (nonconvertibility of currency, or others); and when foreign companies or governments default it may be very expensive and time consuming to take collection action. The Foreign Credit Insurance Association (FCIA) is an agent of the Export–Import Bank of the United States. Exporters may purchase credit insurance from the FCIA, which also has special insurance programs for banks, foreign commercial lease payments, and others.

Bibliography

Trieschman, J. S. & Gustavson, S. G. (1993). *Risk management and insurance.* 9th edn, Cincinnati, OH: Southwestern College Publishing.

JOHN O'CONNELL

foreign currency Accounting regulations for foreign currency vary internationally. Foreign currency accounting regulations are contained in Statement of Financial Accounting Standard No. 52, "Foreign Currency Translation", (1981) (SFAS 52) in the USA; Statement of Standard Accounting Practice No. 20 (SSAP 20) in the UK; CICA 1650, "Foreign Currency Translation," in Canada; AASB 1012 and AAS 20, "Foreign Currency Translation" in Australia; International Accounting Standard IAS 21, "The Effects of Changes in Foreign Exchange Rates"; standards issued by the Business Accounting Deliberation Council in Japan; recommendations issued by Sweden's Authorized Accountant Association; the Plan Comptable Général in France, and other forms of regulation in various countries. Not all countries' regulations regulate all foreign currency accounting issues; nor do all countries' regulations concur. It is noteworthy that the European Community's (EC's) Fourth and Seventh Directives are both silent concerning foreign currency accounting, requiring merely the disclosure of exchange rates used to translate foreign currency balances.

Offshore investments

To incorporate a firm's equity investment in operations with foreign-currency denominated accounts into the firm's own group accounts, it is necessary to translate the foreign operation's accounts into the investor's reporting currency. Of the following translation methods the current rate and temporal methods are those most frequently adopted.

The *current rate method* was used by British accountants in the 19th century and has been followed by UK, European, Asian, Australian, and New Zealand firms. It is currently permitted for self-sustaining operations under international, US, Canadian, UK, European, Australian, and Asian accounting standards. All the foreign operation's assets and liabilities are translated at the exchange rate ruling on balance date. Profit and loss statement items are translated using exchange rates ruling at the times of the transactions or approximations thereto. Because a self-sustaining operation operates independently of the investor, the investor's currency risk is limited to its "net investment." Most international standards therefore require that the net investment in self-sustaining operations, i.e., assets less liabilities, be translated using the current rate method.

A claimed advantage of the current rate method is that it preserves the relativity of measures in the foreign operation's accounts. A claimed disadvantage is that when assets valued at other than current values are translated using a current exchange rate, the resultant measure is devoid of economic meaning.

The *temporal method* is sometimes required by international, US, Canadian, UK, European, and Australasian countries' accounting standards, and generally is to be applied only where the foreign investment is "integrated," i.e., where the overseas firm frequently exposes the reporting firm to currency risk because of financial and/or operating interdependencies. Under the temporal method, assets and liabilities are translated using exchange rates corresponding to their valuation: historical-cost-valued items are translated using historical exchange rates; items at current or revalued amounts are translated using exchange rates ruling at their (re)valuation. Revenues and expenses are translated using exchange rates at the time of the transactions.

The current rate and temporal methods often produce translation differences of the opposite sign. Because all assets and liabilities are translated at current rates under the current rate method, and assets generally exceed liabilities, the accounting exchange rate exposure arises from net assets. In contrast, the temporal method generally yields an exposure from net liabilities since liabilities are more frequently measured at current values than are assets. While the temporal method retains the subsidiary's measurement system, the current rate method yields exchange rate gains or losses consistent with the parent entity's economic currency exposure from the subsidiary's net

assets and does not distort the relationships of items in the offshore operation's accounts.

The *monetary–non-monetary method* translates monetary items using balance-date exchange rates and non-monetary items using historic exchange rates, yielding effects similar to the temporal method if assets are not revalued. Where revaluations are common, as in some European and most Australasian countries, the differences can be material.

The *current–non current method* entails translating current assets and liabilities at balance-date exchange rates; non current items are translated at historic rates. The method was common when rates moved gently, as within a stabilization system like the European Monetary System. It was advocated on the grounds that current items were likely to be settled at rates approximating the current rate. In contrast, exchange rates might have returned to prior levels by the time long-term items were settled.

Translation policies under hyperinflation

For subsidiaries in countries with high inflation, a particular problem arises due to two economic relationships:

(1) Purchasing power parity, whereby an inverse relation between currency strength and inflation rates ensures that asset values in countries with different exchange rates remain relatively constant in terms of either currency.
(2) The "Fisher effect," where there is an inverse relation between interest rates and currency movements so that as a currency strengthens relative to another, the interest rate weakens.

Over extended periods, both effects tend to operate. Translating the accounts of an operation in a hyperinflationary country can therefore distort the accounts relative to the parent's. US and UK standards respond differently to the problem: US Statement of Financial Accounting Standard (SFAS) 52 requires temporal translation if prices more than double in three years; while Statement of Standard Accounting Practice (UK) (SSAP) 20 requires inflation adjustments to the foreign operation's accounts before using the current rate method. International Accounting Standard (IAS) 21 permits either method.

Treatment of Translation Gains and Losses

Translation gains or losses (differences) can pass through earnings or go directly to reserves such as a foreign currency translation reserve. Internationally, regulations require different practices for different translation methods. In turn, the extent of integration of the investor and investee operations determines the translation method. The current rate method is required for self-sustaining operations and combines with taking translation gains and losses to reserves; the temporal method combines with taking translation differences to earnings for integrated operations.

Foreign currency transactions of the reporting firm

Foreign currency transactions are recorded at exchange rates ruling when the transactions occur. When resultant debts or receivables are settled before balance date, realized gains or losses are recorded in earnings: there appears to be no international or national accounting regulation requiring that they be taken directly to reserves.

At balance date, any unsettled monetary assets or liabilities are translated using the balance-date exchange rate. Most countries' accounting standards require the unrealized gains or losses to be taken to earnings if the item is short term (current). For long-term monetary items there has been greater diversity. IAS 21 and US, UK, Australian, and New Zealand standards require unrealized gains or losses on long-term monetary items that are not hedges to be recognized as income or expenses of the period when the exchange rate moves. The Canadian accounting standard recently adopted this practice. Previously, it required them to be deferred to a balance sheet account and amortized the related items' lives. Deferral and amortization policy was once required under Australian regulations also.

Foreign currency hedges

Countries vary considerably in their treatment of foreign currency hedges, and many countries' standards do not cover hedge accounting. International Accounting Standard (IAS) 21 does not deal with hedge accounting except to require equity classification of exchange differences from monetary items forming part of an enterprise's net investment in a foreign subsidiary or hedging a net investment until the investment is disposed. Then, these differences are recognized as income or expenses (IAS 21, para. 17). US Statement of Financial Accounting Standard (SFAS) 52, requires identical treatment, as do UK Statement of Standard Accounting Practice (SSAP) 20, paras 51, 57, AASB 1012, para. 31 (Australia) in AASB 1012, para. 31 and CICA 1650.50 (Canada).

Where foreign currency transactions such as forward contracts hedge an identifiable, specific foreign currency commitment such as a purchase or sale commitment, Australian, New Zealand, and US accounting standards require the unrealized gains or losses on the hedge transaction to be deferred and included in measuring the hedged commitment (AASB 1012 (XXV); as in New Zealand; SFAS 52, para. 21). The Canadian approach defers the gain or loss until monetary item settlement (CICA 1650.54).

The treatment of premiums or discounts on forward contracts can depend upon the purpose of the contracts. Under Australian, New Zealand, and US regulations, if the purpose is not to hedge a specific identifiable foreign currency commitment, the premiums or discounts are deferred to the balance sheet and amortized over the lives of the contracts. If a contract hedges a specific identifiable commitment, the portion related to the commitment may be included in measuring of the commitment (AASB 1012, Commentary; SSAP 21, para. 5.5; SFAS 52, para. 19). International, UK, and Canadian standards are silent on the treatment.

Disclosure

Almost all countries with foreign currency accounting standards require disclosure of the amount of exchange rate differences included in the period's net profit or loss; net exchange differences classified as a separate component of equity; and a reconciliation of amounts at the start and end of the period. Additional disclosures sometimes required include details of changes in the classification of significant foreign operations and the financial impact of the changes (IAS 21, para. 44); and the amounts and currencies of payables and receivables (AASB 1012, para. 60).

Reactions to Proposed and Actual Accounting Standards

Most research investigating reactions to proposed and actual foreign currency accounting standards emanates from the USA. Research indicates that firms increased foreign exchange risk management to reduce exposure to earnings variability subsequent to the introduction of Statement of Financial Accounting Standard, the predecessor to SFAS 52 (SFAS) 8. Further studies of lobbying and changes in financing or operating activities in response to SFAS 8 indicate managerial risk aversion to increased reported income variability and that managers adopted the new standard when it had the potential to most reduce their contracting and political costs.

While their results have been mixed, researchers have generally found negative stock price reactions to SFAS 8 and positive reactions to SFAS 52 and that the share price effects are associated with the extent to which the SFAS-induced earnings variability affected firms' earnings-based contracts and political vulnerability.

Foreign Currency Accounting Policy Choices

In one of the few publications to examine firms' voluntary foreign currency accounting policies, Taylor, Tress & Johnson (1990) note that most Australian firms prefer current rate translation. They investigate why firms varied in taking the consequential translation differences to reserves, operating earnings, or extraordinary earnings and find that the selected policies facilitated risk sharing between shareholders and managers. Godfrey (1992) finds evidence that voluntary policies were optimal in sharing risk between Australian lenders, shareholders, and managers. She finds that Australian companies' policies for translating accounts of overseas subsidiaries and for foreign currency long-term debt combined to yield an accounting hedge if the firm hedged its economic exchange rate risk, and did not give an accounting hedge if the firm did not hedge the economic risk.

Godfrey (1994) investigates whether, prior to regulation of accounting for foreign currency long-term debt, Australian managers used accounting policies to reflect firms' underlying exchange rate risk exposure, or whether the policies were used opportunistically to influence reported earnings levels. Policies included taking all currency differences to current earnings; deferring and amortizing them over the life of the debt; or recognizing them in earnings only when the debt was repaid. She finds that managers chose methods that reflected the firms' underlying economic exposures to currency risk. In particular, when foreign debt hedged currency exposure for foreign currency-export-earning assets, managers selected the method that best reflected the results of the hedging objective.

Generally, research indicates that Australian firms' voluntary reporting practices reflected the underlying nature of the firms' foreign currency exposures and that alternative practices imposed costs on the firms and their shareholders.

Bibliography

Financial Accounting Standards Board (1995). *Original Pronouncements–Accounting Standards as of June 1995*, Vol. 1. New York: John Wiley & Sons, Inc.

Godfrey, J. M. (1992). Foreign Currency Accounting Policies: Reporting the exchange rate/asset value correlation. *Accounting and Finance*.

Godfrey, J. M. (1994). Foreign currency accounting policies: The impact of asset specificity. *Contemporary Accounting Research*, Spring.

Taylor, S., Tress, R. B. & Johnson, L. W. (1990). Explaining intraperiod accounting choices: The reporting of currency translation gains and losses. *Accounting and Finance*.

JAYNE M. GODFREY

foreign distributors   *see* DISTRIBUTOR

foreign exchange   Foreign exchange is the currency of one country located in a second country. A country generally uses the foreign currency it has on hand to pay debts owed in the issuing country. Foreign exchange may also refer to the actual process of exchanging one currency for another. Foreign exchange markets have been established throughout the world for such exchanges to take place.

Bibliography

Agenor, P. R. (1992). *Parallel currency markets in developing markets: Theory, evidence, and policy implications.* Princeton, NJ: Princeton University.

Miletello, F. C. & Davis, H. A. (1994). *Foreign exchange management.* Morristown, NJ: Financial Executives Research Foundation.

Peters, C. C. & Gitlin, A. W. (eds) (1993). *Strategic currency investing: Trading and investing in the foreign exchange markets.* Hinsdale, IL: Probus Publishing Company Inc.

JOHN O'CONNELL

foreign exchange arbitrageur   A person who purchases the currency of two or more countries simultaneously in hope of profiting from differences in exchange rates of the purchased currencies.

JOHN O'CONNELL

foreign exchange broker   An intermediary who brings together buyers and sellers of currency. Foreign exchange brokers may represent banks, private companies, governments, and individuals seeking to exchange currencies.

JOHN O'CONNELL

foreign exchange dealers   Persons who buy and sell currency on the foreign exchange market. The majority of foreign exchange dealers are employed by banking institutions although they could also work for large organizations with frequent exchange needs.

JOHN O'CONNELL

foreign exchange loans   If a company takes out a loan in other than the currency of its home country, the loan is considered a foreign exchange loan. Foreign exchange loans are commonly made to companies which want to take advantage of lower interest rates or other favorable loan terms offered in a foreign country.

The major drawback to such loans is that if exchange rates change, all advantages from the better terms may be wiped out.

JOHN O'CONNELL

foreign exchange markets   Foreign exchange markets are the institutional frameworks within which currencies are bought and sold by individuals, corporations, banks and governments. Trading in currencies no longer occurs in a physical marketplace or in any one country. London, New York, and Tokyo, the major international banking centers in the world, have the largest share of the market, accounting for nearly 60 percent of all transactions. The next four important centers are Singapore, Switzerland, Hong Kong, and Germany. Over half of transactions in the foreign exchange markets are cross-border, that is between parties in different countries. Trading is performed using the telephone network and electronic screens, like Reuters and Telerate. More and more, however, trading is conducted through automated dealing systems which are electronic systems that enable users to quote prices, and to deal and exchange settlement details with other users on screen, rather than by telex machine or telephone. Counterparties in foreign exchange markets do not exchange physical coins and notes, but effectively exchange the ownership of bank deposits denominated in different currencies. In principle, a tourist who makes a physical exchange of local currency for foreign currency is also a participant in the foreign exchange market and indeed for some currencies seasonal flows of tourist spending may alter exchange rates, though in most markets rates are driven by institutional trading. Other currencies may not be officially converted except for officially approved purposes and the currency rate is then determined by a parallel market which is more indicative of market trends than officially posted rates by the central bank or by the commercial bankers (Kamin, 1993).

According to the Bank for International Settlement's latest triennial survey of the global foreign exchange market, around US$880 billion worth of currencies are bought and sold daily. This represents a 42 percent growth in size compared to the previous survey of 1989 and makes the foreign exchange market the world's biggest and most liquid market. The time zone positions of major international financial markets make the foreign exchange market a 24-hour global market. Unlike the different stock exchanges and securities markets around the world, the foreign exchange market is virtually continuously active with the same basic assets being traded in several different locations. Throughout the day, the center of trading rotates from London to New York and then to Tokyo. Less than 10 percent of the daily turnover in foreign exchange transaction is between banks and their customers in response to tangible international payments. The remaining transactions are mostly between financial institutions themselves and are driven by international financial investment and hedging activities that are stimulated by the increasing deregulation of financial markets and the relaxation of exchange controls. Trading activity in foreign exchange markets shows few abnormalities and with the exception of late Friday and weekends, day of the week distortions are minimal. Trading activity in most centers is characterized by a bimodal distribution around the lunch hour. New York, however, has a unimodal distribution of activity, peaking at the lunch hour which coincides roughly with high activity in London and Frankfurt at the end of the business day in those locations (Foster and Viswanathan, 1990).

Currencies

Although its share is a declining trend, the US dollar remains predominant in foreign exchange turnover. About 83 percent of all foreign exchange transactions involve the US dollar with main turnover between the US dollar and the deutsche mark, Japanese yen, British pound, and the Swiss franc. This small group of currencies accounts for the bulk of interbank trading. Significant amounts of trading occur in other European currencies and in the Canadian dollar, but these can be considered second-tier currencies in that they are not of worldwide interest mostly because of the limited amount of trade and financial transactions denominated in those currencies. In the third tier would be the currencies of smaller countries whose banks are active in the markets and in which there are significant local markets and some international

scale trading. The Hong Kong dollar, the Singapore dollar, the Scandinavian currencies, the Saudi rial, and Kuwait dinar are such currencies. Finally, the fourth tier would consist of what are called the exotic currencies, those for which there are no active international markets and in which transactions are generally arranged on a correspondent-bank basis between banks abroad and local banks in those centers to meet the specific trade requirements of individual clients. This group includes the majority of the Latin American currencies, the African currencies, and the remaining Asian currencies. A currency needs to be fully convertible to be traded in international foreign exchange markets. If there are legal restrictions on dealings in a currency, that currency is said to be inconvertible or not fully convertible and sales or purchases can only be made through the central bank often at different rates for investment and foreign transactions.

Transactions

A spot transaction in the currency market is an agreement between two parties to deliver within two business days a fixed amount of currency in return for payment in another at an agreed upon rate of exchange. In forward transactions the delivery of the currencies, the settlement date, occurs more than two business days after the agreement. In forward contracts short maturities, primarily up to and including seven days, are dominant. There are two types of forward transactions: outright forwards and swaps. Outright forwards involve single sales or purchases of foreign currency for value more than two business days after dealing. Swaps are spot purchases against matching outright forward sales or vice versa. Swap transactions between two forward dates rather than between spot and forward dates are called "forward/forwards." Spot transactions have the largest share in total foreign exchange transactions, accounting for just under half of the daily turnover. However, forward transactions have increased in volume faster and now nearly match the share of spot transactions. Activity in currency futures and options, which approximately represents 6 percent of the market, accounts for the rest of the turnover.

Market Efficiency

Market efficiency is of special interest to both academics and market participants with respect to the foreign exchange markets. Modern finance theory implies that prices in the foreign exchange markets should move over time in a manner that leaves no unexploited profit opportunities for the traders. Consequently, no foreign exchange trader should be able to develop trading rules that consistently deliver profits. This assertion seems to be supported by the traders' performance in real life. However, published research results, so far, show evidence of *ex post* unexploited profit opportunities in the currency markets. Dooley and Shafer (1983) also reported that a number of filter rules beat the market even in the *ex ante* sense. Some authors have argued that the filter profits found in exchange markets are explicable in the light of the speculative risk involved in earning them and may perhaps not be excessive or indicative of inefficiency.

A filter rule refers to a trading strategy where a speculator aims to profit from a trend by buying a currency whenever the exchange rate rises by a certain percentage from a trough and selling it whenever it falls by a certain percentage from a peak. If foreign exchange markets were efficient, the forward rate today would be an optimal predictor of future spot rate and by implication would be the best forecaster. The empirical evidence suggests that the forward rate is not an optimal predictor of the future spot rate, i.e. it is a biased predictor. The rejection of forward market efficiency may be attributable to the irrationality of market participants, to the existence of time-varying risk premiums, or to some combination of both of these phenomena (Cavaglia et al., 1994). Crowder (1994) is one of the examples which argues that once allowance is made for fluctuations in the risk premium, efficiency is preserved. Currently there is no consensus among the researchers on the existence of market inefficiency or on the explanations for the inefficiency.

Participants

The major participants in the foreign exchange markets are banks, central banks, multinational corporations, and foreign exchange brokers.

Banks deal with each other either directly or through brokers. Banks are the most prominent institutions in terms of turnover and in the provision of market-maker services. The interbank market accounts for about 70 percent of transactions in the foreign exchange markets. Banks deal in the foreign exchange market for three reasons. First, banks sell and buy foreign currency against customer orders. Second, banks operate in the market in order to meet their own internal requirements for current transactions or for hedging future transactions. Finally, banks trade in currencies for profit, engaging in riskless arbitrage as well as speculative transactions. In carrying out these transactions the banks both maintain the informational efficiency of the foreign exchange market and generate the high level of liquidity that helps them to provide effective service to their commercial customers. According to the BIS survey in April 1992 in London, the top 20 banks out of 352, acting as foreign exchange market makers, account for 63 percent of total market turnover. In all international markets there is a continuing trend towards a declining number of market-making banks as a result of both mergers among banks and of the withdrawal of some smaller banks who have inadequate capital to trade at the level needed for profitability in such a highly competitive business.

Non-financial corporations use the foreign exchange market both for trade finance and to cover investment/disinvestment transactions in foreign assets. In both activities the objective of the corporation is to maximize its profits by obtaining the most advantageous price of foreign exchange possible. Although small in scale, the corporations' involvement in foreign exchange markets extends to management of their foreign exchange exposure through derivative products and, in the case of larger corporate entities, to actively seeking profit opportunities that may exist in the market through speculative transactions.

In their role of regulating monetary policies, central banks of sovereign states are often in the position of both buying and selling foreign exchange. The objective of central banks' involvement in the foreign exchange markets is to influence the market-determined rate of their currencies in accordance with their monetary policy. Central banks often enter into agreements with one central bank lending the other the foreign exchange needed to finance the purchase of a weak currency in the market to maintain the value of their currencies within a mutually agreed narrow band of fluctuations. Stabilization is intended to prevent wild fluctuations and speculations in the foreign exchange market, but central banks are increasingly cautious about signaling a commitment to a fixed intervention rate. Even the Exchange Rate Mechanism (ERM) of the European Union, in which currencies were contained within narrow bands of their central rate, was unable, in spite of the committed support of all European central banks, to prevent a concerted market adjustment. In September 1992 the Bank of England lost many millions of foreign currency reserves in a short and unsuccessful defense of sterling. Both sterling and the Italian lira were on that occasion forced out of the ERM bands.

Risks

Counterparty credit risk, settlement risk, and trading risk are the three major risks that are faced by market participants in the foreign exchange markets. Credit risk relates to the possibility that a counterparty is unable to meet its obligation. Settlement risk arises when the counterparty is able and willing but fails to deliver the currency on settlement day. The settlement of a foreign exchange contract is not simultaneous; therefore, counterparties are usually not in a position to insure that they have received the countervalue before irreversibly paying away the currency amount. In the foreign exchange markets there are unequal settlement periods across countries. Different time zones may expose the party making the first payment to default by the party making the later payment. In 1974 US banks paid out dollars in the morning to a German bank, Bankhaus Herstatt, but did not receive German marks through the German payment system when German banking authorities closed at 10.30 a.m. New York time. Herstatt received the dollars in the account of its US correspondent but did not pay out the marks. Market risk refers to the risk of adverse movements in the rate of foreign exchange. A market participant in the foreign exchange market risks loss when

rates decline and it has a long position (owns the asset) or when rates rise and it has a short position (has promised to supply the asset without currently owning it).

Quotation and Transaction Costs

The exchange rate quoted for a spot transaction is called the spot rate and the rate that applies in a forward transaction is called the forward rate. If a currency is trading at a lower price against another currency on the forward market than on the spot market, it is said to be at a discount. If, however, the currency is more expensive forward than spot, it is said to be at a premium. What determines whether a currency trades at a premium or discount is the interest rate differential in money markets. The currency with higher/lower interest rate will sell at a discount/premium in the forward market against the currency with the lower/higher interest rate. However, some research has shown a small bias in the forward rate explained by a time-varying risk premium.

Traders in the foreign exchange markets always make two-way prices, that is they quote two figures: the rate at which they are prepared to sell a currency (offer) and the rate at which they are willing to buy a currency (bid). The difference is called the spread and represents the market maker's profit margin. The spread is conventionally very narrow in stable currencies with a high volume of trading. Liquidity is usually extremely good for major currencies and continuous two-way quotations can be obtained. However, in unstable, infrequently traded currencies, it can become a good deal wider. It widens with uncertainty – spreads on internationally traded currencies such as British pound, US dollar, or deutsche mark will widen if the international financial markets are in turmoil. The evidence from foreign exchange markets, however, does not support an unequivocal relationship between the market liquidity and the transaction costs. Bid–ask (offer) spreads are not necessarily lowest when the liquidity is high. More trading by informed risk averse participants brings about higher costs. Bollerslev and Domowitz (1993) report that small traders (banks) in foreign exchange markets tend to increase both the quoted spread and market activity at the beginning and at the end of their regional trading day, because they are more sensitive with respect to their inventory positions at the close than larger banks and have less information based on retail order flow at the beginning than larger banks that operate continuously. Another factor which may effect the transaction cost in foreign exchange markets is unobservable news. News events which change traders' desired inventory positions result in order imbalances, changing the relative demand and supply for the currency, with the potential of changing the spreads (Bollerslev and Domowitz, 1993).

Exchange Rate Systems

From the end of World War II until 1971 the leading industrialized countries under the hegemony of the US economy committed themselves to a fixed exchange rate system. This period in the international monetary system is known as the Bretton Woods system and aimed to preserve a fixed exchange rate between currencies until fundamental disequilibrium appeared, at which point through devaluation or revaluation a new fixed parity was established. The Bretton Woods system was based on the strength of the US economy whereby the US government pledged to exchange gold for US dollars on demand at an irrevocably fixed rate (US$35 per ounce of gold). All other participating countries fixed the value of their currencies in terms of gold, but were not required to exchange their currencies into gold. Fixing the price of gold against each currency was similar to fixing the price of each currency against each other.

With the increasing competitiveness of the continental European economies and the Japanese economy against the US economy, the USA had become unable to meet its obligations under the Bretton Woods system and the fixed exchange rate system gave way to the floating exchange rate system in 1973. Under the floating exchange rate system currencies are allowed to fluctuate in accordance with market forces in the foreign exchange markets. However, even in systems of floating exchange rates where the going rate is determined by supply and demand, the central banks still feel compelled to intervene at particular stages in order to help maintain stable markets. The Group of Seven (G7) council of economic ministers has in the past attempted co-ordinated

interventions in the foreign exchange markets with a view to stabilizing exchange rates. The exchange rate system that exists today for some currencies lies somewhere between fixed and freely floating. It resembles the freely floating system in that exchange rates are allowed to fluctuate on a daily basis and official boundaries do not exist. Yet it is similar to the fixed system in that governments can and sometimes do intervene to prevent their currencies from moving too much in a certain direction. This type of system is known as a managed float. Economists are not in agreement as to which of the exchange rate systems, fixed or floating, can create stability in currency markets and is a better means for adjustments to the balance of payments positions (Friedman, 1953; Dunn, 1983). A fixed exchange rate system is unlikely to work in a world where the participating countries have incompatible macroeconomic policies and the economic burden of adjustments to the exchange rates usually fall on the deficit countries. The floating exchange rate system, on the other hand, has not delivered the benefits that its advocates put forward. The exchange rate volatility during the floating rate period is severe and is not consistent with underlying economic equilibria due to the activities of short-term speculators. The European Union's aim is not to create a fixed exchange rate system, but to create a monetary union where the exchange rate fluctuations are eliminated with adoption of a single currency by the member countries. However, to reach this goal a transitional period where a stability in exchange rates through conversion of member countries' macroeconomic performances to a specified desirable level is necessary. Since the Maastricht Treaty of 1989 the European Union countries have not been successful in achieving these macroeconomic targets, thus raising serious concerns about the monetary union.

Bibliography

Bollerslev, T. & Domowitz, I. (1993). Trading patterns and prices in the interbank foreign exchange market. *The Journal of Finance*, 48, 1421–1443.

Cavaglia, S. M., Verschoor, W. F. & Wolff, C. C. (1994). On the biasedness of forward foreign exchange rates: irrationality or risk premia?. *Journal of Business*, 67, 321–343.

Committeri, M., Rossi, S. & Santorelli, A. (1993). Tests of covered interest parity on the Euromarket with high quality data. *Applied Financial Economics*, 3, 89–93.

Copeland, L. S. (1994). *Exchange rates and international finance.* 2nd edn, Wokingham: Addison-Wesley.

Crowder, W. J. (1994). Foreign exchange market efficiency and common stochastic trends. *Journal of International Money and Finance*, 13, 551–564.

Dooley, M. P. & Shafer, J. R. (1983). Analysis of short run exchange rate behaviour: March 1973 to November 1981. *Exchange rate and trade instability.* Bigman, D. & Taya, T. (Ed.) Cambridge, MA: Ballinger,. 187–209.

Dunn, R. M. (1983). *The many disappointments of flexible exchange rates.* Princeton Essays in International Finance. Princeton: University of Princeton Press..

Eichengreen, B., Tobin, J. & Wyplosz, C. (1995). Two cases for sand in the wheels of international finance. *The Economic Journal*, 105, 162–172.

Foster, D. & Viswanathan, S. (1990). A theory of intraday variations in volumes, variances and trading costs. *Review of Financial Studies*, 3, 593–624.

Friedman, M. (1953). The case for flexible rates. *Essays in positive economics.* Chicago, IL: University of Chicago Press.

Group of Ten Deputies (1993). *International capital movements and foreign exchange markets.* Rome: Bank of Italy.

Kamin, S. B. (1993). Devaluation, exchange controls, and black markets for foreign exchange in developing countries. *Journal of Development Economics*, 40, 151–169.

Krugman, P. (1991). Target zones and exchange rate dynamics. *Quarterly Journal of Economics*, 51, 669–682.

The Bank of England (1992). The foreign exchange market in London. *Bank of England Quarterly Bulletin*, November 408–417.

Tucker, A. L., Madura, J. & Chiang, T. C. (1991). *International financial markets.* St Paul, MN: West Publishing Company.

ISMAIL ERTURK

foreign exchange rate *see* EXCHANGE RATE

foreign exchange restrictions *see* EXCHANGE CONTROLS

foreign exchange risk *see* EXCHANGE RISK

foreign exchange risk management Companies that realize the potential for loss associated with various transactions involving foreign exchange may seek to limit their losses. A number of strategies are available to manage the foreign exchange risk. One strategy is to purchase currency forward contracts. Forward contracts allow the purchase of specified amounts of currency at a set rate on a future date. Even if currency rates fluctuate, the forward price remains static. Another strategy is to purchase currency options. Options give the purchaser the right but not the obligation to make the purchase at a preset price before a stated future date. If it is advantageous, the option is exercised, if not the option is allowed to expire.

Bibliography

Daigler, R. T. (1993). *Managing risk with financial futures: Pricing, hedging, and arbitrage.* Hinsdale, IL: Probus Publishing Company Inc.

Kenyon, A. (1990). *Currency risk and business management.* Cambridge, MA: Blackwell Publishers.

JOHN O'CONNELL

foreign exchange swaps Also referred to as a bank swap. It is the purchase of a foreign currency (left on deposit with a bank) combined with a forward sale of the same currency. The forward sale date and the maturity date of the original sale are the same.

JOHN O'CONNELL

foreign exchange traders Employees of an organization whose job it is to purchase and sell foreign currency for that organization.

JOHN O'CONNELL

foreign freight forwarder *see* FREIGHT FORWARDER

foreign income Income that is obtained from sources that are outside the home country. A Pepsi subsidiary in Amsterdam sending its profits back to the US would be an example of foreign income.

JOHN O'CONNELL

foreign income information returns program This is an agreement between the United States and certain foreign countries (generally those with which the US has reciprocal tax agreements) under which US citizens working in those countries will have their tax records forwarded to the United States Internal Revenue Service (IRS). The IRS uses this information to coordinate tax payments as specified in tax agreements and under US tax law.

See also **Withholding tax**

Bibliography

Nexia International Staff (1994). *International handbook of corporate and personal taxes.* New York: Chapman & Hall.

JOHN O'CONNELL

foreign investment Investments made in a country by citizens of another country. Foreign investments are commonly classified as being either "direct" or "portfolio" investments. Direct foreign investment describes situations in which the investor gains a considerable amount of control of the company or enterprise in which the investment was made. Portfolio foreign investment is the purchase of stock, etc. with little or no control of the company being acquired.

Bibliography

Houthakker, H. S. & Williamson, P. J. (1994). *The economics of financial markets.* New York: Oxford University Press Inc.

JOHN O'CONNELL

foreign investment codes Many countries have laws against foreign investors owning or controlling certain industries. These laws were passed during times when public and political sentiment moved against foreign acquisitions of formerly domestic businesses. Laws usually restrict foreign ownership of certain industries such as munitions or other government-related defense production. Foreign investment codes may also be the place to look for information regarding a country's intellectual property right protections as well as repatriation of profits regulations.

See also **Intellectual property; Repatriation of profits**

Bibliography

International Intellectual Property Alliance Staff (1992). *Copyright piracy in Latin America: Trade losses due to piracy and the adequacy of copyright protection in 16 Central and South American countries.* Washington, D.C.: International Intellectual Property Alliance.

JOHN O'CONNELL

foreign manufacture's agent   *see* EXPORT AGENT

foreign national An employee of an organization who comes from another country. When hiring takes place on a geocentric basis (from employees throughout the world) it is very common to have employees of several countries in a company's home or regional offices. Foreign nationals are citizens of countries other than the one to which they are assigned.

See also **Employee categories; Staffing**

JOHN O'CONNELL

foreign payoffs   *see* BRIBERY

foreign sales agent (FSA)   *see* EXPORT AGENT

foreign service premium   *see* EXPATRIATE ALLOWANCE

foreign source income When a person receives income from a source outside of his/her own country it is considered "foreign source income." Depending upon the countries involved and the duration of stay (if any) in another country taxes may have to be paid in either or both of the countries involved. It is very important to determine the consequences of receiving income from foreign sources before entering into contracts or other relationships overseas.

Bibliography

Langar, M. (1992). *Tax exile report: How to escape confiscatory taxes in the U.S. and other high tax countries.* Rolands Castle, Hants: Scope International.

JOHN O'CONNELL

foreign sourcing   *see* SOURCING

foreign subsidiaries   Often a company will see fit to establish a separate corporation in a foreign country to handle the parent company's activities in that country. The corporation established in the foreign country is referred to as a foreign subsidiary. Foreign subsidiaries may be formed to take advantage of foreign tax laws and rates, or as a business decision to establish themselves locally in all of the parent company's foreign markets.

JOHN O'CONNELL

foreign tax credit   Some countries allow their citizens a credit on their income taxes for taxes paid to foreign countries. For example, if a US citizen worked in Europe and paid income taxes on the foreign income, he/she would be allowed to offset US taxes payable on that same income. Tax credits recognize that taxes must be paid, but they also recognize that it is unfair in most cases to have to pay them twice.

Bibliography

Ferris, K. R. (1993). *Financial accounting and corporate reporting: A casebook.* 3rd edn, Homewood, IL: Irwin.

JOHN O'CONNELL

foreign trade zone (FTZ)   Foreign trade zone is the term used in the United States to refer to specific geographic area(s) within a country in which foreign goods enter and are eventually re-exported without payment of local duties or tariffs. A country can take advantage of employment opportunities offered by foreign producers of products by allowing those products to enter FTZs for assembly, processing, transshipment, or other activities needed to forward the export to its final destination. Foreign trade zones allow exporters to take advantage of low cost labor or other services provided by the FTZ without duties/tariffs further increasing the final sale price of the goods. As long as foreign goods do not move into the country housing the FTZ, no duties/tariffs are paid. That is, all goods must be re-exported in order to remain duty/tariff free. Duties/tariffs are collected by the country to which the goods are finally exported.

FTZs are also commononly located in international airports. Travelers may purchase foreign goods, duty free at these locations. Airport FTZs are normally referred to as duty free ports (DFP) or duty free zones (DFZ).

Foreign trade zones are also referred to as: free economic zones (FEZ); export processing zones (EPZ); or special economic zones (SEZ).

JOHN O'CONNELL

FOREX   The abbreviation for foreign exchange. Whenever this term is used, one can substitute the words "foreign exchange." (This sometimes helps people new to international trade to better comprehend what is going on.)

JOHN O'CONNELL

FOREX broker   *see* FOREIGN EXCHANGE BROKER

forfaiting   Forfaiting is a method of financing export debt. A bank or other financial institution purchases foreign receivables from an exporter at a discount. The amount of the discount depends upon the financial institution's perceived risk of foreign buyers not paying their debts. The purchase is on a nonrecourse basis, thus the exporter takes the money and is not responsible for any unpaid debts.

Bibliography

Kim, Taeho (1984). Changing international banking: Proceedings of the 1984 International Banking Conference. *American Graduate School of International Management Faculty Publication.* Glendale, AZ.

JOHN O'CONNELL

fortress Europe   Fortress Europe was a term used by people who felt that the plans of the European Community after 1992 might include shutting out foreign interests. EC plans to restrict operations of companies which did not have actual physical presence in one or more EC countries by 1992 were of great concern to those foreign organizations not yet ready to move some of their operations to Europe. The market would become inaccessible to foreign companies, in other words a fortress protecting Europe from economic invasion. Fortunately these fears seem to be unfounded. Europe remains today an active and growing world marketplace.

JOHN O'CONNELL

forward contract   A contract in which a buyer purchases or a seller sells a specified amount of currency, securities, or even commodities at an agreed price for a fixed payment amount. Forward contracts lock in a price today for items to be delivered at a later date.

JOHN O'CONNELL

forward covering   International transactions often obligate a company to pay a debt or other obligation at some future date in a foreign currency. Risk of currency value fluctuations accompany such contracts. Thus, if the organization had to borrow the money or sell assets to secure foreign exchange a loss could occur based upon the decreased value of the currency at the time it was acquired. Forward covering is a way to reduce the risk of currency fluctuations. By purchasing a forward contract at the same time

the debt obligation was made, the company locks in a value of the currency which will eventually be used to pay the debt. The forward contract matures at the same time as the debt and foreign currency is available to make payment.

Bibliography

Mathis, F. J. (1990). International risk analysis in *Global Business Management in the 1990s.* R. T. Moran (Ed.), Washington, D.C.: Beacham.

JOHN O'CONNELL

forward exchange rate   An exchange rate quoted today for currency to be delivered at a specific time in the future.

JOHN O'CONNELL

forward market   *see* FOREIGN EXCHANGE

forwarding company   A forwarding company arranges transportation for goods. Also known as a freight forwarder, the forwarding company can also offer a variety of other services including: advising of documentation required for exports/imports; processing items through customs; and offering other advice as needed.

See also **Freight forwarder**

JOHN O'CONNELL

FOT   (pre-1990 trading term) *see* FREE ON TRUCK

foul bill of lading   A bill of lading for goods which were received by the carrier in damaged condition. A notation on the bill indicates the existence of damage.

See also **Bill of lading; Clean bill of lading**

JOHN O'CONNELL

FPAAC *see* FREE OF PARTICULAR AVERAGE; GENERAL AVERAGE

FPAEC *see* FREE OF PARTICULAR AVERAGE; ENGLISH CONDITIONS

franchise agreement This is an agreement in which a company holding the rights to a product, trademark, process, etc. allows another company to make and distribute the product or use the trademark under a contractual agreement. The franchise agreement spells out the details, which usually include the geographic area in which the franchise is good; the fees to be paid to the franchisor; as well as any other requirements the franchisor is able to place in the contract. A franchise agreement is a method of entering a foreign market by having a local business (hopefully an established and highly reputable business) distribute and/or produce a foreign firm's product. This builds name recognition and provides a good foundation from which to add more foreign franchisees or to begin the company's own operation overseas.

See also **Market entry strategies**

Bibliography

Prahalad, C. K. & Doz, Y. L. (1987). *The multi-national dimension: Balancing local demands and global vision.* New York: The Free Press.

JOHN O'CONNELL

free alongside ship – named port of shipment (FAS) Under this trading term, the seller is responsible for delivering goods to a place where they can be loaded directly upon a vessel (alongside). The charge for delivery alongside is paid by the seller and included in the purchase price. The buyer is responsible for all costs and other charges to move the goods onto the ship; freight charges; securing and paying for export insurance; costs of unloading the vessel; import duties; and any inland freight charges in the buyer's country. Title to the goods transfers when the goods are placed alongside the vessel. The buyer is also respon-sible for obtaining both the export license from the seller's country and the import license from his/her country of import.

Bibliography

International Chamber of Commerce (ICC) (1990). *Incoterms 1990.* New York, NY: ICC Publishing Corp.

JOHN O'CONNELL

free carrier – named place (FCA) This trading term indicates that the seller's respon-sibility ends when the goods are delivered to a carrier at a specified place. The term refers to a carrier as any party who has made (or in whose name has made) a contract of carriage with a trucking firm, an ocean carrier, an air carrier, or any other form of transportation. This term takes the place of former trading terms which specified an air carrier (free on air – FOA), or a trucker (free on truck – FOT), or other carrier. The term is especially applicable in today's world of intermodal carriers.

Under FCA the seller or the buyer may be responsible for inland freight in the seller's country depending upon the sales agreement. The buyer is responsible for costs of loading a vessel; ocean/air, etc. freight charges; securing and paying for export insurance; costs of unloading the vessel; import duties; and any inland freight costs in the buyer's country. The seller is responsible for securing the export license and the buyer is responsible for securing the import license. Title to goods transfers when the goods reach a named carrier at a specified point.

Bibliography

International Chamber of Commerce (ICC) (1990). *Incoterms 1990.* New York, NY: ICC Publishing Corp.

JOHN O'CONNELL

free of all average A clause in a marine insurance policy which states that only losses resulting in total loss will be covered. There is no coverage for partial or average losses.

Bibliography

Rodda, W. H., Trieschmann, J. S. & Hedges, B. A. (1978). *Commercial property risk management and insurance*. Malvern, PA: American Institute for Property and Liability Underwriters.

JOHN O'CONNELL

free of particular average (FPA) A marine contract provision in which the insurer is not responsible for partial losses unless certain conditions are met. FPA clauses are normally one of two types:

Free of particular average – American Conditions (FPAAC): Excludes partial losses except when caused by specified sources of loss (burning, collision, sinking, or stranding). The American conditions also restrict coverage to all but larger ships.

Free of particular average – English Conditions (FPAEC): Excludes partial losses except when caused by burning, collision, sinking, or stranding of the ship. English conditions have no restrictions on ship size.

JOHN O'CONNELL

free on air (FOA) Pre-1990 trading term indicating that the seller's responsibility for goods ceases when the goods are transferred to an air carrier at a named location.

See also **Free carrier – FCA.**

Bibliography

International Chamber of Commerce (ICC) (1990). *Incoterms 1990*. New York, NY: ICC Publishing Corp.

JOHN O'CONNELL

free on board (FOB) The seller of goods is responsible for delivering goods to a particular point designated in the sales contract. The sales price of goods includes all transportation costs and insurance for damages to the goods until such point as stated in the contract. If goods are sent FOB point of destination, the seller is responsible for the goods until they reach the specified destination point. If the goods are shipped FOB point of departure, the buyer is responsible for the goods as they leave the seller's premises. FOB may be designated in a number of different ways including: FOB vessel (seller pays transit and insurance costs until goods are on board a specified vessel); FOB airport (seller pays transit and insurance costs until goods are delivered to an air carrier at a specified airport); and FOB named inland carrier (seller pays transit and insurance costs until goods are delivered to a specified inland carrier – e.g., trucking firm). The title to goods transfers when the goods are loaded onto the described mode of transit. The seller is responsible for securing the export license and the buyer is responsible for securing the import license.

Bibliography

International Chamber of Commerce (ICC) (1990). *Incoterms 1990*. New York, NY: ICC Publishing Corp.

JOHN O'CONNELL

free on rail (FOR) Pre-1990 trading term meaning that the seller is responsible for delivering goods to and loading them onto railroad cars at a specified location. The buyer assumes all costs and responsibilities from that point on. The 1990 INCOTERM which replaced FOR is FCA.

See also **Free carrier; INCOTERMS**

Bibliography

International Chamber of Commerce (ICC) (1990). *Incoterms 1990*. New York, NY: ICC Publishing Corp.

JOHN O'CONNELL

free on truck (FOT) Pre-1990 trading term meaning that the seller is responsible for delivering goods to and loading into trucks at a specified location. The buyer assumes all costs and responsibilities from that point on. The 1990 INCOTERM which replaced FOT is FCA.

See also **Free carrier; INCOTERMS**

Bibliography

International Chamber of Commerce (ICC) (1990). *Incoterms 1990.* New York, NY: ICC Publishing Corp.

JOHN O'CONNELL

free out   A trade term meaning that the seller of goods pays all costs of transportation, insurance, etc. until the goods reach the port of destination.

See also **INCOTERMS**

Bibliography

International Chamber of Commerce (ICC) (1990). *Incoterms 1990.* New York, NY: ICC Publishing Corp.

JOHN O'CONNELL

free trade area (FTA)   A free trade area is established when several countries agree to initiate actions to reduce and eventually abolish all barriers to trade between the countries. Countries which are signatories of such agreements will enjoy freedom of trade with all other members of the FTA. A free trade area is not necessarily a common market because common markets normally seek a greater degree of integration between countries than do FTAs. FTAs may well lead to closer relationships and common markets in the future. The newest example of a free trade area is comprised of Canada, Mexico, and the United States, which were signatories to the North American Free Trade Agreement (NAFTA).

Bibliography

Simmonds, K. R. Musch, D. J. (eds) (1992). *Law and practice under the GATT and other trading agreements, North American Free Trade Agreements, United States–Canada Free Trade Agreements: Binational panel reviews and reports.* Dobbs Ferry, NY: Oceana Publications Inc.

JOHN O'CONNELL

free trade zone   *see* FOREIGN TRADE ZONE

Freedom of Commerce and Navigation Treaty   *see* FRIENDSHIP, COMMERCE AND NAVIGATION TREATY

freight   Freight comprises any kind of goods, raw materials, finished products, commodities, or other items shipped by a carrier. Freight, in a different context, refers to the charges made by a carrier for hauling goods from one point to another.

JOHN O'CONNELL

freight broker   *see* CARGO BROKER

freight forwarder   A freight forwarder is a trade intermediary who arranges for the transportation of goods. Freight forwarders can also offer additional services to exporters and importers because of the expertise they gain in dealing with trade transactions.

Bibliography

Johnson, T. E. (1994). *Export–Import procedures and documentation.* New York: Amacom.

JOHN O'CONNELL

Friendship, Commerce, and Navigation Treaty (FCN)   FCN treaties are very important to world trade. They many times form the basis for countries being able to use one another's airspace, waterways, communications systems, and other important domestic infrastructures which are essential to successful international trade. FCN treaties also may include important agreements with respect to property rights and other legal questions commonly considered in the context of international trade.

JOHN O'CONNELL

fringe benefits   Items of indirect compensation provided to employees. Fringe benefits include: insurance (life, health, disability, dental, legal services, and other types); company-sponsored education programs; scholarship programs for employee children; vacation time; employer paid or subsidized lunches; company car; sick leave; retirement programs; and many others depending upon the country of employment and the agreement with the employer. Fringe benefits are provided for a number of reasons including the following: (1) incentives for persons to begin and continue employment; (2) to increase morale; (3) due to local customs; (4) union agreements. Many fringe benefits also receive favored tax treatment for both the employer and the employee. For example, in the United States, employer paid insurance premiums are generally not taxed as income (subject to some specific exceptions) to employees and are deducted as a business expense by the employer. Fringe benefits which are not taxable or taxable at a lower rate for employees (e.g., employer paid life insurance in the United States) are referred to by some people as "perqs" or "perquisites."

Bibliography

Teagarden, M. B., Butler, M. C. & Von Glinow, M. A. (1992). Mexico's maquiladora industry: Where strategic human resource management makes a difference. *Organizational Dynamics*, **Winter**, 34–47.

Von Glinow, M. A. & Chung, B. J. (1989). Comparative HRM practices in the U.S., Japan, Korea and the PRC. *Research in Personnel and HRM, A Research Annual.*

JOHN O'CONNELL

frozen account *see* BLOCKED ACCOUNT

frozen assets Frozen assets are those that the government of a country has seized pending the solution to a legal or political problem. Assets of foreign governments have been frozen in times of war. Assets of foreign business ventures have been frozen pending criminal trial resolution. If the solution to the problem includes return of some or all of the assets to their owners, the government will consider releasing them.

JOHN O'CONNELL

FTA *see* FREE TRADE AREA

functional currency A multinational company (MNC) may have earnings and disbursements in a large number of currencies. When it comes to reporting the results of its transactions in various accounting reports, the currency unit used in the reports is the currency of its country of incorporation. Thus, a firm whose home country is in Australia may do business in 40 countries, but when its accounting reports are issued all values are expressed in Australian dollars. The Australian dollar is the company's functional currency.

JOHN O'CONNELL

functional intermediary A functional intermediary is a person, or firm, who has actual physical involvement in a trade transaction. Examples of functional intermediaries are freight consolidation firms, ocean shipping companies, railroad carriers, and lighter firms which offload cargo from larger ships.

JOHN O'CONNELL

furnishing allowance An amount of money made available to an expatriate to furnish the apartment or home selected in the host country.

See also **Compensation package**

JOHN O'CONNELL

futures A contract in which a buyer agrees to pay a specified amount for a financial instrument or a commodity with delivery taking place at a future date.

JOHN O'CONNELL

futures contract *see* FUTURES

G

Gaijin (Japanese) The name given to foreigners working in Japan. Its literal meaning is "outsider."

JOHN O'CONNELL

gap analysis Gap analysis is a marketing tool that allows an organization to determine if there are portions of a market which are not being served. Gap analysis seeks to explain why sales are lower in a market than first expected. The reasons are usually related to how products are used, the types of products being distributed in the market, the distribution system itself, and the competitive climate. Gap analysis can be used to compare markets within a country or between countries in order to determine which markets hold the most opportunities. Gap analysis provides a useful albeit somewhat standardized basis for cross-country .comparisons of marketing opportunities.

Gap analysis involves a study of the needs of the market and the specific attributes of a product. The analysis attempts to match product features with consumer wants and needs.

If consumers are using less of the product than expected, advertising or other information gathering steps may be in order. If the product line being offered does not meet the needs of the market, changes in the line (new products, packaging, etc.) or a realignment of products in different markets may be necessary. The distribution system in effect may not be getting the product to those who are most likely to make purchases or it is too slow. Competitors may be found to be selling more of the same type of product than would normally be expected and new ways of competing may have to be considered. When gaps are found in a market, action can be taken to fill them.

Bibliography

Terpstra, V. (1993). *International dimensions of marketing.* Belmont, CA: Wadsworth Publishing Company.

JOHN O'CONNELL

GATT *see* GENERAL AGREEMENT ON TARIFFS AND TRADE

General Agreement on Tariffs and Trade (GATT) The General Agreement on Tariffs and Trade is a treaty related to development of free trade throughout the world. GATT came into being in 1948 as a temporary multilateral trade treaty pending the formation of the United Nation's International Trade Organization (ITO). The ITO was never approved and the temporary GATT has been functioning now for almost 50 years. GATT was originally authorized to seek reductions in tariff and non-tariff barriers to trade, as well as establish a mechanism for settling international disputes related to trade. Agreements under GATT are developed during extended meetings of members. These meetings are called "rounds." Thus far there have been eight GATT rounds. Each round is referred to by a different name. The names of the rounds and its dates are as follows:

1 Geneva Round   1947
2 Annecy Round   1949
3 Torquay Round   1950
4 Geneva Round   1956
5 Dillon Round   1960–1

6 Kennedy Round 1962–7

7 Tokyo Round   1973–9

8 Uruguay Round 1986–94

The first several rounds of negotiations involved reductions or elimination of tariffs between countries. Rounds seven and eight, however, added new dimensions to negotiations. The Tokyo Round added discussions of governance of GATT and procedural questions related to the functioning of the agreement. Nontrade barriers were also added for discussion. The Uruguay Round added discussion about intellectual property rights, trade in services, and further procedures for dispute resolution. Probably the most significant action coming out of the most recent GATT rounds was the establishing of the World Trade Organization (WTO) GATT members will replace GATT's temporary status with a permanent organization, the WTO.

See also **World Trade Organization**

Bibliography

Bowker, R. R. (1994). *Results of the GATT Uruguay round of multilateral trade negotiations – executive summary.* Chester, PA: Diane Publishing Company.

Grosse, R. & Kujawa, D. (1995). *International business: Theory and managerial applications.* 3rd edn, Boston, MA: Richard D. Irwin Inc.

Leaffer, M. A. (Ed.) (1990). *International treaties on intellectual property.* Washington, D.C.: BNA Books.

Simmonds, K. R. (Ed.) (1991). *Law and practice under the GATT and other trading agreements: The Association of South-East Asian Nations (ASEAN).* Dobbs Ferry, NY: Oceana Publications Inc.

JOHN O'CONNELL

general average   General average is a maritime term used to determine who is responsible for payment of costs incurred to save a vessel in eminent peril of destruction. Essentially, general average clauses state that all financial interests in the voyage will proportionately share in this type of cost. (An example of general average will be given after a review of the circumstances which

must be present for this clause to apply to a loss or cost incurred.) General average applies if the following three circumstances occur:

1 The vessel is in peril – the vessel is in high seas and is taking on water more quickly than the pumps can handle; a rudder is lost and the ship cannot be steered; cargo shifts causing the vessel to list (tilt to one side); cargo breaks free and causes damage to the ship; and many other situations.

2 The master of the vessel takes steps to save the vessel and these steps incur costs or losses of property – the vessel is listing, so cargo on the low side of the vessel is thrown over board (jettisoned) in an attempt to stabilize the vessel; the ship's steering goes out in high seas and an ocean-going tugboat is called to rescue the ship before it runs aground; a cargo of flammable goods is thrown overboard when a fire breaks out in another part of the ship.

3 The actions of the ship's master are successful in saving the voyage – the ship is no longer listing because the jettisoned cargo righted the ship; the tugboat successfully kept the ship from running aground; the fire was successfully put out

The above losses to cargo or additional costs to save the voyage will be paid for by contributions from all property interests in the voyage. Thus, the shipowner contributes and each of the cargo owners contributes to the cost of loss. Contribution is proportionate. Thus, if the costs of loss of property value was $100,000; the ship's value $10,000,000 and the total cargo value $20,000,000 the loss would be paid as follows:

Ship value ($10,000,000)/total value ($30,000,000) x loss = 1/3

Cargo value ($20,000,000)/total value ($30,000,000) x loss = 2/3

In this case the shipowner is responsible for one-third of the costs and the cargo owners will share in the remaining two-thirds of the losses. This sharing occurs under general average because if it was not for the incurred losses all property would have been lost. General average losses are normally covered by ocean marine insurance contracts.

See also **Marine insurance**

Bibliography

Rodda, W. H., Trieschmann, J. S. & Hedges, B. A. (1978). *Commercial property risk management and insurance.* Malvern, PA: American Institute for Property and Liability Underwriters.

JOHN O'CONNELL

general license   Although referred to as a license, a general license (US) is actually a broad government statement allowing goods to be exported. Thus, exporters have "license" to send goods abroad. Some export transactions (certain types of goods) may require actual written certificates or permits. Exporters must check with the appropriate government agency of each country from which exports will be taken, to assure licensing requirements are met.

Bibliography

Zodl, J. A. (1992). *Export–Import: Everything you and your company need to know to compete in world markets.* Cincinnati, OH: Betterway Books.

JOHN O'CONNELL

general visa   A general visa allows entry to a country for any purpose (business or pleasure). A general visa essentially combines a tourist visa with a commercial visa. A general visa normally limits a pleasure visit to six or twelve months and a business visit to a time period close to that expected to carry out the business but normally not more than three or six months. General visa holders must be coming to a country for a temporary visit after which they will depart the country. Visitors also must normally maintain a foreign residence during their time in the host country and prove that they have sufficient financial resources to support themselves while visiting. Normally, visitors cannot engage in productive work for which payment is provided by any organization in the host country.

Business visitors – business visitors using a general visa are normally restricted as to activities or earnings in the host country. The business visitor must also normally be engaged (with some exceptions) in trade or other international activities of which the visitor's activities benefit a foreign entity or the visitor his/herself. Allowable activities of a business visitor include sales calls, purchasing goods for export, consulting work, attending professional meetings, research, and other activities. If a general visa is not used in a country, business visitors have to apply for what is commonly called a "commercial visa."

Visitors for pleasure – visitors coming to a country as tourists, attending nonbusiness conventions, making a shopping trip, or visiting relatives or friends. Any person working in the host country is technically ineligible for the general visa's pleasure visitor category. If a visitors for pleasure category is not available under a general visa, visitors will have to apply for what is normally referred to as a "tourist visa."

Even though general visas are for broad categories of visitors, each country has its own eligibility criteria. Care must be taken to obtain the correct type of visa for the activities being undertaken in another country.

See also **Visa**

JOHN O'CONNELL

generalized system of preferences (GSP)   The GSP refers to agreements made by the more industrialized countries to allow imports from less developed countries (LDCs) to enter with lower import duties than the same goods coming from more developed countries. The intent of the agreements is to make goods from LDCs more competitive in order to increase LDC production and speed up their economic development. Thus, LDCs are granted preferences over other countries. Industrialized nations essentially accepted any injuries to domestic companies due to less expensive imports as justifiable if the economic development of LDCs is enhanced.

JOHN O'CONNELL

geocentric approach to hiring   Under this approach to hiring, people are viewed in the context of how well they can accomplish a particular job or task rather than on the basis of their home country, religion, culture, or other factors. Employees are selected from throughout the organization without regard to nationality with a resulting workforce that is quite diverse. This approach to hiring is truly global in nature.

See also **Staffing**

JOHN O'CONNELL

geocentrism Viewing one's business as being truly global. Decisions related to the best interests of the organization are carried out without respect to home country domination or staffing. A geocentric approach to international business sees the entire world as its market and all of its employees as able to substantially contribute to the organization's goals and objectives regardless of their country of origin. Products will be produced on a standardized basis with modifications (if necessary) for local market conditions.

JOHN O'CONNELL

geographic structure Geographic structure refers to the organization of a company to coincide with the geographic areas in which the company operates. A multinational firm may have a Far Eastern, a North American, and a European Division.

See also **Regional structure**

JOHN O'CONNELL

global alliance *see* STRATEGIC ALLIANCE

global branding The use of the same brand name for products everywhere they are sold in the world. Global branding has the advantages of building name identification, new products take on the good name of established products, and there are economies in developing packaging, advertising, trademarks, etc. It is also simpler to move into new markets when the name of your product is well known in surrounding markets.

Coca Cola is probably the best known product that uses global branding. Global branding, however, may cause some problems as well. A product which suffers problems because of, for example, consumer injuries from its use, may put the company's entire product line in question throughout the world. There are also potential problems related to words having different meanings in different countries. Advertising print, product names, and distribution materials must be carefully reviewed for words, colors, or even numbers which may be offensive in certain cultures. Global brands may also infer support for a particular political view (British Airlines, American Express, etc.) which may be unacceptable in some countries.

Bibliography

Pradeep, A. R. & Preble, J. F. (1987). Standardization of marketing strategy by multinationals. *International Marketing Review*, Autumn, 18–28.

JOHN O'CONNELL

global cash management *see* CASH MANAGEMENT

global companies The term global company has in the past referred to a company whose operations span the world with operations on all continents and in most of the countries. Names like Coca Cola, McDonald's, Ford, General Electric and others are considered global because of the extent of their international presence.

In today's world, the term global company is taking on a new meaning. A global company is one that views the world as one market. Every country offers possibilities for sales, placement of facilities, sources of employees, as well as other potential benefits. A global company seeks to standardize its products for sale through a coordinated worldwide distribution network. Although the term global company still denotes the vast assets of a General Motors or Mitsubishi it also now describes a way of management thinking and action.

Bibliography

Ricks, D. A. (1974). *International business blunders.* Columbus, OH: Grid Inc.

JOHN O'CONNELL

global enterprise   A global enterprise is an organization which is not bound by a country's borders, thrives in multinational settings, is flexible in style and application, responds to change as part of its everyday itinerary, and pictures the entire world as its home and market. Although there are relatively few truly global enterprises, expansion of international trade and travel, and the breakdown of controlled systems of government, are moving more organizations toward achieving true global status.

Bibliography

Morrison, A. J. (1990). *Strategies in global industries: How U.S. businesses compete.* New York: Quorum Books.

JOHN O'CONNELL

global information technology   *see* INFORMATION TECHNOLOGY

global leadership   In a recent article (Handy, 1996), it was noted that a German senior manager described organizations in Germany as "organizations largely run by engineers. Such people think of the organization as a machine, something that can be designed, measured, and controlled – managed in other words." Today, our metaphors for organizations are changing from a machine image to more organic images such as organizations as networks, communities, or knowledge systems. With such change has come a renewed focus on leadership being critical to organizations.

In the past, most studies of leadership have been based on the assumption that leadership derives from position: leaders became leaders by virtue of their roles in the organization. As companies change from hierarchy-based management structures to more delayered, empowered systems, our conceptions of leadership also

need to change (Hesselbein *et al.*, 1996). The more widely distributed knowledge becomes, the more that leadership needs to be distributed amongst a variety of individuals in the organization. For example, employees in customer-interface roles must be leaders in their interactions with customers and in disseminating the knowledge which they gain in these interactions to other parts of the organization.

In addition to the challenge of distributing leadership due to the shift to distributed knowledge, organizations today are facing the challenge of developing leaders who will be effective in global organizations that span numerous cultures. Companies are focusing on developing the set of leadership competencies which enable individuals to lead across cultures. Although there may be some born global leaders, this set is too small to meet the needs of today's global organizations. For the most part, global leadership must, and can, be learned (Ashkenas *et al.*, 1995).

What does this leadership look like? Leaders of knowledge-based, global organizations will behave and lead in a variety of ways, but they share a focus on several key issues (Drucker, 1996):

- They begin with the question "What needs to be done?"

- They follow with "What can and should I do to make a difference?"

- They focus on performance and results.

- They are supportive of diversity in people and do not seek to reinforce mirror images of themselves.

- Relatedly, they develop their followers and are not fearful of strong, competent followers (Kouzes & Posner, 1995).

- They test themselves against high standards of leadership and role model the behaviors and qualities which they wish to see in others. They are doers.

In summary, global leaders share a common focus on articulating a vision which leads to measurable results and by leading through action, notably personal action.

Much of the research on leadership has focused on transformational leadership, or leadership which leads to changes in followers of organizations and in the leader him- or herself (Kouzes & Posner, 1995). Change and global leadership are inextricably linked. The key change challenges which face global leaders are linked to the changes that are occurring as organizations move from being bureaucratic machines to being knowledge-based networks. Specifically, leaders must guide their organizations to produce results today, even as they push for transformation which will positively impact the future.

Finally, the work of Ulrich (1996) generates some useful thoughts about the importance of credibility and capability. Ulrich argues that successful leaders must be both personally credible and must be able to create organizational capability. Credible leaders engender trust and commitment from those who follow their vision. Organizational capability results from a leader who shapes a stronger organization through development, systems, and processes.

To conclude, organizations are changing rapidly. Global leaders are faced with the challenge of leading this transformation even as the role of leadership is being transformed. Often, leaders are finding that they, themselves, need to change personally and to develop new abilities. The future promises to be a time of exciting, rapid change, with the effective leaders being those individuals who can transform and be transformed in the midst of this change.

Bibliography

Ashkenas, R., Ulrich, D., Jick, T. & Kerr, S. (1995). *The boundaryless organization.* San Francisco, CA: Jossey-Bass.

Drucker, P. (1996). Leading the organizations of the future. In Hesselbein, F., Goldsmith, M., & Beckhard, R. (eds), *The leader of the future.* San Francisco, CA: Jossey-Bass.

Handy, C. (1996). The new language of organizing and its implications for leaders. In Hesselbein, F., Goldsmith, M., & Beckhard, R. (eds) *The leader of the future.* San Francisco, CA: Jossey-Bass

Hesselbein, F., Goldsmith, M. & Beckhard, R. (Eds), (1996). *The leader of the future.* San Francisco, CA, Jossey-Bass.

Kouzes, J. & Posner, B. (1995). *The leadership challenge.* San Francisco, CA: Jossey-Bass.

CAREN SIEHL

global sourcing   Sourcing is the acquiring of goods, labor, and materials necessary to produce a product. An origination that seeks the resources to produce its goods from any place that may have an availability of resources is said to employ a global sourcing strategy. Global sourcing has come about because of differences in supply and price of various resources. When sufficient supplies are not available locally or the cost of any resource is very high locally, firms begin to seek resources elsewhere. Global sourcing is not without its problems: increased transportation costs, increased possibilities of interruption of supplies (natural disaster, political problems, etc.), delays in shipment (weather, strikes, etc.) (*see* SOURCING STRATEGIES), and becoming too reliant on foreign sources of supply, all add to the risks of doing business through foreign sourcing.

Bibliography

Swan, A. C. & Murphy, J. F. (1991). *Cases & materials on the regulation of international business and economic relations.* New York: Mathew Bender & Co.

JOHN O'CONNELL

global strategy   A company's plans to meet goals and objectives with respect to how that company has defined its overall position in the global marketplace. It is important to recognize that a strategy is a plan to achieve specific goals and objectives. Sound global strategy is based upon a realistic appraisal of a company's strengths and weakness as well as the opportunities and threats posed by the global environment.

See also **SWOT analysis**

Bibliography

David, K. (1991). *"Field research" in the cultural environment of international business.* Cincinnatti, OH: South-Western.

JOHN O'CONNELL

globalization   Globalization is the process of organizing an enterprise to establish activities or operations in other parts of the world. It is usually the endpoint of a long process of moving domestic operations into the international arena. Globalization seeks markets for products or services without regard to international borders, while at the same time developing the capability to service those markets chosen for activity. In a truly global company there is no market that cannot be serviced; rather the decision of the company is whether it desires to provide services under current circumstances.

Bibliography

Bartlett, C. A. & Sumantra, G. (1987). Managing across borders: New organizational response. *Sloan Management Review*, Fall, 43–53.
Daniels, J. D., Pitts, R. A. & Tretter, M. J. (1985). Organizing for dual strategies of product diversity and international expansion. *Strategic Management Journal*, 6, 223–37.

JOHN O'CONNELL

governing law   International contracts will often specify the country whose laws will be used to deal with any disputed areas of the contract. The law specified is referred to as governing law. Problems may arise when governing law is not the same as that which is stated to be jurisdictional (i.e., the country in which the dispute is lodged is different than the governing law country in the contract). Countries tend to allow governing specifications of a contract to stand when a contract has been properly drawn. There are no guarantees, however, that contract governing law statements will be upheld by the courts.

JOHN O'CONNELL

government procurement codes   The rules and practices associated with the purchase of goods and services by a government entity. These are important because governments are a very large market for the sale of goods and services of all kinds. If procedures are not strictly followed parties seeking to sell goods or services will be precluded. Another problem associated with government procurement is that preferences may be given to domestic goods or services over those imported, regardless of cost or quality. Although such preferences are frowned upon by the General Agreement on Tariffs and Trade (GATT) the practice is very common.

gradual internationalization   *see* EVOLUTION OF GLOBAL ORGANIZATION

gray market   The term gray market formerly described a market outside of the normal market in which goods that are in short supply are sold at a premium. Gray markets were (and still are) found in countries suffering distribution problems, wars, extreme inflation embargoes or trade sanctions, or shortages of various goods for a number of other reasons. The gray market has come to mean the market for illegal copies or knock offs of popular products. Gray markets (sometimes called parallel markets) are common in Southeast Asia and eastern Europe, although gray market goods show up in virtually every country.

JOHN O'CONNELL

gray money   Money derived from gray market activities or questionable business transactions.

See also **Black market; Gray market**

JOHN O'CONNELL

grease payment   *see* BRIBERY

green card/green card holder   In the United States the holder of a green card is a foreign citizen who has been granted permission by the government to work in the US. Green card holders are documented workers and legally work in the country.

JOHN O'CONNELL

green clause letter of credit   A letter of credit which does not allow an exporter to draw against the letter until such time as all required documentation is presented to the advancing bank.

See also **Letter of credit; Red clause letter of credit**

JOHN O'CONNELL

Gregorian calendar A twelve-month calendar developed by Pope Gregory I in 1582. The calendar year is based upon the movement of the sun (solar year). Most of the western world has adopted this calendar as the basis for keeping track of time.

See also **Hijrah calendar**

JOHN O'CONNELL

group norms Group norms are expectations of behaviors, attitudes, and beliefs which are expected by the group. They are an important determinant of behavior in an individual's personal and business life. The importance of group norms and the amount of control they exert is greatly affected by the culture of the persons in the group. Norms are illustrated by the way people greet each other (a handshake or a hug); the respect given to management (strong respect or feeling of unjustified superiority). Knowledge of group norms is essential to successful international management.

See also **Cultural diversity; Cultural norms**

Bibliography

Adler, N. J. (1983). A typology of management studies involving culture. *Journal of International Business Studies*, 14 (2), 29–47.
Axtell, R. E. (1993). *Do's and taboos around the world.* 3rd edn, New York: John Wiley & Sons.
Briody, E. K. & Chrisman, J. B. (1991). Cultural adaptation on overseas assignments. *Human Organization*, 50 (3), 264–82.
Graham, J. L. (1985). The influence of culture on business negotiations. *Journal of International Business Studies*, 16 (1), 81–96.

Johnson, M. & Moran, R. T. (1985). *Robert T. Moran's cultural guide to doing business in Europe.* 2nd edn, Oxford: Butterworth-Heinemann.
Punnett, B. J. (1995). Cross-national culture and management in M. Warner (Ed.) *International Encyclopedia of Business of Management.* London: Routledge.

JOHN O'CONNELL

GSP *see* GENERALIZED SYSTEM OF PREFERENCES

guaranteed letter of credit Another name for a confirmed letter of credit. This letter guarantees payment by requesting a bank from the exporter's country to make good on payments under the letter if the importer and the importer's bank default on the letter of credit.

See also **Confirmed letter of credit; Letter of credit**

Bibliography

Johnson, T. E. (1994). *Export–Import procedures and documentation.* New York: Amacom.

JOHN O'CONNELL

guest workers A multinational business may occasionally have a need to send workers to one of their foreign operations for short periods of time. For example, equipment failures or other accidents may require short-term assistance form outside of a country. Since work is being performed by a foreign citizen it is necessary in many countries to secure a temporary permit to conduct such work. "Guest worker" status is granted in some countries for noncitizens who are on temporary assignment to complete a project or specific task.

JOHN O'CONNELL

H

hard currency   A hard currency is one which is readily convertible into other currencies. Hard currencies include the: British pound, Canadian dollar, French franc, German mark, Italian lira, Japanese yen, Swiss franc, and United States dollar.

JOHN O'CONNELL

hard money   *see* HARD CURRENCY

hardship allowance   An organization sending employees overseas may offer additional pay for the inconvenience or because the location of overseas employment is considered less than desirable. Such pay is often referred to as a "hardship allowance."

See also **Compensation package**

JOHN O'CONNELL

harmonization   A movement toward standardization, generally referring to standardization of trade regulations, monetary systems, accounting procedures, laws protecting property rights, and other areas where differences exist between countries. Harmonization does not mean a movement towards a single culture, in fact most economic agreements are careful to preserve such differences. Harmonization is a movement toward freedom of movement of people, goods, and capital between nations.

JOHN O'CONNELL

HCN   *see* HOST COUNTRY NATIONALS

health certificate   A form on which a record of a person's vaccinations appear. A health certificate is often required to enter certain countries because of past and present health problems in that country.

JOHN O'CONNELL

hedge   To hedge is to attempt to reduce the risk associated with an investment or a bet. When a person or company fears that future events will cause fluctuations in the value of assets or the flow of valuable goods, he/she may hedge or act to reduce the impact of future change.

See also **Hedging**

JOHN O'CONNELL

hedging   Profits in international transactions are somewhat dependent upon the values of currency or other commodities at the time of sale versus the time of delivery or payment. In order to plan for the amount of funds necessary to pay for goods or repay loans, many international companies employ hedging strategies. For example, if a company is fearful that the exchange rate of a currency might fall (the currency is worth less) that currency could be purchased today at a specified price for delivery later when the organization's need arises. The organization now knows what the exchange rate will be because it has locked in its future price. Therefore, the organization's currency risk has been reduced it has hedged its currency position.

See also **Futures; Options**

Bibliography

Bishop, P. & Dixon, D. (1992). *Foreign exchange handbook: Managing risk and opportunity in global currency markets.* New York: McGraw-Hill Inc.

Daigler, R. T. (1993). *Managing risk with financial futures: Pricing, hedging, and arbitrage.* Hinsdale, IL: Probus Publishing Company Inc.

JOHN O'CONNELL

high contact cultures   Cultures in which there is a high degree of physical contact or proximity. This is reflected in the extent which people within a culture touch, embrace, shake hands, or stand close to one another. South American cultures are for the most part high contact cultures whereas United States and Canadian cultures are low contact. Difficulties occur when people of both types of culture meet: feeling your space is being invaded by someone standing too close; feeling that friendship and trust are lacking because someone is standing too far away during conversation; uncomfortable feelings from being touched; or a feeling of unfriendliness from not being touched may arise. In order to successfully manage living and working in a culture, knowledge about the degree of contact expected is helpful.

Bibliography

Ahmad, K. (1976). *Islam: Its meaning and message.* London: Islamic Council of Europe.

Johnson, M. (1992). *Cultural guide to doing business in Europe.* 2nd edn, Boston, MA: Butterworth-Heinemann.

JOHN O'CONNELL

high context cultures   A culture in which feelings or emotions are not directly expressed. In a high context culture knowing the true meaning of what is being said requires the building of a relationship over time. Once a relationship is built, knowing the other person's true feelings is easier because one now understands the various visual and other nonverbal cues (nods of the head, smiles, posture, intonation, and others). High context cultures are found in Japan, China, Middle Eastern countries, and others.

Bibliography

Tabatava'i, S. M. (1989). *Islamic teachings: An overview.* Canada: John Deyell.

JOHN O'CONNELL

Hijrah calendar   The calendar used in Islamic countries of the Middle East. The calendar has eleven months and is based upon the movement of the moon (a lunar year).

See also **Gregorian calendar**

JOHN O'CONNELL

hiring   *see* STAFFING

historically planned economy (HPE)   This term is used by the World Bank to refer to countries which have recently changed from communist governments to movement toward market economies. Those countries included as HPEs are Russia and the other newly-formed states of the former Soviet Union and most of eastern Europe.

JOHN O'CONNELL

home country   The country of which an employee is a citizen. This is different from the host country in which that employee would be considered a foreigner.

JOHN O'CONNELL

home country national   Multinational companies are legally formed in a given country and expand from there. Citizens from the country in which the organization was formed are referred to as "home country nationals."

JOHN O'CONNELL

home currency   Generally the currency of the country in which a parent company was originally formed and still has residence. The home currency of a US company is the US dollar; the home currency of a British company is the pound sterling; etc.

JOHN O'CONNELL

home leave   An expatriate (including family) is often given paid leave each year to return to his/her home country. Normally all expenses of the trip home are paid by the company. Home leaves were developed to allow expatriates and their families to maintain ties with relatives, friends, and others. This eases problems commonly associated with the transition to and from the foreign location.

JOHN O'CONNELL

host country   When an employee is sent from his/her own country to another, the new country is referred to as the "host country." To most expatriates, a host country is a temporary location from which they will move either to a new host country or back to their home country.

JOHN O'CONNELL

host country nationals   Citizens of those countries to which a multinational corporation expands. If the multinational company was formed in France but also had operations in Spain, Spanish workers would be host country nationals (French workers would be home country nationals).

JOHN O'CONNELL

house air waybill   Often a freight forwarder will combine goods from many shippers into a shipment by air to a single location. The freight forwarder issues a receipt for goods being shipped. This receipt is referred to as an airbill. Included in the airbill is the house air waybill. The waybill lists the specifics of the shipment transaction (destination, owners, types of goods, values, etc.).

JOHN O'CONNELL

household effects   All of the furnishings and other property which go into a home. Although the exact nature of property differs it is generally comprised of furniture, cooking and serving equipment, beds and bedding, and other items of personal selection. This term may become important to an expatriate whose employer has agreed to move household effects to the new assignment location. If the employee has any unusual or uncommon property (grand piano, valuable collection of antiques, etc.) these may or may not fit into the normal household effects category. Also, it must be remembered that some countries have restrictions related to types of property which may be brought into the country (e.g., pets, plants, guns, etc.). Depending on the home and host country accommodations, it is common to ship a portion of an expatriate's household effects to the new location and store the rest.

JOHN O'CONNELL

housing allowance   A common benefit provided to expatriates. Housing allowances are provided in several forms - additional salary to help pay housing costs; provision of employer owned housing in the foreign country; and reimbursement (or paid directly to the landlord) of the actual cost of housing incurred by the expatriate.

JOHN O'CONNELL

human relations   A human relations approach to management views each employee as a separate entity, motivated by individual wants and needs and capable of accomplishments at different levels. To enable managers to motivate employees an employee's needs (not just money) must be identified and ways found to meet more of them in the workplace.

JOHN O'CONNELL

human resource management   *see* INTERNATIONAL HUMAN RESOURCES MANAGEMENT

human resource strategy The term human resource strategy (HRS) currently lacks definitional precision, but it generally refers to a construct denoting the coherent set of decisions or factors that shape and guide the management of human resources (acquisition, allocation, utilization, development, reward) in an organizational context. It is directly related to the business strategy and focuses on the formulation and alignment of human resource activities to achieve organizational competitive objectives.

HRS is a relatively new concept in the field of human resource management (HRM). It has emerged as the HRM function has assumed a more strategic perspective and organizations have come to view employees as essential resources who are to be managed effectively to achieve strategic business goals. There are at least three basic concepts of HRS that have been articulated: the decisional concept, the human resource issue/action concept, and the human resources priorities concept.

The Decisional Concept

Drawing upon the business strategy literature, Dyer (1984) has formulated a longitudinal or retrospective decisional concept of HRS. He defines the organizational HRS "as the pattern that emerges from a stream of important decisions about the management of human resources" (p. 159). This concept requires a review of important HRM-related organizational decisions over a period of time to determine consistencies and observable patterns. In effect, the emergent pattern of coherent and consistent decisions revealed upon retroactive investigation would indicate the strategy that guides HR activity.

In a later work, Dyer and Holder (1988) offer a more proactive decisional concept of HRS. In this case, the HRS is viewed as the collection of major human resource (HR) goals and means to be used in pursuit of organizational strategic plans. When an acceptable business strategy is formulated, key HR goals are defined to support this strategy and the necessary means (i.e. programming and policies) are designed and implemented to meet the goals. For example, if an organization chooses a competitive strategy of low-cost producer, major HR goals to support this strategy could be higher performance and lower headcounts. These, in turn could lead to programs including reduction in force and more increased investment in employee training. This combined set of HR goals and means would be the organizational HRS.

The HR Issue/Action Concept

This approach is based on an issue-oriented focus to develop an organizational HRS. Schuler and Walker (1990) and Walker (1992) argue that in a dynamic, fast changing environment, managers have to deal effectively with a series of emerging business issues that can have a significant impact on competitive success. Business issues will involve HR issues that are critical to successful strategy implementation.

These HR issues can be considered gaps that represent opportunities for people to contribute more effectively to the achievement of business strategies. Line managers have to respond to these HR issues in their decision processes. As is necessary, they will define directional actions to address the people-related business issues. These managerial actions and plans will focus, mobilize, and direct the HR activities toward the business issues most important to the firm; and they will form the essence of the organizational HR strategies.

The HR Priorities Concept

This concept of HRS posits that each organization has an identifiable set of dominant HR priorities that are used to align its HR activities, policies, and programs with its strategic business goals (Craft, 1988, 1995). This cluster of key HR priorities, which constitutes the HRS, defines the organization's orientation and attitude toward its employees and it guides the development of HR plans that deal with the personnel aspects of basic business issues. For example, in an organization competing on the basis of innovation, core HR priorities might include employee risk taking, initiative, teamwork and high competence.

The priorities will be basic factors guiding and configuring the HR system (acquiring, developing, rewarding) in response to business needs. Each organization's cluster of priorities (HRS) will differ based on the mix of its competitive strategy, internal organizational factors (e.g. culture, technology), and external environmental factors (e.g. labor market, competitor practice).

While the HRS tends to be stable in the short term, over time it is a dynamic concept since the priorities will evolve and be crafted to meet changing business situations.

Bibliography

Craft, J. A. (1988). Human resource planning and strategy. *Human Resource Management: Evolving Roles and Responsibilities*, Dyer, L. (Ed.) Washington, DC: Bureau of National Affairs. 47–87.

Craft, J. A. (1995). Human resources strategy (unpublished working paper).

Dyer, L. (1984). Studying human resource strategy: an approach and an agenda. *Industrial Relations*, 23, 156–69.

Dyer, L. & Holder, G. W. (1988). A strategic perspective of human resource management. *Human Resource Management: Evolving Roles and Responsibilities*, Dyer, L. (Ed.) Washington, DC: Bureau of National Affairs.

Schuler, R. S. & Walker, J. W. (1990). Human resources strategy: focusing on issues and actions. *Organizational Dynamics*, 19, 4–19.

Walker, J. W. (1992).. *Human Resource Strategy*, New York: McGraw-Hill.

JAMES A. CRAFT

human resources   Human resources are the employees, management, and other parties having personal input into an organization. Human resources, like all other resources (materials, capital, etc.) must be used to their fullest potential in order for the organization to be successful. Assuring the most advantageous use of human resources is the task of human resource management.

See also **Human resource management**

Bibliography

Cohen, R. B. (1988). The new international division of labor and multinational corporations; in *The Transformation of Industrial Organization: Management, Labor, and Society in the United States*. Belmont, CA: Wadsworth.

Schuler, R. S. (1993). World class HR departments: Six crucial issues. *The Singapore Accounting and Business Review*, Inaugural Issue, September.

JOHN O'CONNELL

human rights policies   Although human rights policies are normally associated with governmental functions, concern over the plight of mankind has become of great concern in the international business world. Feelings about a country's treatment of its citizens, especially those who speak out against the government or seek changes or freedoms which other citizens may have, are often transferred to the businesses located in the country. For example, when South Africa was considered to have a poor record regarding human rights, foreign companies doing business in South Africa were criticized, boycotted, and some were even terrorized. Now that the system has begun to change, former investors are coming back to South Africa. Perception of a company's feelings or positions can greatly harm or assist in successful international activities. Many companies stay away from taking stands, while others seem to make a point of explaining their corporate view. Either way, a company must carefully consider its public and private positions, especially on questions involving such sensitive areas as human rights.

See also **Advocacy advertising**

Bibliography

Litka, M. (1991). *International dimensions of the legal environment of business.* 2nd edn, Boston, MA: PWS-Kent Publishing Company.

JOHN O'CONNELL

hyperinflation   A state of extreme inflation in an economy. Germany suffered hyperinflation in the 1920s and 1930s during which time a loaf of bread cost billions of marks. Brazil suffered inflation rates of hundreds of percentage points during parts of the 1970s and 1980s. Hyperinflation destroys the purchasing power of domestic currency, causes social unrest, and commonly brings down the government.

Bibliography

Austin, J. E. (1990). *Managing in developing countries: Strategic analysis and operating techniques.* New York: Free Press.

JOHN O'CONNELL

hypothetical tax In order to determine the appropriate compensation package for an expatriate, taxes must be taken into consideration. A "hypothetical tax" is an estimated tax based upon the best information available related to the employee's total income and allowable deductions. The hypothetical tax gives an idea of how much money is left from the proposed compensation package for necessary goods and services while on assignment. If necessary, the compensation package can be adjusted to reflect the expected tax liability.

See also **Compensation package**

Bibliography

Hamill, J. (1984). "Labour relations practices" and "Multinational corporations and industrial relations.". *Industrial Relations Journal*, **15** (2), 30–4.

JOHN O'CONNELL

— I —

IAA *see* INTER-AMERICAN ACCOUNTING ASSOCIATION

IAC *see* IMPORT ALLOCATION CERTIFICATE

IASC *see* INTERNATIONAL ACCOUNTING STANDARDS COMMITTEE

IBF *see* INTERNATIONAL BANKING FACILITY

IBRD *see* INTERNATIONAL BANK FOR RECONSTRUCTION AND DEVELOPMENT

ICA *see* INTERNATIONAL CONGRESS OF ACCOUNTANTS

ICC *see* INTERNATIONAL CHAMBER OF COMMERCE

ICG *see* INTERNATIONAL COMMODITY GROUP

ICO *see* INTERNATIONAL COMMODITY ORGANIZATION

ICSID *see* INTERNATIONAL CENTER FOR THE SETTLEMENT OF INVESTMENT DISPUTES

IDA *see* INTERNATIONAL DEVELOPMENT ASSOCIATION

IDB *see* INTER-AMERICAN DEVELOPMENT BANK

IDF *see* IMPORT DECLARATION FORM

identical reciprocity When two countries enter into trade agreements, the result is often concessions from both parties to reduce import/export barriers which may exist between them. When two countries reduce barriers in response to one another, this is generally referred to as reciprocity. Identical reciprocity describes a situation in which countries allow foreign firms to operate but only to the extent that current local laws and regulations allow. Foreign firms also may not undertake activities not allowed in their home country. For example, insurance companies in the United States generally cannot own or operate banks, whereas in Europe joint banking and insurance is common. If identical reciprocity was in effect, a French insurance company could operate in the US but would have to accept the restriction on bank relationships. On the other hand, a United States insurer could operate in France and even though France allows banking relationships, the US insurer could not enter into such an arrangement because US law precludes it.

See also **Reciprocity**

Bibliography

Simmonds, K. R. Musch, D. J. (eds) (1992). *Law and practice under the GATT and other trading agreements, North American Free Trade Agreements, United States–Canada Free Trade Agreements: Binational panel reviews and reports.* Dobbs Ferry, NY: Oceana Publications Inc.

JOHN O'CONNELL

IFC   *see* INTERNATIONAL FINANCE CORPORATION

IIC   *see* INTER-AMERICAN INVESTMENT CORPORATION

ILO   *see* INTERNATIONAL LABOR ORGANIZATION

illegal alien   *See* ALIEN

IMF conditionality   *see* INTERNATIONAL MONETARY FUND

imitation   Although imitation is sometimes referred to as the highest form of flattery, in international business it is at the very least a costly activity and at the most an illegal act. When a company copies or counterfeits another company's product or process it literally takes money out of the original company's pocket. A number of international agreements have been established in attempts to dissuade imitators but not all countries strictly enforce the agreements.

See also **Intellectual property**

Bibliography

Schultz, J. S. & Windsor, S. (1994). *International intellectual property protection for computer software: A research guide and annotated bibliography.* Littleton, CO: Fred B. Rothman & Company.

JOHN O'CONNELL

immersion approach, to training   *see* EXPATRIATE TRAINING

immigrant visa   A visa that permits a foreign person to enter into a country and to stay there for a fixed amount of time or permanently. An immigrant visa normally allows a person the freedom to obtain employment or to conduct business in that foreign country.

Bibliography

Grant, L. (1994). *Immigration lawyer's transaction pack.* Bristol: Jordon Publishing.

JOHN O'CONNELL

immigration   Immigration takes place when a person seeks to enter a country to establish permanent residency. Immigration patterns have changed over the last several hundred years, reflecting the opportunities people see at different times in different countries or problems which exist on a temporary basis (wars, famine, etc.) Immigration restrictions are enforced by a number of countries as to numbers or nationalities of persons allowed immigration rights.

Bibliography

Light, I. Babchu, P. (eds) (1993). *Immigration and entrepreneurship: Culture, capital, and ethnic networks.* New Brunswick, NJ: Transaction Books.
Lutton, W. & Tanton, J. (1994). *The immigration invasion.* Petrosky, MI: Social Contract Press.
Stewart, D. W. (1993). *Immigration and education: The crisis and the opportunities.* Lexington, Maine: D. C. Heath & Company.

JOHN O'CONNELL

immigration regulations   Each country establishes its own regulations with respect to foreign citizens seeking permanent residency. One can learn about the regulations by contacting the appropriate government department of a particular country. Regulations are subject to change depending upon the actions of government related to various international conditions (war, etc.).

Bibliography

Grant, L. (1994). *Immigration lawyer's transaction pack*. Bristol: Jordon Publishing.

JOHN O'CONNELL

import   Importing is the act of transferring goods and/or services across international boundaries. For example, clothing is imported into countries in which the local clothing industry is not capable of meeting the demand. The term may also refer to the goods themselves. For example, oil is an import which is very important to the United States.

Bibliography

Appleyard, D. R. & Field, Jr., A. J. (1994). *International economics: Trade theory and policy*. Chicago, IL: Richard D. Irwin Inc.

JOHN O'CONNELL

import allocation certificate (IAC)   A document required by the Japan Ministry of International Trade and Industry authorizing foreign exchange for imports. This purpose of the certificate is to assist the government in regulating foreign exchange expenditures. The importer must submit the certificate to the appropriate governmental agency in order to secure an import license. A Japanese importer may not receive an import license without this completed document.

Bibliography

Korth, C. (1985). *Barriers to international business*. Englewood Cliffs, NJ: Prentice-Hall.

JOHN O'CONNELL

import barriers   Most countries do not allow unlimited importation of all types of goods and services. Generally barriers to importation are established to allow local markets to grow while being protected from competition from outside the country. As local markets grow and efficiencies develop trade restrictions tend to be reduced. The particular type of restriction varies with the type of goods being protected and the countries involved.

See also **Barriers**

Bibliography

Bowker, R. R. (1993). *GATT, General Agreement on Tariffs and Trade: What it is and what it does*. Chester, PA: Diane Publishing Company.

JOHN O'CONNELL

import broker   Many persons who are involved in exporting activities do not have the knowledge or contacts to successfully conduct trade activities. An import broker is hired by exporters to locate buyers (importers) for the exporter's goods. Typically, the import broker receives a commission for services rendered.

Bibliography

United States Customs Service (1994). *A basic guide to importing*. Lincolnwood, IL: NTC Publishing Group.

JOHN O'CONNELL

import declaration form (IDF)   An IDF is required by some countries (generally those having foreign exchange restrictions in place) of importers desiring to pay for imports with the currency of another country. The appropriate government authority must act on an application (the import declaration form) prior to making foreign exchange available.

See also **Foreign exchange; Mark sheet**

JOHN O'CONNELL

import deposit   A country may require an importer to deposit funds with governmental authorities as a type of good faith offering that all taxes, etc. will be paid. The deposit is returned after a relatively short period of time. Although this sounds fair, in reality the deposit has been used by some countries to restrict the importation of items. The practice of collecting import deposits is not widespread.

Bibliography

Zodl, J. A. (1992). *Export–Import: Everything you and your company need to know to compete in world markets.* Cincinnati, OH: Betterway Books.

JOHN O'CONNELL

import (direct)   A buyer who handles the import transaction without help from intermediaries is said to have made a direct import. Although handling importation of goods without intermediaries may save money for the buyer, a great deal of knowledge is normally required to successfully carry out the transaction. Thus, the use of intermediaries is very common.

Bibliography

Zodl, J. A. (1992). *Export–Import: Everything you and your company need to know to compete in world markets.* Cincinnati, OH: Betterway Books.

JOHN O'CONNELL

import license   Generally a person is required to secure government permission before moving goods from one country to another. An import license is issued by the appropriate government office to provide specific permission for the importation of goods into a country. Without the license, a person is unable to legally import goods. Licenses are issued by governments desiring to control the amounts or types of goods, or to collect taxes associated with importation.

Bibliography

Johnson, T. E. (1994). *Export–Import procedures and documentation.* New York: Amacom.

JOHN O'CONNELL

import quotas   In order to limit the importation of certain goods, a government may establish maximum numbers or values of the goods which may be imported. Limitations are commonly established to protect domestic industries from foreign competition or as retaliation for trade practices of other nations.

Import quotas may also be established to improve a country's balance of payments position.

See also **Barriers**

JOHN O'CONNELL

import restrictions   Many countries attempt to limit the importation of certain goods and/or services. A country may impose a total ban on certain items or services or restrict the numbers of or total value of goods or services imported. Restrictions can apply to a specific country of origin or to the world as a whole with respect to specific goods or services.

See also **Import quotas**

JOHN O'CONNELL

in bond   It is common for the buyer of goods to take delivery prior to the buyer's peak selling season. Goods delivered, but warehoused until the selling season, are said to be held "in bond."

Bibliography

Zodl, J. A. (1992). *Export–Import: Everything you and your company need to know to compete in world markets.* Cincinnati, OH: Betterway Books.

JOHN O'CONNELL

import substitution   Import substitution involves substituting local production of goods for the importation of those goods. As a country develops economically certain goods may not be available locally even though there is a demand for them. In order to promote local development of production, a government may institute controls over the importation of certain items. Examples of controls include charging high import duties for certain goods or restricting the amount of goods allowed to be imported. Duties or quotas restrict the amount of goods imported, thereby giving local industry time and incentive to develop.

See also **Barriers**

JOHN O'CONNELL

import tariff Many countries place taxes on certain types of merchandise entering a country. Such taxes (tariffs) usually serve the purpose of reducing the local demand for such goods because of higher prices. Tariffs not only provide income for the taxing authority but also serve to protect local industry by raising the price of competing imports.

Bibliography

Grosse, R. & Kujawa, D. (1995). *International business: Theory and managerial applications*. 3rd edn, Boston, MA: Richard D. Irwin Inc.

JOHN O'CONNELL

import trade control order notices If a country decides that it is in its best interest to restrict importation of certain goods, a written directive is normally issued by the appropriate governmental authority. This written directive provides information related to quotas placed on specific imports.

Bibliography

Johnson, T. E. (1994). *Export–Import procedures and documentation*. New York: Amacom.

JOHN O'CONNELL

import wholesalers Often it is not economically feasible for a retailer to import goods directly from a foreign manufacturer. Problems and costs commonly associated with establishing contacts and carrying out the trade transaction act to exclude many small retailers from direct importing activities. An import wholesaler helps to solve this problem. The wholesaler makes all arrangements to import large quantities directly from foreign sources. Local retailers then arrange for delivery from the wholesaler.

JOHN O'CONNELL

in transit After goods have left the seller's possession until such time they are received by the buyer they are considered to be "in transit." It is very important to determine who is responsible for damage to goods, securing and paying for insurance, and other details of delivery while goods are in transit. Normally, responsibility for the various aspects of the trade transaction are determined by the terms of the contract between seller (exporter) and buyer (importer).

See also **INCOTERMS**

JOHN O'CONNELL

income tax treaties The United States is a party to a dizzying array of international agreements with other nations, including over 80 income tax treaties now in force or being negotiated. Even the best income tax advice can be thrown to the winds if the subject transaction is between taxpayers from different countries and the taxpayers fail to consider the effects of tax treaties that may exist between their nations. The language of the treaties, although a little stilted with the formulas of international legal expression, is generally understandable in context, and the goal of income tax treaties is clear: to harmonize and simplify tax laws between the two countries, promoting commerce, while avoiding double taxation and fiscal evasion.

Each income tax treaty is a separate agreement between two nations who are a party to the agreement. While in theory each treaty could differ widely from each other treaty, in practice all treaties to which the United States is a party tend to look very much alike, and tend to look like most other income tax treaties in the world, owing largely to the Organization for Economic Cooperation and Development (OECD). In 1963, the OECD member nations developed a model treaty, a basic framework designed to serve as the starting point for tax treaty negotiations between member nations. Modified in 1977, the Model Treaty was accompanied by a Commentary prepared by the OECD that has become a key guide to interpreting the meaning to the terms and expressions used in modern treaties. As a consequence of this general international understanding of the meaning of treaty terms, conflicts between nations over treaty obligations are actually rather rare. If they do occur, the International Court at The Hague adjudicates the dispute. In 1977 and in 1981, the United States adopted its own version of a model treaty, but the Commentary developed by the OECD remains a major guide to interpretation of this U.S. Model Treaty, as well as the OECD versions.

The status of a treaty obligation is a matter for domestic law to determine in each country. Where a treaty obligation is in conflict with a domestic tax law, a country must decide which has priority over the other. In the United States, tax law clearly provides that a treaty provision controls in the event of a conflict of laws if the conflict existed on April 16, 1954, but, thereafter, the later expression of sovereign will controls. As a result, it is possible for Congress to override a treaty obligation by passing a law that contravenes the clear language of a treaty obligation already in existence. In this event, the treaty as a whole remains in force, but the contravened provision is deemed abrogated, and usually the two countries renegotiate the treaty.

In the United States, treaties are negotiated by the executive branch of the federal government, and once approved by the President, sent to the Senate for its advice and consent. Once ratified by the Senate, treaties come into force on the date the two parties to the treaty exchange instruments of ratification – conformed copies of the final treaty. Because all recent U.S. tax treaties start from the same model, it is possible to generalize a great deal about the contents of an income tax treaty, although the specific points that are agreed upon vary from treaty to treaty.

Each income tax treaty must determine what persons have treaty standing, and what taxes are covered by the treaty. Treaty standing is critical because a taxpayer may take advantage of a provision in a treaty only if that taxpayer is covered by the treaty. U.S. tax treaties generally follow the OECD model in providing that all U.S. residents and domestic corporations may benefit from a U.S. tax treaty. Interestingly, this means that a nonresident U.S. citizen may not obtain benefits from a U.S. tax treaty, even though the U.S. asserts its right to tax its citizens – not just its residents – on their worldwide income. Residency is usually carefully described in terms of the geographic area that creates residency for treaty standing purposes, and generally excludes U.S. territories. Residency can be a difficult matter to determine, and treaties often go to great lengths to avoid dual residency by prescribing "tie breaker" rules, designed to insure that any taxpayer is

deemed a resident of only one of the two contracting nations in a tax treaty. A treaty may also contain a set of anti-treaty shopping provisions, designed to thwart taxpayers' efforts to obtain treaty benefits by creating shell corporations or other subterfuges that appear to create residency.

The taxes covered by the treaty tend to include only U.S. federal income taxes, often exclusive of the personal holding company tax and the accumulated earnings tax. In only a few cases are state income taxes explicitly covered in U.S. treaties, although the fact that nearly 40 states in the United States begin their tax computations with federal income makes these states implicit signatories to each U.S. income tax treaty. Similarly, other countries may or may not cover taxes other than basic federal income taxes.

Once a treaty has established the issues of treaty standing and taxes covered by the treaty, treaties based on the OECD Model Treaty often include permanent establishment provisions. To simplify the issue of the income taxation of business income of a foreign entity or individual, these treaties provide that the business income of a foreign person is taxable in the foreign country only if that person has a permanent establishment in that foreign country. Otherwise, this business income is taxable only in the country of that persons residency. If there were no permanent establishment provision, foreign business income would be taxable in a foreign country if the tax laws in that foreign country sourced the transaction in that foreign country. The rules governing sourcing of transactions vary widely, often leading to double taxation without a permanent establishment provision to harmonize the tax laws of the two countries in a treaty.

A permanent establishment is defined in the U.S. Model Treaty of 1981 to be:

> a fixed place of business through which the business of an enterprise is wholly or partly carried on.

A place of management, a branch, an office, a factory, a workshop, a mine or well, a building site used for 12 months, or an installation, drilling rig, or ship used for more than 12 months to discover or exploit natural resources all qualify as permanent establishments. In addition, if another party other than an agent of independent status has and habitually exercises the power to bind a foreign person to contracts in a foreign country, this person is deemed to create a permanent establishment on behalf of the person that he or she represents in that country.

Following the permanent establishment provisions in treaties are a number of special sourcing rules for nonbusiness income, such as dividends, interest, rents, royalties, and capital gains. These types of income are often taxed to nonresident recipients by using withholdings taxes – taxes withheld by the payor and sent directly to the government – obviating the need to file tax returns in the foreign country. To encourage commerce, treaties often reduce or eliminate these withholdings taxes. In addition, the treaty may include special taxing rules for other types of income, such as the income of teachers or students, or that of artists or sportsmen. Often this kind of income is determined to be tax free, or very beneficially taxed, in the foreign country.

Treaties usually contain a savings clause that clearly limits the applicability of the treaty to international transactions, by providing that nothing in the treaty should be construed as interfering with the right of the country of residency to tax its own residents. As a result, even though a U.S. treaty may declare gains on the sale of personal capital assets tax free, gains on the sale of such assets by a U.S. citizen or resident are clearly taxed in the U.S.

Treaties also commonly include the identification of a person or official to serve as competent authority to negotiate with the other government to insure that the goal of avoiding double taxation without evasion is met. Competent authorities are often invoked to determine fair transfer prices for goods or services provided by residents of one country to those of the other country, where the parties are related, for example.

Information sharing provisions are also commonly included in treaties, providing for specified levels of cooperation between the contracting states in the pursuit of income taxes in the other country. The United States refuses to enter into such information sharing agreements unless foreign governments agree to treat the information so received with the same level of confidentiality that is required of U.S. tax authorities.

While the language of treaties appears to be somewhat technical in character, reference to model treaties and their commentaries provides a ready basis for reading and understanding the nature of the mutual obligations that nations incur in the network of income tax treaties, and the often extraordinary benefits that the treaties confer on the residents of the contracting states. Clearly, tax planning and practice require that treaty law be carefully screened to insure that international transactions are appropriately taxed.

DALE L. DAVISON

inconvertibility of currency coverage   The inability to convert local currency into a company's home currency. This is an important consideration for an organization seeking to repatriate profits or dividends from a foreign operation. Insurance against losses arising from inconvertibility is available from specialty international insurance markets. Insurance commonly protects against one or both of the following situations:

1 A change in a law or regulation which restricts the right to convert currency. As long as there was an official method of currency conversion before the insurance contract goes into force, coverage usually applies for changes in the law from that point forward. Most policies require that normal convertibility be delayed at least 60 to 90 days beyond the normal conversion period.

2 An administrative delay on the part of the country's exchange authority which delays the ability to exchange currency. Most policies require the delay to be a minimum number of days beyond the period normally required for conversion.

If either of these situations occur, the insurer converts the currency for the insured into the currency designated in the contract.

See also **Political risk; Political risk insurance**

JOHN O'CONNELL

INCOTERMS Standardized terminology used to assist in describing the responsibilities of parties (usually buyer and seller) in international trade transactions. INCOTERMS were approved by a committee of the International Chamber of Commerce. Trading terms have been standardized in order to reduce misunderstandings between parties to trade transactions. The terms specify which party is responsible for delivery of goods to a given place, providing and paying for insurance, and other transportation requirements. The most recent revision of INCOTERMS took place in 1990. The following chart lists the 1990 INCOTERMS:

EXW	Ex works (named place)
FAS	Free alongside ship (named port of shipment)
FCA	Free carrier (named place)
FOB	Free on board (named port of shipment)
CFR	Cost and freight (named port of destination)
CIF	Cost, insurance and freight (named port of destination)
CAP	Carriage and insurance paid to (named place of destination)
CPT	Carriage paid to (named place of destination)
DAF	Delivered at frontier (named place)
DDP	Delivered duty paid (named place of destination)
DDU	Delivered duty unpaid (named place of destination)
DEQ	Delivered ex quay duty paid (named port of destination)
DES	Delivered ex ship (named port of destination)

Each INCOTERM is explained in detail under its name.

JOHN O'CONNELL

indigenization laws In order to restrict (and therefore control) foreign ownership of organizations operating within its borders a government may establish a minimum percentage of ownership by local nationals. These restrictions are referred to as indigenization laws. It is not uncommon for developing countries to require that at least 51% of ownership be held locally. This allows foreign investment to take place while still retaining local control. This protectionist position may allow a greater percentage of foreign ownership as time passes, thus allowing the industry to become more firmly embedded in the host country's economy.

See also **Barriers**

JOHN O'CONNELL

indirect exchange rate An exchange rate is determined by valuing one currency in terms of another. It is common to see the value of a US dollar expressed in yen or the value of a British pound expressed in marks. However, when two currencies are compared and neither of the currencies is well known an indirect exchange rate may be used. Thus, the Colombian bolivar and the Nigerian naira may each be compared to the German mark in order to determine their comparable value.

JOHN O'CONNELL

indirect exporting Producers of goods may not desire or have the expertise to undertake export operations of their own. In order to take advantage of foreign purchasers of goods, many producers turn to indirect exporting or use the services of export agents or other intermediaries. The intermediary generally receives a commission for services rendered. This is a common way to begin export activities. As activities increase it then becomes more likely that producers will begin to develop internal expertise in the export area and reduce the use of intermediaries.

Bibliography

Johnson, T. E. (1994). *Export–Import procedures and documentation*. New York: Amacom.

JOHN O'CONNELL

indirect quote (foreign exchange cross rate)   An indirect quote is when the value of two currencies are compared by determining the exchange rate of each currency in relation to a third country's currency. Currencies which are not often traded for one another may still be compared by relating them to a third, commonly traded, currency. Thus, both currencies may be expressed in German marks or United States dollars for a more meaningful comparison.

Bibliography

Peters, C. C. and Gitlin, A. W. (eds) (1993). *Strategic currency investing: Trading and investing in the foreign exchange markets.* Hinsdale, IL: Probus Publishing Company Inc.

JOHN O'CONNELL

indirect selling   Organizations may not have the desire or the resources to conduct export activities themselves. Many of these organizations enlist the services of export intermediaries to carry out foreign sales activities.

See also **Export agent**

Bibliography

Johnson, T. E. (1994). *Export–Import procedures and documentation.* New York: Amacom.

JOHN O'CONNELL

individually validated export license   A document issued by the appropriate governmental agency to allow an exporter to export a specific good to a specific destination. An individually validated export license may apply to a single shipment or to a series of shipments as specified in the document. This type of export license is used when a general license is unavailable.

JOHN O'CONNELL

industrial countries   The movement from agricultural or trading pursuits to producing products through mechanized methods is a process which has already taken place in a number of countries and is continuing in many more. Countries whose economies have become driven by their industrial base are known as industrial or industrialized countries. Industrialized countries control the vast amount of economic activity taking place throughout the world. The economic impact of just a few nations exceeds that of the remainder of the world. Major industrial countries include Australia, Canada, Germany, Great Britain, France, Hong Kong, Japan, Singapore, and the United States. Virtually all of western Europe is considered to be industrialized as well as some of the states of the former Soviet Union (although the transition to a market economy may delay the realization of the fruits of industrialization for many eastern European countries). As countries become more reliant on industrial output there is a general increase in per capita income and wealth as well as a general awakening of foreign trade and commerce.

Bibliography

Baldasarri (Ed.) (1994). *The international problems of economic interdependence: Central issues in contemporary economic theory and policy.* New York: St. Martin's Press.

JOHN O'CONNELL

industrial espionage   Unethical or illegal activities to obtain information about a competitor's products, processes, or technology. Common targets include new technological developments, research interests, and other proprietary information. Today industrial espionage is commonly carried out through the use of various kinds of electronic equipment (computers, telephone, or other surveillance equipment). Some industrial espionage activities may be subject to criminal prosecution depending upon the exact nature of the espionage and the country in which the activity takes place.

Bibliography

Litka, M. (1991). *International dimensions of the legal environment of business.* 2nd edn, Boston, MA: PWS-Kent Publishing Company.

JOHN O'CONNELL

industrial or producer's goods Whereas goods purchased for individual consumption are referred to as consumer goods, those meant for use in the production of other goods are referred to as industrial or producer's goods. Industrial goods include various kinds of machinery or equipment to process materials into products as well as the raw materials themselves.

Bibliography

Miller, J. G., Demeyer, A. & Nakane, J. (1994). *Benchmarking global manufacturing: Understanding international suppliers, customers and competitors.* Hinsdale, IL: Irwin Professional Publishing.

JOHN O'CONNELL

industrial property There are two definitions of this term which are in common usage. Industrial property may refer to property used for commercial purposes such as factories, storage facilities, research and development facilities, office buildings, and other commercial structures. Industrial property may also refer to intangible property normally associated with commercial ventures such as trademarks, patents, licenses, and other property right protections issued by governments.

Bibliography

Grosse, R. & Kujawa, D. (1995). *International business: Theory and managerial applications.* 3rd edn, Boston, MA: Richard D. Irwin Inc.

JOHN O'CONNELL

industrial relations Industrial relations may refer to any number of interactions between an organization and other parties associated with commercial activity. Examples include, employee/employer negotiations, relations or other activities, interaction between employers and unions, activities associated with trade associations or other industrial associations, as well as many other interactions or activities conducted on behalf of the organization.

JOHN O'CONNELL

infant industry argument When an industry is first beginning to develop in a country (e.g., production of clothing) the government may feel the necessity to institute controls over the importation of that same product. The theory behind these controls is that an infant (just beginning) industry cannot compete with foreign industries of the same type until it becomes established and efficient. Trade protection, either through quotas or tariffs, will give the infant industry a chance to grow and become self-sufficient. A problem can exist, however, if protectionist activities of government are not repealed after the industry grows from its infant stage.

See also **Barriers; Quotas.**

JOHN O'CONNELL

inflation Inflation occurs when the price level of goods and services rises over time. Increased price levels erode the purchasing power of local currency. Inflation rates (the percentage increase in prices normally measured on an annual basis) vary from country to country and even within a country as time passes. Major problems associated with purchasing power or investment returns/values arise when the inflation rate is high. A number of countries have at times had inflation rates in excess of 200–300%. Hyperinflation has been known to occur at times of war causing thousands of percentage points of inflation in very short periods of time. Such inflation literally destroys a country's economy and its ability to actively partake in international trade. Foreign investments in times of high inflation are very risky and normally decrease in countries showing inflation instability. Small amounts of inflation are quite normal. When inflationary pressures begin to mount, however, governments attempt to stem the rise through a combination of monetary policies, price controls, and adjustments in governmental spending.

Bibliography

Ellsworth, P. T. (1990). *The international economy.* New York: Harper & Row.

JOHN O'CONNELL

inflation accounting   An accounting practice that attempts to explain the effects of inflation on an organization's financial activities. By taking inflation into account, an organization can determine its real rate of growth or the value of assets in current financial terms. If this type of accounting is not used, the real return on investment as well as real values of assets are difficult to determine.

Bibliography

Ferris, K. R. (1993). *Financial accounting and corporate reporting: A casebook*. 3rd edn, Homewood, IL: Irwin.

JOHN O'CONNELL

influence peddling   Persons may be influential because of their governmental contacts, family name, position in the military, or for other reasons. These people may seek to achieve personal gain by using this influence to assist others. For example, a person uses his/her contacts to assist a firm secure a government contract. The firm then names the person (or a relative of that person) to an important management position in the firm. The person has peddled his/her influence in return for the management position.

Bibliography

Scarpello, V. & Ledvinka, J. (1987). *Personnel/human resource management*. Boston, MA: Kent.

JOHN O'CONNELL

information giving approach to training   *see* EXPATRIATE TRAINING

information technology   The electronic transfer of information has revolutionized the management of organizations throughout the world. The term "information technology" describes the various electronic devices which are used to store, interpret, and transfer data. Devices include computers, satellite links (both portable and fixed base), electronic mail systems, various types of telephone links, and the associated cables and other connecting devices. The development of new information technol-ogy proceeds at a blinding rate. The effect of such change on future management of firms remains uncertain, but exciting.

Bibliography

Deans, P. C. & Kane, M. J. (1992). *International dimensions of information systems and technology*. 2nd edn, Boston, MA: PWS-Kent Publishing Company.

JOHN O'CONNELL

infrastructure   When viewing the economic condition of a country, important factors considered in most inquiries include the transportation system (roads, airways, railways, etc.), the financial system (banks, credit system, stock market activity, etc.), and the communications system (telephone, media, electronic transfer capabilities, etc.). These systems comprise the basic "infrastructure" of a country.

Bibliography

Adler, N. J. (1991). *International dimensions of organizational behavior*. 2nd edn, Belmont, CA: Wadsworth Inc.

JOHN O'CONNELL

injury   This term is sometimes used to describe the financial impact of imports on domestically-produced goods and services. A domestic enterprise is considered "injured" if it perceives itself as being damaged by imports. Damages could include reduced market share, lower profits, downsizing employment opportunities, or any other real or perceived injury.

Bibliography

Serko, D. (1991). *Import practice: Customs and international trade law*. New York: Practicing Law Institute.

JOHN O'CONNELL

inland bill of lading   The name given to a bill of lading when goods are shipped over land by truck or rail. Many times several bills will have to be prepared when goods are transported by different types of carriers (inland, ocean, etc.)

See also **bill of lading**

JOHN O'CONNELL

INMARSAT *see* INTERNATIONAL MARITIME SATELLITE ORGANIZATION

innovation   Historically, this term has meant a new approach or way of doing things. An innovative organization was one which sought out and implemented new or unique ways of accomplishing its tasks. In recent years innovation has been associated with developments of technology and the adoption of advances by firms. Development of, and implementation of, new technology is considered to be innovative.

JOHN O'CONNELL

insurance certificate   Trading transactions normally require either the seller or buyer to secure and pay the cost of insurance protection. In order to supply proof to the remaining parties to the transaction an insurance certificate is commonly required. The certificate indicates the dates of coverage, values insured, and coverage territory. This is not an insurance policy, but merely certification (usually by the insurance company or insurance broker) that a policy exists.

Bibliography

Kunreuther, H. K. & Pauly, M. V. (1990). *International trade in insurance*. Philadelphia, PA: Huebner Foundation for Insurance Education.

JOHN O'CONNELL

intellectual property   Most property can be seen, touched, and is capable of physical measurement and valuation. This is not true of all property. With technological advancements over the past several decades, a new type of property in the form of ideas or unique processes has been recognized. Especially valuable are ideas and developments associated with advances in computers or communications technology. The person having these ideas or the firm developing a process or way of doing things is said to have developed intellectual property. Intellectual property has become

valuable and subject to protection in many countries. Patents and copyrights are two examples of measures to protect intellectual property rights.

The owner of intellectual property can protect it against unauthorized use by filing the forms documenting its existence with the appropriate governmental authorities. A real problem exists in the world today because of the failure of some countries to allow intellectual property rights to be protected or to enforce existing property right protections. Failure to protect intellectual property rights may slow the spread of certain technological advances throughout the world. Unless intellectual property rights protection is provided (with the accompanying right to profit from those rights) organizations may be unwilling to share technological developments with certain countries.

Several international initiatives and organizations have begun work toward establishing better methods of controlling unauthorized use of intellectual property. The United Nations established the World Intellectual Property Organization (WIPO) and began operations in 1970. The WIPO is charged with promoting international cooperation and coordination related to intellectual property rights protection.

See also **Berne Convention, Patent Cooperation Treaty; World Intellectual Property Organization**

JOHN O'CONNELL

Inter-American Accounting Association (IAA)   This association was established to increase standardization of accounting practices and rules in the region. Standardization eases problems associated with reconciling financial reports of organizations conducting cross-border business. This has the effect of encouraging international business activities.

Bibliography

Arpan, J. S. & Al Hashim, D. D. (1984). *International dimensions of accounting*. Boston, MA: Kent Publishing Company Inc.

JOHN O'CONNELL

Inter-American Convention on Invention, Patents, Designs and Models This 1910 convention was one of the early attempts of countries to enter into agreements protecting property rights. Concerns over illegal use of proprietary information (patents, inventions, designs, etc.) by organizations in other countries caused a number of Latin American countries (the United States is now also a signatory to the convention) to enter into agreements to abide by one another's rules and regulations pertaining to such property rights.

Bibliography

Hautmann, R. A. & Sullivan, R. A. (1989). Intellectual property: Maximising protection of an employer's rights. *Employee Relations Journal*, **15**, 253–65.
Seminsky, M. & Bryer, L. G. (eds) (1994). *The new role of intellectual property in commercial transactions*. New York: John Wiley & Sons.
Stewart, G. R. (Ed.) (1994). *International trade and intellectual property: The search for a balanced system*. Boulder, CO: Westview Press.

                                    JOHN O'CONNELL

Inter-American   Development   Bank (IDB) The bank's purpose is to assist in the economic development of its member countries. The bank is the financial institution charged with responsibility for implementing projects sponsored by the United Nations Development program. The IDB was founded in 1959 and is responsive to the needs of 25 regional members and 18 nonregional members. In addition to providing funding for projects, the bank also offers support by providing information related to a number of important basic economic activities (technological development, communications, transportation, and other areas of potential investment). The bank's headquarters are located in Washington, D.C.

Bibliography

Ludlow, N. H. (1988). *A practical guide to the development bank business: How to identify it, market to it, and win it*. Washington, D.C.: Development Bank Associates Inc.

                                    JOHN O'CONNELL

Inter-American   Investment   Corporation (IIC) The Inter-American Investment Corporation is associated with the Inter-American Development Bank (IDB). Whereas the IDB was primarily concerned with what may be considered to be infrastructure projects in Latin America (communications, transportation, education, etc.) the IIC was established to promote private enterprises in the region.

See   also **Inter-American   Development Bank; Private Sector Development Program**

Bibliography

Ludlow, N. H. (1988). *A practical guide to the development bank business: How to identify it, market to it, and win it*. Washington, D.C.: Development Bank Associates Inc.

                                    JOHN O'CONNELL

interbank market A market in which the major participants are various banking units. Interbank markets include the foreign exchanges market (as far as bank to bank transfers are concerned), the Eurocurrency market (even though many transactions are between banks and their customers), and the practice of banks lending to one another within a country.

Bibliography

Ricks, D. A. (1978). *International dimensions of corporate finance*. Englewood Cliffs, NJ: Prentice-Hall.

                                    JOHN O'CONNELL

interbank offered rate This is the interest charged when one bank loans funds to another bank within the same country. The rates normally charged for interbank loans are nearer the actual cost of funds for the bank than are loans to commercial customers. That is, the rates charged for interbank loans are generally lower then regular commercial loans. Probably the most well-known interbank rate is the London Interbank Offered Rate (LIBOR). This rate is the average of five London banks and is used not only as a true interbank rate, but also as the basis for rates on short-term international loans.

Bibliography

Eiteman, D. K., Stonehill, A. J. & Moffett, M. H. (1992). *Multinational business finance*. 6th edn, Reading, MA: Addison-Wesley Publishing.

JOHN O'CONNELL

interdependence   Interdependence is a relatively simple concept referring to organizations or groups relying upon the actions of each other in order to function. An import firm is reliant upon an export firm to stay in business, as well as the export firm being reliant on the import firm for the same reason. The two firms are thus interdependent. Regardless of its simplicity, it is an extremely important concept in the context of international trade. Organizations which are too dependent upon the operations of other organizations (suppliers, buyers, distributors, etc.) may have their very existence threatened by the demise of that other organization or a change in contract, etc.).

Interdependencies must be identified and dealt with by management. When situations are identified in which the dependence is too great for management, alternate sources of supply, sale, or distribution must be found. Failure to deal with interdependency situations places the organization's continued existence in the hands of others. To most managements this is an unacceptable condition which must be remedied if at all possible.

Bibliography

Egelhoff, W. G. (1988). Strategy and structure in multinational corporations: A revision of the Stopford and Wells Model. *Strategic Management Journal*, **9**, 1–14.
Grosse, R. & Kujawa, D. (1995). *International business: Theory and managerial applications*. 3rd edn, Boston, MA: Richard D. Irwin Inc.
Humes, S. (1993). *Managing the multinational: Confronting the global–local dilemma*. Englewood Cliff, NJ: Prentice-Hall.
Rosenweig, P. M. & Singh, J. V. (1991). *Organizational environments and the multinational enterprise*. The Academy of Management Review, **16**, 340–61.

JOHN O'CONNELL

interest arbitrage   A process by which one takes advantage of higher interest rates in different countries by lending or investing wherever the rates are highest. One can borrow in one country and lend in another and profit by the difference in rates of interest. At the same time, however, the investor is also taking on any additional risks associated with doing business in the second country. The overall effect of interest arbitrage is to make rates of interest more equal between countries. Interest arbitrage takes place through the trading of short-term funds (usually 90 days or less).

Bibliography

Houthakker, H. S. & Williamson, P. J. (1994). *The economics of financial markets*. New York: Oxford University Press Inc.

JOHN O'CONNELL

interest rate   The amount paid for the use of capital. Interest rates can vary greatly between countries, over time and between various uses of funds. Interest rates are expressed as a percentage. Comparison of rates of return between countries must not be based solely upon the percentage rate interest; other factors should also be considered, such as security of investment principle, guarantee of return, and stability of the country's economic system.

Bibliography

Ashegian, P. & Ebrahimi, B. (1990). *International business*. Philadelphia, PA: HarperCollins.

JOHN O'CONNELL

intermediated market   *see* INTERMEDIATION

intermediation   Intermediation is the process of securing funds from savings or investors and in turn offering those funds to borrowers. Since the lenders are not the direct source of loanable funds they perform an "intermediary" or go-between function. Lenders performing intermediary functions include banks, insurance companies, building societies, and savings and loan companies. Each institution secures deposits and loans funds to others who are not necessarily the original depositors.

Bibliography

Agenor, P. R. (1992). *Parallel currency markets in developing markets: Theory, evidence, and policy implications.* Princeton, NJ: Princeton University.

JOHN O'CONNELL

intermerchant   Some currencies are more readily convertible then are others. The so-called "hard" currencies are regularly traded and generally pose no problems in the exchange process. "Soft" currencies, however, are many times difficult to exchange. An intermerchant is a person specializing in solving problems associated with hard and soft currency exchange. The intermerchant makes necessary arrangements for paying for goods sold between countries with hard currencies and those with soft currencies.

Bibliography

Murray, F. & Murray, A. (1991). *SRM forum: Global managers for global businesses.* Ann Arbor, MI: The University of Michigan Press.

JOHN O'CONNELL

intermodal containers   *see* CONTAINER

International Accounting Standards Committee (IASC)   One of the major administrative problems facing a multinational company is complying with a variety of accounting procedures which exist in different countries. In 1973, representatives from a group of powerful trading nations formed the International Accounting Standards Committee. The objective of the committee was to develop accounting standards which could be applied on an international basis. Over the past 22 years, the committee has made strides towards this objective. The nations represented on the committee are Australia, Canada, France, Germany, Ireland, Japan, Mexico, the United Kingdom, and the United States. Associate membership is also available and numbers more than 40 countries.

JOHN O'CONNELL

international agreement   A country many times seeks the support of other countries in order to achieve a common goal. Goals may relate to environmental concerns, human rights questions, or deal with any number of other topics. A stand taken by a single country is generally not as effective as the same position when endorsed by several countries. International agreements are achieved when several countries become signatories to a written document proclaiming a specific stand on an issue. The agreement then becomes a part of each country's obligations to the others or to the world as a whole.

JOHN O'CONNELL

International Bank for Reconstruction and Development (IBRD)   This was the original name given to what is now commonly referred to as the World Bank. The bank's major goals are to foster international economic growth. Its goals are achieved by offering financing for long-term development projects mainly to developing and less developed countries.

JOHN O'CONNELL

International Banking Act of 1978   In an attempt to regulate the impact of foreign banks, the United States adopted the International Banking Act of 1978. The banking act restricted the activities of a foreign bank to a single state. The act also limits the bank to conducting either commercial banking activities or activities related to investment banking, but not both.

Bibliography

Sarachek, B. (1994). *International business law: A guide for executives with case examples.* Pennington, NY: Darwin Press Inc.

JOHN O'CONNELL

international banking facility (IBF) If a United States bank desires to accept Eurocurrency deposits and make Eurocurrency loans, it can establish an IBF. Upon proper notice to the Federal Reserve, a US bank may enter into Eurocurrency transactions. That is, it may accept deposits from or make a loan to non-US residents as well as to other international banking facilities. The IBF must keep separate accounts for all Eurodollar transactions. IBF status allows a bank to compete in offshore banking activities. IBF status also allows the bank to be free of many of the US banking regulations, reserve requirements, and some taxes but only for those transactions falling under the international banking facility activities).

Bibliography

Bowker, R. R. (1994). *International banking: Strengthening the framework for supervising international banks*. Chester, PA: Diane Publishing Company.

JOHN O'CONNELL

international business International business takes place when business is carried out across national borders. International business includes import and export activities, tradè in services, consulting activities, and any other business related endeavors which cross a nation's borders. International business activities have grown to be a major part of the world's total economic picture. Changes in political positioning of countries and the drive toward privatization of formerly governmental operations will assure the continued growth of international business.

Bibliography

Alkhafaji, A. F. (1990). *International management challenge*. Acton, MA: Copley.

JOHN O'CONNELL

International Center for the Settlement of Investment Disputes (ICSID) International business transactions are not without problems and disagreements. In order to assist in bringing disputes to an equitable end, the World Bank established the International Center for the Settlement of Investment Disputes in 1966.

The Center arbitrates disputes between private parties concerning commercial ventures. Countries which are signatories to the convention establishing the Center are bound by the Center's decisions and the courts of those countries are instructed to act to enforce the decisions if necessary.

JOHN O'CONNELL

International Chamber of Commerce The International Chamber of Commerce (ICC) is an association of business persons with its home office located in Paris. The ICC was established to foster the growth and development of trade throughout the world. The ICC provides international contacts for business activities; supports the expansion of free trade in goods and services; and provides a place to which people interested in international business can go for assistance. One of the most important programs sponsored by the ICC is the development and dissemination of International Commerce Terms (INCOTERMS). INCOTERMS are used throughout the world to define the parties, responsibilities, and other details of the trade transaction. Virtually everyone in business has heard of FOB (free on board) or FAS (free along side) in relation to shipping goods. These are examples of INCOTERMS developed by special committees of the International Chamber of Commerce in conjunction with governments and other interested parties.

See also **INCOTERMS; International Maritime Bureau**

JOHN O'CONNELL

international code of business ethics Can international codes of professional ethics be developed to regulate, successfully, professional behavior? Put differently: are the rules of the game the same in Boston, Berlin, and Tokyo? There is evidence that local "customs" may override universal principles, thus making for ethical "diversity." By identifying and understanding the factors which make local cultures unique, and addressing their requirements, the potential effectiveness and acceptability of an "international" code might be enhanced. There is no guarantee of success in this venture: to illustrate the problems, we will examine the code of conduct or guidelines used by the International Federation of Accountants (IFAC) in July 1990.

On the face of it, there are two major reasons why worldwide acceptance of the current version of this Guideline may be problematic. First, societies tend to resist guidelines imposed from without where they are perceived as inconsistent with a society's entrenched cultural norms. Second, as socio-economic conditions vary dramatically from country to country, so, too, do levels of professional proficiency in the countries in which guidelines are to be implemented. While all accountants encounter ethical conflicts, those arising in the context of the high technical proficiency required of accountants in a developed country may be entirely different in kind from those encountered by accountants in developing countries. In this article we will concentrate on highlighting the cultural issues.

Cultural Influences on Ethical Conduct

We will argue that culture plays an important role in relation to ethical standards. If we restrict the meaning of culture to a national or local unit of analysis, as opposed, say, to ethnic or corporate cultures, Hofstede's (1980) definition provides a useful framework. Culture in this sense is "the collective mental programming of the mind which distinguishes the members of one human group from another" (p. 25). As he considered cultures, he concluded that four measures – power distance, uncertainty avoidance, poles of individualism and collectivism, and poles of masculinity and femininity – could be used to differentiate the "collective mental programming" which is culture.

Power distance, a construct originally identified by Mulder (1977), measures how a less powerful subordinate perceives the degree of inequality in power which separates him or her from a more powerful superior.

Uncertainty avoidance, which indexes tolerance for uncertainty in culture, considers three indicators: rule orientation, employment stability, and stress. *Reluctance to break rules*, even when doing so is in the interests of the company, indicates an aversion to uncertainty. *Employment stability* captures a collective tolerance of the risks associated with job change. (Long-term employers who hold scrupulously

to rules would measure high on the uncertainty avoidance scale.) While recognizing that *stress* certainly reflects organizational and personality variables, Hofstede attributes some part of it to culture and sees it as reflecting the level of anxiety in a society.

The poles of *Individualism* and *Collectivism* form the third dimension of national culture. Put simply, this dimension captures the extent to which a culture values individual achievement over group cohesion. Individualist societies, such as the United States, regard achievement as personal; collective contributions to one's success tend to be discounted. In contrast, collectivist cultures prize group well-being and group achievement over individual self-interest.

The poles of *Masculinity* and *Femininity* form the final dimension of national culture. This dimension measures the extent to which a culture emphasizes assertive ("masculine") rather than supportive ("feminine") values and also captures the degree to which a culture identifies jobs as gender-based.

Where cultures differ, international codes of ethics, even for a relatively homogenous profession such as accounting, may encounter difficulties. Two broad difficulties suggest themselves: lack of consensus as to what constitutes acceptable behavior and divergent interpretations of the code.

Lack of consensus on acceptable behavior. Since cultures embody generally held beliefs and norms of appropriate behavior in a country, they have consequences for ethical behavior. Consider bribery. Pressure on a subordinate to cover up a supervisor's illegal action, such as accepting bribes, might be evaluated differently by Japanese than Americans because of cultural influences. While an American might interpret this pressure as coercion, a Japanese might willingly participate in a cover-up for collective motives – to save face and protect the reputation of the group.

Intellectual property presents another interesting contrast. In the typically collectivist cultures of Asia, the individual artist or writer is expected to share his or her creation. In contrast, individualist societies emphasize protecting the artist or writer by establishing copyright and patent laws.

Figure 1 A framework for evaluating international codes of conduct applied to IFAC's "Guideline on Ethics"

| | Consistency with Cultural Values | | | |
	Power distance	*Individualism/ Collectivism*	*Uncertainty/ Avoidance*	*Masculinity/ Femininity*
Integrity	Loyalty to supervisor	Conflicting loyalties	Compromising professional standards	Exaggeration of ability
Objectivity	Loyalty to supervisor	Value of others' opinions		
Confidentiality	Willingness to follow instructions	Loyalty to family and friends		Acceptability of self-promotion
		Loyalty to professional colleagues	Resolution of ethical conflicts	"Lowballing" and aggressive promotion of the firm
Professional behavior		Independence of audit		Sex discrimination

Diversity of interpretation. Cultural differences, in the second place, might limit the application of an international code by spawning a diversity of interpretations of the code, with corresponding consequences for implementation. The ideal of a self-regulating profession, in which members identify not with the organization by which they are employed but instead with the code of a profession, may be based on an individualist value system. Several researchers have argued that individualism values prize allegiance not to a group of people, but to a set of standards. As a consequence, practitioners in an individualist society may assume that if a professional chooses in light of the profession's guidelines, this will produce the best long-term results for that profession and for the society. But such an assumption may be antithetical to a collectivist culture.

An Evaluation of the IFAC Guideline

The Guideline identifies six principles fundamental to the accounting profession: Integrity, Objectivity, Professional Competence and Due Care, Confidentiality, Professional Behavior, and Technical Standards. Some of these could conflict with some cultural norms, and others are geared more toward the needs of developed economies than those of less-developed countries. Figure 1 shows a matrix consisting of Hofstede's cultural dimensions and the IFAC Guideline: cells with text identify areas where cultural diversity might create problems.

Power Distance and the dilemmas of the faithful follower. Power distance captures the extent to which subordinates in an organization expect to be instructed by superiors, and willingly obey those instructions. In a "high" power distance culture, the International Guideline's requirements on integrity, objectivity, and confidentiality are likely to create cultural conflicts for subordinates. Consider the first column of Figure 1: a subordinate in such a culture would be likely to acquiesce to a superior s unauthorized request for confidential information, and such acquiescence would be regarded as acceptable behavior. A subordinate would also be more likely to remain loyal to his or her supervisor out of respect for the supervisor's position, even when the supervisor acts unethically, or even illegally. More important, such behavior on the part of the subordinate would be culturally acceptable.

Individualism/Collectivism and the dilemmas of personal loyalty. The integrity principle requires the professional accountant to be "straightforward and honest in performing professional services," and the objectivity principle requires that "a professional accountant should be fair and not allow prejudice or bias or influence of others to override objectivity" (IFAC, p. 8). If we take "straightforward and honest" to involve a willingness on the part of individuals to be open to non-members of their group, then cultures will differ markedly. As the second column indicates, a member of a collectivist culture would value the opinion of peers, and indeed would be unwilling to make a decision without their input. A code of conduct which forces individuals to compromise relationships with group members in favor of client confidentiality also conflicts with collectivist cultural norms.

The confidentiality principle states that a professional accountant "should respect the confidentiality acquired during the course of performing the professional services and should not use or disclose any such information without proper and specific authority" (IFAC, p. 9). If a professional discovered that his or her client was close to bankruptcy, the Guideline requires that this information be withheld from close friends and family. However, in a collectivist culture, a failure to warn family and friends who were owed money would be a serious breach of collectivist norms.

Uncertainty Avoidance and the dilemma of being "professional". In the process recommended for the solution of an ethical conflict, the Guideline recommends a hierarchical approach whereby the professional is to review the conflict with his or her superior, or a higher authority if the superior is involved in the conflict problem. While this hierarchical approach might be suitable for a strong uncertainty avoidance culture, with its preference for written rules and intolerance of deviance, a weak uncertainty avoidance culture would be more tolerant of whistleblowing. Furthermore, a professional from a collectivist culture would value the advice of colleagues rather than superiors.

Masculinity/Femininity and the question of professional "presentation". The masculinity dimension has important implications for the accounting profession, in which Western norms

of professional conduct include restrictions on advertising and promotion. A masculine culture might be more tolerant of exaggerated self-promotion, and aggressive bidding for new clients.

The norms of a masculine culture which include acceptance of gender-based work-role differences in a country such as Japan (which has the highest masculinity score) would be interpreted as sex discrimination by members of a more feminist culture (such as Sweden).

Toward Internationally Acceptable Ethical Guidelines

As our review of the IFAC's guidelines suggests, "international" professional guidelines may turn out to be ethnocentric, reflecting the ethical and cultural standards of the developed countries whose organizations are most influential in writing them. They therefore risk failing to address ethical dilemmas found primarily in developing countries. Truly international guidelines must be sensitive to the need for guidance of the profession in its normal practice in all countries in which the code will operate.

Bibliography

Hofstede, G. (1980a). *Culture s Consequences.* Beverly Hills, Calif.: Sage.

Hofstede, G. (1980b). Organizational Dynamics. *Motivation, leadership, and organization: Do American theories apply abroad?* Summer, 42–63.

Mulder, M. (1977). *The Daily Power Game.* Leiden, Netherlands: Martinus Nijhoff.

LAURIE PANT
JEFFREY COHEN
DAVID SHARP

International Commodity Agreement (ICA) A number of developing countries have entered into agreements with one another in order to control the supply, and therefore the price, of certain commodities. The agreements are usually entered into by countries which have little else to trade except for the protected commodity. Examples of commodities currently subject to such agreements are: coconuts, rubber, coffee, sugar, and petroleum. There has been some difficulty in the past with policing some of the agreements either because all countries which produce a particular commodity are not signers of the agreement or because self-interest of one nation has led it to breach the agreement.

See also **International Commodity Group; International Commodity Organization**

Bibliography

Winham, G. R. (1992). *The evolution of international trade agreements.* Toronto, Ontario: University of Toronto Press.

JOHN O'CONNELL

International Commodity Group (ICG) - Generally thought of as a group of nations coming together to establish control over a particular commodity, an ICG could also refer to a group of economists interested in supplying the world with statistical reports related to a particular commodity. Probably the most recognizable of all commodity groups is the Organization of Petroleum Exporting Countries (OPEC), which has been very active in controlling price and distribution of oil in international markets.

International commodity groups often administer commodity agreements for members. When this occurs the IGC becomes eligible for financial support from the United Nations and is recognized as an International Commodity Organization (ICO).

See also **International Commodity Organization; Organization of Petroleum Exporting Countries; Cartel; International Commodity Agreement**

Bibliography

Yannopoulos, G. N. (1988). *Customs unions and trade conflicts: The second enlargement of the European Community.* London: Routledge.

JOHN O'CONNELL

International Commodity Organization (ICO) When a group of countries enters into formal written agreements to stabilize prices and supply of a particular commodity (rubber, coffee, etc.), that group may become recognized

by the United Nations. The United Nations refers to such groups as International Commodity Organizations or ICOs.

See also **International Commodity Group; International Commodity Agreement**

JOHN O'CONNELL

international companies An international company is one which does business across national borders. International companies are of all sizes, types and interests, but have a common stake in international activity. Companies enter into international business at a number of different levels and also reach their current status through varying methods.

See also **Evolution of global organization**

JOHN O'CONNELL

International Congress of Accountants One of the problems associated with operating an international business is that accounting standards and methods vary from country to country. It becomes quite difficult to compare operational results and activity when the accounting methods used to chart such activity differ. The International Congress of Accountants is an association made up of accountants from throughout the world. The purpose of the Congress is to study methods of standardizing accounting methods to allow easy application and comparison across international borders. The Congress meets every five years to discuss ongoing issues as well as new ideas or problems.

Bibliography

Gray, D. (1993). *Foreign currency translation by United States multinational corporations: Towards a theory of accounting standard selection.* New York: Garland Publishing Inc.

JOHN O'CONNELL

International Court of Justice (ICJ) The ICJ is probably better known as the World Court. The court is actually the judicial branch of the United Nations. The purpose of the court is to hear and rule upon disputes between nations. Although members of the United Nations agree to abide by decisions of the court, this has not always been the case in the past. The court may offer decisions but must seek the backing of the United Nations if compliance with its decisions is not achieved.

The court is based in the Hague, the Netherlands, and has fifteen sitting justices. The court presides over United Nation's Charter issues, breaching of international treaties or agreements, or any other question brought to its attention by a member of the United Nations.

JOHN O'CONNELL

international debt rating The success of a financial institution or other organization with high capital needs is closely tied to its ability to secure funds and the price paid for those funds. Banks and other large lenders and borrowers of capital are judged by debt-rating services as to their creditworthiness. A low debt-rating results in funds being difficult to obtain, and if obtained only at a high cost. An organization with a good debt-rating will normally find funds readily available at favorable rates.

Bibliography

Johnson, H. (1993). *New global banker: What every U.S. bank must know to compete internationally.* Hinsdale, IL: Probus Publishing Company Inc.

JOHN O'CONNELL

International Development Association (IDA) Many of the developing nations of the world do not have the ability to meet the financial or other requirements for loans through most programs of the World Bank or other fund providers. Thus, money for development is hard to come by through normal channels. In 1960, the International Bank for Reconstruction and Development (IBRD) established the IDA to provide funding (at subsidized rates) to the poorest nations to facilitate economic development. The IDA's efforts expedite the development of countries, thereby making them eligible

for other types of assistance with the aim of, eventually, making them financially self-supporting.

Bibliography

Bowker, R. R. (1988). *Development aid: A guide to national and international agencies.* Worburn, Maine: Butterworth-Heinemann.

JOHN O'CONNELL

international division One of the ways of carrying out international operations is to establish a separate division in the company dedicated to international business activity. International divisions are normally only included in larger organizations where international activity is sufficient to warrant the time and expense of establishing such an entity.

It is important to recognize the implications of establishing an international division. Close coordination between this division and all other divisions of the company is extremely important. It must be remembered that if the only responsibility for international activity is held by a particular division, misunderstandings about the overall role in the organization of the division and its personnel are common. Clear delineation of responsibilities and communications channels must be established if an international division is to be a successful part of the organization.

See also **Evolution of global organization**

JOHN O'CONNELL

International Finance Corporation (IFC) The International Finance Corporation was established in 1956 by the World Bank. The purpose of the IFC is to provide funding for private investments in member countries. By concentrating on private investments and enterprises instead of government sponsored and/or guaranteed projects, the IFC hopes to develop private interests separate from those of the government. Without the IFC, capital for private investments may be very difficult to secure in many countries.

JOHN O'CONNELL

international human resources management (HRM)   International human resources management involves managing the factors dealing with persons employed in various fashions by an organization. These factors include: planning for human resource needs; staffing per the plans; training and development, if necessary; developing compensation systems; and evaluating the performance of employees. These factors are the same as those for domestic operations except international HRM must also take into consideration cultural variables between employees' countries of origin, language differences, religious preferences, and a myriad of other factors which differ from country to country. International HRM involves keeping a balance between all employees, thereby allowing employee transfer from country to country. It also allows different management styles to coexist and value differences to be recognized and accommodated.

Bibliography

Acuff, F. (1984). International and domestic human resource functions. *Innovations in International Compensation*, **September**, 3–5.
Brewster, C. & Tyson, S. (1991). International comparisons in *international human resource Management*. London: Pitman.
Dowling, P. J. & Schuler, R. S. (1990). *International dimensions of human resource management*. Boston, MA: PWS-Kent.
Edstron, A. & Lorange, P. (1984). Matching strategy and human resources in multinational corporations. *Journal of International Business Studies*, **15** (2), 125–37.
Ishidi, H. (1986). Transferability of Japanese human resource management abroad. *Human Resource Management*, **259** (1), 103–20.
Martinez, Z. L. & Ricks, D. A. (1989). Multinational parent companies' influence over human resource decisions of affiliates: U.S. forms in Mexico. *Journal of International Business Studies*, **20** (3), 465–87.
Punnett, B. J. (1989). International human resource management in A. Rugman (Ed.) *International Business in Canada*. Toronto, Canada: Prentice-Hall, Canada.
Reynolds, C. (1986). Compensation of overseas personnel in *Handbook of Human Resource Administration*. 2nd edn, New York: McGraw-Hill.
Schuler, R. S. (1993). World class HR departments: Six crucial issues. *The Singapore Accounting and Business Review*, Inaugural Issue, September,

Tung, R. L. (1984). Strategic management of human resources in the multinational enterprise in *Human Resource Management*. New York: John Wiley & Sons.

JOHN O'CONNELL

international integration   This is the process of molding a company's various international activities into a single, unified organization. The integration process centralizes management decisions, thereby reducing the autonomy of foreign subsidiaries or affiliates. The process of international integration allows management to view the organization as truly a single entity with focused goals and objectives instead of a group of independent operations which may or may not have the best interests of the parent company in mind. International integration is generally a precursor to the development of a true global organization.

Bibliography

Peak, M. H. (1991). Developing an international style of management. *Management Review*, **80**, 32–5.

JOHN O'CONNELL

International Labor Organization (ILO)   The International Labor Organization was founded by the League of Nations in 1919 and integrated into the United Nations in 1946. The ILO membership is made up of representatives from labor, management, and government. The ILO's purpose is to establish minimum labor standards as well as provide assistance to governments regarding various issues affecting labor, management, and government.

JOHN O'CONNELL

International Law Commission   A United Nations Commission composed of a group of experts involved in the ongoing development of international law and its codification. The purpose of the Commission is to make international law a more effective means of implementing the principles set forth by the United Nations. The Commission consists of 34 members serving five-year terms.

Bibliography

Weiss, E. B. (1995). *Compliance with international law.* Irvington, NY: Transnational Publishers Inc.

JOHN O'CONNELL

international location   The international location decision is one which is concerned with the location of facilities at the highest level. It is a decision that needs to be made by any organization involved in international operations. Such organizations can include subsidiaries of multinational enterprises, international joint ventures, licensees or franchising operations. They may be involved in a range of different activities such as local assembly, offshore manufacturing or the complete production of goods for global markets. International organizations are also increasingly becoming involved in the delivery of services, particularly since the barriers preventing them being transferred across national boundaries are progressively being removed.

In many respects the international location decision is similar to any decision regarding the location of facilities for a domestic organization. Tangible factors can be taken into account, such as the cost of land, cost of buildings, labor costs, transport costs, etc. Similarly there are intangible factors to be considered, such as environmental constraints and ease of communications.

Perhaps the main thing that distinguishes an international location decision from a domestic one is its strategic dimension. Many organizations choose a particular international location with a view to exploiting the long-term possibilities offered and not simply to meet short-term objectives. Therefore, many of the established techniques for evaluating alternative locations or determining an "optimum" location are only of partial relevance.

The actual method used to determine the location of an international operation will tend to vary according to its type.

Local assembly normally takes place where tariff barriers exist on imported goods, or the assembly costs in the parent company are high, thereby making the products too expensive in the local market. The solution is therefore to use local labor to assemble CKD (complete knock down) or SKD (semi-knock down) kits, thereby avoiding import tariffs or taking advantage of lower local labor costs. Location decisions in this case need to consider the logistics of supplying parts and the availability of suitable low-cost labor.

Offshore manufacturing is where products are made in a foreign country to the design of, and often using parts supplied by, an original equipment manufacturer (or OEM), then reexported to the country of the OEM or to third countries. Therefore it is often restricted to assembly operations with the purpose of exploiting one or more of the local advantages such as reduced labor costs, specialized skills or lower overheads. Where there is a tariff on imported materials this is often overcome by locating in an "export processing zone," which is a tariff free area for export-oriented companies. Location decisions in such situations are influenced by the local costs of production, the incentive and taxation regime, and the ease with which materials, parts, and finished goods can be transported into and out of the country in question.

Complete production of goods for the global market is the approach to international operations commonly encountered in multinational corporations. It is often chosen because it offers the opportunity of achieving good economies of scale since production for every market takes place at just one single location and is fully integrated. Here, the location decision involves finding the best place to manufacture the product, taking into account a wide range of factors such as design capability, engineering competence, and availability of low-cost productive resources, as well as the need to minimize transport costs. This last factor is not too easy to determine because the materials, parts and finished goods can come from, and go to, an enormous number of other countries. The distribution of finished goods can also present difficulties because of the ever changing nature of the market in terms of customer location and product mix.

An alternative and overlapping approach to international location is to consider the configuration of a company's network at an international level. Four configuration strategies have been identified.

Home Country Configuration

The simplest strategy for an organization trading around the world is not to locate plants outside its home country and to export its products to foreign markets. The reason for this might be, for example, that the technology employed in the product is so novel that it needs to be manufactured close to its research and development headquarters. Alternatively, the home location of the company might be part of the attraction of a product (e.g. high fashion garments from Paris).

Regional Configuration

An alternative strategy is to divide the company's international markets into a small number of regions and make each region as self-contained as possible. So, for example, the Pacific region's market would be served by an operation or operations, in that region. Companies might adopt this strategy because their customers demand speedy delivery and prompt after-sales service. If products or services were created outside the region it might be difficult to provide such a level of service without regional warehouses and service centers.

Global Co-ordinated Configuration

The opposite of the regional strategy is the global co-ordinated configuration. Here each plant concentrates on a narrow set of activities and products and then distributes its products to markets around the world. So, for instance, a company might take advantage of low labor costs in one region and the technical support infrastructure in another in order to seek to exploit the particular advantages of each site or region. However, by doing so it does place a co-ordination requirement on the headquarters of the company. All product allocations, operations capacities and movement of products are planned centrally.

Combined Regional and Global Co-ordinated Configuration

The regional strategy has the advantage of organizational simplicity and clarity, the global co-ordinated strategy of well exploited regional advantages. Firms often attempt to seek the advantages of both by adopting a compromise between them. Under such a strategy regions might be reasonably autonomous, but certain products could still be moved between regions to take advantage of particular regional circumstances.

Bibliography

Dicken, P. (1992). *Global shift*. London: Paul Chapman.

DuBois, F. C. & Oliff, M. D. (1992). International manufacturing configuration and competitive priorities. In C. A. Voss (Ed.), *Manufacturing strategy: Process and content*. London: Chapman and Hall.

DAVID BENNETT

international management   The process of planning, staffing, organizing, and controlling international business activities. International management thinking is normally not a part of domestic business operations. When an organization first ventures into international trade activities, management is not prepared to face its challenges. Consultants are often used to fill in the gaps in knowledge and approach to multinational business activities. As the organization grows in terms of its reliance on international business for market growth and profits, managers begin to more fully appreciate other cultures and economic systems. Language skills and cultural awareness increase. More growth results in managers striving to standardize their products for worldwide distribution. The world begins to appear as a single market and management must be prepared to deal with all aspects of that market.

Bibliography

Austin, J. E. (1990). *Managing in developing countries: Strategic analysis and operating techniques*. New York: Free Press.

Beamish, P., Killing, J. P. & Lecraw, D. J. (1991). *International management text and cases*. Homewood, IL: Irwin.

Daniels, J. D. & Radebaugh, L. H. (1993). *International dimensions of contemporary business*. Boston, MA: PWS-Kent Publishing.

Davidson, W. H. & de la Torre, J. (1989). *Managing the global corporation*. New York: McGraw-Hill.

Deresky, Helen (1994). *International management*. 1st edn, New York: HarperCollins.

Hodgetts, R. H. & Luthans, F. (1994). *International management.* 2nd edn, New York: McGraw-Hill Inc.

Lane, H. W. & Distefano, J. J. (1988). *International management behavior.* Scarborough, Ontario: Nelson Canada.

Lessem, R. (1989). *Global management principles.* London: Prentice-Hall International.

Mahini, A. (1988). *Making decisions in multinational corporations – managing relations with sovereign governments.* New York: John Wiley & Sons.

Mendenhall, M., Punnett, B. & Ricks, D. (1995). *Global management.* Cambridge, MA: Blackwell Publishers.

Punnett, B. J. & Ricks, D. (1992). *International business.* Boston, MA: PWS-Kent.

JOHN O'CONNELL

international manager (evaluation) *see* PERFORMANCE EVALUATION

International Maritime Bureau (IMB) The International Chamber of Commerce has established the International Maritime Bureau to identify and inform the proper authorities of ocean transit related crime and fraud. The Bureau operates under the authority of a multilateral treaty entered into by the largest and most economically developed nations of the world. These nations stand to lose the most from piracy, fraud, and other crimes associated with the international transportation of goods over the seas. Although the IMB has not stopped all of the criminal activity associated with maritime trade, its existence does act as a deterrent for such activity.

See also **International Chamber of Commerce**

JOHN O'CONNELL

International Maritime Organization (IMO) This agency of the United Nations has responsibility for promoting safety associated with maritime activities. The organization develops and implements shipping safety standards and acts as the enforcement bureau for the international Rules of Navigation. Through its research and training activities, the IMO seeks to implement changes to make the entire process of maritime transportation safer. A relatively new, but major, responsibility of the organization is to develop programs to educate people and governments about fighting pollution associated with marine transportation. The organization began in 1948 and continues today as a major force affecting marine transportation.

See also **International Maritime Satellite Organization**

JOHN O'CONNELL

International Maritime Satellite Organization (INMARSAT) The advent of satellite tracking capabilities has extended man's ability to keep track of what is going on around the world. One area of great importance is that of transport by ship. Prior to satellite technology it was very difficult to track and communicate with ships throughout the world. In time of distress a ship might not be able to be located. INMARSAT began in 1976 to monitor shipping movements and establish communications through the use of satellites. This allowed for quicker response in time of distress as well as communication whenever necessary. In the 1980s INMARSAT was extended to cover aircraft movement and land-based transportation. It is now possible to track even a single truck on the road. The use of INMARSAT for emergencies and for logistical applications is just now being fully realized. INMARSAT's homebase is in London.

JOHN O'CONNELL

international marketing International marketing may refer to two situations: (1) the activities of organizations to determine and take advantage of opportunities to sell goods or services internationally. This type of marketing may involve both large and small companies. Or (2) the standardization of products by an organization which seeks to take advantage of the large-scale production and distribution of those products throughout the world. This type of marketing is normally carried out by the largest of organizations.

Bibliography

Albaum, Gerald, Strandskov, Jesper, Duerr, Edwin & Dowd, Lawrence (1994). *International marketing and export management.* 2nd edn, Wokingham: Addison-Wesley.
Buzzell, R. D., Quelch, J. A. & Bartlett, C. A. (1995). *Global marketing management: Cases and readings.* Reading, MA: Addison-Wesley.
Kaynak, E., & Ghauri, P. N. (eds) (1994). *Euromarketing: Effective strategies for international trade and export.* Binghamton, NY: Haworth Press Inc.
Pradeep, A. R. & Preble, J. F. (1987). Standardization of marketing strategy by multinationals. *International Marketing Review*, Autumn, 18–28.
Ricks, D. A. (1983). *Big business blunders: Mistakes in multinational marketing.* Homewood, IL: Dow Jones-Irwin.
Root, E. R. (1994). *Entry strategies for international markets.* New York: Lexington Books.
Toyne, B & Walters, Peter, G. P. (1993). *Global marketing management.* Boston: Allyn and Bacon.
Tse, D. K., Lee, K., Vertinsky, I. & Wehrung, D. A. (1988). Does culture matter? A cross-cultural study of executive choice, decisiveness, and risk adjustments in international marketing. *Journal of Marketing*, 52 (4), 81–95.
Turnbull, P. W. (1987). Interaction and international marketing: An investment process. *International Marketing Review*, Winter, 7–19.

JOHN O'CONNELL

International Monetary Fund (IMF)   The International Monetary Fund began operations in 1947 as a result of agreements reached at the Bretton Woods Conference. Key operations of the IMF can be placed into two categories: (1) developing standardized rules for the financing of international trade; and (2) providing funds for nations with temporary balance-of-payments difficulties. The IMF undertakes a number of different loan activities depending upon the type and extent of need of any particular country. The IMF sets forth the criteria which must be met in order to qualify for a loan as well as the terms of the loan itself.

From the time of its first activities in 1947, the International Monetary Fund expanded its operations to include funding for nations suffering temporary declines in export revenues, the establishment of what are referred to as Special Drawing Rights (SDRs), and the development of standards which country borrowers must abide by in order to maintain access to IMF funds and other services. The IMF has over 150 country members. In recent years the IMF has focused on lending to less Developed Countries (LDCs).

See also **World Bank**

Bibliography

Humphreys, N. K. (1993). *Historical dictionary of the International Monetary Fund.* Lanhau, Maryland: Scarecrow Press Inc.
Salda, A. C. (1992). *The International Monetary Fund: A selected bibliography.* New Brunswick, NJ: Transaction Publishers.
Stiles, K. (1991). *Negotiating debt: The IMF lending process.* Boulder, CO: Westview Press.

JOHN O'CONNELL

international organizations (IOs or INTORGs)   Although the term may seem to describe any organization operating across borders, its actual meaning is much more specific. International organizations are those long-term or permanent organizations which advocate a cause (e.g., environmental concerns), promote specific interests (e.g., trade or economic development institutions), or generally seek to advocate cooperation and understanding on a worldwide basis (e.g., health organizations). International organizations may be formalized by governmental action (trade agreements, etc.) or stay in the private sector (environmental concerns) but the end product of each type of organization is the pursuit of members' goals and objectives on an international scale.

JOHN O'CONNELL

international patenting   One of the most troublesome problems associated with international distribution of products is protecting the design, process, or other intellectual property rights associated with the product. Unless a country offers protection against the theft of intellectual property rights the maker of a product is in danger of having the product copied and sold by locals of that nation. In 1970 the World Intellectual Property Organization (WPO) adopted the Patent Cooperation Treaty (PCT) to assist in protecting property rights of inventors. The PCT has been signed by approximately 50 countries and attempts to provide patent protection in all member countries through a single application (instead of the 50 applications formerly required).

It is important for patent holders to determine the extent of any particular country's adherence to patent agreements. There have been times in the past when a country has agreed to adhere to safeguarding intellectual and other property rights, but has failed to carry out that agreement.

Bibliography

Stewart, G. R. (Ed.) (1994). *International trade and intellectual property: The search for a balanced system.* Boulder, CO: Westview Press.

JOHN O'CONNELL

international planning   Planning is the process of determining the steps to achieve specific goals and objectives. In the international arena the planning process includes reviewing the various factors normally associated with business functions (sources of labor, materials, financing, etc.) as well as additional factors associated with differences in culture, monetary systems, language, and legal systems. The planning process includes an evaluation of an organization's strong and weak points and the identification of core competencies from which to build a strong organization. One of the most important aspects of international planning is the identification of possible threats to the viability of the organization. Such threats are normally associated with foreign governments, competitors, or cultural differences which may overwhelm an otherwise strong organization.

Bibliography

Alkhafaji, A. F. (1995). *Competitive global management.* Delray Beach, FL: St. Lucia Press.
Bartlett, Christopher, A. & Ghoshal, Sumantra (1992). *Transnational management.* 2nd edn, Chicago: Irwin.

Beamish, P. W., Killing, J. P., Lecraw, D. & Morrison, A. J. (1994). *International management: Text and cases.* 2nd edn, Burr Ridge, Illinois: Irwin.
Deresky, Helen (1994). *International management.* 1st edn, New York: HarperCollins.
Mead, Richard (1994). *International management: Cross cultural dimensions.* Cambridge, MA: Blackwell Publishers.
Mendenhall, M., Punnett, B. & Ricks, D. (1995). *Global management.* Cambridge, MA: Blackwell Publishers.

JOHN O'CONNELL

international product life cycle   This is a relatively new theory (originating in the mid-1960s) attempting to describe the evolution of products through various stages: (1) local sales in the country in which the product was first produced; (2) exporting the goods; (3) production in a country which formerly imported the goods; and (4) becoming an import to the country in which the production process for the goods was originally developed. Through the cycle the original producing country eventually becomes an importer of the goods.

When an organization develops the technology to successfully produce a quality product (which is in demand) at low cost, that product will secure a local market relatively quickly. Take for example, color televisions. When color televisions first came on the market, local companies which had the technology produced and sold most of the TV sets. As more and more sets were sold more companies entered the market to produce and sell goods. TVs were exported as the local demand was met. As exports grew, the demands of high quantity production brought about standardization of product to take advantage of economies of scale.

As overseas sales prospered, it became evident that if the costs of transportation, tariffs, etc. could be saved, lower costs and competitive advantage would accrue to the company. Overseas production units are then established to service the foreign markets. More and more of domestic product is transferred to foreign factories as it becomes evident that labor and materials costs are also less. As more production takes place overseas, competition develops in foreign countries to meet their own demand. Eventually, production in developing countries supplants the production of the originator of the color television. Less costly production may eventually lead the original innovative country (the developer of the color TV) to become an importer of the item to meet its own demand. In the advanced industrialized nations this has occurred with automobile production, textiles, computers, and other products as well.

Bibliography

Albaum, Gerald, Strandskov, Jesper, Duerr, Edwin & Dowd, Lawrence (1994). *International marketing and export management.* 2nd edn, Wokingham: Addison-Wesley.

Davidson, W. H. & de la Torre, J. (1989). *Managing the global corporation.* New York: McGraw-Hill.

Root, E. R. (1994). *Entry strategies for international markets.* New York: Lexington Books.

Toyne, B & Walters, Peter, G. P. (1993). *Global marketing management.* Boston: Allyn and Bacon.

JOHN O'CONNELL

international product standards *see* INTERNATIONAL STANDARDS ORGANIZATION

international selection   This is the process used to determine which employees will be considered for overseas assignments. The factors associated with international selection have both similarities to and differences from the selection process for home country (domestic) employment. Both types of selection include basic qualifications for work competency (work skills, technical knowledge, etc.); work ethic (absenteeism rate, etc.) and general managerial skills. The expatriate, however, must have a number of additional qualities in order to be successful. These qualities normally include among other factors: flexibility in thought and action; ability to listen; empathy; acceptance of change; tolerance of cultural differences; and good language skills.

One of the major problems with expatriate selection is that having a different selection process for local and international positions may run afoul of laws against discrimination in some countries. For example, it is difficult for a person in a country which provides equal rights to men and women to accept that in other countries women may not be able to obtain driver's licenses, cannot go out unescorted, or a number of other things which would be blatant discrimination in their own countries. Is it justifiable under these conditions to avoid hiring women for jobs in such a country? A difficult question and one which must be dealt with considering both the laws against discrimination in various countries and practical considerations of getting a job done.

Bibliography

Brown, R. (1987). How to choose the best expatriates. *Personnel Management,* **June,** 67.

Harvey, M. (1985). The executive family: An over-looked variable in international assignments. *Journal of International Business Studies,* Columbia Journal of World Business, 785–800.

Heller, J. E. (1980). Criteria for selecting an international manager. *Personnel,* May–June, 47–55.

Martinez, Z. L. & Ricks, D. A. (1989). Multinational parent companies' influence over human resource decisions of affiliates: U.S. forms in Mexico. *Journal of International Business Studies,* **20 (3),** 465–87.

Punnett, B. J., Crocker, O. & Stevens, M. A. (1992). The challenge for women expatriates and their spouses: Some empirical evidence. *International Journal of Human Resource Management,* **3 (3),** 585–92.

Tung, R. L. (1984). Strategic management of human resources in the multinational enterprise in *Human Resource Management.* New York: John Wiley & Sons.

Zeira, Y. & Banai, M. (1985). Selection of expatriate managers in MNC's: The host environment point of view. *International Studies of Management and Organization,* **15 (1),** 33–51.

JOHN O'CONNELL

International Standards Organization (ISO)   The ISO was established in 1946 to develop standards for measurements used in the scientific field, international trade, commerce, and industry. The development of the organization was in response to common problems associated with differing systems of measurement existing in different countries. It is the goal of the ISO to develop uniformity of measures applicable to international commerce.

JOHN O'CONNELL

international trade administration   *see*
UNITED STATES INTERNATIONAL TRADE
ADMINISTRATION

International Trade Commission (ITC)
The ITC along with several other government
departments and commissions oversees international trade between the US and the rest of the
world. The International Trade Commission is a
Untied States government agency which provides advice, statistics on trade, and information
reports to the President and the Congress of the
United States.

JOHN O'CONNELL

international union   A labor union with
membership which spans international boundaries. Probably, the most powerful of the
international unions with respect to international
trade is the International Longshoremen's and
Warehousemen's Union. International unions
may be able to provide support for trade
activities through their impact in many different
countries. On the other hand they may also be
problematic, for exactly the same reason. With a
local union, only local production or transit are
normally affected by a strike or other labor-
related problem. With an international union,
however, the impact may be much broader
geographically.

JOHN O'CONNELL

inventory management   Many organizations rely upon a supply of raw materials or
products to complete their daily tasks. Manufacturers rely upon materials or subproducts,
food processors rely upon a steady supply of
agricultural products, retailers and wholesalers
rely upon finished products to distribute.
Businesses may invest large amounts of money
to keep stocks of needed materials or products
readily available. Inventory levels must be carefully managed or problems could occur. If
inventory levels are higher than necessary an
organization ties up funds which may be better
used elsewhere. High inventory levels also run
the risk of becoming outdated or unsuitable for

use. If too little inventory is kept, an organization
runs the risk of being unable to fill customer
demand, thus paving the way for competition to
enter the market. A great deal of skill is necessary
to plan for the correct balance between inventory, customer demand, and production needs.

A Japanese system of inventory control has
become popular in some organizations. The
system is referred to as "just-in-time" inven-
torying. Although the concept of having just
enough inventory to meet current needs makes
sense from an efficiency point of view, there are
also some potential problems associated with
just-in-time measures. For example, what if an
organization's supplier of goods goes out of
business or suffers a loss forcing a shutdown?
Just-in-time systems may result in a shutdown
of multiple businesses which are dependent
upon one another for supplies. This potential
problem must be weighed against the possible
inventory financing savings during normal
operations.

See also **Just-in-time**

Bibliography

Daniels, J. D. & Radebaugh, L. E. (1994). *International business: Environments and operations.* 7th
   edn, Reading, MA: Addison-Wesley Publishing.
Rugman, A. M. & Hodgetts, R. M. (1995). *International management: A strategic management
   approach.* New York: McGraw-Hill Inc.
Steudel, H. J. (1992). *Manufacturing in the nineties:
   How to become a mean, lean, world-class competitor.*
   New York: Van Nostrand Reinhold.

JOHN O'CONNELL

investment banking   Investment bankers
perform three important functions for organizations: (1) They purchase new issues of securities
from the issuing company in hopes of reselling
them at a profit. This is referred to as under-
writing an issue. (2) They act as an agent of the
issuing company in selling its securities. A
commission is generally received from sales.
And (3) investment banks offer management
advice with regard to securities issued by a
company. Investment bankers offer the above

three services to private organizations and governmental units both domestically and internationally.

Bibliography

Bendaavid, D. Rosenbloom, A. (eds) (1990). *The handbook of international mergers and acquisitions.* Englewood Cliffs, NJ: Prentice-Hall.
Logue, D. E. (Ed.) (1995). *The WG&L handbook of international finance.* Cincinnati, OH: South-Western Publishing Company.

JOHN O'CONNELL

investment barriers   *see* BARRIERS

investment guarantee program   An investment guarantee program offers protection against some of the risks associated with international operations. Investment guarantee programs seek to provide incentives for local investors to invest overseas. Examples of guarantee programs include: insurance for the credit risk (failure or inability of buyers to pay for goods after delivery) and for political risk (expropriation, inconvertibility of currency, etc.). Programs such as these reduce the overall risk for an exporter, thereby providing incentive to enter foreign trade.

JOHN O'CONNELL

investment incentives   Investment incentives are offers which are intended to lure prospective investors to place their money in a particular country or in a particular city or region. Incentives often include: tax holidays (reduction or elimination of property taxes for a stated period of time); sharing of development costs (plant sites, roads, communications systems needed for operations, etc.); low interest financing; changes in regulations to allow certain types or operations; and others. Incentives are offered in return for a foreign investor building a plant or increasing the size of existing facilities. Capital investments are normally long term and give benefit to local economies for years to come.

JOHN O'CONNELL

irrevocable letter of credit   An irrevocable letter of credit cannot be withdrawn without the consent of all parties. Parties to a letter of credit include the importer, the exporter, and the importer's and exporter's banks. Payment of the exporter is more certain when using an irrevocable letter of credit.

See also **Letter of credit, Revocable letter of credit**

JOHN O'CONNELL

irrevocable transferable letter of credit   The transferable nature of this type of letter of credit allows an exporter to convey a portion of its proceeds to another party. For example, this type of letter may be used to guarantee payment to an exporter's suppliers or for anyone else's benefit as determined by the exporter. The irrevocable nature of the letter means that the details of the letter cannot be changed without the consent of all parties to the letter of credit.

See also **Letter of credit**

JOHN O'CONNELL

Islamic Development Bank (ISDB)   One of the products of the 1973 Islamic Conference was the establishment of the Islamic Development Bank. Unlike most banks in the world, the ISDB's financing activities are based upon the principles of Islam. Thus, the activities of the bank are limited to Arab member countries and to investment projects which are considered worthwhile undertakings under Islamic law. Other than being governed by the principles of Islam, the bank is much like any other development institution. It provides loans for economic development sponsored by government or private sectors of member nations.

Bibliography

Ludlow, N. H. (1988). *A practical guide to the development bank business: How to identify it, market to it, and win it.* Washington, D.C.: Development Bank Associates Inc.

JOHN O'CONNELL

ISO 9000   In 1987 the International Standards Organization (ISO) introduced a number of product and service quality standards. The intent of the ISO 9000 standards (known as EN 29,000 in Europe) was to entice firms to make quality their highest priority. The ISO 9000 standards set forth a series of requirements related to product research, development and testing, purchasing, installation and inspection, employee training, and the institution of a quality management system to continually monitor the remainder of a company's operations. ISO 9000 makes provision for companies to become certified as complying with its procedures. A company that qualifies is normally viewed as above average by buyers and sellers alike. Thus, certification is a good image builder as well as a commitment to quality production and service.

Bibliography

Daniels, J. D. & Radebaugh, L. E. (1994). *International business: Environments and operations.* 7th edn, Reading, MA: Addison-Wesley Publishing.

JOHN O'CONNELL

issuing bank   In relation to international trade, this is a bank that prepares and issues a letter of credit or a documentary draft for a client. The bank is referred to as the issuing bank.

See also **Documentary draft; Letter of credit**

JOHN O'CONNELL

ITC *see* INTERNATIONAL TRADE COMMISSION

—— J ——

Jamaica Agreement (Jamaica Accord)
After years of discussion, the international community entered into one of the most important monetary agreements in history. In 1976, the Jamaica Agreement eliminated pegging of the price of gold to the US dollar (then valued at $32 per ounce) and accepted the concept of managed float.

See also **Managed float**

JOHN O'CONNELL

Japan Sea Basin (economic cooperation zone)   Although still in the idea stage (in 1996), the Japan Sea Basin economic cooperation zone could develop into one of the major trading blocs in the world. The seeds for the trade zone came from officials of the Japanese Ministry of International Trade and Industry with the help of university theorists. The zone would have included China, Japan, North Korea, South Korea, and the former USSR. Doubts exist as to its viability because of recent problems between North and South Korea and the demise of the USSR. The idea, however, still has a good deal of support. If political problems could be overcome, the trading zone would be a formidable competitor to the other trading blocs of the world.

JOHN O'CONNELL

jettison   There are times when a ship captain must take action to save a vessel from sinking or running aground. One of the actions which may be necessary is to jettison cargo or equipment. Jettisoning means to purposefully throw goods overboard in order to save the venture. For example, if a ship is taking on water and begins to list, the captain may elect to jettison deck cargo in order to right the ship. The decision to jettison is entirely up to the master of the ship.

Cargo jettisoned in order to save the venture is subject to general average. Briefly, general average means that all interests in the venture share proportionately in compensating the owners of any jettisoned cargo.

See also **General average**

JOHN O'CONNELL

joint venture   An agreement by companies to share a business venture. This is a very common method of entering a foreign market because it allows firms to share their strengths (the host company's knowledge of the local market and cultural differences; the foreign company's products, processes or financial strength) in the production and marketing of products or services.

Joint ventures may be formally established through the formation of a third organization (owned by the joint-venture parties) or informally by means of a contractual arrangement specifying the responsibilities of each party. As more countries reduce barriers to foreign ownership of domestic businesses, more and more foreign companies are opting for equity positions of higher and higher percentages in domestic firms. Although equity positions are actually a form of joint venture, recent activity suggests that most companies are moving toward full ownership or solid control of foreign operations.

See also **Market entry strategies**

Bibliography

Beamish, P. W. (1985). The characteristics of joint ventures in developed and developing countries. *The Columbia Journal of World Business*, **20**.

Bubant, J. (Ed.) (1992). *Joint ventures in East Asia: Legal issues*. Norwell, Maine: Kluwer Academic Publishers.

Butterworth Legal Publishers (1993). *Joint ventures with international partners: Analysis and forms.* Salem, NH: Butterworth Legal Publishers.

Contractor, F. J. (1986). Strategies for structuring joint ventures: A negotiations planning paradigm. *Columbia Journal of World Business*, Summer, 30–9.

Geringer, J. M. (1991). Strategic determinants of partner selection criteria in international joint ventures. *Journal of International Business Studies*, **22** (1), 41–62.

Shan, W. (1991). Environment risks and joint venture sharing arrangements. *Journal of International Business Studies*, **22** (4), 555–78.

JOHN O'CONNELL

just-in-time An inventory system which keeps as little inventory in stock as possible. A just-in-time system continuously orders small amounts of needed raw materials or products to coincide with their use in the sales or production function of a business. This allows a business to operate more efficiently.

Just-in-time inventory systems are very popular in Japan. A problem arose with this type of inventory system after the 1995 Kobe earthquake when many suppliers were knocked out of business. Many Japanese buyers using just-in-time inventory systems did not have sufficient inventory on hand to continue operations for even a few days after the earthquake. This resulted in a ripple effect that had a dramatic short-term impact on the Japanese economy.

Bibliography

Daniels, J. D. & Radebaugh, L. E. (1994). *International business: Environments and operations*. 7th edn, Reading, MA: Addison-Wesley Publishing.

JOHN O'CONNELL

K

kanban   The Japanese word for "just-in-time" inventory methods. The just-in-time inventory system does not allow the stockpiling of inventory. Instead inventory is ordered as needed. The system is closely linked to electronic inventory reordering systems which automatically order small amounts of inventory as existing inventory is being used.

See also **Just-in-time**

JOHN O'CONNELL

key currency   Because of their strength and international acceptance several currencies are referred to as being "key" or important to world trade. Key currencies include those issued by Japan, West Germany, France, Britain, Italy, Canada, or the United States. Many international financial valuations are pegged to these currencies, including establishing exchange rates and settling international trade financial issues.

JOHN O'CONNELL

key industry   A key industry is one which plays a major role in the economy of a country. The industry may be key because it is the only major industry, the industry employing the most people, the largest source of foreign trade, or for other reasons. Key industries are often the focal point of protectionist activity by a country. In order to protect the viability of a key industry, a government may impose restrictions on importation of goods produced by that industry or subsidize the industry to assure its competitive standing.

JOHN O'CONNELL

kickbacks   Kickbacks are a form of bribery. They are usually associated with purchases of goods or services. When the order is made a portion of the sales price is secretly given back (kickback) to the purchasing agent. Kickbacks are considered illegal in most countries.

See also **Bribery**

JOHN O'CONNELL

knock-offs   *see* BRAND PIRACY

Kyoto Convention   At a meeting in Kyoto, Japan in 1973, representatives of the Customs Cooperation Council agreed to adopt standardized rules pertaining to the handling of cargo and its documentation. The purpose of the agreement was to attempt to reconcile procedures related to cargo handling and documentation between countries. Member countries of the Customs Cooperation Council agreed to comply with practices adopted at the Kyoto meeting. Standardization of practices reduces the problems associated with international trade. The actual name given to the Kyoto conference was the Kyoto Convention on the Simplification and Harmonization of Customs Procedures.

Bibliography

Serko, D. (1991). *Import practice: Customs and international trade law.* New York: Practicing Law Institute.

JOHN O'CONNELL

—— L ——

labeling   Labeling involves the packaging, design, color, and wording used to enclose goods for sale. Labeling is an important part of marketing a product. International marketing people must be sensitive to the meaning given to a certain color, number, design, or symbol by a particular culture. Designs and color schemes have been known to offend or even bring possible legal or religious sanctions against a manufacturer or distributor of a product. It is important to seek local review of designs and wording before attempting to distribute a product in another country.

Bibliography

Ricks, D. A. (1983). *Big business blunders: Mistakes in multinational marketing*. Homewood, IL: Dow Jones-Irwin.

JOHN O'CONNELL

labor agreements   A labor agreement is an agreement between management and employees concerning the terms of employment. Generally, labor agreements are pursued through the process of collective bargaining between management and labor unions. The strength of labor unions varies considerably throughout the world. Some countries are virtually controlled by unions while others are relatively free from union influence.

JOHN O'CONNELL

labor contract   Periodically, business management and employees meet to work out details related to continued employment. Wages, hours of work, work conditions, etc. generally become a part of a written labor contract. In some countries (Japan, for example) public demonstrations by employees to bring attention to their demands occur on an annual basis. In other countries, strikes or labor unrest are common around negotiation time. Many developing countries still do not have large numbers of actual labor contracts because the system of employer/employee relations and negotiation is just developing. When a labor contract is concluded between employer and employees the process is generally referred to as "collective bargaining."

JOHN O'CONNELL

labor intensive   This term may be used to describe either a job or an entire industry which relies heavily on manual labor rather than mechanical means to produce a product or service. A situation in which investment in facilities or materials is emphasized is referred to as capital intensive. Labor-intensive activities include delivering pizza, insurance sales, psychotherapy, landscaping, and many others. Industries which are capital intensive include automobile production and steel production. As technological advances continue labor-intensive jobs and industries are becoming more capital intensive. Agricultural pursuits in industrialized countries are an example of this phenomena. Where formerly it was relatively simple to enter the farming business in the United States, it now takes a great deal of capital investment.

JOHN O'CONNELL

labor law   This is a very important topic for managers of multinational companies (MNCs). The rights of employees, compensation items, severance pay, benefits, right to strike and other important labor issues are many times spelled out in the labor laws of each country. Because such laws vary so greatly between countries it is extremely important for someone in a company to be responsible for becoming familiar with them. A few examples will verify the importance of labor law knowledge and understanding. Some countries make it very difficult to fire an employee or to downsize an operation (re-engineering as it is now referred to). One way to make it difficult is to require severance payments, which can exceed $100,000 US per employee in some countries. In some countries employers are legally responsible for work-related injuries or diseases contracted by the employee. This causes high insurance rates and other additional costs for employers. Some countries require an employer to provide retraining for employees released from employment. Others require an extension of certain employee benefits for employees and family members for a period of time after the employee leaves employment. Knowing the laws which apply to workers will allow an organization to make better decisions regarding location of operations or the most effective entry strategy. It may be that franchising or some other form of partnership is best in countries with strict and costly labor laws, while a subsidiary is better in another country.

Bibliography

Litka, M. (1991). *International dimensions of the legal environment of business.* 2nd edn, Boston, MA: PWS-Kent Publishing Company.
Sarachek, B. (1994). *International business law: A guide for executives with case examples.* Pennington, NY: Darwin Press Inc.
Weiss, E. B. (1995). *Compliance with international law.* Irvington, NY: Transnational Publishers Inc.

JOHN O'CONNELL

labor markets   A labor market is the source of employment for workers in a particular country. This means the industries and institutions which offer employment and the methods used to link workers to those sources of employment. When the labor market is good, jobs are plentiful. When the labor market is poor, jobs are scarce.

With the opening of international borders and the privatization of formerly government operations in some countries, the labor market is becoming more regional. Thus, workers are prone to move from country to country in search of employment opportunities.

JOHN O'CONNELL

LAFTA   *see* LATIN AMERICAN FREE TRADE ASSOCIATION

lags   When local companies enter into joint ventures or borrow funds from foreign investors, payments made to partners or debt payments are usually made in the home currency of the local company (unless the contractual arrangements specify otherwise). Under these circumstances it may be beneficial from time to time to delay (lag) payments to partners or creditors. For example, if the value of the local currency has increased, delaying payments will allow the local company to take advantage of the situation.

See also **Leads**

Bibliography

Celi, L. J. & Rutizer, B. (1991). *Global cash management.* 1st edn, New York: Harper Business (HarperCollins).
Eiteman, D. K., Stonehill, A. J. & Moffett, M. H. (1992). *Multinational business finance.* 6th edn, Reading, MA: Addison-Wesley Publishing.

JOHN O'CONNELL

LAIA   *see* LATIN AMERICAN INTEGRATION ASSOCIATION

land bridge   The old adage "a straight line is the shortest distance between two points" applies to the shipping of goods as well. This poses problems, however, when shipment is to be made by sea but a continent lies between the point of origin and the point of destination. For example, to ship by sea from Europe to Hawaii one would have to face the treacherous seas off the tip of South America, as well as travel thousands of miles away from a straight line course. The concept of a land bridge is a simple one: where land interrupts the sea transport of goods, ship across the land and reload on ships to complete the voyage. Thus, goods shipped by sea from Europe to Hawaii may go by ship to New York; by land to California and back on ship for the remainder of the journey. Efficient use of land bridge shipping requires a good deal of coordination between modes of shipment.

JOHN O'CONNELL

landed value   Landed value is the market value of goods on the day they are offloaded from a vessel. It is possible that the market could change substantially on long voyages. Thus, the landed value of goods could be different than the value of the same goods when first shipped.

JOHN O'CONNELL

landing costs   A charge made for unloading cargo from a ship when it reaches its destination. Such charges become a part of the ultimate price of the goods.

JOHN O'CONNELL

Latin American Free Trade Association (LAFTA)   This was one of the original regional organizations seeking to improve trading conditions between member countries. Founded in 1960, LAFTA attempted to promote trade between member nations by eliminating tariffs and other barriers between association countries. LAFTA consisted of eleven countries: Argentina, Bolivia, Brazil, Chile, Colombia, Ecuador, Mexico, Paraguay, Peru, Uruguay, and Venezuela. The association was reorganized into the Latin American Integration Association in 1980. The membership in the old and new organization remained the same.

See also **Latin American Integration Association**

Bibliography

Winham, G. R. (1992). *The evolution of international trade agreements.* Toronto, Ontario: University of Toronto Press.

JOHN O'CONNELL

Latin American Integration Association (LAIA)   The LAIA is the successor of the Latin AMERICAN FREE TRADE ASSOCIATION (LAFTA). The LAIA carries on the same types of activities to increase the possibility of trade between association countries. The association is developing agreements between its members which are planned to lead to a trading bloc of Latin American countries. This should prove to be a very important economic development for the region. Members of the Latin American Integration Association are: Argentina, Bolivia, Brazil, Chile, Colombia, Ecuador, Mexico, Paraguay, Peru, Uruguay, and Venezuela. The association is located in Montevideo, Uruguay.

Bibliography

Winham, G. R. (1992). *The evolution of international trade agreements.* Toronto, Ontario: University of Toronto Press.

JOHN O'CONNELL

laundering   *see* MONEY LAUNDERING

law of the sea   *see* MARITIME LAW

LDC   *see* LESS DEVELOPED COUNTRY

leads   To pay financial obligations before they are due. Unless the contractual agreement specifies otherwise, joint-venture partners or other interests are paid in the currency of the host country. When this occurs, there may be times when it is beneficial to the host organization to pay off debt or other obligations prior to the date actually due. For example, if a currency is devalued it benefits the local company to pay foreign partners or creditors with low value currency ahead of time. That is, the local company "leads" its payments.

See also **Lags**

JOHN O'CONNELL

leads and lags The acceleration (lead) or delay (lag) in paying foreign partners or creditors in order to take advantage of changing currency valuations.

See also **Lags; Leads**

JOHN O'CONNELL

League of Arab States In 1945 a group of Arab nations entered into an agreement forming the League of Arab States. The League is currently involved in promoting economic and cultural cooperation among its members. The members of the League are: Algeria, Bahrain, Djibouti, Egypt, Iraq, Jordan, Kuwait, Lebanon, Libya, Mauritania, Morocco, Oman, Syria, Tunisia, United Arab Emirates, and Yemen. The League has sponsored the Arab Bank for Economic Development and the Arab Monetary Fund to assist with economic development of the region. The League is also known as the Arab League.

JOHN O'CONNELL

least developed country (LLDC) A least developed country is the lowest on the scale of economic development. Generally, an LLDC developed has few natural resources; lacks an industrial base of almost any kind; has problems in continually feeding its population; has a very high rate of illiteracy; and has a government which is prone to instability. The largest number of least developed countries is in Africa. Although the United Nations and other organizations have special programs for such countries, the economic problems are so great that even assistance from outside sources does little to stem the tide of poverty.

Bibliography

Kozminski, A. K. (1993). *Catching up? Organizational and management change in the ex-socialist block.* Albany, NY: State University of New York Press.

JOHN O'CONNELL

legal system A legal system dictates the process used to arrive at decisions concerning disputes between parties. Although the exact nature of legal systems vary throughout the world there are three major categories into which most systems would fit.

1 Civil law: This system of law depends upon a written body of laws to determine the outcome of legal disputes. Unlike common law, which relies upon past decisions, civil law is linked to the codes and statutes in force in a particular country. This means that as one moves from country to country (assuming all have civil law systems) the legal interpretation of an action or a contract will vary. When organizations seek to become multinational, they should also seek expert assistance in reviewing the various codes and statutes which demand their compliance. Civil law systems exist in most of Europe, Latin America, some African countries, and Japan.

2 Common Law: Under this system of law each situation is subject to review based upon the precedents established through prior court rulings and from custom of the country. Although not restricted to them, common law is found mainly in English-speaking countries. Matters of law and dispute are dealt with by the system employing a judge and jury. Contract interpretation under common law is often more liberal than under other systems. Thus the terminology used in contractual agreements must be precise and clearly express the intent of the parties.

3 Code law: A system of law based upon the interpretation of teachings included in a religious text. For example, Muslim Law is a code law based upon the Koran. Because of its deep religious roots, code law is sometimes referred to as "revealed" law or as in being sent from the scriptures. For interna-

tional businesses from common or civil law countries, code law is probably the most difficult of all to understand. Since the basis of code law is a religious text, those not familiar with the writing may be at a great disadvantage in seeking decisions under its rules.

A problem associated with varying legal systems is determining which system has jurisdiction over contracts or dispute settlement. This problem is normally dealt with in the contractual arrangement between the parties and also on the basis of the jurisdiction in which the contract was signed. Because of problems dealing with different systems of law, many organizations rely upon other methods of settling legal differences. These methods are referred to as alternate dispute resolution methods (ADR). Arbitration is probably the most common ADR.

See also **Alternative dispute resolution**

Bibliography

Enderlein, F. & Maskow, D. (1992). *International sales law: U.N. Convention on Contracts for the International Sale of Goods.* Dobbs Ferry, NY: Oceana Publications Inc.
Kiss, A. & Sheeton, D. (1994). *International environmental law: 1994 supplement.* Irvington, NY: Transnational Publishers Inc.
Litka, M. (1991). *International dimensions of the legal environment of business.* 2nd edn, Boston, MA: PWS-Kent Publishing Company.
Sarachek, B. (1994). *International business law: A guide for executives with case examples.* Pennington, NY: Darwin Press Inc.
Weiss, E. B. (1995). *Compliance with international law.* Irvington, NY: Transnational Publishers Inc.

JOHN O'CONNELL

less developed country (LDC)   Although better off than "least developed countries" (LLDC), LDCs are still impoverished with little hope of overcoming their economic problems without further industrialization. LDCs are mainly agrarian economies that rely on exports of coffee, fruits, and other commodities for income. Hope for some LDCs rests with the development of mineral or energy resources and the accompanying industrial growth which normally follows. Those countries seeking growth because of natural resources may still be considered less developed if the funds from those resources do not go to education, infrastructure building, and further economic development. As a group, LDCs are also known as the Third World countries. LDCs include most Middle Eastern countries, China, India, Brazil, Malaysia, as well as many other mainly southern hemisphere countries.

JOHN O'CONNELL

less than fair value (LTFV)   When the sales price of an item exported from a country is significantly lower than the price for the same item sold in the exporting country, it may be that the item is being sold at less than fair value. When it is shown that this price differential occurs, it is probable that the exporting country is "dumping" the item on the international market. Anti–dumping regulations in many nations forbid this type of pricing structure. When lower prices are charged for exports versus locally sold items the importing country may impose duties to offset the lower price. In this way local producers and markets can be protected against low priced imports.

See also **Dumping**

JOHN O'CONNELL

letter of credit (L/C)   A document which provides payment to a seller of goods upon proof of the seller's compliance with requirements set forth by the document. A letter of credit is normally issued by a bank (which represents the purchaser – importer – of goods) to the exporter of goods. The exporter may then draw payments from the letter of credit upon submitting proof to the bank that the details of the purchase transaction have been strictly complied with. The term "issuing bank" refers to the importer's bank which issues the letter of credit.

There are a number of different kinds of letters of credit. The exact nature of the letter of credit used in any particular situation is based upon specific needs of a particular transaction or set of transactions as well as the degree of trust between buyer and seller. Letters of credit differ from one another in many areas. It is very important to understand the exact content and requirements of a letter of credit or difficulties in securing payment may occur. In alphabetical order, the types of letters of credit are:

1 Advised letter of credit – When an exporter's bank informs the exporter of the requirements to collect payment on a letter of credit, the exporter is said to be "advised." Thus, the term "advised letter of credit."

2 Back-to-back letter of credit – Often an exporter does not have the goods on hand to fill the orders of foreign buyers. An exporter commonly relies upon payment from the foreign buyer to pay its own suppliers. When this occurs a back-to-back letter of credit may be required. Whereas a letter of credit from the foreign buyer agrees to pay the exporter, it guarantees nothing for the exporter's supplier. If, however, the exporter causes a second letter of credit to be issued in favor of the supplier with the original letter acting as collateral, both the exporter and the supplier are guaranteed payment. When delivery of goods is made to the buyer, the bank honors both letters of credit paying off the supplier and remitting the remainder to the exporter. Without such financing, many export transactions would be impossible to complete.

3 Circular letter of credit – A circular letter of credit is also referred to as a "traveler's letter of credit" or "traveler's credit." This document is used to provide payments to a person who will be traveling in a foreign country. The person holding the letter of credit presents it to a bank specified in the letter and is able to withdraw funds up to the limit established by the letter.

4 Confirmed letter of credit – This form of letter of credit poses the least risk for the exporter of goods. A bank in the exporter's own country guarantees payment even if the importer, or the importer's bank, fails to remit funds to the exporter. Normally, the local bank requires the foreign bank to deposit funds before the goods are shipped, in order to guarantee payment. Upon

presentation of the letter of credit and compliance with all terms of the letter, payment is made to the exporter.

5 Documentary letter of credit – A seller under this form of letter of credit is paid by a bank upon presentation of the shipping papers. By itself, this type of letter of credit does not guarantee that the letter might not be revoked by the bank prior to presentation or that any other safeguards for the seller are in effect.

6 Green clause letter of credit – A letter of credit which does not allow an exporter to draw against the letter until such time as all required documentation is presented to the advancing bank.

7 Guaranteed letter of credit – Another name for a confirmed letter of credit. This letter guarantees payment by a bank from the exporter's country if the importer and the importer's bank default on the letter of credit.

8 Irrevocable letter of credit – One of the problems associated with international trade is the risk the seller of goods takes with respect to payment for those goods upon delivery. In order to make the transaction more palatable to the seller, noncancellable letters of credit were devised. An irrevocable letter of credit cannot be canceled, amended, or rescinded by the buyer unless agreed to by all parties to the transaction (buyer, seller, and applicable banks).

9 Irrevocable transferable letter of credit – This type of letter of credit allows the exporter to convey a portion of its proceeds to another party. For example, this type of letter may be used as a guarantee of payment to an exporter's suppliers or for anyone else's benefit as determined by the exporter.

10 Red clause letter of credit – Often an exporter does not have the funds to produce products to fill current orders. A letter of credit may have already been issued by the importer in anticipation of goods being exported. If allowed by the terms of the letter of credit, the exporter may draw upon the letter to obtain funds to produce goods. Once the goods are delivered the exporter may then submit the proper documentation to obtain the balance of the letter of credit. This type of interim financing is referred to

as coming from a "Red clause letter of credit."

11 Revocable letter of credit – A revocable letter of credit may be withdrawn by the issuing bank without prior notice or explanation. Unlike the irrevocable letter of credit, this type does not require the permission of the other parties to the transaction. As such, this letter exposes the seller of goods to more risk. Sellers seeking to reduce their risk should always demand an irrevocable letter of credit.

12 Revolving letter of credit – This type of letter of credit is used for an exporter with whom the issuing bank has had favorable past experience. The exporter also deals with customers of the issuing bank on a continuous basis over a period of time. Instead of issuing a new letter of credit each time this exporter sells to a given importer, the issuing bank arranges to offer a revolving letter of credit. This document allows the exporter to use the same letter for each transaction with the amount of payment on the letter being recredited after the completion of each transaction. As long as a single draw is for less than the overall limit, the letter's line of credit is renewed automatically over a specified period of time.

13 Standby letter of credit – A letter of credit may perform the same function as a surety bond in terms of being used as a financial guarantee of performance. International transactions may not be easily bondable, but a letter of credit may perform the same function. For example, an organization is seeking to bid on the construction of a dam in another country. Generally, bids on such projects require a good faith guarantee on the part of the bidder to assure the bid will be accepted if granted and that work will be done on time and in a workman-like manner. Ten percent of the bid amount is not uncommon. One of the methods of securing this guarantee is to obtain a Standby letter of credit in favor of the government of the foreign country. If the bidder defaults, the foreign government is paid from the letter of credit. The bank issuing the letter then has recourse against the bidding company.

14 Traveler's letter of credit – A letter of credit issued to a person who will be traveling in another country. The letter allows drafts to be written against the letter up to the value set forth in the letter. Another name for this type of letter of credit is "circular letter of credit."

Bibliography

Albawn, Gerald, Strandshov, Jesper, Duerr, Edwin & Dowd, Lawrence (1994). *International marketing and export management.* 2nd edn, Wokingham: Addison-Wesley.

Eiteman, D. K., Stonehill, A. J. & Moffett, M. H. (1992). *Multinational business finance.* 6th edn, Reading, MA: Addison-Wesley Publishing.

Johnson, T. E. (1994). *Export–Import procedures and documentation.* New York: Amacom.

United States Customs Service (1994). *A basic guide to importing.* Lincolnwood, IL: NTC Publishing Group.

Zodl, J. A. (1992). *Export–Import: Everything you and your company need to know to compete in world markets.* Cincinnati, OH: Betterway Books.

JOHN O'CONNELL

letter of indication   A person traveling overseas may purchase a letter of credit from a bank. The letter can be drawn upon by the traveler, by writing drafts against the credit amount. A "letter of indication" is provided by the bank to the traveler in order to identify the traveler as the party to whom the letter of credit was issued.

JOHN O'CONNELL

level   In order to determine the approximate value of a currency a person may seek the "level" at which the currency is being traded. A "level" is an informal quotation indicating the present rate at which a currency is being traded. Parties indicating the level of a currency are not bound by the level quoted.

JOHN O'CONNELL

licensed production   The holder of a patent, trademark, or copyright may allow another organization to use its property rights in the production of goods. An organization is "licensed" to use the rights or processes of another. A commission or royalty is commonly paid in such licensing arrangements. This arrangement is common when an organization in one country desires to legally use the rights or processes of an organization in another country.

See also **Licensing**

JOHN O'CONNELL

licensing   Licensing provides the right to a foreign company to use trademarks, patents, and other protected property rights in return for a licensing fee. The company holding the property rights is able to obtain distribution through an established business in a foreign country and avoid the problems associated with high capital outlays and competing in a country in which it is relatively unknown. Licensing may also be a way of gaining some protection against pirating or other invasion of intellectual property rights because it sells these rights to an existing foreign company which is more likely to be able to protect them in the host country. Licensing also allows a company to enter a market in which foreign entry restrictions are high or currency convertibility problems exist. A license fee flows out of the country as an expense of the local business, instead of a repatriation of profits to a foreign parent company.

See also **Market entry strategies**

Bibliography

Root, E. R. (1994). *Entry strategies for international markets*. New York: Lexington Books.

JOHN O'CONNELL

licensing agreement   The written document specifying the details of the understanding between two companies related to use of proprietary rights in a second country. The agreement authorizes a second company to use a patented process or produce a patented product in a second country in return for a royalty or fee payment.

See also **Licensing**

JOHN O'CONNELL

licensing fees   In international business it is common for one organization to allow another to use its patented products, copyrighted processes, or trademarks in return for a royalty payment or fee. It is also possible for a multinational company to charge fees to its subsidiaries for use of the MNC's proprietary processes or products. This type of payment is usually treated as a franchise or other type of royalty (therefore, an expense to the subsidiary). In countries having restrictions on the flow of currency, the above arrangement may be a way of repatriating funds to the parent company (since funds flow as an expense instead of profits or dividends).

See also **Licensing**

JOHN O'CONNELL

lifetime employment   Some cultures promote the well-being of the employee to such an extent that employment is considered a right and may be expected to be offered for the lifetime of the employee. Japan's culture has been a supporter of lifetime employment for many decades. Lifetime employment is not expected (or offered) in most countries. Even in Japan, lifetime employment is not as certain as it used to be because of recent reversals in Japan's economy and stagnation of certain industries.

JOHN O'CONNELL

lingua franca   The extensiveness of today's international activities makes it common for two people to meet who do not speak one another's language, but share a third language. By speaking the common third language, communication between the parties is possible.

Lingua franca can also refer to the language of business in any particular area. For example, the language of business in Latin America is Spanish between Latin American Countries but English with most other countries. In the

Middle East, the native language is Arabic but the business language with the rest of the world is English. Knowing the "lingua franca" of an area can assist a traveler or businessperson in effectively communicating without having to know a large number of different languages. English is the most common business language used between nations.

JOHN O'CONNELL

linkage   A very large industry can have a major impact on a country's economy in terms of employment, productive capacity, and balance of trade. As such, that industry also may be able to exert a tremendous amount of pressure on the remainder of the economy. This pressure is referred to as "linkage." For example, a very large company may be able to obtain preferential tax treatment or land-use permits from its own government. The automobile industry is an example of an industry able to exert great pressure in the United States. Energy-related extractive industries (oil especially) are also capable of exerting tremendous amounts of pressure in their country of origin. Without these industries entire economies could fail or be heavily damaged.

JOHN O'CONNELL

liquid assets   Liquid assets are those which can be easily and quickly converted to cash. Liquid assets include: hard currencies, marketable securities, and various kinds of negotiable papers or documents.

JOHN O'CONNELL

liquidation of entry   An importer may not receive imported items until all entry requirements have been met. Goods must be classified by customs and the amount of duty determined. Once this is accomplished, the importer pays any fees or duties then due and the liquidation is normally complete. Goods are then released to the importer.

See also **Entry documents**

JOHN O'CONNELL

liquidity   This term is associated with two meanings: (1) The ability of an organization to convert its assets into cash. One of the measures of the ability of a firm to respond to current cash needs is its liquidity position. (2) In international monetary dealings, the amount of transferable currency available to a particular country to meet balance-of-payments needs. The more currency held in reserve the greater the ability of a country to satisfy any temporary imbalances in its balance-of-payments accounts.

JOHN O'CONNELL

living allowance   An additional amount of compensation to account for additional costs of living in an expatriate's host country versus the home country. Examples of costs of living which are commonly higher in other countries are: food, housing, transportation, and services. If the expatriate would normally take advantage of goods and services while in the home country, a living allowance is normally provided for those same goods and services in a host country. This is an important consideration for an employee considering an overseas assignment. It is also important to recognize that the degree or quality of goods or services may also vary and must be taken into consideration as well.

See also **Compensation package**

Bibliography

Reynolds, C. (1986). Compensation of overseas personnel in *Handbook of Human Resource Administration*. 2nd edn, New York: McGraw-Hill.

JOHN O'CONNELL

LLDC   *see* LEAST DEVELOPED COUNTRY

Lloyd's agent   A representative of Lloyd's of London. A Lloyd's agent's responsibility, however, is different than what may first come to mind. In marine insurance, a Lloyd's agent is responsible for surveying and certifying losses on property insured by Lloyd's. Lloyd's agents are located throughout the world to assist in the fair settlement of claims. Information provided by Lloyd's agents is invaluable to insurance companies, shipping companies, and others with interests in the movements of vessels and cargo.

Bibliography

Lloyd's of London Press Staff (1991). *Leading developments in international marine insurance: An industry report.* New York: Lloyd's of London Press.

JOHN O'CONNELL

local hire   This is a person hired to do a job at the location of the job. Thus, if a British citizen applied for and was hired for a job in the United States he/she would be considered a "local hire." The place where the actual hiring takes place is more important to this term than the nationality of the person being hired.

JOHN O'CONNELL

local national   Multinational companies commonly operate through subsidiaries in various countries. Citizens of the host country are sometimes referred to as local nationals.

See also **Employee categories; Host country nationals**

JOHN O'CONNELL

localization (of employees)   This concerns replacing expatriates with host country nationals (HCNs) as the opportunity arises. The cost of sending expatriates overseas is extremely high. High level management personnel may cost an additional several hundred thousand dollars to send overseas. Although that figure may be extreme the cost for any expatriate is much higher than local labor. Localization of employees is the process of replacing expatriates with local hires as expatriate assignments come to an end. The need for expatriates is usually the greatest in the early periods of a company's

overseas activities. Once time has allowed local labor to be trained (in technical as well as managerial pursuits) lower cost employees can successfully take the place of expatriates.

Bibliography

Black, J. S. (1988). Work role transitions: A study of American expatriate managers in Japan. *Journal of International Business Studies,* **19** (2), 277–94.
Pulatie, D. (1985). How do you ensure success of managers going abroad. *Training and Development Journal,* December, 22–4.
Ronen, S. & Tung, R. L. (1981). Selection and training of personnel for overseas assignments. *Columbia Journal of World Business,* Spring, 68–78.

JOHN O'CONNELL

localization of industry   Industries tend to locate in areas in which there is a ready supply of raw materials, labor, or other services necessary for the production of goods. In the past some organizations developed "company towns" where workers not only lived but shopped for goods and services and went to work in the company facility. With the advent of global enterprises the tendency to localize industry has declined. With the entire world as a potential location for various segments of a company's operations, localization of industry is not as common as in the past.

JOHN O'CONNELL

location theory   An economic theory that a manufacturer will consider transportation costs as a major location determinant. If true, this theory states that a manufacturer will locate its manufacturing and distribution activities at locations having the lowest transportation costs for incoming raw materials and outgoing finished products.

JOHN O'CONNELL

lockout   Lockout occurs when employees are kept from work by the employer in order to influence collective bargaining. Employer/employee bargaining does not always result in a labor agreement. When failure occurs management may decide that employee demands or actions are unacceptable and attempt to force concessions by not allowing employees to work until an agreement is reached. This is referred to as a "lockout." Lockouts may be considered an unfair labor practice in some countries.

JOHN O'CONNELL

logistics The overall costs to supply a product to a user are determined by factors associated with the production and distribution process. Logistics is the study of relationships between these processes. Theoretically, if one could optimize the securing and storage of raw materials and inventory, the cost and timing of production, and the distribution process, the cost to supply goods to the user would be the lowest.

See also **Just-in-time**

JOHN O'CONNELL

long service leave An Australian business practice which allows an employee to take a leave of absence with pay after working for a company a minimum number of years. Years of employment must generally exceed ten to fifteen years. Duration of leave time varies from three to six months.

JOHN O'CONNELL

low context culture A culture in which communications must be clearly expressed either in writing or in words. Low context

cultures do not rely upon body language, facial expression, or tone of voice to complete the communication. Examples of countries having low context cultures are the United States, Canada, Germany, and Switzerland. In this type of culture important information must be set out and if problems exist they must be explained fully. Although working within a low context culture is generally not a problem for people from that culture, people from other cultural backgrounds may have considerable trouble adapting.

See also **High context cultures**

Bibliography

Deresky, Helen (1994). *International management.* 1st edn, New York: HarperCollins.
Mendenhall, M., Punnett, B. & Ricks, D. (1995). *Global management.* Cambridge, MA: Blackwell Publishers.

JOHN O'CONNELL

luncheon voucher (LV) Although not important in the overall scheme of things, if you are an employee of a British firm, luncheon vouchers take on a whole new meaning. LVs are just what the name implies: an employment benefit in the form of a voucher which may be exchanged for food at various eating establishments. The vouchers are tax free (up to a specified amount per day) in Great Britain.

JOHN O'CONNELL

LV *see* LUNCHEON VOUCHER

M

macrorisk   The risk associated with changes in the overall economy of a country. This is contrasted with risks associated with sets of individual factors which cause uncertainty.

JOHN O'CONNELL

Madrid Agreement   The full name of this multilateral treaty is The Madrid Agreement Concerning the International Registration of Marks. This was one of the early agreements related to the protection of industrial trademark rights. The Madrid Agreement allows a company from one of the signatory countries to obtain international protection through a single application. The Agreement is overseen by the World Intellectual Property Organization (WIPO). Signatories to the Agreement also provide an automatic additional 20 years protection for a trademark.

Bibliography

Stewart, G. R. (Ed.) (1994). *International trade and intellectual property: The search for a balanced system.* Boulder, CO: Westview Press.

JOHN O'CONNELL

managed currency   Central banks often seek to control fluctuations in their currency exchange rate. Through the purchase and/or sale of its currency the central bank can directly impact the exchange rate. When a central bank contributes to the control on exchange rates, the country has what is referred to as a "managed currency." The currency in the free market operates on the forces of supply and demand alone, but this is not common with most of the predominant currencies in the world today.

JOHN O'CONNELL

managed float   A floating currency in the foreign exchange market which is not being allowed to float freely along with the direction of the open market, but is being managed in a desired direction is considered a managed float. The central bank accomplishes this through the buying and selling of the currency. This is done quite often and is not considered unusual as the central bank revises its monetary policies and exerts its influence on the markets.

JOHN O'CONNELL

managed floating exchange system   The term itself is an example of how far we have come to accept at least some governmental intervention in most levels of an economy. One could make a point that you either have a "managed exchange rate system" in which government monetary authorities are heavily involved in curing the problems of fluctuating exchange rates; or you have a "floating exchange rate system" in which market forces determine values. A "managed floating exchange system" is one in which there is some monetary authority activity to control short-term exchange rates.

JOHN O'CONNELL

managed trade   Trade is "managed" when it is impacted in any way by restrictions or barriers set forth by an individual country or a group of countries. The term does not infer that managed trade is good or bad, but merely that it does not flow of its own accord. Managing trade includes actions to limit exports/imports, a system of tariffs, quotas, taxation differences on domestic versus imported goods, and many other governmental activities. With a definition this broad, it is difficult indeed to find a situation involving trade between two countries which is not managed in some fashion.

See also **Barriers; Reciprocity**

JOHN O'CONNELL

management contracting   A firm can enter foreign markets under a contract to manage a new or existing commercial operation in those markets. For example, a manufacturer has a proven record of aggressive and efficient management in its home country. The manufacturer may be approached not to provide product but instead management expertise for a start-up operation or an existing operation having problems in a foreign country. This places the management of the original manufacturer into a foreign operation in which international experience may be gained. Success in one management contract may lead to additional contracts and eventually equity ownership in foreign firms. The only real problems associated with management contracts is that they remove top management from the home country operation, are normally temporary, and may incur the blame for a problem which previously existed in a foreign company.

See also **Market entry strategies**

JOHN O'CONNELL

management contracts   Many organizations do not have the desire or the experience to manage their operations in every country. When this occurs the organization may arrange with another company to manage and operate its foreign subsidiary. Management contracts are normally compensated by means of a fee for services or a percentage of profits.

JOHN O'CONNELL

management fee   Many organizations use the services of a professional fund manager to invest their capital. In return the investment manager normally charges a fee based on the value of the portfolio or the amount of profit made during a given period of time. In international business a management fee may also be charged by a foreign partner to operate a joint venture for the remaining partners.

JOHN O'CONNELL

manufacturing   The establishing of capability to produce goods in a foreign country is one method of entering into international operations. This method allows the greatest control of the overseas operation but also the greatest investment in capital, management time, and effort. Often direct investment in facilities is achieved through the purchase of an existing company's assets in a foreign country but many large companies build new facilities when they expand. The decision to purchase or build manufacturing plants in another country may be forced upon a company by competition or foreign government demands for local representation.

See also **Market entry strategies**

Bibliography

Dunning, J. (1981). *International production and multinational enterprise.* London: Allen and Unwin.
Mefford, R. N. (1986). Determinants of productivity differences in international manufacturing. *Journal of International Business Studies,* **17** (1), 63–82.
Miller, J. G., Demeyer, A. & Nakane, J. (1994). *Benchmarking global manufacturing: Understanding international suppliers, customers and competitors.* Hinsdale, IL: Irwin Professional Publishing.
Steudel, H. J. (1992). *Manufacturing in the nineties: How to become a mean, lean, world-class competitor.* New York: Van Nostrand Reinhold.

JOHN O'CONNELL

maquiladora   This Spanish term refers to a special area in Mexico along the US border. In this area many firms carry out the production of goods for export. The Maquiladora area was created by the Mexican government to offer employment to Mexican workers. To make the area more attractive from a business point-of-view, firms doing business in the area are granted certain tax exemptions. Goods produced in the area are taxed on the basis of a type of value added tax (on only the value of labor and materials added during production). Maquiladoras have become very popular not only with parent companies from the United States but also with companies from Europe and Asia.

Bibliography

Daniels, J. D. & Radebaugh, L. E. (1994). *International business: Environments and operations.* 7th edn, Reading, MA: Addison-Wesley Publishing.

JOHN O'CONNELL

marine insurance   Insurance on ocean-going vessels and their cargo – marine insurance – is the oldest form of insurance protection. In addition to a vessel and its cargo, marine insurance can also be written on offshore drilling rigs and sometimes even for inland pipelines and facilities connected to port oil facilities. In addition to the perils of the sea, marine insurance is one of the only forms of coverage which can cover war risks. War risk insurance is normally not a standard part of a marine contract, but must be requested at an additional premium. Marine insurance is very important to international commercial transactions because it is usually required to be purchased by one of the parties to the transaction. The party responsible for purchasing marine cargo insurance is determined by the terms of the purchase agreement.

There is no standard policy to cover marine risks. However, coverage is generally divided into four coverage areas:

1 Hull coverage – Coverage against damage or destruction to the ship itself. Coverage may be written for a ship under construction (builder's risk), a ship in active use, or when in dry-dock for repairs. Policies may provide coverage on a worldwide basis or for operation of a ship only within a specified port of call (port risk only). Coverage may be written on a ship as a single entity or on a number of jointly-owned ships (fleet). Hull coverage can also be written on a total loss only basis. Under a total loss only form there is no coverage for partial losses. A deductible normally applies to hull losses. The deductible can be as high as 25% of the loss. A "collision" clause may be included in a hull policy to provide coverage for damage to other ships caused by the negligence of the insured. This is actually a liability coverage but is an option to hull coverage under marine forms.

2 Cargo coverage – Coverage against damage or loss to goods being carried by a vessel. Policies may be written for a single voyage (single risk or trip policies) or for all trips over an extended basis (open policy). Most marine cargo insurance is written on open forms of coverage. Open cargo forms may be written on a warehouse to warehouse basis. This means that coverage is provided for not only the ocean portion of transit but also the land portion if necessary to reach the buyer's warehouse.

3 Freight coverage – this is the cost of hauling goods or the charges made by the carrier for transporting goods. This cost is often included in the insurance for cargo. It is common to insure cargo for 110% of its value to include the value of insurance premiums and freight charges. Freight coverage may also be included with hull coverage to protect the shipowner from loss of income for hauling goods.

4 Protection and indemnity (P&I) coverage – This is a form of liability coverage for owners/operators of vessels. However, P&I provides more than just normal liability protection. P&I provides coverage for injury or illness to crew members, injury or illness to passengers, negligent damage to cargo carried by the vessel, and damage to docks or piers caused by the vessel. Additional amounts of coverage may be obtained through the purchase of excess protection and indemnity protection.

See also **INCOTERMS; Perils of the sea**

Bibliography

International Chamber of Commerce (ICC) (1990). *Incoterms 1990.* New York, NY: ICC Publishing Corp.

Rejda, G. E. (1995). *Principles of risk management and insurance.* 5th edn, New York: HarperCollins.

Rodda, W. H., Trieschmann, J. S. & Hedges, B. A. (1978). *Commercial property risk management and insurance.* Malvern, PA: American Institute for Property and Liability Underwriters.

Trieschman, J. S. & Gustavson, S. G. (1993). *Risk management and insurance.* 9th edn, Cincinnati, OH: Southwestern College Publishing.

JOHN O'CONNELL

marine perils   *see* PERILS OF THE SEA

maritime law   The branch of law that relates to navigation or trade on the high seas or other areas under the jurisdiction of Admiralty courts. These special courts oversee disputes and enforce the laws of the sea.

See also **Admiralty court**

JOHN O'CONNELL

maritime perils   *see* PERILS OF THE SEA

mark of origin   Goods traded internationally normally must be labeled in some fashion to allow customs and other inspectors to identify the shipment's country of origin and its point of destination. The "mark" or label must appear on the cargo itself and the bill of lading.

See also **Bill of lading**

JOHN O'CONNELL

mark sheet   The Japanese government requires importers seeking to use foreign exchange to pay for imports to submit a "mark sheet" to the Bank of Japan. Mark sheets are used only for imports with total values in excess of one million yen. A mark sheet allows the government to control the flow of large amounts of foreign exchange out of the country. Thus, mark sheets assist the government in managing foreign exchange.

JOHN O'CONNELL

market disruption   A market disruption occurs when there is a threat to its very existence either from within the economy or from foreign sources. Disruption causes unemployment of persons working in particular sectors, investments to lose value, and sometimes the way of life of a people to change. Many circumstances can cause market disruptions, but one of the most common is associated with a rapid increase in importation of products which directly compete with domestic production. This is why many countries have instituted various kinds of trade barriers in attempts to reduce the problem of market disruption.

See also **Barriers**

JOHN O'CONNELL

market entry strategies   The method chosen by a company to begin selling, or conduct other activities, in a foreign country. Entry into a foreign market can be as easy as picking up a telephone and contacting an overseas buyer for your goods. Entry could also involve a start-up operation which duplicates a company's operations in its home country. The type of market entry strategy chosen depends upon a number of factors, including the following: amount of available investment capital; degree of risk one is willing to assume; knowledge of foreign markets; knowledge of working with diverse cultures; knowledge of export/import transactions; available distribution systems; time commitment; ability to handle stress and uncertainty; potential profit; and a number of other factors as well. The following lists some of the more common market entry strategies.

1   Assembly operations – An organization sends parts for a product to a foreign plant for final assembly. The products are then sold in the foreign market or exported to other countries. Assembly plants may allow a company to take advantage of low cost labor in the most labor-intensive portion of production. There may also be lower duties and other taxes because unfinished products are imported instead of finished products. Assembly plants also allow a foreign manufacturer to meet host country requests for

more domestic production while at the same time allowing the manufacturer to maintain control over production by using its own subproducts as supplies and materials for the foreign assembly plant. A potential problem, especially with plants located to pacify foreign governments needs for domestic production, is that the foreign government may institute quotas on the amount of foreign parts which may be used in the host country.

2 Contract manufacturing – Some companies use manufacturers in foreign countries to make (or assemble) their product and distribute them through the foreign manufacturer's existing marketing channels. Thus, entry to the country is achieved with the assistance of local companies using proven marketing channels. Although the cost of this type of method is usually a substantial portion of the product revenues, it allows a company to test the market for its goods and become more familiar with doing business overseas.

3 Exporting – This is one of the simplest methods of foreign market entry. The product is exported to a buyer who then distributes it to the foreign market. Market entry of the product is achieved without considerable investment of either time or capital. The key to exporting is knowing the components of the export transaction very well. If knowledge is not present there are a number of export agents available to assist the exporter of products (*see* EXPORT AGENT).

4 Joint venturing – A joint venture is an agreement between two companies to coproduce and distribute a product. A separate entity is commonly established to handle a joint-venture arrangement. Joint ventures normally involve a foreign company and a host country company. Some countries require some local equity participation in all companies operating within their borders. A joint venture is a way of meeting equity participation requirements. One of the major problems associated with joint ventures (in addition to usually high capital investment needs) is obtaining the right joint-venture partner. If partners are not compatible, do not understand each other's

cultures, do not have a common language, or do not share basic intentions regarding the outcome of the joint venture, the chances of the arrangement succeeding are reduced.

5 Franchise agreement – This is an agreement in which a company holding the rights to a product, trademark, process, etc. allows another company to make and distribute the product or use the trademark under a contractual agreement. The franchise agreement spells out the details, which usually include the geographic area in which the franchise is good, the fees to be paid to the franchisor, as well as any other requirements the franchisor is able to place in the contract. A franchise agreement is a method of entering a foreign market by having a local business (hopefully an established and highly reputable business) distribute and/ or produce a foreign firm's product. This builds name recognition and provides a good foundation from which to add more foreign franchises or to begin owned operations overseas.

6 Licensing – Licensing provides the right to a foreign company to use trademarks, patents, and other protected property rights in return for a licensing fee. The company holding the property rights is able to obtain distribution through an established business in a foreign country and avoid the problems with high capital outlays and competing in a country in which it is relatively unknown. Licensing may also be a way of gaining some protection from pirating or other invasion of intellectual property rights because it sells these rights to an existing foreign company, which is more likely to be able to protect them in the host country. Licensing also allows a company to enter a market in which foreign entry restrictions are high or currency convertibility problems exist. A license fee flows out of the country as an expense of the local business, instead of a repatriation of profits to a foreign parent company.

7 Management contracting – A firm can enter foreign markets under a contract to manage a new or existing commercial operation in those markets. For example, a manufacturer has a proven record of aggressive and efficient management in its home country. The manufacturer may be approached not

to provide product but instead management expertise for a start-up operation or an existing operation having problems in a foreign country. This places the management of the original manufacturer into a foreign operation in which international experience may be gained. Success in one management contract may lead to additional contracts and eventually equity ownership in foreign firms. The only real problems associated with management contracts is that they remove top management from the home country operation, are normally temporary, and may incur the blame for a problem which previously existed in a foreign company.

8 Manufacturing – The establishing of capability to produce goods in a foreign country. This method allows the greatest control of the overseas operation but also the greatest investment in capital, management time, and effort. Often direct investment in facilities is achieved through the purchase of an existing company's assets in a foreign country but many large companies build new facilities when they expand. The decision to purchase or build a manufacturing plant in another country may be forced upon a company by competition or foreign government demands for local representation.

9 Piggyback exporting – Piggyback exporting describes a situation in which one company markets its products through the. distribution channels of a second company. Two major reasons for piggyback marketing are: (1) a local company desires to enter multinational markets but lacks the money, experience or possibly the inclination to learn what is necessary to be successful in the international marketplace; (2) an existing multinational company is seeking to fill out its product lines to stay competitive overseas. Piggybacking involves products which compliment one another instead of competing. This method of exporting is one of the least problematic of all of the methods of entering foreign markets. Of course, success is dependent upon who the partners are and the commitment to making the partnership function effectively.

10 Wholly owned subsidiaries – This form of market entry provides a company full control over its foreign operations. This method of market entry requires large capital investment, commitment of time and effort, and normally a willingness of some employees/management to travel to and live in a foreign country. Fully owned subsidiaries are commonly existing businesses acquired by the company. If this is so the investment in management and expatriate time and effort may not be as significant as with a start-up operation.

Bibliography

Albaum, Gerald, Strandskov, Jesper, Duerr, Edwin & Dowd, Lawrence (1994). *International marketing and export management*. 2nd edn, Wokingham: Addison-Wesley.

Buzzell, R. D., Quelch, J. A. & Bartlett, C. A. (1995). *Global marketing management: Cases and readings*. Reading, MA: Addison-Wesley.

Cateora, P. R. (1993). *International marketing*. 5th edn, Homewood, IL: Irwin.

Grosse, R. & Kujawa, D. (1995). *International business: Theory and managerial applications*. 3rd edn, Boston, MA: Richard D. Irwin Inc.

Kaynak, E., & Ghauri, P. N. (eds) (1994). *Euromarketing: Effective strategies for international trade and export*. Binghamton, NY: Haworth Press Inc.

Majaro, S. (1977). *Marketing: A strategic approach to world markets*. London: George Allen and Unwin.

Mendenhall, M., Punnett, B. & Ricks, D. (1995). *Global management*. Cambridge, MA: Blackwell Publishers.

Toyne, B. & Walters, Peter, G. P. (1993). *Global marketing management*. Boston: Allyn and Bacon.

JOHN O'CONNELL

market penetration   Generally expressed as a percentage, market penetration is a measure of a particular product's or an entire company's share of any given market. The greater the percentage share the greater the penetration. Market penetration may be difficult to measure in some foreign markets because of the difficulty in obtaining data from which to measure share. Companies seeking to determine how well they are doing overseas (and possibly how to do better) may be assisted by a gap analysis.

See also **Gap analysis**

JOHN O'CONNELL

marketing intelligence There is a tremendous supply of information that must be continually evaluated in order to make informed and effective marketing decisions. Information on competitor's products, research and development efforts, consumer wants and needs, and hundreds of other types of information may assist a company in its marketing efforts. The more useful information that is available for input, the more valuable and accurate the analysis will be. Marketing intelligence is the process of securing information from all available sources (internal and external to the company), screening that information for relevant data, and using that data to make more informed marketing decisions.

An interesting sidelight to marketing intelligence has arisen over the past several years in terms of who gathers the intelligence. With the fall of communism and the end of the cold war many former government workers or contractors are becoming consultants gathering various kinds of intelligence information for business interests. Using the most up-to-date methods, information of many kinds may be identified and transferred to clients.

JOHN O'CONNELL

marking In international trade the term "marking" refers to the conspicuous placement of the name of an import's country of origin and final destination point. Marking helps customs officials easily identify property which may be subject to special duties or import restrictions.

JOHN O'CONNELL

marking duty "Marking" is the indication on imports as to the country of origin. If improper marking occurs an additional duty is applied as a penalty.

See also **Duty**

JOHN O'CONNELL

married status When an employee is sent on an overseas assignment and is accompanied by his/her spouse or children, the employee's assignment status is "married." Assignment status determines many of the compensation allowances and benefits available to an employee when transferred overseas.

See also **Assignment status**

JOHN O'CONNELL

massify To massify is to produce a standard product with attributes which are sufficient to meet the demand of buyers. Essentially, a company seeks to produce a product for the masses or the largest group possible. A product with sufficient qualities (but not all available qualities) to meet the needs of most consumers should be cheaper to produce than a product which must be tailor-made for one market and changed for each different market.

JOHN O'CONNELL

master air waybill A single shipper of goods may have a number of cargoes destined for a single destination. Once these cargoes are put together (consolidated) for shipment the air carrier issues an airbill as a receipt for the cargo. Included in the airbill is a master air waybill which lists the details of the air shipment (destination, owner of goods, types of goods, values, etc.)

JOHN O'CONNELL

matrix organizational structure Generally, organizations are structured so that clear chains of command, communication, reward, and responsibility are provided for employees. In these organizations, employees have responsibility for one area and usually answer to one manager or department. The matrix organization is one in which employees have at least a dual responsibility. International organizations are very often matrix organizations due to the complexity of the international business process. Employees and managers must successfully operate the foreign subsidiary, but do so in a way that meets the objectives of the parent organization. Thus, responsibility is dual: to the foreign operation and to the parent organization.

Such a system usually results in less formal communications channels; use of task forces to solve problems or discover opportunities; an emphasis on the ability to adapt to situations; and a constant reminder of the overall organizational goals and objectives, lest they be forgotten in the stressful times often associated with managing a foreign operation. Managers are hired for their ability to be flexible in their actions and ability to display independence, while continuing to meet the objectives of the parent company.

Bibliography

Adler, N. J. (1991). *International dimensions of organizational behavior*. 2nd edn, Belmont, CA: Wadsworth Inc.
Bleicher, K. (1986). Corporate governance systems in a multinational environment: Who knows what's best. *Management International Review*, 3, 4–15.
Mendenhall, M., Punnett, B. & Ricks, D. (1995). *Global management*. Cambridge, MA: Blackwell Publishers.

JOHN O'CONNELL

mature economy   An economy experiencing stable growth. Usually a nation which has industrialized to the point that continued capital investment is not as essential as it once was. Purchases of goods changes from factory equipment to automobiles and other personal goods. The economy is not stagnant, but its growth pattern is moving from industrial goods to consumer goods production.

JOHN O'CONNELL

Medivac   Medivac is the name given to services which are available to transport an ill or injured employee from one place to another for medical care. Evacuation for medical purposes may be to another part of the host country, to the closest country in which appropriate care may be provided, or to the home country. Commercial services are available to companies who can sign-up for either group or individual plans in anticipation of possible medical problems. Remember, the medical care and facilities in a host country may be quite different and possibly inferior to those provided in the home country. Medivac services not only provide

security for the expatriate, but possible reduction of potential employer liability for placing an employee in a known area of danger without providing for proper medical care.

JOHN O'CONNELL

meet and greet   Many organizations who send employees overseas make it a practice for someone representing the organization to meet the expatriate at the airport when he/she first arrives. Problems concerning immediate transportation, customs, obtaining a meal as well as providing a certain comfort level can be dealt with more readily by a person familiar with the host country. Meet and greet is not just a problem-solving gesture but also a morale booster for the expatriate and any accompanying dependents.

JOHN O'CONNELL

merchant bank   As with the ordinary definition of the term a "merchant" bank is in the buying and selling business. The buying is the arrangement of commercial loans and the selling is the transfer of the loan to another bank prior to its maturity. Thus, a merchant bank is not in business to make loans to hold until maturity. Instead, loans are made with the intention of reselling them. Merchant banks also underwrite securities; provide investment assistance to companies; and may become an investor in corporate acquisitions or other types of restructuring. Merchant banks also facilitate international trade by often accepting bills of exchange. Merchant banks perform in much the same manner as investment banks in the United States.

See also **Investment banking**

Bibliography

Logue, D. E. (Ed.) (1995). *The WG&L handbook of international finance*. Cincinnati, OH: South-Western Publishing Company.

JOHN O'CONNELL

middle rate   The middle is merely the mid-point between the quoted bid and ask prices for foreign exchange. If the bid price is 1.500 and the ask price is 1.550 the middle rate is 1.525 (the average of the bid and ask prices). The middle rate is used to determine the percentage spread between bid and ask prices of currency.

JOHN O'CONNELL

MIGA   *see*   MULTILATERAL   INVESTMENT   GUARANTEE AGENCY

Ministry of International Trade and Industry (MITI)   Japan's massive industrial base is the envy of most countries around the world. The responsibility for regulating industry and coordinating the distribution of resources to keep industry strong is given to the Japan Ministry of International Trade and Industry. Among other responsibilities, it is MITI's task to develop strategies which lead to further exports of Japanese goods.

JOHN O'CONNELL

MNC strategy   Value activities form the building blocks of MNC strategy and structure. Value activities are the functions performed by an MNC that either directly or indirectly generate revenues. Common activities include R&D, purchasing, logistics, component manu-facturing, assembly, marketing, sales, and ser-vice, as well as the support activities of finance, human resource management, and control. One fundamental choice for an MNC involves determining how these value activities will be geographically configured; a second choice involves determining the degree to which these activities should be coordinated. An MNC's international strategy is manifest in the config-uration and coordination of its activities.

As MNCs configure their activities, they typically think in terms of "concentrating" them in a single country or "dispersing" them in multiple countries. For example, an MNC which concentrates research and development will perform all R&D functions in one central location from which the rest of the world will be served. In contrast, when an activity is dis-persed, the activity is replicated in each country in which the MNC competes. As an example, an MNC which disperses sales activities will employ separate sales teams in each country in which it competes.

Several researchers have found that patterns of MNC configuration vary according to home country affiliation. Japanese-based MNCs, for example, have traditionally relied much more heavily on stand-alone distribution-based affili-ates than U.S.-based MNCs, which tend to combine overseas manufacturing with sales. Some have argued that Japanese-based MNCs tend to concentrate activities at home because they are at an earlier stage in their efforts to transnationalize operations than are U.S.-based MNCs. The geographic proximity of concen-trated activities generally makes them easier for MNC managers to control.

How an MNC configures its operations directly impacts its capacity to exploit the differences in comparative advantage across countries. Differences in comparative advantage can stem from a variety of factors including variations in labor rates, unequal levels of labor productivity, and disparities in raw material costs and energy costs. MNCs that exploit differences in comparative advantage concen-trate activities in whichever location an advan-tage can be gained. In theory, this concentration should produce an advantage over MNCs which broadly dispersed their activities or over wholly domestic competitors. In practice, however, exploiting differences in comparative advantage can be more difficult than suggested by theory. The evidence suggests that most world trade takes place within developed countries where differences in comparative advantage are often small. Governments also often subsidize or tax away differences in comparative advantage.

Transportation expenses can also diminish the impact of comparative advantages.

In addition to making decisions about the geographic configuration of activities, MNCs also decide the degree to which activities are coordinated. Coordination is related to the integration or interdependence of value activ-ities within an MNC. Coordination can range from very low – where each value activity is performed independently – to very high, where like activities are tightly integrated across geographic locations. For example, if an MNC has highly coordinated manufacturing, each manufacturing facility will have identical control systems, use common production processes, rely on the same parts, and have integrated production schedules. Manufacturing facilities that are loosely coordinated have a high degree of autonomy and would produce output with different designs, relying on different equipment, and utilizing unique parts.

One advantage of tight coordination is the minimization of redundancies. Tight coordination also leads to greater power over buyers and sellers. For example, coordinated purchasing has saved automobile MNCs billions of dollars in the 1990s. Other advantages stemming from tight coordination include savings through the use of common brand names, speedier communication of market knowledge, and ease of management functions through standardization of control procedures.

While coordination focuses on horizontal linkages between similar activities, MNCs are also concerned about vertical linkages, say between R&D and manufacturing, or between manufacturing and marketing. Vertical linkages can minimize internal transaction costs, assure product supply and quality, improve scheduling, and provide important barriers to entry for competitors. Tight vertical integration also insures maximum consistencies in interfacing with customers. To be effective, vertical integration requires enormous teamwork. At AT&T, for example, development work on the company's cordless telephone Model 4200 was cut from two years to one year through the use of integrative teams including engineers, manufacturers, and marketers. Vertical teams have been used effectively at companies as diverse as Boeing, Toyota, and IBM.

Configuration and coordination reflect an MNC's existing strategy. They indicate where an MNC competes and determine how an MNC interacts with different countries. MNCs can exploit particular patterns of configuration and coordination to produce a competitive advantage under appropriate industry conditions. While every MNC strategy has idiosyncratic components, broad patterns of configuration and coordination are generally observable. These patterns make it possible to classify MNC strategies. Research on MNC strategies has generally recognized three broad-based patterns of configuration and coordination. These include stand-alone, simple integration, and complex integration strategies.

Under a traditional stand-alone strategy, activities are both loosely coordinated and geographically dispersed. Affiliate managers are given a high degree of autonomy and control most decision making; each overseas affiliate acts as an independent profit center. The general pattern is to absorb home country offerings and adapt the resulting products to meet local demand. Production, marketing, sales, and service activities tend to be located in each country, with little coordination across countries. Because of the emphasis on generally independent affiliates, stand-alone strategies have also been referred to as multidomestic strategies.

The essence of a simple integration strategy is to design and develop a product to international specifications, produce it in large-scale, modern factories to high quality standards, and sell it around the world at competitive prices. Much of Japan's high profile successes in international markets have come from the adoption of simple integration strategies. In that simple integration strategies are designed to leverage company competencies on a multicountry basis, they are sometimes referred to as integrated regional or pure global strategies. Competitors are defined on a regional or global basis, with the cross-subsidization of national market share battles a common practice.

Complex integration strategies have received growing attention in the 1990s. Sometimes referred to as a multifocal or transnational strategy, a complex integration strategy is designed to concurrently respond to industry pressures to be both globally integrated and locally responsive by emphasizing efficiency, affiliate responsibility, and organizational learning. A complex integration strategy is an attempt to capture the advantages of both stand-alone and simple integration strategies. In order to achieve these benefits, the configuration and coordination of activities are mixed; affiliates play leadership roles for some activities and supporting roles for others. Complex integration strategies can either have a regional or global focus. Under a regionally focused complex integration strategy, activities are configured and coordinated within a region. Under a globally focused complex integration strategy, the world becomes the focus. In both cases, the MNC operates as a network of multifunction affiliates.

See also **multinational corporation**

ALLEN J. MORRISON

monetary union   A monetary union establishes a single currency for all common market members and total freedom of money movement between members. This is one of the steps toward complete economic integration which is sometimes sought after by members of a common market. Such a system would result in fixed exchange rates between countries and full freedom to invest, repatriate, or otherwise use money in any of the member countries.

JOHN O'CONNELL

money laundering   The process of transferring money from one country to another or from one business concern to another in order to conceal the money's original source. Generally, money which is laundered is obtained through illegal sources. Huge sums of money obtained through illegal drug trafficking have been laundered (sometimes successfully and sometimes not) through various countries of the world. Although many countries have laws against such activity, as well as banking procedures to report large sums of cash deposited, money laundering activities are extremely difficult to trace.

JOHN O'CONNELL

money market   Compared to other securities exchanges the money market is a rather unstructured grouping of investors and dealers. Investors represent a broad spectrum of business and government interests. Money market trades are in short-term (normally 90 days or less) liquid investments. Financial institutions that participate in money markets provide much of the financing necessary for local and international commercial ventures and trade finance.

JOHN O'CONNELL

money market instruments   Money market instruments are debt contracts comprised of very liquid investments including commercial paper, CDs that are negotiable, T-Bills, other government short-term paper and short-term tax-exempt securities, among others. The London, Tokyo, and New York financial markets (and other large financial markets) are heavily into trading money market instruments.

JOHN O'CONNELL

money market hedge   *see* HEDGING

most favoured nation status (MFN)   This is generally the highest status a nation can receive with respect to international trade matters between nations. A nation granting most favored status to another nation agrees to offer all tariff reductions it offers to all other MNF countries. Thus, when the United States offered China most favoured nation status, the US agreed to provide China with reduced tariffs and other concessions offered to all other MNF countries. A nation not offered most favoured nation status (or one which has MNF status revoked) normally faces large increases in tariff charges. MNF status, in addition to being a powerful economic tool, can also be used as leverage to attain political and other concessions. For example, MNF status has been used by the United States to reward or punish countries with respect to human rights issues.

Bibliography

Winham, G. R. (1992). *The evolution of international trade agreements.* Toronto, Ontario: University of Toronto Press.

JOHN O'CONNELL

multicultural   Multiculture may be defined as having more than one culture represented. The term is used to describe culturally diverse workplaces, living units, and any other situation or activity where more than one culture exists. The existence of multicultural conditions is so prominent in today's world that managers must become aware of differences and learn how to deal with common problems that arise.

See also **Cross-cultural training**

JOHN O'CONNELL

multidomestic company   When a company decides to allow each facility to operate independently (or is forced to in order to deal with local conditions in various countries), instead of attempting to integrate each under a single corporate operation, that organization is referred to as a multidomestic company or multidomestic industry.

See also **Multinational corporation**

JOHN O'CONNELL

multidomestic industry   *see* MULTIDOMESTIC COMPANY

multidomestic strategies   When a multinational organization elects to establish subsidiaries in different countries and allow each subsidiary to function as if it was a local firm, this is referred to as a multidomestic strategy. Each subsidiary acts as if it were a domestic firm in order to be able to respond more effectively to local conditions. In the final analysis each firm is still a member of the parent organization, but also has roots in the country in which it was formed.

See also **Multinational corporation**

Bibliography

Kim, W. C. & Mauborgne, R. A. (1993). Effectively conceiving and executing multinationals' worldwide strategies. *Journal of International Business Studies*, 24 (3), 419.

JOHN O'CONNELL

multilateral trade agreement   The term multilateral means that several countries have entered into an agreement. A multilateral trade agreement is one that a number of countries have promised to uphold. Trade agreements commonly reduce trade barriers between countries thereby improving the possibility of successful and growing trade between those nations.

JOHN O'CONNELL

Multilateral   Investment   Guarantee Agency (MIGA)   The Multilateral Investment Guarantee Agency (MIGA) was formed by the World Bank in 1987. The purpose of MIGA is to offer support for World Bank member country investors in foreign countries through the provision of country risk (political risk) insurance. MIGA offers coverage against expropriation of property, contract repudiation, breach of contract, war, civil commotion and rebellion, and currency inconvertibility. Insurance of this type reduces the overall risk faced by an investor. Often providers of funds for investors require the purchase of political risk and inconvertibility coverage.

JOHN O'CONNELL

multilateral netting   Multilateral netting is an important cash management tool for organizations having operations and currency flows between a number of nations. Each time currency payments must be made there are transaction costs and delays. If an organization could make fewer, but larger currency transfers, transaction costs could be reduced and delays minimized. This is where multinational netting comes in. As an example, assume an organization has operations in three countries. Each operation transfers currency to each other country once per day. Each operation is paying for some goods or services from a country while at the same time receiving payment from that country for goods or services it provided. Thus, a total of six transactions take place (payments and receipts flowing back and forth between each of the three operations). Instead of transferring money directly to the country, a multilateral netting approach would have each operation transfer its payments to a single "coordination center." The coordination center would "net out" (deduct the outflows from the inflows) the individual transactions between the three country operations. The difference would then be sent to each operation (a total of three transactions) at a lower transaction cost and with greater speed.

See also **Cash management**

Bibliography

Celi, L. J. & Rutizer, B. (1991). *Global cash management.* 1st edn, New York: Harper Business (HarperCollins).

Kuhlmann, A. R., Mathis, F. J. & Mills, J. (1991). *First steps in treasury management: Prime cash.* 2nd edn, Toronto, Canada: Treasury Management Association of Canada.

JOHN O'CONNELL

multimodal bill of lading   A bill of lading is normally issued for a single mode of transportation. However, when two or more modes of transportation are used (truck, rail, water, or air) a single bill of lading for the entire trip may be issued. When a multimodal bill of lading is used, each carrier is responsible only for its portion of the trip. Thus, the air carrier is responsible only for the air portion of the trip; the water carrier for its portion; and the truck carrier for the land portion.

See also **Bill of lading; Combined transport bill of lading**

JOHN O'CONNELL

multinational corporation (MNC)   A corporate entity that is involved in operations in a number of countries. Multinational companies generally view the entire world as their market, taking or making opportunities wherever they arise. Although there is some discussion about whether a multinational company must be very large to properly be referred to as an MNC, there is strong support for the position that the way a company acts is more a determinant of it being classified as an MNC than is its size.

See also **MNC strategy**

JOHN O'CONNELL

multinational enterprise (MNE)   A multinational enterprise is very similar to a multinational corporation except that it does not have to be incorporated. Thus, MNE describes a larger number of organizations working across borders. MNEs include multinational partnerships, trusts, and other noncorporate entities. As with a multinational corporation, MNEs are multinational because they think and act as if the world is their place of business.

JOHN O'CONNELL

multinational firm (MNF)   *see* MULTINATIONAL CORPORATION

multiple column tariff   A multiple column tariff discriminates between countries by assessing different rates for the same types of goods imported from different countries. Multiple column tariffs may be used when imports are purchased from less developed countries (LDCs) in order to make their goods more competitive. Many countries offer preferential tariffs to LDCs to assist in their economic development.

See also **Duty**

JOHN O'CONNELL

multiple option facilities   When lenders offer choices of financial instruments it is referred to as a multiple option facility. Securing large amounts of funds by a corporation or government is sometimes difficult unless a loan is syndicated (a number of banks share in providing the loan). Some syndicated loans offer a variety of financial instruments to choose from. Choices to fill out a loan may include Euronotes, various currencies, or straight syndication.

JOHN O'CONNELL

Muslim law   *see* CODE LAW

mutuality of benefits   *see* RECIPROCITY

— N —

national culture When research and other publications dealing with cultural questions are reviewed it may appear that each country has its own unique culture. This is because most research is carried out in a specific country and the assumption is often made that "country" corresponds with "culture." Nothing could be further from the truth. A "national" culture is that of the majority of a country's citizens. The values, beliefs, and attitudes of the majority can and do coexist with a large number of other cultures. One has only to look at the diversity of cultures within the United States for an example of a multicultural country. Still, the US national culture would probably include descriptors such as: individualism, creative, oriented towards accumulation of material goods, and others. As for cultures remaining only within a certain country's boundaries, one may look to Great Britain as a bold example of national culture spreading to many other parts of the world. If a person goes to most of the former British colonies he/she will find a multitude of British cultural attributes alive and well. A national culture may be capable of definition and useful as a first look at what will face a future expatriate. Closer inspection of most countries will reveal the existence of a great number of other cultures.

JOHN O'CONNELL

national currency National currency is the monetary unit and legal tender of a particular country. It is the official currency 'of a country issued by a government-approved establishment. Debts and other obligations of a country are normally paid using the national currency of that country. At last count there were almost 200 different national currencies. A number of countries do not have their own national currency, but instead use the currency of another country (for example, The Isle of Man uses the pound sterling and Andorra uses the French franc and the Spanish peseta). When dealing in the currencies of different countries it is extremely important to know exactly which currency is being quoted. For example, the currency unit 1 franc could mean the Swiss franc (recently quoted at 1.40 per US dollar); the French franc (quoted at 5.62 per US dollar); the Burundi franc (quoted at 330 per US dollar); the Belgium franc (quoted at 33.8 per US dollar); or the Central African Republic franc (quoted at 594 per US dollar).

JOHN O'CONNELL

national treatment An agreement between countries to treat imported products and services (between signatories of the agreement) in the same manner as domestically-produced goods and services. This is an example of free trade at its highest level. Essentially, national treatment removes barriers which may have hampered free trade. National treatment is the basic goal of the General Agreement on Tariffs and Trade (**GATT**).

See also **General Agreement on Tariffs and Trade; Reciprocity**

JOHN O'CONNELL

national treatment with access National treatment is defined as treating imported goods and services on the same basis as domestically-produced goods and services. Essentially this means the removal of barriers for imported goods and services between agreeing countries. The "with access" terminology is the result of problems in the past with one country offering national treatment to goods of a second country, only to find the second country not completely complying with the agreement. "With access" means that country number one will offer national treatment to country number two only if country number two allows importation of country number one's goods and services. "With Access" wording formalizes what is being expected by each country.

See also **Reciprocity**

JOHN O'CONNELL

nationalism   At its best nationalism portrays a citizen's or government's pride in being a part of their country. At its worst, nationalism results in conflict against those not from a particular country, discrimination, protectionism, and other barriers to free flow of people, materials, and thoughts. Nationalism is a very powerful force. It is a force that shows itself in patriotic celebrations and in trade negotiations. With the world seemingly moving to common market and trade bloc existence, nationalism is being tested. For true economic and other integration to occur countries will have to become a part of some larger political and economic system. Although it is not felt that national feelings will cease, such feeling may slowly be adapted to a larger national (supranational) allegiance.

JOHN O'CONNELL

nationality image   This term refers to a company's desire to project its association with a particular country. A company desiring to project its home country nationality image may keep the same brand name for its products and use similar advertising and distribution as in the home country. If a company desires to project the image of the host country, product naming, advertising, and distribution will resemble that of other local products. Nationality image is important. Sometimes it projects quality and credibility. Other times it projects mistrust, poor

quality products, and even hostile feelings. Care must be taken to view the nationality image of a company or product from the eyes of the host country, instead of the eyes of a market researcher in the home office.

JOHN O'CONNELL

nationalization   Nationalization is the action of a government to transfer possession of private property to the government. Many countries have nationalized whole industries on the premise that ownership transfer is in the public's best interests. Compensation is generally offered but there are no guarantees it will be sufficient to pay for loss of value and future profits of the nationalized firm. Nationalization has been most common in extractive industries (mining, energy), communications and financial services (insurance companies and banks). Nationalization is considered a political risk for which insurance coverage may be available.

See also **Political risk; Political risk insurance**

Bibliography

Coplin, W. D. & O'Leary, M. K. (1994). *The handbook of country and political risk analysis.* New York: Political Risk Services.

Gregory, A. (1989). Political risk management in A. Rugman (ed.). *International Business in Canada*, pp. 310–29. Scarborough, Ontario: Prentice-Hall, Canada.

Kennedy, C. R., Jr. (1991). *Managing the international business environment: Cases in political and country risk.* Englewood Cliffs, NJ: Prentice-Hall.

JOHN O'CONNELL

negotiation   When two or more parties need to reach a joint decision but have different preferences, they negotiate. They may not be sitting around a bargaining table; they may not be making explicit offers and counteroffers; they may even not be making statements suggesting that they are on different sides. However, as long as their preferences concerning the joint decision are not identical, they have to negotiate to reach a mutually agreeable outcome.

Over the last decade, the topic of negotiation has captivated the field of Organizational behavior, and more broadly, business schools. It has grown to be one of the most popular topics of instruction, and the current state of research is very different as a result of the interest in this topic. This review will highlight the five dominant areas of research in negotiation:

(1) individual differences;
(2) situational characteristics;
(3) game theory;
(4) asymmetrically prescriptive/descriptive; and
(5) cognitive.

More detailed reviews can be found elsewhere (Neale & Bazerman, 1991).

Individual differences

During the 1960s and early 1970s, the majority of psychological research conducted on negotiations emphasized dispositional variables (Rubin & Brown; 1975), or traits; individual attributes such as demographic characteristics, personality variables, and motivated behavioral tendencies unique to individual negotiators. Demographic characteristics (e.g., age, gender, race, etc.), risk-taking tendencies, locus-of-control, cognitive complexity, tolerance for ambiguity, self-esteem, authoritarianism, and machiavellianism were all hot research topics in 1960s negotiation literature (Rubin & Brown, 1975).

Since bargaining is clearly an interpersonal activity, it seems logical that the participants' dispositions *should* exert significant influence on the process and outcomes of negotiations. Unfortunately, despite numerous studies, dispositional evidence is rarely convincing. When effects have been found, situational features imposed upon the negotiators often reduce or negate these effects. As a result, individual attributes typically do not account for significant variance in negotiator behavior.

A number of authors have reached the conclusion that individual differences offer little insight into predicting negotiator behavior and negotiation outcomes: ". . . there are few significant relationships between personality and negotiation outcomes" (Lewicki & Litterer, 1985).

In addition to the lack of predictability from individual differences research, this literature has also been criticized for its lack of relevance to practice. Bazerman and Carroll (1987) argue that individual differences are of limited value because of their fixed nature, i.e., they are not under the control of the negotiator. Furthermore, individuals, even so-called experts, are known to be poor at making clinical assessments about another person's personality in order to formulate accurately an opposing strategy (Bazerman, 1994).

In summary, the current literature on dispositional variables in negotiation offers few concrete findings. Future research in this direction requires clear evidence, rather than intuitive assertions, that dispositions are important to predicting the outcomes of negotiations.

Situational Characteristics

Situational characteristics are the relatively fixed, contextual components that define the negotiation. Situational research considers the impact of varying these contextual features on negotiated outcomes. Examples of situational variables include the presence or absence of a constituency, the form of communication between negotiators, the outcome payoffs available to the negotiators, the relative power of the parties, deadlines, the number of people representing each side, and the effects of third parties.

Research on situational variables has contributed much to our understanding of the negotiation process and has directed both practitioners and academics to consider important structural components. For example, situational research has found that the presence of observers in a negotiation can dramatically affect its outcome. This effect holds whether the observers are physically or only psychologically present. Further, whether the observers are an audience (i.e., those who do not have a vested interest in the outcome of the negotiation) or a constituency (i.e., those who will be affected by the negotiation) is of little importance in predicting the behavior of the negotiator (Rubin & Brown, 1975).

One of the main drawbacks of situational research is similar to that of individual differences research. Situational factors represent aspects of the negotiation that are usually external to the participants and beyond the individual's control. For example, in organizational settings, participants' control over third-party intervention is limited by their willingness to make the dispute visible and salient. If and when the participants do, their manager usually decides how he or she will intervene as a third party (Murnighan, 1987).

The same criticism holds true for other situational factors, such as the relative power of the negotiators or the prevailing deadlines. While negotiators can be advised to identify ways in which to manipulate their perceived power, obvious power disparities resulting from resource munificence, hierarchical legitimacy, or expertise are less malleable. Negotiators are often best served by developing strategies for addressing these power differentials instead of trying to change them.

The Economic Study of Game Theory

The earliest attempts at providing prescriptive advice to negotiators were offered by economists. The most well-developed component of this economic school of thought is game theory. In game theory, mathematical models are developed to analyze the outcomes that will emerge in multiparty, decision making contexts if all parties act rationally. To analyze a game, specific conditions are outlined which define how decisions are to be made; e.g., the order in which players get to choose their moves; and utility measures of outcomes for each player are attached to *every* possible combination of player moves. The actual analysis focuses on predicting whether or not an agreement will be reached, and if one is reached, what the specific nature of that agreement will be. The advantage of game theory is that, given absolute rationality, it provides the most precise prescriptive advice available to the negotiator. The disadvantages of game theory are two-fold. First, it relies upon being able to completely describe all options and associated outcomes for every possible combination of moves in a given situation – a tedious task at its best, infinitely complex at its worst. Second, it requires all players to act rationally at all times. In contrast, individuals often behave irrationally in systematically predictable ways that are not easily captured within rational analyses.

Asymmetrically Prescriptive/Descriptive

As an alternative to game-theoretic analyses of negotiation which take place in a world of "ultrasmart, impeccably rational, supersmart people," Howard Raiffa developed a *decision-analytic approach* to negotiations – an approach more appropriate to how "erring folks like you and me actually behave," rather than "how we should behave if we were smarter, thought harder, were more consistent, were all knowing" (Raiffa, 1982, p. 21). Raiffa's decision-analytic approach focuses on giving the best available advice to negotiators involved in real conflict with real people. His goal is to provide guidance for a focal negotiator given the most likely profile of the expected behavior of the other party. Thus, Raiffa's approach is prescriptive from the point of view of the party receiving advice, but descriptive from the point of view of the competing party. Raiffa's approach offers an excellent framework for approaching negotiations. However, it is limited in the insights that it provides concerning the behaviors that can be anticipated from the other party.

Raiffa's work represents a turning point in negotiation research for a number of reasons. First, in the context of developing a prescriptive model, he explicitly acknowledges the importance of developing accurate descriptions of opponents, rather than assuming they are fully rational. Second, by realizing that negotiators need advice, he recognizes that they do not intuitively follow purely rational strategies. Most importantly, he has initiated the groundwork for dialogue between prescriptive and descriptive researchers. His work demands descriptive models which allow the focal negotiator to anticipate the likely behavior of the opponent. In addition, we argue that decision analysts must acknowledge that negotiators have decision biases that limit their ability to follow such prescriptive advice.

Cognitive

The cognitive approach (Neale & Bazerman, 1991; Bazerman & Neale, 1992) addresses many of the questions that Raiffa's work leaves behind. If the negotiator and his or her opponent do not act rationally, what systematic departures from rationality can be predicted? Building on work in behavioral decision research, a number of deviations from rationality have been identified that can be expected in negotiations. Specifically, Neale and Bazerman's research on two-party negotiations suggests that negotiators tend to:

(1) be inappropriately affected by the positive or negative frame in which risks are viewed;

(2) anchor their number estimates in negotiations on irrelevant information;

(3) overrely on readily available information;

(4) be overconfident about the likelihood of attaining outcomes that favor them;

(5) assume that negotiation tasks are necessarily fixed-sum and thereby miss opportunities for mutually beneficial trade-offs between the parties;

(6) escalate commitment to a previously selected course of action when it is no longer the most reasonable alternative;

(7) overlook the valuable information that is available by considering the opponent's cognitive perspective; and

(8) retroactively devalue *any* concession that is made by the opponent (Ross, 1994).

These tendencies seriously limit the usefulness of traditional prescriptive models' rationality assumption, i.e., the belief that negotiators are accurate and consistent decision makers. Further, these findings better inform Raiffa's prescriptive model by developing more detailed descriptions of negotiator behavior.

Collectively, these five prospectives provide a summary of the recent history and current state of knowledge of the topic of negotiation. Future research is moving in a cognitive direction, which will hopefully serve the need to better resolve disputes in personal, organizational, and societal affairs.

Bibliography

Bazerman, M. H. (1994). Judgment in managerial decision making. (3rd edn) New York: Wiley.

Bazerman, M. H. & Carroll, J. S. (1987). Negotiator cognition In B. Staw & L. L. Cummings (eds) Research in organizational behavior. Vol. 9, pp. 247–288). Greenwich, CT: JAI Press.

Bazerman, M. H. & Neale, M. A. (1992). Negotiating rationally. New York: Free Press.

Lewicki, R. J. & Litterer, J. A. (1985). Negotiation. Homewood, IL: R.D. Irwin.

Murnighan, J. K. (1987). The structure of mediation and "intravention." Negotiation Journal. 2, (4), 351–356.

Neale, M. A. & Bazerman, M. H. (1991). Cognition and rationality in negotiation. New York: Free Press.

Raiffa, H. (1982). The art and science of negotiation. Cambridge, MA: Belknap.

Ross, L. (1994). Psychological barriers to dispute resolution. In K. Arrow, R. Mnookin, L. Ross, A. Tversky & R. Wilson (eds) Barriers to conflict resolution. New York: Norton.

Rubin, J. Z. & Brown, B. R. (1975). The social psychology of bargaining and negotiation. New York: Academic Press.

MAX H. BAZERMAN

nepotism   Nepotism is favoritism toward relatives in hiring, advancement, job reviews, etc. In many countries nepotism is frowned upon and companies have written rules against such behavior. In some countries, however, nepotism is a way of life in business. Family-owned businesses make it a practice to place relatives in positions in their companies based upon family ties rather than job competence. Workers and/or managers not used to nepotism in the workplace should be aware of local practices, or misunderstandings and uncomfortable situations may arise.

JOHN O'CONNELL

netting   *see* MULTILATERAL NETTING

newly industrialized countries (NICs)   A newly industrialized country is one which has moved beyond the low income level, agrarian-based economy of a less developed country (LDC). It has not yet achieved, however, full industrialization, increased personal income, educational opportunities, etc. of an industrialized nation. Although this category of nation may seem superficial or useless, it does have an impact on a country especially in the area of available economic development funds from various sources. Many providers of funds offer them only to LDCs. Thus, when a country moves from that category to higher level economic status it loses the ability to secure economic development funds from some sources. Countries currently falling into the newly industrialized category include, Thailand, Malaysia, Brazil, and Mexico.

JOHN O'CONNELL

noncommodity agreement   Agreements between countries dealing with things other than products or other goods. Noncommodity agreements address areas such as intellectual property rights, application of laws, technology transfer, human rights, and other intangible concerns.

JOHN O'CONNELL

nonfinancial incentives   Nonfinancial incentives are those not measured in increased pay to an employee but instead are related to status (a new title or new office), greater feeling of stability or well-being (being placed on exempt status instead of hourly payroll), assistance with coping with overseas assignment problems (training in stress management and cultural awareness), and others. Often the nonfinancial benefits are more important to success than are monetary compensation items. It is important to determine not only what incentives are normal for a country or culture but also for individual workers. Although information collection concerning viable incentives is a time-consuming task, the resulting information will allow the structuring of an overall compensation (financial and nonfinancial) system that will be more effective in motivating employees.

See also **Compensation package**

Bibliography

Harvey, M. (1985). The executive family: An overlooked variable in international assignments. *Journal of International Business Studies*, Columbia Journal of World Business 785–800.
Pulatie, D. (1985). How do you ensure success of managers going abroad. *Training and Development Journal*, December, 22–4.

JOHN O'CONNELL

nonresident convertibility   A nonresident of a country normally has the right to exchange local deposits of that country's currency for any other currency. Thus, a Canadian citizen with pound sterling in a London bank could exchange the pound sterling for any other currency. This is referred to as "nonresident convertibility."

JOHN O'CONNELL

non-tariff barriers   These are barriers, other than tariffs or duties, which reduce or restrict the free flow of trade. Such barriers include customs delays, subsidies to local businesses, domestic content requirements, and others.

See also **Barriers**

JOHN O'CONNELL

North American Free Trade Agreement (NAFTA)   NAFTA is a trilateral agreement between Canada, Mexico, and the United States. The agreement seeks to reduce or eliminate tariffs and other trade barriers between the signatory countries. NAFTA is seen as potentially the first step in uniting all of North and South America into a Hemispheric Trading Zone. Relaxation of restrictions should quicken Mexico's economic development, making it into even more of an importer of Canada's and the United States' goods and services. Mexico, on other hand, offers both of its partners inexpensive labor (which is certain to increase in cost as development occurs) and a genuine need for the partner's industries. The agreement is still too new to determine its impact, but all indications seem to point to a successful trade relationship.

Bibliography

Bowker, R. R. (1994). *The North American Free Trade Agreement: A guide to customs procedures*. Chester, PA: Diane Publishing Company.
Bowker, R. R. (1994). *The NAFTA: Supplemental agreements*. Chester, PA: Diane Publishing Company.

JOHN O'CONNELL

O

ocean bill of lading A bill of lading used when goods are consigned to an ocean-going transportation company for shipment to a foreign country. The ocean bill provides details of the shipping transaction as well as of the goods, buyers, sellers, etc.

See also **Bill of lading**

Bibliography

Johnson, T. E. (1994). *Export–Import procedures and documentation.* New York: Amacom.

JOHN O'CONNELL

offset deals   *see* COUNTERTRADE

offset trade   *see* COUNTERTRADE

offsets Offsets can refer to financial transactions in which an investor nullifies a requirement imposed by a previous purchase or to an agreement between importers and exporters. An example of the financial transaction offset is when a person buys a future contract for the delivery of a commodity at a specific time and then purchases another contract for the sale of the same commodity at the same future date. The two transactions cancel or offset each other. With respect to import/export agreements offsets refer to agreements between parties to exchange goods for goods instead of goods for money. This is a countertrade transaction.

See also **Countertrade**

JOHN O'CONNELL

offshore In international trade and finance the term offshore refers to any situation in which deposits, investments, production, or other activities take place in a country other than the home country of the investor, producer, or owner of the deposits. Thus, a US resident placing dollars in a bank in Switzerland would have an offshore deposit. The Swiss bank would be considered an offshore banking facility.

JOHN O'CONNELL

offshore banking Locations that offer services, tax benefits, and confidentiality to foreign depositors. The term offshore banking is often synonomous with "tax haven."

See also **Tax haven**

JOHN O'CONNELL

offshore financial centers An offshore financial center is a place (city or country) to which foreign currency (Eurocurrency) is drawn for deposit. Offshore financial centers usually offer lower tax rates, more confidentiality for transactions, a variety of financial services and security, and lower rates of interest for loans to multinational companies. The most important offshore financial centers are located in Bahrain, the Bahamas and Cayman Islands, Hong Kong, London, New York, Singapore, and Switzerland. A point of confusion may be associated with the term "offshore." It does not mean an island nation, but rather that the currency center is in another country than most of the parties transacting business there.

See also **Tax haven**

JOHN O'CONNELL

offshore funds Funds kept in banks outside of the owner's country are referred to as offshore funds.

See also **Offshore financial centers; Tax haven**

JOHN O'CONNELL

on-board bill of lading When cargo is placed on board a ship for transportation, an on-board bill of lading is given to the exporter when the ship leaves port. The bill provides a list of goods loaded by the carrier. An on-board bill is used as proof of shipment and is often part of the documentation required for the exporter to be paid.

See also **Bill of lading**

Bibliography

Albaum, Gerald, Strandskov, Jesper, Duerr, Edwin & Dowd, Lawrence (1994). *International marketing and export management.* 2nd edn, Wokingham: Addison-Wesley.

JOHN O'CONNELL

on-deck bill of lading When cargo is placed on the deck of a ship for delivery, an on-deck bill of lading is given to the exporter when the ship leaves port. The bill provides a list of goods loaded on the deck of the ship. An on-deck bill is used as proof of shipment and is often part of the documentation required for the exporter to be paid. On-deck transit is more dangerous than if cargo is carried in the hold of a ship. Insurance and financing for such transit may be more difficult to obtain or may be more costly.

Bibliography

Albaum, Gerald, Strandskov, Jesper, Duerr, Edwin & Dowd, Lawrence (1994). *International marketing and export management.* 2nd edn, Wokingham: Addison-Wesley.

JOHN O'CONNELL

OPEC *see* ORGANIZATION OF Petroleum EXPORTING COUNTRIES

open account A method of arranging payment for exports which provides a stated number of days in which the importer must make payment. Open accounts are normally used only when the importer is well known to the exporter.

JOHN O'CONNELL

open cargo policy *see* CARGO INSURANCE

open door treatment Generally the result of a reciprocal trade agreement in which two or more countries agree to allow free (or with very few restrictions) flow of goods between countries. Also called equal treatment.

JOHN O'CONNELL

open insurance policy *see* CARGO INSURANCE

operational centers A financial center in which actual banking transactions take place. A center where money is deposited or passed through is referred to as a "booking" center. New York financial centers are considered operational centers, whereas a financial center in the Bahamas is usually considered a booking center.

JOHN O'CONNELL

OPIC *see* OVERSEAS PRIVATE INVESTMENT CORPORATION

options   An option gives the right to its owner to purchase a specified amount of securities, currency, or commodities at a specified price at a stated time in the future. Options are commonly used to hedge purchases or sales of securities, currency, or commodities. An option is a right and not an obligation, thus the holder does not have to exercise his/her rights under the option.

Bibliography

Eiteman, D. K., Stonehill, A. J. & Moffett, M. H. (1992). *Multinational business finance.* 6th edn, Reading, MA: Addison-Wesley Publishing.

Luft, C. F. (1994). *Understanding and trading futures: A hands-on study guide for investors and traders.* Hinsdale, IL: Probus Publishing Company Inc.

Robbins, J. (1994). *High performance futures trading: Power lessons from the masters.* Hinsdale, IL: Probus Publishing Company Inc.

JOHN O'CONNELL

order bill of lading   This type of bill of lading is a negotiable instrument. That is, it may be used to transfer title to goods being shipped to another party. The transfer may occur at any time during the transit process simply by conveying the order bill to another party. This form of bill of lading was previously referred to as a "uniform bill of lading."

See also **Bill of lading; Straight bill of lading**

Bibliography

Zodl, J. A. (1992). *Export–Import: Everything you and your company need to know to compete in world markets.* Cincinnati, OH: Betterway Books.

JOHN O'CONNELL

Organization for Economic Cooperation and Development (OECD)   In the late 1950s and early 1960s representatives from a number of developed nations began meeting to examine ways to stimulate economic growth in developing countries. In 1961, the Organization for Economic Cooperation and Development was founded. Membership in the OECD include: Australia, Austria, Belgium, Canada, Denmark, Germany, Finland, France, Greece, Iceland, Ireland, Italy, Japan, Luxembourg, the Netherlands, New Zealand, Norway, Portugal, Spain, Sweden, Switzerland, Turkey, the United Kingdom, the United States, and Yugoslavia. The Organization has established committees and centers which assist in its goal of promoting economic development and trade.

See also **Development Assistance Committee; Development Center of the Organization for Economic Cooperation and Development**

Bibliography

Ludlow, N. H. (1988). *A practical guide to the development bank business: How to identify it, market to it, and win it.* Washington, D.C.: Development Bank Associates Inc.

JOHN O'CONNELL

Organization for European Economic Cooperation (OEEC)   After the devastation of Europe caused by World War II there was a need for large-scale, coordinated efforts to assist in rebuilding the economies of European nations. With this in mind, the Organization for European Economic Cooperation was formed in 1948. Essentially, the OEEC had the responsibility to administer the Marshall Plan as well as seeking to expand and liberalize international export/import activities.

JOHN O'CONNELL

Organization of Petroleum Exporting Countries (OPEC)   This is probably the best known of the producer cartels. OPEC was formed in 1960 by a number of major oil-producing nations. The intent of the organization is to establish oil production limits and pricing structures for members. OPEC membership consists of: Algeria, Ecuador, Gabon, Indonesia, Iran, Iraq, Kuwait, Libya, Nigeria, Qatar, Saudi Arabia, the United Arab Emerates, and Venezuela.

See also **Cartel; International commodity group**

JOHN O'CONNELL

organizational culture   The interest in organizational culture during the 1980s – to practitioners and researchers alike – was stimulated by two factors. The first of these was the impact of Japanese enterprises in international markets, and the search to identify a possible link between national culture and organizational performance. The second factor was the perceived failure of the "hard S's" – systems, structure, and strategy – to deliver a competitive advantage, and the belief that this elusive success was more a matter of delivering the "soft S's," such as staff, style, and shared values. However, the early attempts to prescribe a specific culture and manipulate cultural change met with little success, and have led to a reappraisal of what the concept of "culture" involves.

Smircich (1983) provides a useful framework for reappraising the concept. She classifies the perspectives of culture as falling into two broad camps. In the first perspective culture is seen as a "product," something an organization "has." In such an approach, organizational culture is deemed to be as capable of classification and manipulation (usually by management). By contrast, in the second perspective organizational culture is regarded as more of a "process," something an organization "is." According to this perspective, "culture" is much more difficult to pin down and pigeon-hole, and does not lend itself to manipulation.

Culture as a "Product"

This perspective generates a spectrum of definitions, ranging from those that emphasize the surface indicators to those that try to tap some deeper meaning. The surface manifestations include definitions such as "how things get done around here," or culture as a "stock of values, beliefs, and norms widely subscribed to by those who work in an organization." In this vein, an influential approach has been Handy's division of cultures into four types: power, role, task, and person (Handy, 1978). Deeper definitions refer more to culture as "mental processes or mindsets characteristic of organizational members."

Hofstede (1990) defines culture as the "software of the mind." His work, conducted in over 50 countries, has concentrated on unearthing national cultural differences and determining how these influence organizational life. He claims that organizations have to confront two central problems: how to distribute power and how to manage uncertainty. He then identifies five value dimensions which, he claims, discriminate between national groups, and which influence the way in which people perceive that an organization should be managed to meet these two key problems. The dimensions are as follows:

- power distance, i.e., the extent to which people accept that power is distributed unequally

- uncertainty avoidance, i.e., the extent to which people feel uncomfortable with uncertainty and ambiguity

- individualism/collectivism, i.e., the extent to which there is a preference for belonging to tightly knit collectives rather than a more loosely knit society

- masculinity/feminity, i.e., the extent to which gender roles are clearly distinct (masculine end of the spectrum) as opposed to those where they overlap (feminine end of the spectrum)

- Confucian dynamism, i.e., the extent to which long-termism or short-termism tends to predominate

Hofstede's work is only based on employees of one organization. Furthermore, the extent to which one country can be said to have an homogenous culture is problematic. Nevertheless, Hofstede's work has been highly influential. It attempts to explain why differing national cultural mind-sets will cause difficulties when a manager from one country goes to work abroad. Difficulties can also be predicted when two organizations from countries with different cultural mind-sets attempt to merge. Adler's work (1991) on differing national negotiating styles is also useful for gaining an understanding of cultural differences between nations. It is interesting to speculate whether globalization will increase the need to understand national cultural differences (as multinationals seek to manage diverse workforces) or whether the need will decrease as globalization brings about an homogenization of national cultures.

In terms of the desire to "learn from Japan," it is possible to identify specific cultural values in Japanese society which might influence economic performance, such as the importance attached to reciprocity between those of different status. However, there are successful organizations in other parts of the world in which these conventions are flouted. Indeed, even within Japan, there is a range of organizational practices as to how employees are treated. It is also difficult to disentangle the effects of culture on performance from other factors, such as industrial structure, manufacturing practices, and the role of the state (Dawson, 1992). The evidence on the attempts to introduce Japanese practices in other countries is also mixed (for the UK experience, see Oliver & Hunter, 1994).

The "culture as a product" perspective has also focused on the role of comparative organizational cultures within a country. Here an attempt has been made to provide a rigorous test as to what sort of a culture will lead to high performance. Denison (1991) argues that the four specific variables that influence performance are involvement, consistency, adaptability, and mission. Denison notes how these variables are, to some extent, contradictory: for example, consistency in terms of having agreement can sometimes inhibit adaptability. It is also important that a culture is appropriate to its environment, so it is unlikely that there is one universal culture that suits all environments. On the other hand, environments change much more rapidly than organizational cultures, which can take many years to develop. Kotter & Heskett (1992) claim that cultures in which there is a strong consensus that key stakeholders should be valued, leadership at all levels is seen as important, and the culture underpins an appropriate strategy, can serve as valid generalizations, but these claims have yet to be put to the test. Brown (1994) carries a useful summary of both this issue and of the literature on models of organizational cultural change, of which Schein's model (1985) is the best-known.

Culture as a Process

Smircich's other perspective sees culture as a root metaphor for understanding organizations. This perspective makes it difficult to define culture. Organizations do not so much *have* cultures; it is more that they *are* cultures. This

has implications for those who wish to try to change a culture.

The "culture as root metaphor" concept sees culture as something that is collectively enacted, where all who experience a culture at first hand become part of its generation and reproduction. To assume that one group (usually management) can unilaterally modify a culture is thus to mistake its essential properties. This is not to deny that culture changes – indeed, its enactment is a continuous process – but it usually changes in unintended ways. It is important also to recognize that collective enactment does not mean harmony and agreement; the power to enact is not equally shared amongst all groups.

The concept also has implications for those who wish to research cultures: the researcher inevitably becomes part of the enactment process (Weick, 1983). Trying to fix a culture and establish typologies is just an interpretation, one more part of the enactment process. As Martin (1993, p. 13) puts it: "Culture is not reified – out there – to be accurately observed."

However, this does not mean that the concept of "culture" is valueless except as a stick to beat those who see it as a product. Morgan (1986) argues that culture can be a powerful metaphor for enabling thought about organizations, drawing attention to the importance of patterns of subjective meaning, of images, and of values in organizational life.

Conclusion

The life cycle of organizational culture mirrors that of many other alleged managerial panaceas, running through the stages of initial enthusiasm, followed by a critical backlash, and ending up with a more widely based consensus on the limited applicability of the concept, which often highlights the complexity of management as a discipline.

Culture as a "product" has already gone through this cycle. It soon became clear that "culture" is not something that can easily be manipulated. Indeed, culture as a "process" seems a more powerful perspective in that it recognizes that culture depends upon human interaction – it is continuously being produced and re(created). To believe that one group can unilaterally change an existing culture according to some blueprint is mistaken. Culture does change – but often slowly and in unpredictable ways. Managers who wish to establish a blue-print might be better advised to go for a greenfield site and then carefully control recruitment and selection (Wickens, 1987). There is also the danger of thinking of culture as a monolithic entity to which all organizational members subscribe. Martin (1993) terms such a view "integrationist" and contrasts it with a "differentiation" focus, which stresses the importance of subcultures and the potential for conflict between these subcultures.

Even if a particular culture could be established by managerial fiat, the links between culture and organizational performance are not well-established. Assuming that cultures can be measured and pigeon-holed, there is no clear evidence that one particular type of culture is always associated with success – indeed, some of the features which are claimed to be linked with success are themselves contradictory. Further-more, the sheer complexity of the factors involved in organizational performance makes it difficult to pin-point the exact contribution made by culture alone.

Bibliography

Adler, N. (1991). *International dimensions of organisa-tional behaviour*, Boston, MA: PWS-Kant.

Brown, A. (1994). *Organisational culture*, London: Pitman.

Dawson, S. (1992). *Analysing organisations*, (2nd edn), London: Macmillan.

Denison, D. (1991). *Corporate culture and organisa-tional effectiveness*, New York: John Wiley.

Handy, C. (1978). *The gods of management*, Har-mondsworth, UK: Penguin.

Hofstede, G. (1990). *Cultures and organisations: software of the mind*, Maidenhead, UK: McGraw-Hill.

Kotter, J. P. & Heskett, J. L. (1992). *Corporate culture and performance*, New York: The Free Press.

Martin, J. (1993). *Cultures in organisations*, Oxford: Oxford University Press.

Morgan, G. (1986). *Images of organisations*, Sage.

Oliver, N. & Hunter, G. (1994). The financial impact of Japanese production methods in UK companies. Paper no. 24 Cambridge, UK: Judge Institute of Management Studies.

Schein, E. H. (1985). *Organisational culture and leadership*, London: Jossey–Bass.

Smircich, L. (1983). Concepts of culture and organisational analysis. *Administrative Science Quarterly*, **28**, 339–58.

Weick, K. (1983). Enactment processes in organisations. B. Staw, G. Salancik (Ed.), *New directions in organisational behaviour*, Malabar, FL: Robert E. Krieger.

Wickens, P. (1987). *The road to Nissan: flexibility, quality, teamwork*, London: Macmillan.

MICHAEL BROCKLEHURST

orientation Orientation is a process that prepares an expatriate (and in some cases, family members) for an overseas assignment. The orientation process can take little time or effort or may be very involved and time consuming depending upon the person being transferred and the location of the transfer.

See also **Cross-cultural training; Expatriate training**

JOHN O'CONNELL

overall reciprocity This takes place when two countries agree to offer one another virtually unrestricted trade concessions. It is the broadest form of reciprocity. Overall reciprocity is one of the ultimate goals of nations belonging to trading groups or blocs. Achievement of overall reci-procity has been found to be an extremely difficult objective.

See also **Reciprocity**

JOHN O'CONNELL

overbase compensation Base salaries between the home country and the host country are usually equalized for an expatriate. That is the pay in the host country would be the same for the same job in the home country. Adjust-ments in the form of higher pay to offset inconveniences and dangers not occurring in the home country or longer periods of work (as expected in some countries) are referred to as "overbase" compensation.

See also **Compensation package**

JOHN O'CONNELL

Overseas Private Investment Corporation (OPIC) The Overseas Private Investment Corporation is a United States government agency which is a part of the overall effort of the US government to encourage private business investment in developing countries as well as those countries emerging from communist forms of government. In order to encourage investment by US businesses, OPIC offers three important tools for their use: (1) business financing through direct loans and by guaranteeing loans to business investors; (2) political risk insurance to cover many of the actions of a foreign government which may deprive the investor of some or all of the investment assets; and (3) a number of services to make the task of overseas investment simpler. The Overseas Private Investment Corporation is located in Washington, D.C.

See also **Political risk; Political risk insurance**

JOHN O'CONNELL

P

Pacific Economic Cooperation Group (PECG) A number of Pacific Ocean region countries have entered into an agreement to pursue discussions of ways to promote cooperation and economic development in the area. Virtually all of the countries surrounding the Pacific Ocean are members of the group.

JOHN O'CONNELL

Pacific Rim countries The countries that surround the Pacific Ocean. These countries include some of the largest and most powerful economies in the world. Often people define the Pacific Rim as those countries that are poised for economic growth (i.e., Southeast Asian countries). Strictly speaking, however, all countries bordering the ocean must be included.

JOHN O'CONNELL

packing list When goods are placed in a container a record of the contents is kept. This record is used to verify the container's contents, if necessary, during shipment as well as when the goods are eventually delivered. A "packing list" is also helpful in verifying contents if a loss of the container was to occur.

JOHN O'CONNELL

Pan American Copyright Convention One of the early attempts to protect intellectual property rights. Countries which are signatories to the agreement (many Latin American countries and the United States) will recognize copyrights of other signatory countries as long as the copyrighted piece is properly marked as being protected.

See also **Intellectual property**

Bibliography

Seminsky, M. & Bryer, L. G. (eds) (1994). *The new role of intellectual property in commercial transactions.* New York: John Wiley & Sons.

JOHN O'CONNELL

parallel loans A loan between two organizations in a foreign country which turns out to actually involve four organizations in two countries. A parallel loan is a method of offsetting a loan made to a subsidiary in another country. Here is how it works: A subsidiary company in country A needs money to operate. Instead of getting money directly from its parent company (which would involve selling parent company currency and buying subsidiary country currency) a parallel loan agreement is worked out. Subsidiary company number 1 borrows local funds from subsidiary company number 2. The parent companies of both subsidiaries (which are both located in a second country) arrange another loan between each other in their home currency. The second loan offsets the first loan.

Bibliography

Eiteman, D. K., Stonehill, A. J. & Moffett, M. H. (1992). *Multinational business finance.* 6th edn, Reading, MA: Addison-Wesley Publishing.

JOHN O'CONNELL

parent company Groups of companies are often formed by incorporating companies as the need may arise or through acquisition of organizations. Generally one company in the group owns the majority of shares in each of the other companies. The majority shareholder is usually referred to as the "parent company." Other terms also refer to parent companies: (1) a "holding" company is a parent, but has no actual business of its own except buying, selling, and holding other companies (e.g., a holding company may buy and sell a variety of other organizations - from financial organizations to manufacturers and processors); (2) an "operating" company is the parent of similar subsidiaries (e.g., one insurance company owns other insurance companies.)

JOHN O'CONNELL

parent country national (PCN) Citizens of the country in which the parent company is established. Parent country nationals may be called upon to become expatriates if the company decides to offer them overseas positions.

JOHN O'CONNELL

Paris Convention *see* PARIS UNION

Paris Union Formally known as the Paris Convention for the Protection of Industrial Property, the Paris Union is an early example of a multilateral agreement to protect patents, trademarks, and industrial designs. The agreement afforded national treatment (same protections as in each signatory country's laws) for property rights registered in any signatory country to the agreement. The agreement also supports the so-called "first to file" standard, which gives exclusive rights to the individual who first files for registration of a patent or other right in "any" of the member countries. Thus, if two inventors filed for the same invention, the one with the earliest filing date would receive the patent.

See also **World Intellectual Property Organization**

Bibliography

Leaffer, M. A. (Ed.) (1990). *International treaties on intellectual property*. Washington, D.C.: BNA Books.

JOHN O'CONNELL

passport Citizens who desire to travel abroad must apply to their government for a passport. Passports offer official certification of the identity and citizenship of the holder.

See also **Visa**

JOHN O'CONNELL

patent A government license granting exclusive rights to an invention. Exclusive rights include the right to use, sell, or produce the patented item. Patent rules and procedures vary from country to country. An inventor or possessor of a patent is well advised to seek professional assistance in seeking protection for patents in other nations. There is a serious international problem regarding unauthorized use of patents and other intellectual property rights. Most nations have some form of intellectual property rights protection (for properly applied for and issued patents, etc.) but the enforcement of such rights varies from strict to almost nil.

See also **Intellectual property; Patent Cooperation Treaty; World Intellectual Property Organization**

Bibliography

Leaffer, M. A. (Ed.) (1990). *International treaties on intellectual property*. Washington, D.C.: BNA Books.
Stewart, G. R. (Ed.) (1994). *International trade and intellectual property: The search for a balanced system*. Boulder, CO: Westview Press.

JOHN O'CONNELL

Patent Cooperation Treaty (PCT) The Patent Cooperation Treaty is one of the most beneficial treaties in existence with respect to the international protection of patents (at least amongst the signatory nations of the treaty). Under this treaty an inventor begins the international patent process by making a single PCT application in his/her own country (assuming the country has membership in PCT). The application is then reviewed to assure that it meets the criteria set forth for the granting of a patent. An international search takes place of member country records, to ascertain if a patent has already been issued. If no problems arise, a patent will be issued which is honored by all signatory countries. The applicant pays only once for the application process and that is in the home country of the prospective patent holder. There are approximately 50 signatories to the PCT including most European nations, Australia, Japan, and the United States. The PCT program operates under the World Intellectual Property Organization.

See also **Intellectual property; World Intellectual Property Organization**

Bibliography

Leaffer, M. A. (Ed.) (1990). *International treaties on intellectual property*. Washington, D.C.: BNA Books.
Stewart, G. R. (Ed.) (1994). *International trade and intellectual property: The search for a balanced system*. Boulder, CO: Westview Press.

JOHN O'CONNELL

pay equity A government regulation requiring all organizations in a country to provide equal pay for equal work. Not all countries have such laws. The law's intent is to correct past discrimination in pay between men and women or between different races. Organizations seeking to do business in a country with pay equity statutes (the United States, for example) must strictly comply with the law. This means that some companies will have to treat workers in the United States differently than in the company's home country. Severe penalties apply to those not following the law.

See also **Affirmative action; Equal opportunity**

JOHN O'CONNELL

PCN *see* PARENT COUNTRY NATIONAL

peg To peg is to stabilize or link the value of something to some base value or other measure. For example, the value of a currency may be pegged or linked to the value of another currency. Changes in the value of the base currency result in corresponding changes in the pegged currency.

JOHN O'CONNELL

pegged exchange rates Pegged exchange rates are those which are tied to a specific currency or a derived monetary unit such as the European Currency Unit (ECU) of the European Community. If a currency is "pegged" its value rises or falls with that of the currency to which it is tied. Pegging a currency to a more stable currency or to a market basket currency such as the ECU acts to stabilize the first currency.

See also **European Currency Unit**

JOHN O'CONNELL

penalty duty Any duty which is in addition to regular duties. Penalty duties are imposed to add additional costs on an exporter/importer for not complying with fair trade practices or the customs laws of a country. Penalty duties include "marking" duties, "exclusionary" duties, "anti-dumping" duties, and "retaliatory" duties.

See also **Anti-dumping duty; Dumping; Duty**

Bibliography

Viner, J. (1991). *Dumping: A problem in international trade*. Caldwell, NJ: Augustus M. Kelley Publishers.

JOHN O'CONNELL

performance evaluation (international managers) Managers (or any other employee) are expected to successfully perform a number of tasks and/or assignments for an organization. In order to determine the extent of a manager's success in carrying out required activities, periodic appraisals of performance are strongly advised. To be effective, a performance evaluation must concentrate on those factors which are within a manager's control and are included in a clear statement of the manager's scope of authority and responsibility. To judge the performance of a manager on the basis of factors which are uncontrollable or not within the scope of authority or responsibility granted is unfair and not responsive to the purpose of an evaluation. Although an evaluation system that includes factors over which a manager has no control may not result in a poor rating of the manager, it will result in a rating that does not realistically portray the achievements of the manager within his/her stated job objectives.

Areas of performance measurement usually used for managers include: meeting budgets; production goals; sales goals; quality of product or service measures; profitability of department; and market share. All of these items are normally subject to measurement and control on the part of the manager when a domestic operation is being reviewed. However, international managers may not have the same degree of control over these or other factors when business is carried out in another country. Evaluation factors must be reviewed in terms of the conditions in the host country. Profits may be restricted because of local laws or tax structures; market penetration may be closely monitored and governed by the host government; production figures, etc. may be partially determined by the continued availability of trained labor, raw materials and other resources, some of which may be in short supply or in intermittent supply in a foreign country; and quality and service measures may not be comparable with home country operations because of the inability to obtain data or different standards which may apply in the host country.

Evaluating the managers of foreign operations requires a good deal of work to establish the standards by which comparisons will be made. Using the experience of former expatriate managers and sharing of ideas in professional meetings are two ways of gaining additional insight into the problem. The three most important things to remember are: (1) the areas of evaluation must be under the control of the manager to be evaluated; (2) the evaluators must be well versed and aware of the host country environment in which the manager is expected to perform; and (3) the input of the expatriate manager must become a part of the evaluation process in order to explain the peculiar differences the manager has encountered in running an overseas operation.

Bibliography

Carroll, S. J. & Schneier, C. E. (1982). *Performance appraisal and review systems*. Glenview, IL: Scott, Foresman.

Caudron, D. (1991). Training ensures success overseas. *Personnel Journal*, **70**, 27–30.

Dowling, P. J. & Schuler, R. S. (1990). *International dimensions of human resource management*. Boston, MA: PWS-Kent.

JOHN O'CONNELL

perils of the sea A marine insurance term used to describe some of the causes of loss which may affect property on an ocean voyage. Generally speaking, perils of the sea are those causes over which the captain of a vessel has no control. Thus, if a peril of the sea causes damage to cargo, the carrier may or may not be responsible depending upon the nature of the loss. If there was no negligence on the part of the captain of the ship, the carrier would probably not be held responsible for compensating cargo owners for loss or damage. Cargo insurance coverage is available to cover for such losses for the benefit of the cargo owner. Perils of the sea include: severe weather causing high waves; high winds; lightning strikes; fog; striking ice; stranding; sinking; or collision with another vessel.

See also **Marine insurance**

JOHN O'CONNELL

permanent assignment The term "permanent assignment" infers that the employee will not return from the assignment during his/her work career with the company. Permanent assignment actually has different meanings in different companies. Some companies use the term to mean an assignment of at least one year, while other companies use two, three or more years. Each company will have its own way of describing assignment duration. There is no standard which is used throughout the world.

JOHN O'CONNELL

perq *see* PERQUISITE; FRINGE BENEFITS

perquisite Generally, a perquisite refers to an indirect form of compensating an employee which results in favored tax treatment of that compensation. For example, in some countries the premium paid by an employer for company paid insurance programs is not taxable as income to the employee. Thus, the employee gets the additional benefit (insurance) with no income tax payable and the employer is able to deduct the premium payment as a business expense.

See also **Fringe benefits**

JOHN O'CONNELL

phytosanitary inspection certificate A phytosanitary inspection certificate is an official government statement from the exporting country that exports of plants, animals, meat, and other commodities have been inspected and are free from disease or insects which might damage the health or agriculture of the importing country.

JOHN O'CONNELL

piggyback exporting Piggyback exporting describes a situation in which one company markets its products through the distribution channels of a second company. Two major reasons for piggyback marketing are: (1) a local company desires to enter multinational markets but lacks the money, experience, or possibly the inclination to learn what is necessary to be successful in the international marketplace; (2) an existing multinational company is seeking to fill out its product lines to stay competitive overseas. Piggybacking involves products which compliment one another instead of competing. This method of exporting is one of the least problematic of all of the methods of entering foreign markets. Of course, success is dependent upon who the partners are and the commitment to making the partnership function effectively.

See also **Market entry strategies**

Bibliography

Cateora, P. R. (1993). *International marketing*. 5th edn, Homewood, IL: Irwin.

JOHN O'CONNELL

piracy This term is used to describe two situations related to the management of international enterprises. Both definitions are related to the illegal taking of property but in vastly different contexts. (1) The unauthorized use of a patent, trademark, copyright, or other protected intellectual property. This form of illegal activity removes billions of dollars of income from companies each year. The issuance of fake products using the name of famous manufacturers; illegally copying and distributing computer programs, videotapes, and sound recordings as if they came from the original manufacturer; producing and distributing pharmaceuticals without permission; and using patented industrial processes and machinery without permission are only a few piracy techniques. (2) Piracy of cargo and/or ships. Many people believe that piracy on the seas is a thing of the past. But it is not. There are many specific areas of the world in which armed pirates seize ships and cargo on a frequent basis. The waters just south of Singapore are well known for this problem, as are some of the waters of the southern Caribbean. Piracy also takes place at the hands of bandits who attack overland transportation vehicles in some countries. Regions of the world with special problems with any type of piracy can be identified by requesting information from the International

Chamber of Commerce or domestic governmental officials charged with overseeing trade activities.

See also **Intellectual property; World Intellectual Property Organization**

Bibliography

International Intellectual Property Alliance Staff (1992). *Copyright piracy in Latin America: Trade losses due to piracy and the adequacy of copyright protection in 16 Central and South American countries.* Washington, D.C.: International Intellectual Property Alliance.

JOHN O'CONNELL

point-of-hire   The country in which an employee was originally hired. Point-of-hire generally determines salary range, benefits package, and other compensation items. Many international companies are sending fewer expatriates to foreign operations because of the great expense involved as well as the increase in host country persons who are qualified to take up positions. It is not uncommon for a company to seek out the top foreign students in local universities and colleges to hire them for positions in the student's home country. The actual hiring takes place in the student's home country, which can often dramatically reduce the company's overall employee cost. If point-of-hire is in a more expensive labor cost or benefit country, the employee will cost the company more than if point-of-hire is in a less expensive country.

JOHN O'CONNELL

political risk   Political risks are associated with government actions which deny or restrict the right of an investor/owner: (1) to use or benefit from his/her assets; or (2) which reduce the value of a firm. The most well known of the political risks include: war, revolutions, government seizure of property (expropriation, nationalization, or confiscation), and actions to restrict the movement of profits or other revenues from within a country. The impact of political risk sources of loss varies from the total destruction of assets (war); to the ability to operate but without the right to return profits to a home country (currency inconvertibility); to the taking of private property for the social good (expropriation, nationalism, confiscation). The following is a listing of governmental actions which could affect the value of a business or restrict an owner's rights to use or benefit from the business.

1 Confiscation – This is one of the major political risks faced by multinational enterprises. Confiscation is the taking of private property by a government without any offer of compensation. Governments which confiscate privately-owned property of foreign organizations usually use the excuse that the foreign firm was exploiting the country or that relations between the government and the foreign country are too strained to allow any representative of the foreign country to continue in business. Businesses considering large capital investment in a country should check the status of political risk "before" such investment takes place.

2 Contract repudiation – From time to time a contractor will enter into a contract with a foreign government only to find that the contract cannot be fulfilled. This may be because the government terminates the contract without showing cause, refuses to pay for delivered goods, cancels the contractor's license to operate, or otherwise causes cancellation of the contract. Contracts with private buyers are subject to the same set of circumstances, although legal remedies may be available which are lacking when dealing directly with government contracts. Although most contracts are fulfilled without problem, a sufficient number are not honored to support the growth of a specific type of insurance to protect against contract repudiation.

3 Currency inconvertibility – A government may restrict the right of foreign firms to repatriate (send home) profits to their home country. Thus, all profits remain in the foreign country. If an organization does not have other operations in that country, or the owners do not have residence there, this may cause great hardship. Inconvertibility

may arise because of the passage of new laws or because of administrative slowdown. Administrative slowdown refers to situations in which the government bureaucracy of a foreign country slows (either intentionally or unintentionally) the process to convert currency to such a point that it becomes a financial burden to foreign-owned companies. Insurance is available for both causes of currency inconvertibility.

4 Discriminatory taxation – Charging higher tax rates to foreign companies than for domestic companies. This type of protectionist action is not as common as it has been in the past but it still exists in many countries. The system of taxation in a foreign country must be considered when determining the method by which a company will enter that country. For example, if a local company is charged lower tax rates than a foreign-owned company, a local joint venture may be in order.

5 Embargo – To embargo is to prohibit or forbid the movement of certain or all goods to a certain country or countries. One of the most recent embargoes was that placed against Iraq after its invasion of Kuwait in the early 1990s. As of the writing of this book (mid-1996) much of that embargo is still in place. As with the United Nations sanctioned embargo of Iraq, most embargoes are implemented in times of war or to attempt to force political change by other than military force. Embargoes are difficult to implement and even more difficult to enforce over long periods of time. Embargoes not only harm the country to which they are imposed, but also all of the international export of goods to that country.

6 Expropriation of property – The government seizure of private property owned by a foreign company, with compensation being offered. Expropriation is normally aimed at a specific company whereas "nationalization" generally affects an entire industry. Expropriation may occur because of host country feelings that the foreign company is taking advantage of the host country and its people; or because of disagreements between the company and the government; or for any other reason deemed acceptable to the host government.

7 Nationalization – Nationalization is the action of a government to transfer possession of private property to the government. Many countries have nationalized whole industries on the premise that ownership transfer is in the public's best interests. Compensation is generally offered but there are no guarantees it will be sufficient to pay for loss of value and future profits of the nationalized firm. Nationalization has been most common in extractive industries (mining, energy) and communications and financial services (insurance companies and banks). Nationalization is considered a political risk for which insurance coverage may be available.

8 War risk – Actual damage caused by war, rebellion, insurrection, invasion, or use of military force to invade sovereign territory with the intent of exerting governing control. Although the definition of war varies considerably depending upon the legal jurisdiction, the fact that war or warlike actions cause severe damage to property is of the greatest interest in the present context. Generally, war risk insurance is not available in any standard market. When war risk is covered by insurance it is most likely to be under a marine insurance policy with war risk added. Land-based property damage by war is rarely covered by any insurance contract, although it is sometimes available through insurance companies that write political risk insurance.

9 Wrongful calling of guarantees – The unfair collection of a letter of credit, on-demand bond, or other guarantee of performance established by a company on behalf of a government. Companies are often required to put up a good faith guarantee of their performance before being allowed to begin work on a contract for a foreign government. For example, a road contractor may be required to provide 10% of the bid amount to a government before the government will allow construction to begin. The guarantee is supposed to provide the government with leverage to force the contract to be accomplished on time and in a workman-like manner. Wrongful calling occurs when the government causes non-performance to occur. Cancellation of the contractor's

permit to work in a country or restrictions on working hours could result in non-performance, thereby making the guarantee collectible by the government. Such collection is an example of a wrongful calling of a guarantee.

Bibliography

Cosset, J. & Roy, J. (1991). The determinants of country risk ratings. *Journal of International Business Studies*, **22** (1), 135–42.

Gregory, A. (1989). Political risk management in A. Rugman (Ed.) *International Business in Canada*, pp. 310–29. Scarborough, Ontario: Prentice-Hall, Canada.

Howell, L. D. (1994). The political sociology of foreign investment and trade: Testing risk models for adequacy of protection. *AGSIM Faculty Publication*, No. 94–105.

Mathis, F. J. (1990). International risk analysis in R. T. Moran (Ed.) *Global Business Management in the 1990s*. Washington, D.C.: Beacham.

Micallef, J. V. (1981). Political risk assessment. *Columbia Journal of World Business*, **16** (2), 47–52.

Yaprak, A. & Sheldon, K. T. (1984). Political risk management in multinational firms: An interrogative approach. *Management Decisions*, 53–67.

JOHN O'CONNELL

political risk insurance Political risks are associated with government actions that deny or restrict the right of an investor/owner: (1) to use or benefit from his/her assets; or (2) which reduce the value of a firm. The most well known of the political risks include: war, revolution, the government seizure of property (expropriation, nationalization, or confiscation), and actions to restrict the movement of profits or other revenues from within a country. Although not all political risks are subject to insurance coverage, insurance is available for a number of government actions which act to take away or reduce the value of a foreign firm.

Political risk insurance is usually not available for the actions of a company's home government. Thus, if a United States company was subjected to high taxes or fines, political risk insurance would not provide coverage. However, if a US company was confiscated by the Libyan government the confiscation losses could be covered by political risk insurance. The discussion which follows is meant to provide general information on common coverages and restrictions in political risk insurance. Each insurer writing such coverage must be contacted to determine the exact details of their various political risk programs. Common political risk coverage includes:

1 Comprehensive export credit insurance coverage – This insurance provides coverage for losses (above those normally expected in the course of business) caused by a buyer failing to make payment due to political and commercial risks. Political risks are those associated with acts of government, whereas commercial risk includes insolvency of a buyer or other economic reasons for nonpayment. Another type of loss commonly covered by the broader forms of this coverage is if a foreign buyer cannot convert currency in order to make payment to the insured. Coverage is generally very broad, but one cannot rely on the name of an insurance contract (e.g., "comprehensive") to imply coverage. Each contract must be carefully reviewed in making a purchase decision.

2 Confiscation, expropriation, and nationalization coverage – Insurance companies usually do not differentiate between confiscation, expropriation, and nationalization because each involves the actions of a government to deprive a company of its assets or the profits derived from those assets. If compensation is paid by a government the amount received acts to reduce the payment by the insurance company. Depending on the insurance company, coverage is often found for buildings, inventory, or mobile equipment, all of which is located in a foreign country. Policies covering worldwide exposure are preferred by insurers because it provides a good spread of risk. Although single country coverage is available, the company that picks and chooses countries to insure and those to go without, often pays as much as if its entire worldwide exposure was covered. The reason for this is that the countries chosen offer the greatest risk, and thus carry the highest premiums. The insurer would probably be willing to offer an average rate for all exposures which

would have been much lower than that offered for the highest risk countries.

3 Contract repudiation coverage – This type of political risk insurance provides coverage for noncompliance with contracts by a foreign government. An insured doing business with a foreign government faces the risk that the government will not comply with the contract, thereby causing loss to the insured. For example, a building construction contractor expects to be paid when the building is completed, but may not be paid if the government terminates the contract or makes it impossible for the contractor to complete the project on schedule thereby forcing a default. Insurance against contract repudiation commonly provides coverage for: unilateral government termination of a contract without cause; nonpayment of a government for service or other contracts; license termination which forces the company to default; embargoes which make completion impossible; and other government actions as outlined in each policy. Some insurers will also offer coverage for war risk which causes contract cancellation.

4 Inconvertibility of currency coverage – The inability to convert local currency into a company's home currency. This is an important consideration for an organization seeking to repatriate profits or dividends from a foreign operation. Insurance against losses arising from inconvertibility is available from speciality international insurance markets. Insurance commonly protects against one or both of the following situations:

(a) A change in a law or regulation which restricts the right to convert currency. As long as there is an official method of currency conversion before the insurance contract goes into force, coverage usually applies for changes in the law from that point forward. Most policies require that normal convertibility be delayed at least 60 to 90 days beyond the normal conversion period.

(b) An administrative delay on the part of the country's exchange authority which delays the ability to exchange currency. Most policies require the delay to be a minimum number of days beyond the period normally

required for conversion. If either of these situations occur, the insurer converts the currency for the insured into the currency designated in the contract.

5 Wrongful calling of guarantees coverage – The unfair collection of a letter of credit on-demand bond, or other guarantee of performance established by a company on behalf of a government. Companies are often required to put up a good faith guarantee of their performance before being allowed to begin work on a contract for a foreign government. For example, a road contractor may be required to provide 10% of the bid amount to a government before the government will allow construction to begin. The guarantee is supposed to provide the government with leverage to force the contract to be accomplished on time and in a workman-like manner. Wrongful calling occurs when the government causes non-performance to occur. Cancellation of the contractor's permit to work in a country or restrictions on working hours could result in non-performance, thereby making the guarantee collectible by the government. Such collection is an example of a wrongful calling of a guarantee. Exporters are also subject to wrongful calls of guarantees when required to bid on supplying goods to foreign governments. Insurance policies for wrongful calling usually provide coverage if the call on the guarantee was caused by the action of a government, such as the cancellation of an import or export license or other action that causes the non-performance. This is one type of political risk insurance in which the actions of a home government may also be covered. Persons interested in this type of coverage must contact their insurer or broker because coverage details periodically change and differ between insurers.

See also **Political risk**

JOHN O'CONNELL

political union   A political union exists when two or more countries agree to allow some or all of their individual political decisions to be made by a body outside of their own, existing, governments. A third-party government to which countries transfer governing power is referred to as a "supranational" organization or one which spans national boundaries. A good example of a supranational organization is the European Community Parliament which exercises control over the EC, thereby taking some of the powers previously held by each member country of the community.

JOHN O'CONNELL

polycentric approach to hiring   Polycentrism is the belief that managers and employees in a foreign operation should be from the host country. The feeling is that people native to the host country will not have problems with: culture shock, knowing the language, realizing and adhering to the local customs, values and attitudes, and being effective immediately instead of after a learning process has taken place. Key positions in the foreign operation are filled with host country nationals (HCNs). This saves money associated with recruiting, training, and transferring expatriates from other countries in which the company also has operations. There are, however, possible negative aspects of a polycentric approach to hiring. One of the biggest problems relates to parent company control over the foreign subsidiary. The question arises: "Will host country managers be loyal to the parent or to the local operation?" A potential problem arises with coordination of activities, goals, and objectives between parent and subsidiary. The fact remains, though, that polycentric staffing and operation of foreign subsidiaries is successfully being applied by organizations. The parent company must be aware of potential problems and introduce control systems to uncover these problems before they are allowed to get out of hand.

See also **Staffing**

Bibliography

Acuff, F. (1984). International and domestic human resource functions. *Innovations in International Compensation*, **September**, 3–5.
Deresky, Helen (1994). *International management*. 1st edn, New York: HarperCollins.

Dowling, P. J. & Schuler, R. S. (1990). *International dimensions of human resource management*. Boston, MA: PWS-Kent.
Mendenhall, M., Punnett, B. & Ricks, D. (1995). *Global management*. Cambridge, MA: Blackwell Publishers.

JOHN O'CONNELL

polycentric organization   A polycentric organization is one that feels that foreign subsidiaries are best operated with as little parent company input as possible. Host country nationals will staff the subsidiary and local decisions will be made about local product pricing and distribution. Of course, the parent company has review power and probably the right to overrule local decisions, but this does not happen without considerable thought by parent company management and counsel with the foreign subsidiary's management.

JOHN O'CONNELL

portfolio foreign investment   Portfolio foreign investment is the purchase of stock, etc. in a foreign company for an investment rather than seeking to gain a substantial amount of control over the company. Generally, the amount of stock purchased is so small as to offer no possibility of exerting any control.

JOHN O'CONNELL

pourboire   *see* BRIBERY

power distance   This term expresses the ability of a society to accept differences between the highest level of power in an organization and the lowest level of power. The idea that power differences exist in business is not unique. There have always been managers and workers, supervisors and clerks, and owners and employees. However, Hofstede found that different cultures accepted this difference in power better than others. For example, workers in Austria and Israel have a low power distance (low acceptance of unequal power in the workplace) whereas the Philippines and Malaysia readily accept workplace power inequalities. In Malaysia, the manager has the right to be boss and the chain of command is rarely broken. In Austria, however, workers and managers are seen as being equal and more cooperative planning takes place. Workers in the United States and Great Britain are in the low power distance region.

See also **Value dimensions**

Bibliography

Hofstede, G. (1980). Motivation, leadership, and organization: Do American theories apply abroad? *Organizational Dynamics*, Summer, 42–63.

JOHN O'CONNELL

pre-departure briefing   A pre-departure briefing is normally given to expatriates to make certain that important items have been taken care of both as an individual and as an employee of the company. It is the final discussion and farewell before the employee leaves for an assignment. This briefing should emphasize the support systems for the employee and family members which are available as well as bolster their confidence prior to the actual move. The real reason for a pre-departure briefing is to make certain that "surprises" during travel or upon arrival are kept to a minimum.

JOHN O'CONNELL

pre-shipment inspection (PSI)   A buyer may decide that it is appropriate to inspect goods before they are delivered to a carrier for shipment. When this occurs the process is referred to as a pre-shipment inspection. Such inspections are normally carried out at the buyer's expense.

JOHN O'CONNELL

predatory dumping   When a country sells goods in another country at much lower than market prices in either country the practice is called "dumping." Dumping is an unfair trade practice which is subject to additional tax and other penalties. If goods are sold in the manner described above with the intent of putting local competition out of business, the practice is referred to as "predatory dumping." Predatory

dumping is used to achieve market penetration much more quickly than otherwise possible. It is also an unfair trade practice.

Bibliography

Viner, J. (1991). *Dumping: A problem in international trade*. Caldwell, NJ: Augustus M. Kelley Publishers.

JOHN O'CONNELL

preferential duties   A preferential duty is one which is lower for one country than for others. Preferential duties may be the result of trade agreements or agreements with international economic development organizations to reduce duties for less developed countries (LDCs).

See also **Duty**

JOHN O'CONNELL

price escalation   In the international trade context, price escalation refers to the increase in prices of goods when they become exports instead of being consumed locally. Usually, price increases are due to shipment costs and other expenses associated with the export process.

JOHN O'CONNELL

price suppression   Price suppression refers to the downward adjustments often made in domestic prices to stay competitive with low cost imports. Price suppression could be a sign that domestic prices were too high and an adjustment was in order. However, price suppression could also be due to a foreign company "dumping" its products on the market. When foreign products are dumped on a market, it is considered an unfair trade practice.

See also **Anti-dumping duty; Dumping**

Bibliography

Viner, J. (1991). *Dumping: A problem in international trade*. Caldwell, NJ: Augustus M. Kelley Publishers.

JOHN O'CONNELL

Private Export Funding Corporation (PEFCO) PEFCO is a private sector source of funding for financing exports from the United States. PEFCO was formed by a group of commercial banks with the assistance of the United States Export–Import Bank (Eximbank). The Eximbank provides loan guarantees and additional credit when necessary.

JOHN O'CONNELL

Private Sector Development Program (PSDP) As the name implies, this program is aimed at encouraging the privatization of formerly governmental activities. It is felt that private/market oriented economies are more efficient and will assist overall economic development in a region more than a centralized economy approach. The PSDP is aimed at Latin American countries with hopes of eventually developing an effective economic force throughout the region. The program is intended to combine the resources and activities of the Inter-American Development Bank (IDB), the Inter-American Investment Corporation (IIC), and the International Monetary Fund in the Latin American Region.

Bibliography

Ludlow, N. H. (1988). *A practical guide to the development bank business: How to identify it, market to it, and win it.* Washington, D.C.: Development Bank Associates Inc.

JOHN O'CONNELL

privatization The movement of ownership of industry and property from a government to the private sector. Probably the most significant movement to privatize has been experienced by the former states of the Soviet Union and other eastern European countries after the fall of communism in that region. Literally hundreds of thousands of former government-owned and government-operated businesses and industries were put out to sale to private investors. Privatization was a way to quickly remove government from what might be the start of a market economy as well as to unburden businesses from inefficient and ineffective pro-

duction systems. Privatization has occurred to one extent or another in virtually all industrialized nations. Some countries seem to go back and forth between privatization and government ownership whereas others seem to be intent on ridding government of activities which may be accomplished by the private sector.

Some former government operations hold out opportunities for investors. Facilities are intact, workers are on the job, and distribution systems are already in place. The major problem is dealing with a workforce that has been under government control for decades. Waste runs rampant in many former government operations with a workforce which may be lethargic and not used to working for a profit-seeking organization. Still, many private companies see privatization as a means of quick market entry as well as a possibility of picking up some inexpensive business opportunities.

Bibliography

Daniels, J. D. & Radebaugh, L. E. (1994). *International business: Environments and operations.* 7th edn, Reading, MA: Addison-Wesley Publishing.
Deresky, Helen (1994). *International management.* 1st edn, New York: HarperCollins.
Grosse, R. & Kujawa, D. (1995). *International business: Theory and managerial applications.* 3rd edn, Boston, MA: Richard D. Irwin Inc.
Rugman, A. M. & Hodgetts, R. M. (1995). *International management: A strategic management approach.* New York: McGraw-Hill Inc.

JOHN O'CONNELL

privatize The transfer of formerly government activities, operations, industries, and other property to private operation and ownership.

See also **Privatization**

JOHN O'CONNELL

processing When an employee is sent overseas a number of travel and other details have to be managed. The management of these details is referred to as "processing." Details include: travel documents (passports, health certificates, visas, etc.); transportation arrangements (airline tickets, etc.); arrival procedures (customs, person to meet expatriate, etc.); and shipment and/ or storage of personal property (how much can be taken, any restrictions on certain property, etc.). Failure to properly process these items can make the beginning of an expatriate's assignment very stressful.

JOHN O'CONNELL

product life cycle   *see* INTERNATIONAL PRODUCT LIFE CYCLE

production sharing   A creative arrangement under which companies in different countries agree to cooperate in the production and distribution of a product. Differences in customs laws and the prices of resources make such cooperative agreements feasible. Maquiladora production in Mexico is an example of production sharing. Foreign countries ship unfinished or unassembled goods to plants located in special trade zones in Mexico. The goods are finished and/or assembled (at low wage rates) and returned for distribution. Another name for production sharing is "outward processing."

See also **Maquiladora**

Bibliography

Dunning, J. (1981). *International production and multinational enterprise*. London: Allen and Unwin.

JOHN O'CONNELL

pro forma invoice   A pro forma invoice is forwarded by the seller of goods to the buyer as notification that goods have been shipped and that the buyer should be preparing to finalize financing (if necessary) to pay for the goods when they arrive. The invoice provides details of the numbers of units shipped, values, shipping method, etc.

See also **Entry documents**

JOHN O'CONNELL

prohibitive duty   A duty designed to stop the flow of imports of specific goods. Prohibitive duties may be arranged so as to apply at a low rate for a specified number or value of goods, and then at a much higher or prohibitive rate for additional numbers of imports.

See also **Duty**

JOHN O'CONNELL

protectionism   A government practising protectionist actions is attempting to protect local markets and industry from foreign competition. Thus, protectionist acts would include: high duties; quotas on goods entering the country; difficulty in securing import licenses; stringent customs regulations; and other actions aimed at reducing the flow of imported items.

See also **Barriers**

JOHN O'CONNELL

protective duty (tariff)   A tax placed on imported goods to carry out protectionist activities of a government. Taxes increase the cost of imports to consumers thereby reducing their demand. Properly applied duties will increase the development of local industry, as well as protect it from foreign competition.

See also **Barriers; Duty; Protectionism**

JOHN O'CONNELL

PSI   *see* PRE-SHIPMENT INSPECTION

public ownership   Public ownership is when property or organizations are owned by the government. Public ownership is very common around the world. Governmental ownership of property is the most pronounced in the communist countries but is common in many other countries as well. Recent developments in world politics and a general leaning toward private enterprise have moved entire economies from virtual governmental control to attempts by government to relieve itself of as many functions and industries as possible. The drive toward privatization is a phenomena of the 1990s which appears to be the trend of the future.

See also **Privatization**

JOHN O'CONNELL

put   The right to sell currency at a specified price.

See also **Put option**

JOHN O'CONNELL

put option   A "put" is the right to sell currency. An option is a specific amount of currency that may be purchased or sold at a stated price, at a stated time. Thus, a put option is the right to sell a stated amount of currency at a predetermined price within a certain period of time.

JOHN O'CONNELL

Q

quad *see* QUADRILATERAL TRADE MINISTERS

quadrilateral trade Trade taking place between four regions or countries. Bilateral is trade taking place between two regions or countries. Multilateral trade is trade between unspecified numbers of regions or countries.

JOHN O'CONNELL

quadrilateral trade ministers The quadrilateral trade ministers represent a group of four economically powerful countries or regions which have the ability to dramatically affect international commercial activities. The group is commonly referred to as the Quad. The Quad is comprised of the Canadian Minister of International Trade; the European Community's Commissioner for External Relations; Japan's Minister of International Trade and Industry; and the United States Trade representative. The Quad was originally referred to as the Group of Seven until the European Community (which includes four members of the group of seven – France, Germany, Italy, and the United Kingdom) elected to be represented by a single member.

See also **European Community**

Bibliography

Springer, B. (1992). *The social dimension of 1992: Europe faces a new EC.* New York: Greenwood Press.

JOHN O'CONNELL

quality control circle (QCC) One of the objectives in most organizations is to improve productivity and the quality of products and/or services. Japanese organizations first introduced the idea of quality control circles to assist in meeting these objectives. A quality control circle consists of a group of employees (generally volounteers) who meet periodically to identify strengths and weaknesses on the production process. Through the efforts of the circles, suggestions are provided on how to solve problems and increase productivity of quality goods and services.

Bibliography

Mendenhall, M., Punnett, B. & Ricks, D. (1995). *Global management.* Cambridge, MA: Blackwell Publishers.

JOHN O'CONNELL

quality of working life The term "quality of working life" (QWL) refers to people's reactions to work, particularly personal outcomes related to job satisfaction, mental health, and safety. Attention to QWL issues started initially in Scandinavia and Europe in the 1960s and spread to North America in the 1970s. The major impetus was the growing concern among industrialized nations for the health, safety, and satisfaction of workers. In Norway and Sweden, QWL has become a national movement fostered by cultural and political forces advocating employee rights to meaningful work and participation in work decisions. In the United States and Canada, QWL has been more pragmatic and localized, often limited to work situations where unions and management have a strong commitment to improving working conditions.

QWL research has focused on three major issues:

(1) identification of work conditions that contribute to QWL;
(2) development of methods and techniques for enhancing those conditions; and
(3) understanding how QWL affects productivity.

Researchers have discovered a number of conditions that affect whether employees experience work as satisfying, psychologically healthy, and safe. These include: challenging jobs, development of human capacities, safe and healthy work environment, adequate and fair compensation, and opportunity for balancing work and home life. Considerable attention has been directed at developing methods for improving these conditions. Among the QWL innovations that have been implemented successfully in modern organizations are job enrichment, autonomous work groups, flexitime, and employee involvement. A key finding of this applied research is that the success of these QWL interventions depends on a variety of contingencies in the work setting having to do with individual differences, technology, and task environment.

An assumption underlying QWL research is that there is a positive linkage between QWL and productivity. This derives from the idea that increased satisfaction with work will motivate employees to perform at higher levels. Research has shown, however, that the satisfaction-causes-productivity premise is too simplistic and sometimes wrong. A more realistic explanation for how QWL can affect productivity is that QWL innovations, such as job enrichment and participative management, can improve employee communication, coordination, and capability. These improvements, in turn, can enhance work performance. QWL innovations can also improve the well-being and satisfaction of employees by providing a better work environment and more fulfilling jobs. These positive work conditions can indirectly increase productivity by enabling the organization to attract and retain better workers.

Over the past two decades, both the term QWL and the meaning attributed to it have undergone considerable change and development. Concerns about employee well-being and satisfaction have expanded to include greater attention to organization effectiveness, particularly in today's highly competitive, global environment. QWL research and practice have given rise to current attention to employee involvement and empowerment, reflecting the need to make organizations more decentralized and responsive to customer demands. Today, QWL finds expression primarily in union–management cooperative projects in both the public and private sectors. These involve committees, comprised of employees and managers, that seek to address common workplace issues falling outside collective bargaining, such as safety, quality, technology management, and job satisfaction.

Bibliography

Cummings, T. & Molloy, E. (1977). Improving productivity and the quality of work life. New York: Praeger.

Davis, L. & Cherns, A. (eds) (1975). The quality of working life. New York: Free Press.

THOMAS G. CUMMINGS

quantitative quota   One of the ways to constrain the free flow of goods into a country is to institute regulations restricting the numbers or units of goods which can be imported in any given period of time. Generally, such regulations are referred to as quotas. For example, a limit of 10,000 of a certain type of automobile is a quantitative restriction.

See also **Barriers; Quotas**

JOHN O'CONNELL

quantity controls (foreign exchange) Quantity controls are a type of restriction on foreign exchange. The amount of domestic currency which can be transferred (on one's person or by other means) is subject to preset maximums.

JOHN O'CONNELL

quantity restrictions   *see* QUOTAS

quarantine requirements A number of countries regulate the importation of animals and plants as a way of reducing the potentially harmful spread of disease. Animals commonly subject to quarantine are monkeys, birds, cats, and dogs. Quarantine requirements usually include a health certificate and possible actual quarantine for a specified number of days until the animal may be released to its owners. Exporters and importers (and owners moving to another country) of plants and animals must carefully check quarantine requirements or face the possibility of not being able to obtain permission to move some plants and/or animals across international borders.

Bibliography

United States Customs Service (1994). *A basic guide to importing*. Lincolnwood, IL: NTC Publishing Group.

JOHN O'CONNELL

questionable payments *see* BRIBERY

quitas fiscal This is an Algerian term meaning that a clearance is necessary for a foreign resident to leave the country. The clearance verifies that the foreign resident has paid any income taxes due prior to leaving the country.

See also **Fiscal clearance**

JOHN O'CONNELL

quota One of the most common ways of establishing a barrier to free trade is to establish a quota for specific goods. A quota establishes a quantitative limit on the amounts of goods that can be imported. Quotas may be expressed in terms of weight (so many tons of grain), value (no more than $1,000,000 in value of a good), units (no more than 1000 trucks of a certain type), or more recently in terms of a percentage of final value (no more than 50% of the final value of a good may come from outside the country). Quotas are often used as retaliatory measures for what a country perceives as unfair trade practices of another nation.

See also **Barriers**

JOHN O'CONNELL

quotas (commodity agreements) *see* INTERNATIONAL COMMODITY AGREEMENT

quotation A quotation is a statement by a seller as to the expected price (and terms of sale) of goods or services at a specific time. Because the quotation is not associated with an actual order, it is not binding. A quotation may become a binding price if the buyer seeks to enter into a formal purchase agreement. Failure to enter into an agreement in a timely manner usually makes the quotation useless.

JOHN O'CONNELL

quoted currency Currencies that are traded on authorized currency exchanges are referred to as "quoted currencies." This comes from the fact that a value of the particular currency is quoted or referenced in terms of other quoted currencies.

JOHN O'CONNELL

R

R and R   *see* REST AND RELAXATION LEAVE

Ramadan   Ramadan is one of the most important religious observances for Muslims. Ramadan is the holy month of fasting. It is the ninth month of the Muslim year. During this time Muslims refrain from partaking of food, drink, and sexual activity from sunrise to sunset. Ramadan begins and ends with the sighting of the new moon.

JOHN O'CONNELL

rationalization   Rationalization involves seeking efficiency by restructuring an organization. Also known as re-engineering a firm or downsizing, restructuring seeks to reduce the costs of operation through: streamlining processes, reducing unnecessary staff, closing unprofitable operations, concentrating on profitable operations, and generally seeking out the most efficient ways to increase the long-run viability and profitability of a firm. Rationalization has become a very important part of international business activities in the 1990s.

JOHN O'CONNELL

reciprocal trade agreements   *see* RECIPROCITY

reciprocity   Successful international trade sometimes means that countries enter into agreements to reduce barriers to each other's goods and services. Agreements can be as broad as virtually open and free trade to "I'll open my borders for your product, if you will open yours for mine." When an agreement concerning mutual concessions is made it is referred to as "reciprocity." There are a number of types of reciprocity, of which several are listed below:

1 Identical reciprocity – Each country allows organizations to do business across borders but foreign organizations are subject to the same internal regulations as are domestic organizations. Foreign organizations also cannot undertake any activities not allowed in their own country (*see* IDENTICAL RECIPROCITY FOR AN EXAMPLE)
2 National treatment – National treatment is one of the goals of the General Agreement on Tariffs and Trade (GATT). Under this form of reciprocity countries enter into agreements with one another to treat specified foreign goods and/or services in the same manner as their own domestic goods. Barriers for specified goods and/or services between signatories to such agreements are virtually non-existent.
3 Overall reciprocity – Essentially doing away with special barriers and restrictions for all goods and services between two countries.
4 Sectoral reciprocity – Often concessions related to trade begin with limited agreements that affect only portions (sectors) of the economy. For example, two countries may agree to reduce barriers on grains which both countries need. The countries would be exhibiting sectoral reciprocity in grain products.

The idea of equal treatment between foreign and domestic goods and services has been embodied in many trade agreements. The Organization for Economic Cooperation and

Development (OECD) first outlined the concept in 1976. Over the past three decades, however, few, if any, countries have achieved true national treatment in all sectors of their economies.

JOHN O'CONNELL

red clause letter of credit   Often an exporter does not have the funds to produce products to fill current orders. A letter of credit may have already been issued by the importer in anticipation of goods being exported. If allowed by the terms of the letter of credit, the exporter may draw upon the letter to obtain funds to produce goods. Once the goods are delivered the exporter may then submit the proper documentation to obtain the balance of the letter of credit. This type of interim financing is referred to as coming from a "red clause letter of credit."

See also **Green clause letter of credit; Letter of credit**

JOHN O'CONNELL

re-entry (employee)   *see* REPATRIATION

re-entry shock   *see* REVERSE CULTURE SHOCK

re-entry visa   A re-entry visa is issued to a foreign person who has been permitted to work in a country. If that person desires to leave the country for a short period of time a re-entry visa may be issued to expedite the person's readmittance to the host country. Re-entry visas are commonly issued to business people who must return to their home country periodically, but will be back to the host country in a short while to continue their work. Business persons will also have to have a work permit in most countries if they remain resident more than a minimum amount of time.

See also **Visa**

JOHN O'CONNELL

reference price   In order to protect itself from predatory pricing practices or dumping, the European Community (EC) has established minimum prices which must be charged for certain imported commodities. Agricultural commodities are the target of most reference prices. When the price of an import falls below its reference price, a surcharge is imposed on that item. Reference prices are part of the EC's attempt to protect local producers from foreign competition.

See also **Dumping**

Bibliography

Viner, J. (1991). *Dumping: A problem in international trade.* Caldwell, NJ: Augustus M. Kelley Publishers.

JOHN O'CONNELL

regiocentric approach to hiring   A regiocentric approach to hiring selects management personnel from within a region of the world which most closely resembles that of the host country. The company has expanded its search beyond the borders of the host country, but has stopped short of seeking management personnel from its operations throughout the world. The theory behind this selection process is that nationals of the region in which operations actually take place are better able to deal with language and cultural problems than are managers from outside the region. The logic behind this hiring approach is probably sound, but it ignores the potential growth a manager goes through when forced to deal with different situations than those in which he/she is comfortable.

See also **Staffing**

Bibliography

Beamish, P. W., Killing, J. P., Lecraw, D. & Morrison, A. J. (1994). *International management: Text and cases.* 2nd edn, Burr Ridge, Illinois: Irwin.
Deresky, Helen (1994). *International management.* 1st edn, New York: HarperCollins.

Mendenhall, M., Punnett, B. & Ricks, D. (1995). *Global management*. Cambridge, MA: Blackwell Publishers.

JOHN O'CONNELL

regiocentrism   An organization that chooses its management personnel from within a selected region of the world practices regiocentrism. The theory behind this selection process is that nationals of the region in which operations actually take place are better able to deal with language and cultural problems than are managers from outside the region.

See also **Ethnocentrism; Geocentrism, Polycentric approach to hiring**

Bibliography

Beamish, P. W., Killing, J. P., Lecraw, D. & Morrison, A. J. (1994). *International management: Text and cases*. 2nd edn, Burr Ridge, Illinois: Irwin.

JOHN O'CONNELL

regional development banks (RDBs)   Development banks are established by governments to foster economic growth in a particular country, region, or worldwide. There are five regional development banks: The African Development Bank; the Asian Development Bank; the Caribbean Development Bank; Inter-American Development Bank; and the International Bank for Reconstruction and Development (IBRD or World Bank). These banks are also referred to as multilateral development banks (MDBs). The purposes of development banks are to foster the economic development of member countries and to assist in implementing the development programs of the United Nations.

See also **African Development Bank; Asian Development Bank; Caribbean Development Bank; Inter-American Development Bank; World Bank**

Bibliography

Ludlow, N. H. (1988). *A practical guide to the development bank business: How to identify it, market*

to it, and win it. Washington, D.C.: Development Bank Associates Inc.

JOHN O'CONNELL

regional economic integration   This involves the move by groups of countries to establish agreements to reduce trade barriers between the group members as well as to promote cooperation in establishing trade policies between the group and the rest of the world. Trading blocs are either the result of economic integration or the vehicle chosen to assist in achieving economic integration. Examples of successful regional economic integration include: The European Community, which has become one of the most formidable trading associations in the world; and the United States, Canada and Mexico, who through NAFTA, are now attempting to strengthen economic ties. Regional economic integration allows countries to bring real strength of numbers to the international trade negotiating table, while at the same time encouraging internal development of each of the member countries. Other parts of the world are also seeking closer ties. Areas of most recent interest include Southeast Asia (Singapore, Hong Kong, Japan, Korea, and China to mention a few interested countries) and the Middle East. Regional economic integration is the wave of the future. It is expected that within a short period of time world economics will be controlled by fewer and larger blocs of cooperating countries.

See also **Common market; European Community; Trading bloc**

JOHN O'CONNELL

regional structure   Sometimes called "geographic structure," this term refers to a way of structuring an international business by separating responsibility areas into geographic divisions. This method of structuring an organization is commonly used when the organization feels that it is important to recognize cultural differences and local methods of doing business. By organizing on a geographic basis managers may be selected who are familiar with the region, speak the language, and are comfortable with any cultural differences.

JOHN O'CONNELL

regulatory cost advantage Regulatory cost advantage occurs when the cost of complying with regulations governing an organization's actions are extremely high in the home country whereas those regulations do not exist (or if in existence, the cost of compliance is far less) in a host country.

Three current examples of regulatory cost advantage exist in the environmental pollution area; legal liability arena; and health and safety work regulations. Do companies locate in countries because laws are less stringent than in the company's home country? There is some evidence to indicate that companies have moved because of what they consider an oppressive legal system in the United States (high cost of litigation; uncertainty; high liability insurance costs); because of strict pollution liability regulations and responsibility; because of requirements to provide social types of insurance and pension plans; because of reduced safety and loss control requirements; as well as for other reasons. Regulatory cost advantages as a reason to locate a facility are transitory at best. Environmental legislation is sweeping the globe; legal reform is beginning in the United States (the country facing the most serious legal liability exposure); and common markets are slowly equalizing social benefits and programs between member countries.

The real question to be posed to companies taking advantage of regulatory cost advantages is an ethical one. Does an organization have the right to treat the environment or the people of a foreign nation with less respect than in the home country because there are fewer laws in that nation to offer protection? Sometimes taking advantage of reduced regulatory costs adds to the economic development of a nation, but the question must be asked: "At what cost?" Those firms which locate for cost advantages, but also are considerate of the host country, will have a better long-run chance of succeeding than those who are inconsiderate.

JOHN O'CONNELL

reinvoicing Tax considerations play a large role in international trade. One of the methods used by multinational firms to reduce the impact of taxes is to establish an offshore organization which acts as the receiver of imports for the parent corporation. The agent company is established in a country with favorable corporate tax rates and regulations. Goods purchased on behalf of the parent company are sold to the offshore company which then reinvoices the goods to increase their price to the parent company. The parent company has a high cost of raw materials which lowers its domestic taxable income. The offshore company shows high profits which are taxed at favorable rates. The offshore company may then be able to finance the parent company's activities through low- or no-cost loans or through other investments in the parent company.

Bibliography

Celi, L. J. & Rutizer, B. (1991). *Global cash management.* 1st edn, New York: Harper Business (HarperCollins).

Eiteman, D. K., Stonehill, A. J. & Moffett, M. H. (1992). *Multinational business finance.* 6th edn, Reading, MA: Addison-Wesley Publishing.

JOHN O'CONNELL

relativism, cultural and moral *Cultural relativism* is a descriptive claim that ethical practices differ among cultures; that, as a matter of fact, what is considered right in one culture may be considered wrong in another. Thus truth or falsity of cultural relativism can be determined by examining the world. The work of anthropologists and sociologists is most relevant in determining the truth or falsity of cultural relativism, and there is widespread consensus among social scientists that cultural relativism is true.

Moral relativism is the claim that what is really right or wrong is what the culture says is right or wrong. Moral relativists accept cultural relativism as true, but they claim much more. If a culture sincerely and reflectively adopts a basic moral principle, then it is morally obligatory for members of that culture to act in accordance with that principle.

The implication of moral relativism for conduct is that one ought to abide by the ethical norms of the culture where one is located. This position is captured by the popular phrase "When in Rome, do as the Romans do." Relativists in ethics would say "One ought to follow the moral norms of the culture." In terms of business practice, consider the question, "Is it morally right to pay a bribe to gain business?" The moral relativist would answer the question by consulting the moral norms of the country where one is doing business. If those norms permit bribery in that country, then the practice of bribery is not wrong in that country. However, if the moral norms of the country do not permit bribery, then offering a bribe to gain business in that country is morally wrong. The justification for that position is the moral relativist's contention that what is really right or wrong is determined by the culture.

Is cultural relativism true? Is moral relativism correct? As noted, many social scientists believe that cultural relativism is true as a matter of fact. But is it?

First, many philosophers claim that the "facts" aren't really what they seem. Early twentieth-century anthropologists cited the fact that in some cultures, after a certain age, parents are put to death. In most cultures such behavior would be murder. Does this difference in behavior prove that the two cultures disagree about fundamental matters of ethics? No, it does not. Suppose the other culture believes that people exist in the afterlife in the same condition that they leave their present life. It would be very cruel to have one's parents exist eternally in an unhealthy state. By killing them when they are relatively active and vigorous, you insure their happiness for all eternity. The *underlying* ethical principle of this culture is that children have duties to their parents, including the duty to be concerned with their parents' happiness as they approach old age. This ethical principle is identical with our own. What looked like a difference in ethics between our culture and another turned out, upon close examination, to be a difference based on what each culture takes to be the facts of the matter. This example does, of course, support the claim that as a matter of fact ethical principles vary according to culture. However, it does not support the stronger

conclusion that *underlying* ethical principles vary according to culture.

Cultures differ in physical setting, in economic development, in the state of their science and technology, in their literacy rate, and in many other ways. Even if there were universal moral principles, they would have to be applied in these different cultural contexts. Given the different situations in which cultures exist, it would come as no surprise to find universal principles applied in different ways. Hence we expect to find surface differences in ethical behavior among cultures even though the cultures agree on fundamental universal moral principles. For example, one commonly held universal principle appeals to the public good; it says that social institutions and individual behavior should be ordered so that they lead to the greatest good for the greatest number. Many different forms of social organization and individual behavior are consistent with this principle. The point of these two arguments is to show that differences among cultures on ethical behavior may not reflect genuine disagreement about underlying principles of ethics. Thus it is not so obvious that any strong form of cultural relativism is true.

But are there universal principles that are accepted by all cultures? It seems so; there does seem to be a whole range of behavior, such as torture and murder of the innocent, that every culture agrees is wrong. A nation-state accused of torture does not respond by saying that a condemnation of torture is just a matter of cultural choice. The state's leaders do not respond by saying, "We think torture is right, but you do not." Rather, the standard response is to deny that any torture took place. If the evidence of torture is too strong, a finger will be pointed either at the victim or at the morally outraged country: "They do it too." In this case the guilt is spread to all. Even the Nazis denied that genocide took place. What is important is that *no* state replies that there is nothing wrong with genocide or torture.

In addition, there are attempts to codify some universal moral principles. The United Nations Universal Declaration of Human Rights has been endorsed by the member states of the UN, and the vast majority of countries in the world are members of the UN. Even in business, there is a growing effort to adopt universal principles of business practice. In a recent study of international codes of ethics, Professors Catherine Langlois and Bodo B. Schlegelmilch (1990) found that although there certainly were differences among codes, there was a considerable area of agreement. William Frederick has documented the details of six international compacts on matters of international business ethics. These include the aforementioned UN Universal Declaration of Human Rights, the European Convention on Human Rights, the Helsinki Final Act, the OECD Guidelines for Multinational Enterprises and Social Policy, and the United Nations Conduct on Transnational Corporations (in progress) (Frederick, 1991). The Caux Roundtable, a group of corporate executives from the United States, Europe, and Japan, are seeking worldwide endorsement of a set of principles of business ethics. Thus there are a number of reasons to think that cultural relativism, at least with respect to basic moral principles, is not true, that is, that it does not accurately describe the state of moral agreement that exists. This is consistent with maintaining that cultural relativism is true in the weak form, that is, when applied only to surface ethical principles.

But what if differences in fundamental moral practices among cultures are discovered and seem unreconcilable? That would lead to a discussion about the adequacy of moral relativism. The fact that moral practices do vary widely among countries is cited as evidence for the correctness of moral relativism. Discoveries early in the century by anthropologists, sociologists, and psychologists documented the diversity of moral beliefs. Philosophers, by and large, welcomed corrections of moral imperialist thinking, but recognized that the moral relativist's appeal to the alleged truth of cultural relativism was not enough to establish moral relativism. The mere fact that a culture considers a practice moral does not mean that it is moral. Cultures have sincerely practiced slavery, discrimination, and the torture of animals. Yet each of these practices can be independently criticized on ethical grounds. Thinking something is morally permissible does not make it so.

Another common strategy for criticizing moral relativism is to show that the consequences of taking the perspective of moral relativism are inconsistent with our use of moral language. It is often contended by moral relativists that if two cultures disagree regarding universal moral principles, there is no way for that disagreement to be resolved. Since moral relativism is the view that what is right or wrong is determined by culture, there is no higher appeal beyond the fact that culture endorses the moral principle. But we certainly do not talk that way. When China and the United States argue about the moral rights of human beings, the disputants use language that seems to appeal to universal moral principles. Moreover, the atrocities of the Nazis and the slaughter in Rwanda have met with universal condemnation that seemed based on universal moral principles. So moral relativism is not consistent with our use of moral language.

Relativism is also inconsistent with how we use the term "moral reformer." Suppose, for instance, that a person from one culture moves to another and tries to persuade the other culture to change its view. Suppose someone moves from a culture where slavery is immoral to one where slavery is morally permitted. Normally, if a person were to try to convince the culture where slavery was permitted that slavery was morally wrong, we would call such a person a moral reformer. Moreover, a moral reformer would almost certainly appeal to universal moral principles to make her argument; she almost certainly would not appeal to a competing cultural standard. But if moral relativism were true, there would be no place for the concept of a moral reformer. Slavery is really right in those cultures that say it is right and really wrong in those cultures that say it is wrong. If the reformer fails to persuade a slaveholding country to change its mind, the reformer's antislavery position was never right. If the reformer is successful in persuading a country to change its mind, the reformer's antislavery views would be wrong – until the country, did, in fact, change its view. Then the reformer's antislavery view would be right. But that is not how we talk about moral reform.

The moral relativist might argue that our language should be reformed. We should talk differently. At one time people used to talk and act as if the world were flat. Now they don't. The relativist could suggest that we can change our ethical language in the same way. But consider how radical the relativists' response is. Since most, if not all, cultures speak and act as if there were universal moral principles, the relativist can be right only if almost everyone else is wrong. How plausible is that?

Although these arguments are powerful ones, they do not deliver a knockout blow to moral relativism. If there are no universal moral principles, moral relativists could argue that moral relativism is the only theory available to help make sense of moral phenomena.

An appropriate response to this relativist argument is to present the case for a set of universal moral principles, principles that are correct for all cultures independent of what a culture thinks about them. This is what adherents of the various ethical traditions try to do. The reader will have to examine these various traditions and determine how persuasive she finds them. In addition, there are several final independent considerations against moral relativism that can be mentioned here.

First, what constitutes a culture? There is a tendency to equate cultures with national boundaries, but that is naive, especially today. With respect to moral issues, what do US cultural norms say regarding right and wrong? That question may be impossible to answer, because in a highly pluralistic country like the United States, there are many cultures. Furthermore, even if one can identify a culture's moral norms, it will have dissidents who do not subscribe to those moral norms. How many dissidents can a culture put up with and still maintain that some basic moral principle is the cultural norm? Moral relativists have had little to say regarding criteria for constituting a culture or how to account for dissidents. Unless moral relativists offer answers to questions like these, their theory is in danger of becoming inapplicable to the real world.

Second, any form of moral relativism must admit that there are some universal moral principles. Suppose a culture does not accept moral relativism, that is, it denies that if an entire culture sincerely and reflectively adopts a basic moral principle, it is obligatory for members of that culture to act in accord with that principle. Fundamentalist Muslim countries would reject moral relativism because it would require them to accept as morally permissible blasphemy in those countries

where blasphemy was permitted. If the moral relativist insists that the truth of every moral principle depends on the culture, then she must admit that the truth of moral relativism depends on the culture. Therefore the moral relativist must admit that at least the principle of moral relativism is not relative.

Third, it seems that there is a set of basic moral principles that every culture must adopt. You would not have a culture unless the members of the group adopted these moral principles. Consider an anthropologist who arrives on a populated island: How many tribes are on the island? To answer that question, the anthropologist tries to determine if some people on some parts of the island are permitted to kill, commit acts of violence against, or steal from persons on other parts of the island. If such behavior is not permitted, that counts as a reason for saying that there is only one tribe. The underlying assumption here is that there is a set of moral principles that must be followed if there is to be a culture at all. With respect to those moral principles, adhering to them determines whether there is a culture or not.

But what justifies these principles? A moral relativist would say that a culture justifies them. But you cannot have a culture unless the members of the culture follow the principles. Thus it is reasonable to think that justification lies elsewhere. Many believe that the purpose of morality is to help make social cooperation possible. Moral principles are universally necessary for that endeavor.

Bibliography

Benedict, R. (1934). *Patterns of Culture*, New York: Penguin Books.

Bowie, N. (1988). The moral obligations of multinational corporations. In S. Luper-Foy (ed.), *Problems of International Justice*, 97–113. Boulder, Colo.: Westview Press.

Frederick, W. C. (1991). The moral authority of transnational corporate codes. *Journal of Business Ethics*, **10** (3).

Harman, G. (1975). Moral relativism defended. *The Philosophical Review*, **84**, 3–22.

Hatch, E. (1983). *Culture and Morality*, New York: Columbia University Press.

Krausz, M. & Meiland, J. (1982). *Relativism: Cognitive and Moral*, Notre Dame: University of Notre Dame Press.

Ladd, J. (1973). *Ethical Relativism*, Belmont, Calif.: Wadsworth.

Langlois, C. & Schlegelmilch, B. B. (1990). Do corporate codes of ethics reflect national character? Evidence from Europe and the United States. *Journal of International Studies*, **21** (9), 519–39.

Mackie, J. (1977). *Ethics: Inventing Right and Wrong*, Harmondsworth: Penguin Books.

Rachels, J. (1993). *The Elements of Moral Philosophy*, 2nd edn, New York: McGraw-Hill.

Sayre-McCord, G. (1991). Being a realist about relativism (in ethics). *Philosophical Studies*, **61**, 155–76.

Wong, D. (1984). *Moral Relativity*, Berkeley: University of Californina Press.

NORMAN E. BOWIE

relocation allowance   A payment given to employees to cover the cost of moving themselves, family, and personal possessions to the site of a foreign assignment. The costs of transferring employees may be quite high depending upon the assignment location.

See also **Compensation package**

JOHN O'CONNELL

relocation and orientation   International human resources management involves preparing expatriates for transfer to overseas locations. The relocation and orientation process is carried out to assure that the expatriate suffers as little inconvenience as possible. One of the reasons for expatriate failure is improper preparation for the new assignment. Expatriates must be trained in the language, culture, values, forms of communication, and other nuances of the country of assignment. Preparations must also be completed for the move itself: passports and other travel papers; movement of personal property; temporary quarters; schools for children; and other needs. The expatriate must also be compensated in a manner to take care of inconvenience and extra costs not found in the home country. The entire relocation and orientation process is involved, time consuming and expensive, but must be successfully accomplished to give the expatriate the best chance for success.

See also **Compensation package; Expatriate; Expatriate training**

JOHN O'CONNELL

remitting bank   When an international shipment of goods (import or export) is completed it is common for a bank to forward the shipping documents to a second bank for payment. The bank submitting the documents for payment is referred to as the "remitting bank."

JOHN O'CONNELL

repatriation   The return of an employee from a foreign country to the home country upon completion of an assignment or upon illness, injury, or death. Also the return of profits from a foreign company to the home country of the parent.

See also **Repatriation of employees; Repatriation of profits**

JOHN O'CONNELL

repatriation of employees   Moving an employee from a foreign country back to the home country. An expatriate is said to be "repatriated" when he/she is brought home after a foreign assignment. Great care must be taken when bringing expatriates back to the home country. Many employees suffer reverse culture shock due to being out of the country for an extended period of time. Repatriation also may be required upon the illness, injury, or death of a foreign employee. Repatriation costs are normally paid by the employer, but few employers understand the potentially enormous costs associated with bringing home a severely injured or ill employee. If repatriation cannot take place using scheduled commercial transportation methods, special medical evacuation resources must be called upon. It is not uncommon for the cost of special medical evacuation to be $50,000 to $100,000.

See also **Expatriate; Medivac; Reverse culture shock**

Bibliography

Black, J. S. & Gregerson, H. B. (1991). When Yankee comes home: Factors relating to expatriate and spouse repatriation adjustment. *Journal of International Business Studies*, **22** (4), 471–94.

Feldman, D. C. & Thompson, H. B. (1993). Expropriation, repatriation, and domestic geographical relocation: An empirical investigation of adjustment to new job assignments. *Journal of International Business Studies*, **24** (3), 507–30.

Moran, R. T. (1989). Coping with re-entry shock. *AGSIM Faculty Publication*, No. **89–05**.

Napier, N. K. & Peterson, R. B. (1990). Expatriate reentry: What do repatriates have to say? *Human Resource Planning*, **14**, 19–28.

JOHN O'CONNELL

repatriation of profits   Organizations commonly enter into international commerce with the expectation of transferring profits from the foreign market to their home country. Problems arise when foreign countries implement controls over transfer of profits or dividends outside their borders. The foreign country desires to keep investment returns within the country in order to foster further economic growth and stability. Repatriation controls, however, normally have the effect of reducing investor interest in that country.

See also **Barriers; Blocked currency**

JOHN O'CONNELL

reporting currency   A multinational organization normally uses the currency of its home country or place of incorporation to prepare its financial statements. The effect of foreign exchange transactions is also reported in terms of this currency. Using a standard reporting currency assists in viewing the true financial status of an organization over time. The reporting currency is also referred to as functional currency.

JOHN O'CONNELL

representative   *see* EXPORT AGENT

resident alien   *see* ALIEN

resident buying agents   Most organizations conducting international trade do not use their own employees to either buy or sell goods in various countries. The differences between business practices, language, and cultural problems usually make employee arrangements difficult at best. Instead of using employees, organizations may turn to intermediaries in each country to secure goods needed by the organization in its home country (or other country of production). Intermediaries who purchase goods for a foreign company (to be shipped to that foreign company) are referred to as "resident buying agents."

See also **Export agent**

JOHN O'CONNELL

resident selling agents   Most international enterprises do not have actual production taking place in each of the countries. They also normally do not have their own employees in each country because the costs would be prohibitive for all but the largest of organizations. It is very common under these circumstances to use the services of an intermediary to sell a company's goods in overseas markets. Intermediaries who act on behalf of an organization to sell its products in a given country are referred to as "resident selling agents."

See also **Export agent**

Bibliography

Griffin, J. (1994). *International sales and the middleman: Managing your agents and distributors.* London: Mercury.

JOHN O'CONNELL

rest and relaxation leave (R&R)   When an expatriate employee is assigned to a location which is exceptionally inconvenient compared to the employee's home country (some Middle Eastern oil field locations, for example) companies often pay for a week or two-week excursion away from the location to rest and relax. R&R allows employees to reacclimatize themselves in order to avoid burnout.

See also **Compensation package**

JOHN O'CONNELL

rest day   The workweek is not the same in all countries or for all levels of employees. One variation on the workweek is one which includes a "rest day." In some countries employees are paid for a full seven days per workweek. But one or two of the days are considered paid "rest days." Although the total wages paid take into consideration the productivity of the workers during their actual work time, an expatriate manager's failure to recognize this pay practice could result in embarrassment and potential labor problems. New managers must always be aware of local custom concerning wages/pay/ work hours and other employment-related practices.

JOHN O'CONNELL

restricted market   A restricted exchange market is heavily controlled by the government. The government allows the free market (demand and supply) to contribute to the overall valuation of its currency but the major factor affecting the market is the government's willingness to buy or sell currency. A market could also be restricted by linking the value of a currency to that of another country's (e.g., the Luxembourg franc is tied to the Belgian franc). Any restrictions by the second country would also restrict the first country's currency.

JOHN O'CONNELL

retaliation   Retaliation is normally a unilateral action of one country against another. In response to an unfair trade practice, a country may impose substantial duties on a second country's imports. Retaliation is common when dumping of goods takes place. Retaliatory

measures are usually rescinded after the countries come to an agreement regarding proper trade conduct.

JOHN O'CONNELL

retaliatory duty   A penalty duty (in addition to other duties) imposed by a country to punish another country for unfair trade practices. President Clinton's 1995 threat to increase United States duties to 100% on imported Japanese luxury cars was in retaliation for Japan's closed markets with respect to most imports.

See also **Duty; Unfair trade**

JOHN O'CONNELL

revalorization   When a country's monetary system is subjected to numerous devaluations its currency becomes worthless in the eyes of its citizens and the remainder of the world. Repeated devaluations may make the currency essentially unusable for trade or other commerce. When this occurs a country may introduce another currency to take the place of the old. This is thought to give the appearance of more stability and bring about a feeling that the government is actually succeeding in decreasing its monetary problems. Changes in currency names do not have to be substantial. For example, the latest currency could be known as the "new" currency unit as distinguished from the "old" devalued currency unit. There is usually a grace period during which old currency may be exchanged for new (old rubles for new rubles in Russia) but once the new currency is in place, all trading in the old currency ceases.

JOHN O'CONNELL

revaluation   (1) Customs officials in many countries routinely adjust the values of imports from those stated on the import documents. Revaluation or the adjustment of values results in higher import duties being charged. The theory behind revaluation is that exporters routinely undervalue goods in order to decrease duty charges. (2) Revaluation may also refer to a situation in which the central monetary authority of a country changes the value of its currency. Substantial revaluation may lead to the issuance of a new currency.

See also **Devaluation; Revalorization**

JOHN O'CONNELL

reverse culture shock   When an employee returns to the home country after an extended assignment, he/she (or family members) may be subjected to what many refer to as reverse culture shock. Reverse culture shock occurs because things have changed in the home country. Friends and neighbors have moved, new schools are attended, fellow employees have gone into management or departed the company, the clothing fads are different, music has changed, and numerous other things have changed that the expatriate might have felt would be the same. Culture shock may also be the result of a different standard of living than was achieved in the host country. Often expatriates have servants or chauffeurs for the first time, or a larger home, or any number of other items they will not have access to in the home country.

Reverse culture shock can be anticipated and dealt with by an organization in the same manner as culture shock was anticipated when the employee first moved overseas. Orientation programs for coming home, and mentors or other contacts, can keep the family abreast of changes at home. Good communications allow the employee to be aware of what is happening in the home office.

Bibliography

Black, J. S. & Gregerson, H. B. (1991). When Yankee comes home: Factors relating to expatriate and spouse repatriation adjustment. *Journal of International Business Studies*, **22** (4), 471–94.

Feldman, D. C. & Thompson, H. B. (1993). Expropriation, repatriation, and domestic geographical relocation: An empirical investigation of adjustment to new job assignments. *Journal of International Business Studies*, **24** (3), 507–30.

Moran, R. T. (1989). Coping with re-entry shock. *AGSIM Faculty Publication*, No. 89–05.

Napier, N. K. & Peterson, R. B. (1990). Expatriate reentry: What do repatriates have to say? *Human Resource Planning*, **14**, 19–28.

JOHN O'CONNELL

revocable letter of credit   A revocable letter of credit may be withdrawn by the issuing bank without prior notice or explanation. Unlike the irrevocable letter of credit, this type does not require the permission of the other parties to the transaction. As such, this letter exposes the seller of goods to more risk. Sellers seeking to reduce their risk should always demand an irrevocable letter of credit.

See also **Letter of credit**

JOHN O'CONNELL

revolving credit facility   A revolving credit facility is a line of credit which is automatically reinstated as loans are paid off. The reinstated amount equals the amount of repayment. Revolving lines of credit have a maximum amount which may be outstanding at any one time.

JOHN O'CONNELL

revolving letter of credit   This type of letter of credit is used for an exporter with whom the issuing bank has had favorable past experience. The exporter also deals with customers of the issuing bank on a continuous basis over a period of time. Instead of issuing a new letter of credit each time the exporter sells to a given importer, the issuing bank arranges to offer a revolving letter of credit. This document allows the exporter to use the same letter for each transaction with the amount of payment on the letter being recredited after the completion of each transaction. As long as a single draw is for less than the overall limit, the letter's line of credit is renewed automatically over a specified period of time.

See also **Letter of credit**

JOHN O'CONNELL

right of entry (proof of) Documents used to prove ownership or legal possession of goods are needed in order to allow their passage through the customs system of a country. In other words, proof that the goods are being brought to a country by a party who has the legal right to seek entry for those goods. Proof required is normally a bill of lading or other evidence of title or possession.

See also **Entry documents**

JOHN O'CONNELL

right of establishment Right of establishment provides those parties having direct foreign investments with the same protections offered to domestic investors. This means a foreign investor has the right to establish control over a firm in a host country under the same protections (legal and otherwise) as are afforded to a citizen of that country.

See also **National treatment**

JOHN O'CONNELL

Round of Trade Negotiations (RTN) Over the years international trade has increased substantially. This increase has been accompanied by problems arising in virtually all areas of the trade transaction. Problems are usually associated with protectionist actions of one or more countries (*see* BARRIERS). The Round of Trade Negotiations are a series of meetings between country representatives to develop new means to encourage free and open trade throughout the world. The negotiations are normally sponsored by the United Nations Conference on Trade and Development and the countries which are signatories of the General Agreement on Tariffs and Trade (GATT). A series of round of trade negotiations has been held since 1947 and continues to the present day. Consensus agreements of the member nations are referred to as multilateral trade agreements.

JOHN O'CONNELL

royalty Royalties are commonly paid by international enterprises for the use of a company's trademark, patented processes, or other proprietary information. In order to use another company's proprietary information or processes, a licensing arrangement is usually entered into between organizations. The agreement specifies either a percentage of sales or a fee to be paid by the organization using another's property. This payment is a "royalty."

See also **Licensing; Market entry strategies**

JOHN O'CONNELL

— S —

SACUA *see* SOUTHERN AFRICAN CUSTOMS UNION AGREEMENT

SADCC *see* SOUTHERN AFRICAN DEVELOPMENT COORDINATION COUNCIL

safe arrival notification Showing concern for expatriate employees is very important for a business. One of the areas of concern for most employees is that family and friends be notified when they safely reach their destination. An employer can go a long way in showing real concern for employees by notifying selected persons of the expatriate's safe arrival at the assignment destination. This is a simple task, but one that can create goodwill and loyalty between employer and employee.

JOHN O'CONNELL

safeguards Periodically, a nation will have difficulty with a trading partner with respect to the trading partner dumping goods onto the nation's market or engaging in what the first nation feels are unfair trade practices. The first nation may elect to impose unilateral duties or other restrictions on the goods of the trading partner. These restrictions are referred to as sanctions. Sanctions are temporary measures and are used until the offending nation changes its ways or until more formal sanctions can be imposed by the United Nations.

See also **Sanction**

JOHN O'CONNELL

samurai bonds Although the name may be deceiving, a samurai bond is actually issued by a foreign corporation seeking to borrow money in Japan. The bond is denominated in yen and is generally unsecured.

JOHN O'CONNELL

sanction When a country takes actions which endanger the peace and security of other nations, those nations may impose economic or other sanctions on the offending country. The United Nations, acting as a body, may vote for sanctions against a nation when it is felt that outrageous actions of the nation went strongly against the norms the UN sets for its members. The most recent sanction imposed by the United Nations involved a worldwide trade sanction against Iraq following its invasion of Kuwait in 1990. The sanctions have only partially been removed as of mid-1996. Sanctions could also be imposed by a single nation or group of nations against another country for aggression (or support of aggression) aimed at a third nation or one of those imposing the sanction.

JOHN O'CONNELL

secondary boycott *see* BOYCOTT

sectoral reciprocity One country may agree to lower trade restrictions (duties, quotas, etc.) in return for a second nation making similar reductions. When agreements are made to reduce barriers in specific trade areas (sectors such as heavy equipment or automobiles) the exchange of concessions is known as "sectoral reciprocity." Often sectoral reciprocity is the stage from which broader and more widespread trade agreements may flow.

See also **Reciprocity**

JOHN O'CONNELL

Securities and Exchange Commission (SEC) A United States government agency charged with responsibility for overseeing the offering and exchange of securities within the United States. The agency investigates claims of wrongdoing or other securities-related problems. The SEC monitors the issuance of securities, especially in the area of full disclosure to prospective buyers. The SEC was established in 1934 and is governed by five presidentially-appointed commissioners.

JOHN O'CONNELL

selection of expatriates One of the most important tasks associated with managing an international firm is the selection of employees to represent the firm overseas. Expatriate selection is the process used to select employees who will have the best chances of success. Although many companies stress the importance of technical competence, many other factors should also enter into the selection equation. Improperly selected or improperly trained employees can do irreparable harm to an organization's overseas operations and image in a surprisingly short period of time.

The following discussion reviews a number of factors which must be addressed during the expatriate selection process. Failure to address even one of the factors may result in sending an unprepared or unsuitable employee overseas.

1 The task to be completed – Probably the most common concern of employers is whether the employee has the capability of carrying out the work in a foreign country. That is, is the employee well trained and qualified in the job? Is the employee technically prepared to accomplish what the employer expects? This must be judged not only from the actual tasks but also the ability to manage others to carry out the

tasks. Someone who has never managed people should not be sent overseas for their first management position.

2 The country setting – Sending expatriates to a country which is similar to the home country (Canadians to the United States, for example) is a much simpler task than sending them to a country which is much different (US citizen to China). When the assignment country is very different from the home country extensive training should be undertaken to prepare the expatriate (and family members if accompanied) for not only business but daily life. Questions which require answers: "Is the employee a good student?"; "Does he or she enjoy learning and facing challenges?"; "Are the skills too different from existing skills for training to be effective?"; and "Does the company have the ability to train the employee in the appropriate skills needed for personal and business life while on assignment?" Many times employees are prepared for the business side of the assignment, but poorly prepared for dealing with personal or family problems which may arise.

3 Adaptability of expatriate – People being considered for expatriate positions must be flexible in their thinking, willing to learn new things, be able to get along with others well, and be adaptable to whatever situation arises. The inconveniences and surprises associated with overseas life also demand a good sense of humor and an understanding that the assignment is also an experience to be enjoyed. The employee must learn that differences exist and to not be judgmental. Categorizing different customs as wrong or right or good or bad places the expatriate in a precarious position especially when living and working in a culture that expresses the opposite values.

4 Language facility – The ability to converse in the native language of the host country is a positive factor in terms of expatriate success. Although it is true that business is often carried out in English or some language other than the host country's, it is also true that it is easier to get along if the host country language is spoken by the expatriate. People are generally more accepting of someone from a foreign country if

that person knows or at least attempts to learn and use the language. Although fluency is preferred, a good try is also respected in most countries. Not knowing the language also places a manager in a position of having to rely too heavily on others to accomplish even the simplest of tasks. This does not speak well of the manager's ability to take command of a situation when that becomes necessary.

5 Family considerations – If the expatriate has a family all of the items just reviewed also apply to "each" family member (except infants), except that the context is changed from business life to family life. Does the spouse expect to work? Will the spouse be allowed to work under the laws of the host country? Education for the children is also a major consideration. Many foreign assignment locations do not have educational facilities comparable to the home country. Provision of healthcare may be through a completely different system than in the home country. This is also a major consideration especially if children are accompanying the expatriate.

Bibliography

Bird, A. & Dunbar, R. (1991). Getting the job done over there: Improving expatriate productivity. *National Productivity Review*, Spring, 145–56.

Black, J. S. (1988). Work role transitions: A study of American expatriate managers in Japan. *Journal of International Business Studies*, **19** (2), 277–94.

Black, J. S. & Stephens, G. K. (1989). The influence of the spouse on American expatriate adjustment and intent to stay in Pacific Rim overseas assignments. *Journal of Management*, **15** (4), 529–44.

Brown, R. (1987). How to choose the best expatriates. *Personnel Management*, **June**, 67.

Feldman, D. C. & Thomas, D. C. (1992). Career management issues facing expatriates. *Journal of International Business Studies*, **23** (2), 271–94.

Golding, J. (1993). *Working abroad: Essential financial planning for expatriates and their employers.* Plymouth: International Venture Handbooks.

Harris, J. E. (1989). Moving managers internationally: The care and feeding of expatriates. *Human Resources Planning*, **12**, 49–53.

Harvey, M. (1985). The executive family: An overlooked variable in international assignments. *Journal of International Business Studies*, Columbia Journal of World Business, 785–800.

Hays, R. D. (1974). Expatriate selection: Insuring success and avoiding failure. *Journal of International Business Studies*, **5**, 25–37.

Mendenhall, M. E., Dunbar, E. & Oddou, Gary (1987). Expatriate selection, training, and career pathing: A review and critique. *Human Resource Management*, **26**, 331–45.

Napier, N. K. & Peterson, R. B. (1990). Expatriate reentry: What do repatriates have to say? *Human Resource Planning*, **14**, 19–28.

Naumann, E. (1993). Organizational predictors of expatriate job satisfaction. *Journal of International Business Studies*, 61–4.

Nicholson, W. (1989). On the far side: Stories about expatriate life. *The Expatriate Observer*, January, 26–7.

Ronen, S. & Tung, R. L. (1981). Selection and training of personnel for overseas assignments. *Columbia Journal of World Business*, Spring, 68–78.

Shahzad, N. (1984). The American expatriate manager: Present and future roles. *Personnel Administrator*, **29**, 23–5.

JOHN O'CONNELL

services   A service involves the provision of human thought in order to achieve a more effective or efficient use of resources. Service industries include consulting activities of all kinds, legal assistance, most medical care, as well as other areas where the human intellect can be used to accomplish tasks not related to producing a product. In many countries service industries are a major part of the economy. In fact some countries rely upon providing services as their major source of income. For example, many nations depend heavily on tourism to support citizens working in hotels and associated service industries. Other countries see services as a growth business which does not pollute or have physical qualities related to the actual process of production of goods. For example, Bermuda and the Cayman Islands have become centers for international captive insurance companies and banking services.

See also **Captive insurance company**

JOHN O'CONNELL

settling-in allowance   Moving to another country normally takes a considerable amount of time and effort before all of one's personal property and family is settled in a new home. It is common for expatriates to take a minimal amount of personal property when first assigned and to live in temporary quarters until suitable permanent accommodation can be found. This is generally a good idea because an expatriate often does not know the nature of the accommodation and cannot make rational decisions about what property to bring, what amount is appropriate, and what will fit into the new living situation. A settling-in-allowance is an amount of money given to an expatriate for temporary quarters, storage expenses in the new country, and other expenses (known and unknown) likely to be associated with the initial move to a new country.

See also **Compensation package**

JOHN O'CONNELL

shippers agent   Many shippers of goods are not directly involved in locating cargo space on various modes of transportation. Instead, they rely on the efforts of intermediaries who locate space and sell it to the ultimate shipper of goods. Shippers agents perform an important role in the international distribution of goods. Their services allow more businesses to participate in international trade.

Bibliography

Zodl, J. A. (1992). *Export–Import: Everything you and your company need to know to compete in world markets*. Cincinnati, OH: Betterway Books.

JOHN O'CONNELL

shipping terms   The shipping terms are the details of the shipping transaction. Who is responsible for securing the method of transit; who secures and pays for insurance; when transfer of title of goods is made; and other details are specified in the shipping terms. Also known as International Commercial Terms or INCOTERMS, most nations have agreed on their meanings thereby reducing problems in the shipment process.

See also **INCOTERMS**

Bibliography

International Chamber of Commerce (ICC). (1990). *Incoterms 1990*. New York, NY: ICC Publishing Corp.

JOHN O'CONNELL

shunto   Each spring Japanese workers and employers become embroiled in wage negotiations. Although negotiations rarely result in strikes or other serious work stoppages, springtime in Japan does bring marches and other boisterous demonstrations by employees seeking support for their demands.

JOHN O'CONNELL

shutout   A shipping term describing a situation in which a ship's capacity for goods has been reached. This results in cargo being "shutout" or held for later shipment.

JOHN O'CONNELL

sight documentary draft   *see* DOCUMENTARY DRAFT

signatory   When a nation enters into an international agreement an official representing that nation signs the agreement document. That nation then becomes bound by the terms of the agreement. Nations not abiding by signed agreements may suffer sanctions on the part of other signatories.

JOHN O'CONNELL

single status   When an employee is sent on an overseas assignment and is not accompanied by his/her spouse or children, the employee's assignment status is "single." Assignment status helps determine the number and types of compensation allowances and other benefits available to the employee.

See also **Assignment status; Compensation package**

JOHN O'CONNELL

Societas Europaea   *see* EUROPEAN COMPANY

soft currency   If a country's banking and economic system are considered unstable it may be difficult to exchange that country's currency for that of a nation which exhibits more stability. The currency of the unstable system is referred to as a "soft" currency, while the currency of the stable system is referred to as a "hard" currency. Special intermediaries may be employed when trade activities require exchange between hard and soft currencies.

See also **Hard currency; Intermerchant**

JOHN O'CONNELL

sogo shosha (Japan)   This Japanese term refers to the large general trading companies which are so powerful in the Japanese economy. These companies include Sony, Mitsubishi, Matsushida, and Sumitomo. Activities of the "sogo shosha" provide the world with the largest share of Japanese exports.

JOHN O'CONNELL

sourcing   Sourcing is the securing of parts, supplies, materials, labor, and other items necessary to produce merchandise or other items for sale. Domestic companies often purchase resources locally even though the cost may be greater than the same resources (labor, for example) purchased in a foreign country. Global companies may purchase resources wherever the cost is lowest with respect to the overall cost of the finished product. For example, if labor costs are very low in Mexico, a company may locate an assembly plant there, but still source its raw materials from Southeast Asia where they are found for the lowest cost. It is common for a multinational company to use foreign sourcing whenever it is cost effective to do so.

JOHN O'CONNELL

Southern African Customs Union Agreement (SACUA)   A local agreement of five African nations to promote free trade and travel between those countries. In 1969, Botswana, Lesotho, Namibia, South Africa, and Swaziland were signatories to the customs union agreement in hopes of fostering local economic development and cooperation.

JOHN O'CONNELL

Southern African Development Coordination Council (SADCC)   The development of southern Africa for decades has been tied to the success or failure of South Africa. In 1979 a group of South African nations entered into an agreement designed to decrease their reliance on South Africa for economic development. SADCC is comprised of the nations of Angola, Botswana, Lesotho, Malawi, Mozambique, Swaziland, Tanzania, Zambia, and Zimbabwe. Thus far, cooperative activities include upgrading and coordination of infrastructure resources such as transportation and communications systems.

JOHN O'CONNELL

sovereign immunity   This practice dates from the days when countries were ruled by kings and is closely linked with the idea that the king can do no wrong. Thus, the king could not be held legally responsible for his own actions. International law exempts a government from legal actions in its own courts or the courts of other countries unless the government voluntarily accepts the right of legal action against it. Sovereign immunity also protects a country's diplomats (diplomatic immunity) from arrest, as well as a country's property when located in another country.

Many countries have given up sovereign immunity for specific situations thereby allowing legal action against them. In the United

States, for example, immunity has been given up by most governmental entities except for the true governmental function of making or administering the laws. Thus, in the United States a congressional representative cannot be sued for voting a particular way on a bill, but could be sued if involved in an auto accident on his/her way to vote on the bill. Even in today's world, diplomats committing crimes in a country may be subject to expulsion, but not to criminal laws. This also is changing, however, due to agreements by various countries. In general the concept of sovereign immunity is far less protective than it was in the past.

JOHN O'CONNELL

specific duty   A tax levied on imports. The amount of duty is specified as an amount per unit of weight or unit of other measurement. For example, $1.00 per item imported, or $1.00 per pound or hundred weight.

JOHN O'CONNELL

split payroll   Split payroll is a method of compensating an expatriate employee in which part of the pay is made in home country currency (possibly the base salary) and the remainder in host country currency (for all other compensation items). This method is especially common when the income tax rates in the host country are extremely high when compared to the home country. Before entering into a split payroll agreement the employer must be certain that all host and home country tax laws are being followed.

Bibliography

Nexia International Staff. (1994). *International handbook of corporate and personal taxes.* New York: Chapman & Hall.

JOHN O'CONNELL

staffing   One of the most important international management functions is the selection and hiring of employees to staff positions domestically and overseas. International busi-

nesses have a large number of employee sources: their own operations throughout the world; employees from similar operations in other companies; and training new employees from countries in which operations are undertaken. Even though potential employees seem to be almost unlimited, companies tend to select on the basis of top management's feelings which may favor certain geographic regions. Hiring practices usually follow one of four strategies: polycentric approach, ethnocentric approach, regiocentric approach, or geocentric approach. The characteristics of each approach are reviewed below.

1 Polycentric approach to hiring – Polycentrism is the belief that managers and employees in a foreign operation should be from the host country. The feeling is that people native to the host country will not have problems with: culture shock, knowing the language, realizing and adhering to the local customs, values and attitudes, and being effective immediately instead of after a learning process has taken place. Key positions in the foreign operation are filled with host country nationals (HCNs). This saves money associated with recruiting, training, and transferring expatriates from other countries in which the company also has operations. There are, however, possible negative aspects of a polycentric approach to hiring. One of the biggest problems relates to parent company control over the foreign subsidiary. The question arises: "Will host country managers be loyal to the parent or to the local operation?" A potential problem arises with coordination of activities, goals, and objectives between parent and subsidiary. The fact remains, though, that polycentric staffing and operation of foreign subsidiaries is successfully being applied by organizations. The parent company must be aware of potential problems and introduce control systems to uncover these problems before they are allowed to get out of hand.

2 Ethnocentric approach to hiring – If one is ethnocentric in hiring practices, employees of a multinational company who are from the home country will be given preference. This could be because of lack of knowledge of foreign employee's qualifications for

positions or due to bias against workers from outside the home country. Ethnocentric hiring fills all important positions with employees from the home country. This reduces potential for advancement for all other employees. This method of staffing foreign operations is extremely expensive. It also disregards the need to develop management talent in host countries. Ethnocentric hiring may lead to host countries instituting regulations to restrict the number of expatriates coming to the country.

3 Regiocentric approach to hiring – A regiocentric approach to hiring selects management personnel from within a region of the world which most closely resembles that of the host country. The company has expanded its search beyond the borders of the host country, but has stopped short of seeking management personnel from its operations throughout the world. The theory behind this selection process is that nationals of the region in which operations actually take place are better able to deal with language and cultural problems than are managers from outside the region. The logic behind this hiring approach is probably sound, but it ignores the potential growth a manager goes through when forced to deal with different situations than those in which he/she is comfortable.

4 Geocentric approach to hiring – Under this approach to hiring, people are viewed in the context of how well they can accomplish a particular job or task rather than on the basis of their home country, religion, culture, or other factors. Employees are selected from throughout the organization without regard to nationality with a resulting workforce that is quite diverse. This approach to hiring is truly global in nature.

Bibliography

Deresky, Helen (1994). *International management.* 1st edn, New York: HarperCollins.

Dowling, P. J. & Schuler, R. S. (1990). *International dimensions of human resource management.* Boston, MA: PWS-Kent.

Edstron, A. & Lorange, P. (1984). Matching strategy and human resources in multinational corporations. *Journal of International Business Studies*, **15** (2), 125–37.

Heller, J. E. (1980). Criteria for selecting an international manager. *Personnel*, May–June, 47–55.

Ishidi, H. (1986). Transferability of Japanese human resource management abroad. *Human Resource Management*, **259** (1), 103–20.

Martinez, Z. L. & Ricks, D. A. (1989). Multinational parent companies' influence over human resource decisions of affiliates: U.S. forms in Mexico. *Journal of International Business Studies*, **20** (3), 465–87.

Mendenhall, M., Punnett, B. & Ricks, D. (1995). *Global management.* Cambridge, MA: Blackwell Publishers.

Schuler, R. S. (1993). World class HR departments: Six crucial issues. *The Singapore Accounting and Business Review*, Inaugural Issue, September.

JOHN O'CONNELL

standardization   Standardization of product and process is the goal of global companies. Through standardization comes economies of scale related to both production and distribution. Standardization also refers to the goal of economic integration. Standardization, when used to describe integration of laws, standards, and procedures between countries, is also referred to as "harmonization."

Bibliography

Albaum, Gerald, Strandskov, Jesper, Duerr, Edwin & Dowd, Lawrence (1994). *International marketing and export management.* 2nd edn, Wokingham: Addison-Wesley.

Cateora, P. R. (1993). *International marketing.* 5th edn, Homewood, IL: Irwin.

Toyne, B & Walters, Peter, G. P. (1993). *Global marketing management.* Boston: Allyn and Bacon.

JOHN O'CONNELL

standby letter of credit   A letter of credit may perform the same function as a surety bond in terms of being used as a financial guarantee of performance. International transactions may not be easily bondable, but a letter of credit may perform the same function. For example, an organization is seeking to bid on the construction of a dam in another country. Generally, bids on such projects require a good faith guarantee on the part of the bidder to assure the bid will be accepted if granted and that work will be done on time and in a workman-like manner. Ten percent of the bid amount is not uncommon. One of the methods of securing this guarantee is to obtain a standby letter of credit in favor of the government of the foreign country. If the bidder defaults, the foreign government is paid from the letter of credit. The bank issuing the letter then has recourse against the bidding company.

See also **Letter of credit**

JOHN O'CONNELL

standby line of credit   A standby line of credit is established when the credit-granting institution extends an amount of credit to be drawn upon by the borrower as the borrower sees fit. The maximum amount of credit is preset and cannot be exceeded. There is usually a fee charged by the lending institution for establishing a standby line of credit.

JOHN O'CONNELL

straight bill of lading   This type of bill of lading is a non-negotiable (meaning that it cannot be used to automatically transfer title to goods by simply transferring the bill to another

party) instrument used to establish the details of shipment of goods. The bill specifies the party to whom the goods are to be delivered as well as other information.

See also **Bill of lading; Uniform bill of lading**

JOHN O'CONNELL

strategic alliances   These take the form of coalitions and cooperation agreements, formed between a corporation and others in order to achieve certain strategic goals. Joint ventures may be seen as a specific form of alliance, but in recent times the term has become more widely adopted to describe a variety of forms of cooperative agreement which may or may not involve shareholdings. In particular they have been formed in some industries in which the cost of new model development, technology investment, and the like has emerged as being beyond the resources of the individual corporation. Japanese corporations have been particular users of alliance cooperative agreements with European and North American firms, partially as a way to enter these markets. Such alliances have been identified as important mechanisms for developing a global perspective in the so-called Triad markets.

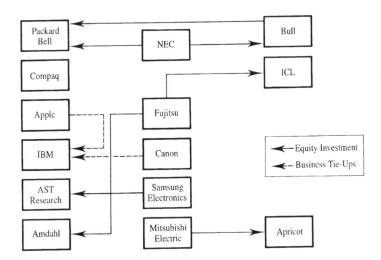

Figure 1 Global networking: international alliances in the PC industry.
Source: companies and Nihon Shimbun.

With an alliance strategy it has been possible for corporations to swiftly gain access to markets, exchange technologies, form defensive shareholding blocs, enter third markets in combination with other partners, and engage in otherwise prohibitively expensive technologies, production facilities, and the like. They have the advantage of being relatively easily formed and disbanded – more so than joint ventures – and by joining in multiple alliances firms may contain risk and hold down costs.

Despite these apparent advantages, however, their value has been seriously questioned by many corporations; and especially by those with proprietary technology, strategic cost advantage, and high market share. For such concerns it has been argued that the potential loss of technical skills, the provision of competitor access to markets, and organizational and cultural clashes may well outweigh any advantage. As a result, perhaps 50 per cent of such alliances are therefore regarded as failures.

The selection of the right partner is critical to the success of an alliance. Any analysis of such a selection should be focused on fundamental, strategic, and cultural fits.

To achieve a fundamental fit between alliance partners, the activities and expertise of each should complement the other in order to add value overall. Questions which need to be considered therefore include the following:

• What are the risks associated with realizing potential of the alliance within a reasonable period of time?

• Is the partner really interested in eventually mounting a bid?

• How stable is the business environment?

• Is the partner really interested in gaining access to our market, technology, and distribution system prior to entering as a competitor?

Strategic alliances should also always form an integral part of the strategy of the partners. It is therefore important to check the harmony and complementarity of partners' business plans, including strategic goals, product market strategies, technological strategy, the common time frame for achieving goals, and an adequate and clearly defined resource commitment.

Many alliances have failed as a result of differences between the cultures of the partner corporations. This has been especially true when they come from countries or regions with significantly different cultures, such as Japan and Western Europe. Regrettably, Western corporations in particular pay too little attention to understanding the underlying cultural and managerial styles of partners from different cultures, despite the fact that this is a major reason for the breakdown of alliances. Analysis of partner cultures is therefore recommended to insure that an acceptable fit is possible before irreversible moves are made.

Bibliography

Bleeke, J. & Ernst, D. (1991). The way to win in cross border alliances. *Harvard Business Review*, 113–33.

Bronder, C. & Pritzl, R. (1992). Developing strategic alliances. *European Management Journal*, **10**,(4) 412–20.

Lorange, P. & Roos, J. (1991). Why some strategic alliances succeed and others fail. *Journal of Business Strategy*.

Ohmae, K. (1985). *Triad power: the coming shape of global competition*, New York: The Free Press.

Ohmae, K. (1989). The global logic of strategic alliances. *Harvard Business Review*, **67**, 143–54.

Sherman, S. (1992). Are strategic alliances working? *Fortune*, 77–8.

DEREK F. CHANNON

strategic business units (SBUs) SBUs represent a movement toward placing management decision-making closer to the operational level of an organization. The formation of a strategic business unit has the following characteristics: product or service oriented; identifiable set of consumers; and an identifiable set of competitors. Thus, in terms of strategic planning, the SBU can literally function by itself in establishing plans related to products or services, customers, and competitive posture. When a corporation establishes SBUs, each SBU becomes the strategic planning unit for its own product/service area.

JOHN O'CONNELL

strategic information systems (SIS) Using today's advanced technology it is possible to receive information on events virtually while those events are taking place. A strategic information system is one that provides timely information related to the company's competitive position. In international business SIS is particularly important because of the inability to secure local information in all countries of operation. Most companies attempt to keep up with trends in the market, competitor activities, consumer demands, potential governmental inputs, and other areas deemed important. A strategic information system gathers information on areas specifically identified as being important to an organization's competitive status and provides that data to management. The difference between today's information systems and those of yesterday is the amount of data that may be accessed and the ability to review that data for relevant information. SIS can be an important source of information as long as proper planning has taken place in order to identify those areas in which information is most needed. Failure to identify areas of need will result in an inundation of information on a variety of unrelated or unnecessary areas, which will have the effect of burdening the planning process instead of providing assistance.

Bibliography

Deans, P. C. & Kane, M. J. (1992). *International dimensions of information systems and technology.* 2nd edn, Boston, MA: PWS-Kent Publishing Company.

Deans, P. C. & Karwan, K. R. (1994). *Global information systems and technology: Focus on the organization and its functional areas.* Harrisburg, PA: Idea Group Publishing.

JOHN O'CONNELL

strategic management   The management of the organization with respect to how it fits into its environment, what its objectives are in that environment, and how the organization expects to achieve its goals and objectives. Strategic management is a process and as such can be broken into steps necessary to complete that process. The steps usually associated with strategic planning are:

1 Mission statement development – A mission statement is an expression of an organization's "reason for being" or a description of why the organization exists in the first place. A mission statement is extremely important because it is upon the mission statement that all corporate goals and objectives are based and evaluated as to their successful attainment. Virtually all actions that take place in an organization should in some way contribute to supporting the basic mission statement of that organization.

2 SWOT analysis – A SWOT analysis develops information on the organizations internal Strengths (core competencies, what the organization does best) and Weaknesses (potential problem areas with supply, management, internal expertise) as well as external Opportunities (new markets, new countries, new products) and Threats (competition, government regulation, trade barriers). The key is to concentrate on an organization's areas of competence to overcome problems and threats.

3 Develop strategic objectives – What exactly do we want to do, when, and how do we measure success. Objectives should be formulated to support the organization's mission statement. The goal is to conduct a concerted effort to plan for successful achievement of objectives which allow the organization to carry out its mission.

4 Develop a strategic plan – In order to achieve objectives a plan has to be developed. The plan includes specific areas that need attention in order to meet the objectives. It is not an operating plan (a detailed plan of how to carry out the everyday activities of the organization), but a plan at a higher level. The strategic plan delineates the overall actions necessary to achieve goals, but not the individual steps to implement the plan.

5 Monitoring phase – Once the strategic plan is placed into action, management must then measure attainment of objectives, monitor the performance of organizational units to determine if control mechanisms must be in place to "guide" certain departments toward organizational objectives, and generally fine tune the plan.

Bibliography

David, F. (1991). *Strategic management.* New York: Macmillan.

Hamel, G. & Prahalad, G. K. (1985). Do you really have a global strategy. *Harvard Business Review*, 63 (4), 139–48.

Herbert, T. T. (1984). Strategy and multinational organization structure: An interorganizational relationships perspective. *Academy of Management Review*, 19 (2), 259–71.

Higgins, J. M. & Vincze, J. W. (1993). *Strategic management and organizational policy.* New York: CBS College Publishing.

Huo, H. P. & McKinley, W. (1992). Nation as a context for strategy: The effects of national characteristics on business-level strategies. *Management International Review*, 32 (2), 103–13.

Huynh, B. S. (1993). Strategy in the open door era. *Columbia Journal of Business*, Fall, 6–8. 13–9.

Majaro, S. (1977). *Marketing: A strategic approach to world markets.* London: George Allen and Unwin.

Prahalad, C. K. & Hamel, G. (1990). The core competence of the corporation. *Harvard Business Review*, May–June, 79–91.

Roth, K. & Ricks, D. (1990). Objective setting in international business: An empirical analysis. *International Journal of Management*, March.

Rugman, A. M. & Hodgetts, R. M. (1995). *International management: A strategic management approach.* New York: McGraw-Hill Inc.

JOHN O'CONNELL

strategic planning   *see* STRATEGIC MANAGEMENT

strike price   When a contract to buy or sell currency or securities at a future date (an option) is actually exercised, the amount paid or received is the "strike" price.

JOHN O'CONNELL

student visa   A student visa is issued to a foreign student seeking to undertake studies in a full-time academic (as opposed to vocational) program approved by the appropriate authorities of the country as being able to offer education to foreign students. While attending school the student must be able to prove that he/she is financially capable of continuing his/her studies and must also maintain a permanent residence outside of the country where school is attended.

See also **Visa**

JOHN O'CONNELL

supranational agencies   One of the basic theories which supports the development of economically integrated groups of countries (common markets) is that single government agencies will make many decisions for all associated countries. Thus, the agency is larger and the decisions have more impact than a single country agency. The name given to such agencies is "supranational." The European Community is a good example of a common market, which includes supranational agencies (EC Parliament, Court of Justice, Monetary Authority, etc.).

JOHN O'CONNELL

switch trade   When an importer cannot fulfill an agreement to purchase goods from an exporter, the importer may be allowed to transfer the contract or "switch" it to another importer. When this occurs there is no guarantee the original payment terms of the contract will be met. For example, it is not uncommon for the new importer to pay for goods with other goods. Exporters allow switching to occur in order to complete the transaction. When switching results in goods being traded for goods instead of a monetary payment, the contract becomes one of "countertrade."

See also **Countertrade**

JOHN O'CONNELL

SWOT analysis   *see* STRATEGIC MANAGEMENT

syndicato (Brazil)   In countries where inflation runs at very high rates it is common to tie prices and wages to an index which attempts to adjust wages and prices to keep up with inflation. In Brazil, the indexing of wages is referred to as "syndicato."

JOHN O'CONNELL

T

targeted production sectors In an attempt to increase international trade activity a government may identify certain domestic products or services as being the most likely to be demanded by foreign buyers. The government then focuses its resources toward the further development of the selected product or service. For example, if technological development is a strong point of local industry, the government may provide grants or other support to increase technological sophistication. Technology itself may then become an exportable item because of its sophistication in that particular country. By identifying specific sectors for support, the government has provided for the best chance of success in its efforts to increase trade activity.

JOHN O'CONNELL

tariff escalation This term describes a situation in which the tariffs of a country reflect the stages of production and the amount each stage can contribute to the local economy. For example, a country with a tariff structure that imposes the highest tariffs on finished goods and the lowest on raw materials imported for local production, recognizes the need for local production and the increased benefits it provides (employment, taxes, exportable goods). On the other hand, the high tariff on imported finished goods forces consumers to buy locally, thereby increasing sales of local goods.

JOHN O'CONNELL

tariff quota A government generally imposes tariffs to raise the price of imported goods to make local goods competitive. Tariffs on specific goods may be set at a given rate until the number imported reaches a pre-established level. At that time the tariff increases for additional goods imported. For example, if the tariff on tires was 5% for the first 100,000 imported, it might move to 10% for any additional importation of tires. Such a quota discourages importers from bringing large quantities of a particular item into the country.

See also **Barriers; Quotas**

JOHN O'CONNELL

tax equalization A process used by international firms to attempt to place the employee in a "no loss/no gain" position with respect to taxes paid on income earned in a foreign country. When an employee is sent on an overseas assignment, income earned is technically subject to taxes in both the home and the host country. However, due to tax agreements between some countries, only a single tax is usually collected. Tax equalization usually takes place if the tax on foreign income is greater than it would be in the home country. Either the employee receives an extra allowance to pay the additional taxes or the employer pays them on behalf of the employee.

See also **Compensation package**

Bibliography

Golding, J. (1993). *Working abroad: Essential financial planning for expatriates and their employers.* Plymouth: International Venture Handbooks.

Pinney, D. L. (1982). Structuring an expatriate tax reimbursement program. *Personnel Administrator,* 27, 19–25.

JOHN O'CONNELL

tax haven   Tax havens are countries having tax rates so low as to attract people and businesses to establish residency or local operations to take advantage of those rates. Tax havens may also establish special rates for certain business ventures (e.g., banks, insurance companies) in order to persuade certain classes of business to locate there. Generally the tax rates that attract the most people and certain types of businesses are those applying to income from foreign sources. Thus a business with mainly foreign source income may benefit greatly by being established in a tax haven country. The number of countries considered tax havens is numerous. The following lists a few of the more well-known tax havens: many of the Caribbean island nations (e.g., Cayman Islands, Bahamas, Antigua, the British Virgin Islands), the Channel Islands (Jersey, Guernsey, and Stark), Costa Rica, Hong Kong, Isle of Man, Liberia, Liechtenstein, Marshall Islands, Netherlands, Panama, Singapore, Switzerland, and many more.

Bibliography

Daniels, J. D. & Radebaugh, L. E. (1994). *International business: Environments and operations.* 7th edn, Reading, MA: Addison-Wesley Publishing.

Eiteman, D. K., Stonehill, A. J. & Moffett, M. H. (1992). *Multinational business finance.* 6th edn, Reading, MA: Addison-Wesley Publishing.

Rugman, A. M. & Hodgetts, R. M. (1995). *International management: A strategic management approach.* New York: McGraw-Hill Inc.

JOHN O'CONNELL

tea money (Australia)   An Australian tradition of providing employees with money to purchase tea or other refreshments during their work breaks. Tea money is formally addressed in Australian labor agreements.

JOHN O'CONNELL

term documentary draft   *see* DOCUMENTARY DRAFT

third-country national (TCN)   A multinational company commonly has operations in several countries. If the company chooses to send an employee from one of its foreign offices to another in a foreign country, that employee is referred to as a third-country national (TCN). This is because the employee is not from the home country and not from the host country, but from a "third" country. Third-country nationals are very common in multinational companies using a regiocentric or geocentric approach to hiring.

See also **Staffing**

JOHN O'CONNELL

Third World   *see* LESS DEVELOPED COUNTRY

Third World countries   *see* LESS DEVELOPED COUNTRY

third-party netting   Netting is a cash management technique in which cash flows, to and from operating units within a company, are forwarded to a netting center. Here inflows and outflows of each unit are netted out with just the balance either being deposited to the unit's account or being taken out of the account to pay other units. Third-party netting takes place when not only the owned units of a company use the netting center but also nonowned entities. If a company has both cash flows to and from another organization, those transactions could be handled more efficiently through a netting center.

See also **Multilateral netting**

JOHN O'CONNELL

through bill of lading   When shipment of cargo must stop at a port enroute special documents are necessary to avoid duties and other costs. A through bill of lading is used to designate cargo that is passing through a port to its final destination.

See also **Bill of lading**

Bibliography

Johnson, T. E. (1994). *Export–Import procedures and documentation.* New York: Amacom.

JOHN O'CONNELL

time draft   A time draft is one that carries a specific maturity date. The maturity date could be a specified number of days after the time the draft was issued or a specific number of days after the draft was accepted.

JOHN O'CONNELL

time orientation   Time orientation can be interpreted in two different ways when applied to international business. (1) A culture's orientation to yesterday, today, and tomorrow. Some cultures place a great deal of emphasis on the past and the traditional ways of doing things. Things that are old are revered and respected. Other cultures seem to live for now and place little stock in tradition. Things that are old are discarded and looked upon as less useful. This form of time orientation impacts the workplace as well. Japan, well known for respect. of tradition, also has widespread life time employment practices. The United States, on the other hand, views work as short term. Employees expect to move several times between employers and few expect a guarantee of lifetime employment. (2) Time orientation with respect to a culture's priorities toward punctuality. Although this may seem like a minor potential problem, there are very real and dramatic cultural differences with respect to punctuality and inferences related to not being on time. In the United States people are very aware of time, especially when concerning business meetings. To be late is considered poor business practice and rude. To be early in the United States may be taken in almost the same manner. Latin Americans view time in relative terms. Families are a priority in Latin America, thus if extra time is spent with family and business appointments are late, it is not considered rude nor out of character. Business can wait.

Problems with time orientation between cultures become evident when persons from two or more cultures must work together. Both cultures may read the other's lateness in different ways (one inferring rudeness and the other merely different priorities). Business meeting times may have to allow for leeway at the beginning and the end even though in an employee's home country, it seems like wasted time. Persons dealing with or living within cultures other than their own must be made aware of cultural differences and time orientation is certainly an important difference.

Bibliography

Deresky, Helen (1994). *International management.* 1st edn, New York: HarperCollins.
Doktor, R. H. (1990). Asian and American CEOs: A comparative study. *Organizational Dynamics,* Winter, 49.
Landis, D. & Brislin, R. (1983). *Handbook on intercultural training.* New York: Pergamon Press.
Mead, Richard (1994). *International management: Cross cultural dimensions.* Cambridge, MA: Blackwell Publishers.
Mendenhall, M., Punnett, B. & Ricks, D. (1995). *Global management.* Cambridge, MA: Blackwell Publishers.

JOHN O'CONNELL

TIR carnet   TIR refers to the French words, Transport International Routier, which translates into International Road Transport. This type of carnet is used for goods that are passing through a country on the way to another country. As long as the goods are not unloaded and reloaded in the country the carnet allows goods to pass without customs duties or customs inspection (of course when the goods reach the final country destination all customs inspections and duties for the final country apply).

See also **Carnet**

JOHN O'CONNELL

Tokyo Round   The Tokyo Round was the first series of negotiations with respect to the General Agreement on Tariffs and Trade. Not unlike other international negotiations the Tokyo Round was quite lengthy, taking six years to complete. It successfully found agreement on the gradual reduction of tariffs, valuation of imports, and overall simplification and harmonization of many details of trade transactions.

See also GATT

JOHN O'CONNELL

total loss only   *see* FREE OF ALL AVERAGE; FREE OF PARTICULAR AVERAGE

total quality control   The founder of TQC as it has developed in Japan was the influential US quality expert, W. Edwards Deming. An annual award named after him, for the most significant quality performance in Japan, is still highly prized. Deming's work strongly emphasized statistical techniques of quality control, and although these are widely used and Japanese workers are highly trained in their use, TQC is today much more than this. It has become a fundamental philosophy which guides all aspects of Japanese manufacturing strategy.

TQC may stand alone but, more commonly, it may be used in conjunction with other concepts, such as kaizen and just-in-time. To implement TQC, all plant personnel are inculcated into the philosophy, and implementation is achieved by the use of a cross-functional management structure and processes. In particular, under the Japanese system all individuals are responsible for their own actions rather than being overseen by quality inspectors and accountants. The concept has been widely used in Japanese industry since the early 1960s, and has been constantly elaborated on and improved such that many companies are still seeking real gains in productivity of 10 per cent or more per annum.

An attempt is made in table 1 to group a number of TQC factors into specific categories. The first of these, organization, consists of the key concept of assigning the primary responsibility for quality to production workers rather than a staff quality control department.

After organizing for TQC, the rate of quality improvement can be accelerated by introducing the items in categories 2–5. These include new goals, principles, facilitating concepts, and

Table 1   Total Quality Control: Concepts and Categories

TQC Category	TQC Concept
1. Organisation Production responsibility	
2. Goals Habit of Improvement	Perfection
3. Basic principles Process Control	Easy-to-see Quality Insistence on compliance Line Stop Correcting ones own errors 100 per cent check Project-by-project improvement
4. Facilitating concepts QC as a facilitator	Small lot size Housekeeping Less than full capacity scheduling Daily machine checking
5. Techniques and aids Exposure of problems	Foolproof devices N = 2 Analytical Tools QC circles

Source: Schonberger p. 51.

techniques for successful implementation of TQC. Some of these concepts are alien to Western production practice, while others have been copied from the West and adapted to Japanese business culture.

Goals

The habit of improvement.   While most Western companies accept one-off improvement programs, Japanese companies have developed the habit of kaizen – continuous improvement, day after day, year after year at all levels within the organization. For example, in some Japanese corporations the workforce meets each morning to confirm and consolidate productivity gains made the previous day.

Perfection.   The goal of perfection is treated differently between Japanese and Western concerns. There is agreement that quality needs to be regularly monitored to insure adherence to specification. However, while Western concerns accept a given standard of defects, Japanese concerns continue to work toward absolute perfection. Similarly, both Japanese and Western concerns accept that quality depends on the efforts of all functions within the corporation. However, while Western concerns place a limit on the costs to be incurred in the pursuit of quality, Japanese companies believe that ever better quality will continue to improve market share and expand the overall market. It must also be seen that for Japanese concerns the TQC concept may well include continuous cost reduction as well as product perfection.

Basic Principles

A number of basic principles are listed as components of TQC. The first two of these are closely related and equally important.

Process control

The concept of process control is a standard Western quality control technique. However, it is undertaken by the inspection of only a number of processes in the production system, together with final inspection. Moreover, this activity tends to be undertaken by the quality control department. In the Japanese system all processes are continuously checked, but by the workforce, who have been trained to undertake this task themselves, thus allowing every work station to become an inspection department.

Easy-to-see quality. This principle, which is an extension of the Deming and Juran concepts that there should be measurable standards of quality, has been finessed by the Japanese such that display boards are located everywhere in Japanese plants. These convey to workers, management, customers, suppliers, and visitors what quality factors are measured, recent performance and what current quality improvement projects are in progress, which groups have won awards, and the like. Many of the displays are graphic rather than numerical and are completed regularly by the workforce. These have much more impact than pages of computer printout, which may well be unread by Western management and perhaps not even shown to the workforce.

Insistence on compliance. In many Western concerns, while lip service is paid to achieving consistent quality standards, these may be sacrificed on occasions for short-term expediency. In most Japanese concerns, the pursuit of quality standards is paramount and takes precedence over output standards and pressures.

Line stop. Closely related to the compliance principle, in Japanese production systems every individual worker has the facility to stop the production line if quality standards are compromised. By contrast, in many Western plants the production line is not expected to stop, and any production identified as deficient is despatched to rework areas. While the Japanese system is initially slow when a new production process is started, as quality problems are gradually resolved, the line speeds up, quality improves, and rework costs are eliminated.

Correcting one's own errors. When errors do occur in the Japanese system, unlike in the West, it is the responsibility of the worker or workgroup to correct its own errors by undertaking its own rework. While the output rate is unimportant in the Japanese system with, for example, the line stop system being open to all workers, daily output is important and in the event of line stops and needed reworks, the workforce is expected to work late to make any necessary corrections. In this way, workers assume full responsibility for quality problems. In general, however, these are limited while JIT keeps lot sizes small, so that any defects detected apply to only a small number of units.

100 per cent check. In Japanese systems this requires every item of output to be inspected – not merely a random sample. This principle applies rigidly to all finished goods and, where possible, to components. When it is impossible to inspect all components, the $N=2$ concept is used (see below), with a long-term goal of achieving a 100 per cent check. By contrast, in Western companies statistical sample inspections are the norm. This technique, which was developed by the US military in World War II, was used initially by the Japanese but later rejected because the concept of a lot implied long production and hence the build-up of inventory – the antithesis of JIT. Second, the

Japanese adopted much tighter standards of defects and ultimately were aiming for true zero defects, which made sampling tables irrelevant. Third, sampling itself was considered inadequate.

Project-by-project improvement. Schemes for project-by-project improvement are visible throughout Japanese production units. The displays may also show partly completed projects, on a type of "scoreboard." Western visitors find such displays impressive, but are skeptical when they understand the number of such projects being undertaken. While it is true that individual projects make little contribution, the overall number, coupled with the cultural environment induced toward quality, results in a massive continuous level of improvement which most Western firms find impossible to replicate.

Facilitating Concepts

The effect of quality improvement can be enhanced by making use of the facilitating concepts once the organizational and quality principles are in place. These facilitators are as follows.

Quality control as facilitator. In Japan, as responsibility for quality is assigned to the line function, specialist quality control departments are reduced in size and used as facilitators for the total process. As a result, they promote the removal of the causes of defects, keep track of quality achievements, monitor as standard procedures are followed, and observe procurement to insure that supplier factories have similar quality standards and conduct QC training. The inspection of goods inwards parts is also passed back to suppliers and, as such, goods inward are sent straight to the production line. One exception to this practice is that parts received from Western suppliers may be inspected by the quality department.

Small lot sizes. This is a key element in JIT production. It is also important in insuring that any defects are detected early. As such, it also forms a basic concept in quality control.

Housekeeping. Japanese factories are carefully laid out to insure scrupulous tidiness and cleanliness. While individual workers are expected to keep their workplace tidy, any production workers not required for their line production jobs may be temporarily assigned to cleanliness and hygiene tasks elsewhere in the factory.

Less-than-full-capacity scheduling. Having available spare capacity insures that the daily production schedules will be met. It is also a quality control concept, as it permits the line to be stopped for quality or other reasons. Moreover, capacity slack avoids over-pressuring the workforce, tools, and equipment – so reducing the probability of errors.

Daily machine checking. Unlike in the West, where production machinery is used as hard as possible and maintenance is the responsibility of specialists, in Japan production workers are expected to perform routine maintenance on their machines at the beginning of each day. Each morning, therefore, the Japanese normally go through a checklist, insuring that the machine functions correctly, oiling, adjusting, sharpening, and the like before operations commence.

Techniques and Aids

In Japanese TQC there are fewer techniques and aids than those found in the West, where specialists using various techniques and aids are common. In Japan, the commonly used tools are fewer and different. They include the following.

Exposure of problems. In the TQC system, discovery of a defect triggers a detailed investigation to discover the cause of the defect and correct it. This process is so valued that management may deliberately remove workers or buffer inventories to expose problems affecting quality. Exposure of problems and correction of causes are also sought out before there is actual evidence of problems. This might involve very careful analysis of product designs and checks at the product start-up phase, before volume production commences. Similarly, workers – both individually and in small groups or quality circles – are constantly seeking ways in which to improve quality.

Foolproof devices. The work process can be redesigned to eliminate many mistakes. Many machines are fitted with *bakayoke*, which automatically check for abnormal production. When such defects are found, the machines stop automatically – the process of "autonomation." The monitoring mechanisms may therefore check for malfunction, excess tool wear, and the like, in addition to dimensions and tolerances. Such devices are also sometimes used in final assembly or when manual systems are used via the line stop system or via worker triggered warning lights.

$N = 2$. While foolproof devices are useful for high-volume operations, for lower volumes manual inspection may be required. High percentages of production are inspected – even as high as 100 per cent, in the case of unstable processes. For more stable processes, sample inspection may be used. Unlike in the West, where random sampling is normal, in Japanese TQC inspection is not random. In practice, the first and last pieces in a production run are inspected – hence the term $N = 2$. The argument is that in a stable process if the first and last units are good, then those produced in between should also all be good.

Tools of analysis. Statistical tools are used in both Western and Japanese quality control systems. In Japan, however, these tend to be used by superiors and workers who have undergone extensive training in their preparation and use.

Many Japanese variants of such tools, however, show greater detail (see, for example, break even analysis, Pareto analysis, and radar mapping). The cause–effect, or Ishikawa, diagram was less known in the West, but is now a normal tool used in quality analysis.

QC Circles. QC circles are used throughout Japanese corporations and almost all employees are members. Such groups meet to develop ideas for quality improvements on a regular basis. Their output is prodigious, with ideas for quality and kaizen improvement often running into millions of suggestions each year per company. Most of these ideas are implemented. While successful ideas are rewarded, the gains in monetary terms are usually small, with prestige awards being more highly thought of.

The TQC concept has been accepted by a number of Western companies, but few have adopted the depth of commitment to the principles and practice found in Japanese

concerns. Without such commitment, the constant improvements in quality and costs experienced in Japan are unlikely to materialize in the West, leading to a continuous loss of competitive advantage.

Bibliography

Kusaba, I. (1981). Quality control in Japan. *Reports of QC circle activities*, (no. 14), pp. 1–5. Union of Japanese Scientists and Engineers.
Ishikawa, K. (1985). *What is total quality control? The Japanese way*, Englewood Cliffs, NJ: Prentice-Hall.
Juran, J. M. (1978). Japanese and Western quality: a contrast in methods and results. *Management Review*, 26–45.
Monden, Y. (1983). *Toyota production system*, Atlanta, GA: Institute of Industrial Engineers.
Schonberger, R. J. (1982). *Japanese manufacturing techniques*, New York: The Free Press.

DEREK F. CHANNON

tourist visa A tourist visa is issued only for sightseeing and other tourist activities. Generally tourist visas are issued for specific periods of time (six months is common). If longer stays are anticipated an extension may have to be applied for. Extensions normally require the traveler to show some form of financial capability of taking care of himself/herself during the extended stay.

See also **Visa**

JOHN O'CONNELL

trade barriers Trade barriers are actions taken by a government to reduce the chances of successful foreign trade. The reasons for barriers range from protection of local industry to retribution for past political activities of a country. For a complete discussion of various types of barriers (*see* BARRIERS).

JOHN O'CONNELL

trade centers A trade center is a location in which trade offices, international consulting firms, educational enterprises, promotional firms, and others are housed and in which international trade is the major business. Probably the most famous of all trade centers are the twin towers of the World Trade Center in New York City. Cities throughout the world have trade centers which, as their name implies, are meant to be the center of international business activity in that particular city.

JOHN O'CONNELL

trade creation When trade barriers are reduced between countries trading opportunities increase. This is not because the opportunity wasn't there before. The opportunities were just not economically feasible with tariff and other barriers increasing the final selling price of goods. Thus, countries which agree to remove barriers tend to create trade opportunities between those same countries.

JOHN O'CONNELL

trade diversion When countries agree to reduce or do away with trade barriers trade increases between those countries. Products that were formerly purchased outside of the agreeing countries are now purchased "between" those countries. Thus, trade has been diverted from countries not part of the trade agreement to those which are signatories to the agreement.

JOHN O'CONNELL

trade fairs One of the ways to advertise newly-developed products or products that are new to a trading area is to open an exhibit at a trade fair. Trade fairs are popular methods of seeing what's new and what the competition is up to. Trade fairs have gotten to be so popular that they are usually very specific as to the types of products they exhibit (computer fairs, video, automobiles, and others are very popular). Trade fairs may be open to the public or strictly for industry producers and buyers.

JOHN O'CONNELL

trade financing The majority of goods traded across borders are financed in one way or another. Most importers of goods will not release funds until they are certain the goods are delivered in good condition. This requires a system of financing to be in place to handle the enormous demand for what are normally short-term funds. Financing is conducted by the exporters themselves, export development banks and agencies in various countries, and by governments, individual investors, and commercial banks throughout the world.

JOHN O'CONNELL

trade mission A trade mission is a group of business people who travel to another country to seek out opportunities for business ventures involving exports/imports, investment in the host country, or contacts for possible foreign investment in the home country. Missions (trips to the foreign country) are a popular method of networking not only with foreign trade officials and business people in the host country, but are also a method of gaining contacts with persons with similar interests in the home country. People going on trade missions usually pay their own expenses. However, government agencies may offer support in some situations. The initial sponsorship of an official trade mission is usually a local, state, or federal government agency.

JOHN O'CONNELL

trade visitor This is usually an influential person in a particular industry who is invited by a government to meet with local producers and exporters with regard to increasing trade between the host and the visitor's countries.

JOHN O'CONNELL

trademark A trademark is a design, symbol, word or series of words that is used to identify a specific company, service, or product(s). A trademark may be registered in order to protect the right of the company to have exclusive use of the trademark in the geographic area of registration. Infringement is a common occurrence in some countries. Even though laws exist in many countries to protect this "property right," lax enforcement of the laws leads to illegal activities by those who would copy products or goods which are trademarked.

See also **Intellectual property; Piracy**

Bibliography

Seminsky, M. & Bryer, L. G.(eds) (1994). *The new role of intellectual property in commercial transactions.* New York: John Wiley & Sons.

Stewart, G. R. (Ed.) (1994). *International trade and intellectual property: The search for a balanced system.* Boulder, CO: Westview Press.

JOHN O'CONNELL

Trademark Registration Treaty (TRT) An international agreement which is administered by the World Intellectual Property Organization (WIPO), the TRT provides a method of registering trademarks internationally using a single application. Once an application has been approved, the trademark protection is valid in all countries which are signatories to the agreement.

See also **Madrid Agreement; World Intellectual Property Organization**

JOHN O'CONNELL

trading area A company's trading area is merely the geographic area in which the company has decided to pursue trade activities. Usually a company begins with a local trading area. As the company grows and products are accepted the trade area expands until it begins to cross international boundaries. Trading areas may be limited by a company's financial condition, laws associated with trade, management's knowledge of the market, or the creativity of the firm's owners/managers.

See also **Evolution of global organization**

JOHN O'CONNELL

trading bloc Trading blocs are a very important development in international trade. Although agreements between groups of countries have existed for decades, it has been only in the 1990s that trading blocs have gained recognition as potentially being able to control large amounts of trade not only within a specific trading bloc but throughout the entire world. Instead of a single country buying and selling goods, virtually all of western Europe (the

European Community) or North America (the North American Free Trade Agreement – Nafta) has become a single market for imports and exports. Trading blocs exert a great deal of economic power. They can control the trade within member countries to make freedom of trade a reality. They can also make demands on other trading nations because of their tremendous purchasing power.

See also **Common market; European Community**

Bibliography

Bartlett, Christopher, A. & Ghoshal, Sumantra (1992). *Transnational management.* 2nd edn, Chicago: Irwin.

Daniels, J. D. & Radebaugh, L. E. (1994). *International business: Environments and operations.* 7th edn, Reading, MA: Addison-Wesley Publishing.

Grosse, R. & Kujawa, D. (1995). *International business: Theory and managerial applications.* 3rd edn, Boston, MA: Richard D. Irwin Inc.

JOHN O'CONNELL

training *see* EXPATRIATE TRAINING

tramp steamer A vessel that does not transport goods on preset schedules or routes. Although the reference to "tramp" may seem to be derogatory, ships of this type are often as seaworthy and dependable as vessels operating on schedules between ports of call. "Tramps" are available for specific voyage needs of charterers. They will take cargo (crude oil tramps are common) when the charterer requires and to wherever the charterer desires. A tramp vessel is akin to a freelance operator in the business of hauling cargo.

JOHN O'CONNELL

transaction exposure This exposure arises when a business enters into transactions in which foreign currency payments are expected to be made "to" the business in the future or in which foreign currency payments are to be made "by" the business in the future. As time passes currency values may change. If foreign currency values fall, the business will be paid in the lower value currency. If foreign currency values increase, the company will have to use more of its domestic currency to purchase foreign currency with which to pay future debt.

See also **Exchange exposures**

Bibliography

Eiteman, D. K., Stonehill, A. J. & Moffett, M. H. (1992). *Multinational business finance.* 6th edn, Reading, MA: Addison-Wesley Publishing.

Miletello, F. C. & Davis, H. A. (1994). *Foreign exchange management.* Morristown, NJ: Financial Executives Research Foundation.

JOHN O'CONNELL

transfer price   The transfer price is the price paid for a good or service between members of the same corporate family. That is, the price charged by a subsidiary to a parent company for goods exported to the parent. Alterations of the transfer price may be used to move excessive amounts of money from a parent company to a subsidiary. This is especially useful if the parent is located in a high tax country and the subsidiary in a low tax country.

See also **Reinvoicing**

Bibliography

Celi, L. J. & Rutizer, B. (1991). *Global cash management.* 1st edn, New York: Harper Business (HarperCollins).

JOHN O'CONNELL

transit visa   As the name implies, a transit visa is issued to a person who is merely passing through a country but must connect with outbound transportation within the borders of a country. If required, a transit visa is in addition to any other visas required by various countries entered by a person during a business or pleasure trip.

See also **Visa**

JOHN O'CONNELL

translation exposure   Translation exposure is an accounting measure. If an organization has assets valued in a foreign currency, it faces the possibility that the foreign currency will fall in value. If this occurs, the decrease in value "translates" into reduced value of business assets.

See also **Exchange exposures**

Bibliography

Eiteman, D. K., Stonehill, A. J. & Moffett, M. H. (1992). *Multinational business finance.* 6th edn, Reading, MA: Addison-Wesley Publishing.

JOHN O'CONNELL

translation risk   *see* TRANSLATION EXPOSURE

transnational corporation (TNC)   A transnational corporation (TNC) is seen by many as being synonymous with a multinational corporation (MNC). Many observers in Europe apply a slightly different view when defining a transnational corporation. The view taken describes a TNC as a merger of existing organizations from different countries into a single transnational corporation. Shell is probably one of the better known transnationals, being of Dutch–English descent.

JOHN O'CONNELL

travel time   As part of the compensation package, most companies allow an expatriate a specified number of days to travel to their assignment country. Full pay and specified expenses are paid during this period of time.

See also **Compensation package**

JOHN O'CONNELL

travelers letter of credit   A letter of credit issued to a person who will be traveling in another country. The letter allows drafts to be written against the letter up to the value set forth in the letter. Another name for this type of letter of credit is "circular letter of credit."

See also **Letter of credit**

JOHN O'CONNELL

treaties   Treaties are official agreements between countries; treaties are generally ratified at the highest levels of government. They are agreements which bind the agreeing nations to actions in areas such as: trade, defense, human rights, environmental protection, and many others. Treaties are extremely important to international commerce as they form the basis of the rules which must be followed when commerce occurs between various countries.

JOHN O'CONNELL

Treaty of Rome   The Treaty of Rome (1957) began the movement toward what is now the European Community. The treaty served as the basis for negotiations which have now spanned five decades. Originally, signatory nations numbered only six (Belgium, France, Italy, Luxembourg, the Netherlands, and West Germany). This number has expanded to a point where within a short period of time there could be nearly twenty member countries.

See also **European Community**

JOHN O'CONNELL

triangular arbitrage   "Three point" or "triangular" arbitrage occurs where three currencies are traded against one another to arrive at a profit. Arbitrage also takes place in the trading of other financial instruments or commodities.

See also **Arbitrage**

JOHN O'CONNELL

trilateral trade agreement   This is a trade agreement in which three countries participate. The North American Free Trade Agreement is an example of a trilateral trade agreement between the United States, Canada, and Mexico.

JOHN O'CONNELL

turnkey plus project   A turnkey project is the construction and outfitting of a facility (usually a building or other structure) with the intent of turning it over to the buyer when complete. A turnkey plus project also entails an agreement to operate the facility for some stated period of time before turning it over to the buyer. The operation time period normally allows for training of local workers and management to successfully begin to operate the facility at a later date.

JOHN O'CONNELL

turnkey project   The construction and outfitting of a facility (usually a building or other structure) with the intent of turning it over to the buyer when complete. The facility is ready to operate, assuming the buyer has the managerial knowledge and employee know-how to undertake operations.

See also **Turnkey plus project**

JOHN O'CONNELL

tying clause   When a loan is provided by lenders from a particular country, the loan agreement may have a clause requiring that proceeds of the loan may only be used to purchase other goods and services within the country in which the loan was granted. This is referred to as a "tying clause." It ties the loan to an agreement to spend the money within the borders of a particular country.

JOHN O'CONNELL

—— U ——

unbundling Companies are sometimes purchased in order to break them into parts for resale. It may be possible to secure higher profits by selling pieces of a company rather than the company as a whole. The process of selling off the pieces is referred to as "unbundling" by the British.

JOHN O'CONNELL

UNCISG *see* UNITED NATIONS CONVENTION ON CONTRACTS FOR THE INTERNATIONAL SALE OF GOODS

UNCITRAL *see* UNITED NATIONS COMMISSION ON INTERNATIONAL TRADE LAW

underselling Underselling occurs when an exporter sells its product in another country at lower than the going price (fair market value). Although such sales may be due to the exporter's lower costs of production, underselling may also be a sign of the "dumping" of products. Dumping is generally considered an unfair trade practice.

See also **Dumping**

JOHN O'CONNELL

understanding cultural differences Many unexpected events happen in international business: some are good, but others are bad. Many problems occur because of cultural differences, which cause six types of problem:

- overestimation of product interest
- product not correctly modified
- wrong name
- wrong packaging
- wrong promotional efforts
- wrong management style

Lack of Product Interest

Many products which sell well in one country do not sell well at all in others. Firms that simply assume that their products are wanted overseas often encounter unexpected losses. One U.S. company, for example, unsuccessfully tried to sell ketsup in Japan. The firm finally realized the Japanese did not like ketsup.

Another U.S. firm tried to sell American-style bed mattresses in Japan. The Japanese did not use such mattresses, did not want them, and therefore did not buy them.

Product Modification

Sometimes the product will sell in another market, but only if it has been modified. Campbell's soup did not sell well initially in Britain, even though it was competitively priced and tasted fine to the British. The problem was that it was condensed soup. The British are used to buying soup in cans with the water already added. To them, it looked as though a buyer of Campbell's condensed soups would only get half as much soup for his or her money. The firm eventually recognized the problem, changed the production method by adding the water, and was then able to sell its soups in Britain.

Similarly, Jell-O was only made available the way it is sold in America – in powder form. The British, however, preferred to purchase such products already made (jelled): they wanted to see what it looked like. Jell-O had to change the way it did business there in order to be successful.

Wrong Name

The name of the product can also be a problem and may need to be changed. General Motors had trouble in Puerto Rico when it tried to introduce its Nova model. The car was popular in the U.S.A., but did not do well in Puerto Rico until its name was changed, because in Spanish *no va* means "does not go."

Wrong Package

Sometimes the problem is the packaging. It might be the wrong color (white is often a problem color in Asia because it represents death), the wrong style, or even have the wrong picture on it.

An animal might be considered "cute" in one culture, but dirty in another. Dogs are seldom pictured successfully on packages sold in the Middle East. An owl might seem like a wise animal in America, but it is a symbol of bad luck in parts of Asia.

Gerber Foods thought that its widely successful baby foods would do well in one African country. Prices were tested. Tastes were tested. Everything looked ready for a successful market entry, but almost no one bought the jars of baby food. When Gerber investigated, it was found that they had failed to test market the packaging. Most of the consumers in that market were illiterate, so they guessed what was in a new product's package by seeing what was shown on the label. Gerber had used its famous (and usually highly successful) smiling baby picture on its jars. Unfortunately, therefore, the local people incorrectly believed that the jars contained ground-up babies.

Wrong Promotional Efforts

Companies have often blundered when trying to market their products in foreign markets. Sometimes they offend the local culture by ignoring religious beliefs. One company, for example, tried to sell its refrigerator in the Middle East by showing it filled with food, including a large ham – a food not eaten there.

Sometimes the promotion is ruined by a simple translation blunder. Pepsi had its famous "Come Alive With Pepsi" slogan come out as "Come Back From the Dead With Pepsi." General Motors had problems in Belgium when its "Body by Fischer" was translated into "Corpse by Fischer." Parker Pens wanted to sell its fountain pens in Mexico with the successful U.S. slogan "Avoid embarrassment, use Parker Pens." However, the Spanish word for "embarrassment" was slang for "pregnancy," and so the promotional effort only brought embarrassment.

Wrong Management Style

Sometimes it is the style of the manager that causes the problem. An aggressive style might work well in one culture, but fail miserably in another.

Some American firms have caused problems by trying to rush negotiations in countries which prefer a slower approach. The Japanese, for example, generally prefer a deliberate style of careful consideration and full discussion. Many people are often involved in the decision making process. One American firm, not aware of this style, incorrectly assumed that its offer was being rejected by the Japanese negotiators, and so it kept improving the offer before even receiving a response to the previous one.

An American mining company had serious problems when its top manager at a mine on a Pacific island had a heart attack. The firm hurriedly flew the manager to the U.S.A. for special medical attention and, on the same day, sent a replacement from California. Unfortunately, the replacement was not prepared. He also arrived tired, nervous, and with his family.

The new manager was told that he could expand mining operations by 50 per cent, so he quickly called a meeting of his top supervisors and told them of the expansion. He then asked the most senior supervisor to take care of hiring the needed new miners.

As soon as the American left the meeting, the supervisors began to argue. This continued during the day, and more and more people were drawn into the discussion. By late afternoon, most of the miners – and even some non-employees – were engaged in a heated conversation. As it grew dark, torches were lit and the apparent mob included most of the local villagers.

The manager grew concerned for the safety of his family. He did not know the local language and could not understand what was happening, so he called on the company's security force to protect his family.

Late in the evening, the mob started moving toward the manager's home, still carrying torches. Fearing for the safety of his family, the manager ordered the guards to fire on the crowd, and several people were killed.

A subsequent investigation revealed that the plant always hired a certain percentage of its employees from each tribe and that each tribe had a representative supervisor. However, the American manager had asked only one supervisor to hire. That supervisor, naturally, felt it necessary to first suggest that all new employees be from his tribe. The other supervisors needed to represent their tribes and put on a good showing. They all knew that they would eventually go back to the old percentage formula, but they enjoyed the discussion. The torches were for light. When an agreement was finally reached, the employees just wanted to tell the new American manager the good news.

Obviously, cultural differences can and do make differences in how we conduct business. Failure to be aware of cultural differences can lead to embarrassing, costly – and even deadly – international business blunders.

DAVID A. RICKS

unfair trade   This term describes transactions which involve goods being "dumped" on foreign markets, black-market goods, copied or otherwise counterfeited goods, or goods that are subsidized beyond normally acceptable levels. Countries that participate in unfair trade practices are subject to retaliatory measures by those countries which are treated unfairly.

See also **Dumping; Intellectual property**

Bibliography

Viner, J. (1991). *Dumping: A problem in international trade.* Caldwell, NJ: Augustus M. Kelley Publishers.

JOHN O'CONNELL

uniform bill of lading   A bill of lading that meets the requirements of the United States Federal Bill of Lading Act of 1915.

See also **Bill of lading**

JOHN O'CONNELL

unilateral duty   A duty imposed by executive order to punish a country for unfair trade practices. It may also be used to reduce the flow of specific types of imports. Unilateral duties are temporary, lasting until the trade problem has been resolved.

See also **Duty; Unfair trade**

JOHN O'CONNELL

United Nations Center on Transnational Corporations   This United Nations center was established in 1974 to assist in the development of standardized procedures for accounting and reporting requirements for multinational businesses.

JOHN O'CONNELL

United Nations Commission on International Trade Law (UNCITRAL)   The expansion of world trade brought about many problems associated with transportation contract interpretation, rights and responsibilities of parties to import/export contracts, and ever-changing rules associated with trade between various countries. Individual countries began to implement regulations and make interpretations concerning responsibilities of parties to trade contracts. The proliferation of rulings led to even more confusion.

In 1966, the United Nations established a permanent commission dedicated to the eventual harmonization of international trade law. The commission acts as a coordinating body between various country efforts to establish trade law, as well as developing wording for and enforcing conventions (agreements) sponsored by the United Nations. Through the work of the commission, great strides have been made in unifying international trade law and practice.

JOHN O'CONNELL

United Nations Convention on Contracts for the International Sale of Goods (UNCISG)   In an attempt to standardize the interpretation of international contracts dealing with imports and exports, the United Nations developed and adopted the UNCISG in 1980. The UNCISG is an attempt to delineate responsibilities of all parties to trade contracts. Although relatively few nations have become signatories of the agreement, efforts are still underway to garner additional support for reducing trade problems through the adoption of standardized rules governing all or parts of trade transactions.

See also **United Nations Commission on International Trade Law**

JOHN O'CONNELL

USITA *see* UNITED STATES INTERNATIONAL TRADE ADMINISTRATION

United States International Trade Administration (USITA)   In 1980, pressures of monitoring and developing international trade prompted the US Congress to establish the USITA as a part of the US Department of Commerce. Assistance was needed in the areas of: developing trade policy; enforcing current trade regulations; and fostering increased exports of United States goods. The USITA is comprised of four operating units: (1) Import administration – This unit develops, implements and oversees regulations associated with international trade. The administration also is responsible for investigating charges of dumping levied against foreign interests. (2) International economic policy – This unit is essentially an information source for those seeking economic information on a country or region of the world. (3) Trade development – This unit is in charge of promoting the export of United States goods. It also offers advice on which types of exports are most likely to be in demand and offers support for specific sectors of the economy as it deems expedient. (4) US and foreign commercial service – This unit sponsors trade missions, exhibitions, conferences, and other activities to promote the export of US goods. The activities of this unit are carried out both in the United States and other countries in which trade promotion is deemed desirable.

Bibliography

United States Customs Service (1994). *A basic guide to importing.* Lincolnwood, IL: NTC Publishing Group.

JOHN O'CONNELL

universal copyright convention   An international agreement which protects the authors of written works from unauthorized use of those works. The agreement calls for protection during the author's life plus an additional 50 years. Under this agreement written work is "automatically" protected if information related to publication (author's name, publication date, or completion date if unpublished), and the copyright symbol are made a part of the work. The agreement applies only to signatory countries.

See also **Intellectual property; Piracy**

JOHN O'CONNELL

— V —

value dimensions (Hofstede's) G. Hofstede's research into cultural differences has yielded perhaps one of the most useful theories to managers and international entrepreneurs. Although readers may not agree with the specific terms used by Hofstede to describe cultural dimensions, it is difficult not to see the usefulness of his work. Hofstede's value dimensions are:

1 Power distance – This expresses the ability of a society to accept differences between the highest level of power in an organization and the lowest level of power. The idea that power differences exist in business is not unique. There have always been managers and workers, supervisors and clerks, and owners and employees. However, Hofstede found that different cultures accepted this difference in power better than others.

   For example, workers in Austria and Israel have a low power distance (low acceptance of unequal power in the workplace) whereas workers in the Philippines and Malaysia readily accept workplace power inequalities. In Malaysia, the manager has the right to be boss and the chain of command is rarely broken. In Austria, however, workers and managers are seen as being equal and more cooperative planning takes place. Workers in the United States and Great Britain are in the low power distance region.

2 Uncertainty avoidance – This is the degree to which people in a given culture are threatened by uncertain situations. High uncertainty avoidance leads to strict rules and regulations, long-term employment opportunities, and a greater sense of a need for stability. This leads to few

decisions being made by any one person and a low state of aggressiveness on the part of workers. Low uncertainty avoidance leads to less structure on the job, fewer work rules and regulations, and workers and managers who are likely to make decisions whenever possible. Japan, Greece, and Portugal express high uncertainty avoidance. Singapore, Denmark, and Sweden express low uncertainty avoidance. The United States and Great Britain are in the low category of uncertainty avoidance.

3 Individualism – This is the degree of independence a person has with respect to his/her organization or society. In the United States and Australia there is a high degree of individualism. A sense of individual achievement seems to be a part of the work ethic in these countries. On the other hand, Ecuador and Panama were measured by Hofstede as having a low degree of individualism. In these countries there is a strong tie between the worker and employer, collective action is common, and social pressures are used to make people conform. Leaders are more easily able to guide the efforts of low individualism countries toward the common goals of the organization and society, than are leaders in high individualism countries.

4 Masculinity – High masculinity denotes aggressiveness, materialism, and women as being housewives and homemakers. Low masculinity denotes women in the workforce, concern for overall quality of life, and lower levels of stress related to performance. Japan is very high on the masculinity scale, while Sweden and Norway are very low on the scale.

When Hofstede's value dimensions are viewed as a whole it may be possible to determine in which cultures a business organization could best operate. Although Hofstede's terminology is probably not as acceptable as it could be in today's world, his ideas do allow for an initial screening of similarities and differences between cultures. The business management implications of his research are many.

See also **Cultural maps**

Bibliography

Evans, W. A., Sculli, D. & Yau, W. S. L. (1987). Cross-cultural factors in the identification of managerial potential. *Journal of General Management*, **13** (1), 52–7.

Ferraro, G. P. (1990). *The cultural dimension of international business.* Englewood Cliffs, NJ: Prentice-Hall.

Hayes, J. & Allison, C. W. (1988). Cultural differences in the learning styles of managers. *Management International Review*, **28** (3), 75–80.

Hofstede, G. (1980). Motivation, leadership, and organization: Do American theories apply abroad? *Organizational Dynamics*, Summer, 42–63.

Kuroda, Y. & Suzuki, T. (1991). A comparative analysis of the Arab culture: Arabic, English, and Japanese language and values. *International Association of Middle Eastern Studies.*

Lane, H. W., Distefano, J. J. & Hollocks, B. (1990). International management behaviour – From policy to practice. *Journal of Operational Research Society*, **41**.

Mendenhall, M., Punnett, B. & Ricks, D. (1995). *Global management.* Cambridge, MA: Blackwell Publishers.

Moran, R. (1988). *Venturing abroad in Asia: Complete business traveller's guide to cultural differences in eleven Asian countries.* New York: McGraw-Hill Book Co.

Ronen, S. & Shenkar, O. (1985). Clustering countries on attitudinal dimensions: A review and synthesis. *Academy of Management Review*, **10** (3), 435–54.

JOHN O'CONNELL

vacation allowance *see* COMPENSATION PACKAGE

validated export license *see* EXPORT LICENSE; INDIVIDUALLY VALIDATED EXPORT LICENSE

valuation   In reference to international trade the term "valuation" means the value established for imported goods by the customs authorities of a country. Prior to guidelines set forth by the General Agreement on Tariffs and Trade (GATT) customs authorities were routinely felt to increase values on imported goods in order to increase revenues from duty payment. The signatory nations of GATT have adopted a set of guidelines which should reduce such occurrences. Usually, major trading countries will have procedures for appealing valuations that are felt to be too high. The major solution to overvaluing, however, is to keep good records of an import's costs and ultimate value and be certain to use these figures to state the value when importing the items. If an importer "underestimates" the true value, customs authorities have been known to assess additional costs to make-up for such oversights.

JOHN O'CONNELL

value added   Value added is the incremental value associated with materials and labor during each of the production stages. Value added becomes important when a tax system such as that found in Europe is based upon the value added at each production stage.

See also **Value-added tax**

JOHN O'CONNELL

value-added tax (VAT)   Value-added taxes separate the taxes on goods so that instead of paying a single tax on the completed value, each party contributing to the production or distribution of a product pays tax on the value added. For example, if a manufacturer produced a product with a final sales price to the consumer of $1,000 the value-added tax might be broken down as follows: the raw materials for the product cost $250 and were processed to a product valued at $500. The processor pays a VAT on the added $250 of value. The processed product is purchased for $500 by the manufacturer who further processes it into a finished product which is sold for $1,000. The manufacturer pays a VAT on the $500 of added value.

Although the value-added tax is mainly a European phenomena, it has made its way to North America via Canada. The United States does not have a VAT, but tax reformists seem to bring it up each time there is debate over the US tax system.

Bibliography

Nexia International Staff (1994). *International handbook of corporate and personal taxes.* New York: Chapman & Hall.

JOHN O'CONNELL

VAT *see* VALUE-ADDED TAX

visa A visa is a document or an entry in a passport giving the passport holder official permission to enter a country. Because of treaties and other agreements not all international travel necessitates the securing of a visa. The international traveler should verify well ahead of departure time whether visas or other documents are necessary for admittance to countries on his/her itinerary.

Visas fall into two basic categories: (1) those issued to business visitors; and (2) those issued to pleasure visitors. Each country establishes the exact nature of the visa (title or number of document, eligibility requirements, etc.) and no two countries are exactly alike. There are general circumstances and uses of visas, however, of which international business persons should be aware. The comments which follow do not apply to any specific nation but are for general understanding only. You must contact the consulate or immigration service of a country to obtain details of its requirements with respect to visas. Common categories of visas include:

1 Commercial visa – A commercial visa is issued to business travelers who are visiting a country on a temporary basis. Usually a business traveler is not allowed to be paid a salary by a company in the host country (local salary earners are usually not eligible for a commercial visa, although exceptions are made). Commercial visa holder activities are also stated in each country's immigration laws. Common activities which are allowed are: attend business conferences or conventions; conduct sales meetings; negotiate business contracts; purchase goods for export; as well as other specifically allowed business activities. Other categories of business visitors may be eligible for special visa status. The party seeking special status must check with a consulate or the immigration authorities of the proposed host country.

2 Exit visa – Exit visas are often required of commercial visa holders who have been permitted to work in a foreign country. The exit visa allows immigration authorities to keep track of work permit holders as well as verifying that all local income and other taxes which may be due are paid "before" the commercial visitor is allowed to leave the country.

3 General visa – A general visa allows entry to a country for any purpose (business or pleasure). A general visa essentially combines a tourist visa and a commercial visa. A general visa normally limits a pleasure visit to six or twelve months and a business visit to a time period close to that expected to carry out the business but normally not more than three or six months. General visa holders must be coming to a country for a temporary visit after which they will depart the country. Visitors also must normally maintain a foreign residence during their time in the host country and prove that they have sufficient financial resources to support themselves while visiting.

Business visitors – Business visitors using a general visa are normally restricted as to activities or earnings in the host country. The business visitor must also normally be engaged (with some exceptions) in trade or other international activities of which the visitor's activities benefit a foreign entity or the visitor him/herself. Allowable activities of a business visitor include sales calls, purchasing goods for export, consulting work, attending professional meetings, research and other activities. If a general visa is not used in a country, business visitors have to apply for what is commonly called a "commercial visa."

Visitors for pleasure – Visitors coming to a country as tourists, attending nonbusiness conventions, shopping trips, or to visit relatives or friends. Any person working in the host country is technically ineligible for the general visa's pleasure visitor category. If a visitors for pleasure category is not available under a general visa, visitors will have to apply for what is normally referred to as a "tourist visa."

Even though general visas are for broad categories of visitors, each country has its own eligibility criteria. Care must be taken to obtain the correct type of visa for the activities being undertaken in another country.

4 Re-entry visa – A re-entry visa is issued to a foreign person who has been permitted to work in a country. If that person desires to leave the country for a short period of time a re-entry visa may be issued to expedite the person's readmittance to the host country. Re-entry visas are commonly issued to business people who must return to their home country periodically, but will be back to the host country in a short while to continue their work. Businesspersons will also have to have a work permit in most countries if they remain resident more than a minimum amount of time.

5 Student visa – A student visa is issued to a foreign student seeking to undertake studies in a full-time academic (as opposed to vocational) program approved by the appropriate authorities of the country as being able to offer education to foreign students. While attending school the student must be able to prove that he/she is financially capable of continuing his/her studies and must also maintain a permanent residence outside of the country where school is attended.

6 Tourist visa – A tourist visa is issued only for sightseeing and other tourist activities, or to visit family or friends. Generally tourist visas are issued for specific periods of time

(six months is common). If longer stays are anticipated an extension may have to be applied for. Extensions normally require the traveler to show some form of financial capability of taking care of himself/herself during the extended stay.

7 Transit visa – As the name implies, a transit visa is issued to a person who is merely passing through a country but must connect with outbound transportation within the borders of a country. If required, a transit visa is in addition to any other visas required by various countries entered by a person during a business or pleasure trip.

Bibliography

Torbiorn, J. (1982). *Living abroad.* New York: John Wiley.

JOHN O'CONNELL

voluntary quota   In the spirit of goodwill (and probably for future bargaining position) countries may enter into voluntary agreements to limit the number of products exported to another country. For example, if a foreign auto manufacturer felt that the government of an important importing country might impose formal quotas for automobile imports, the auto manufacturer may agree to voluntarily limit the number of autos being exported. Voluntary quotas are generally much easier to adjust as time passes than formalized quotas.

See also **Quota**

Bibliography

Winham, G. R. (1992). *The evolution of international trade agreements.* Toronto, Ontario: University of Toronto Press.

JOHN O'CONNELL

W

WAEC *see* WEST AFRICAN ECONOMIC COMMUNITY

war risk Actual damage caused by war, rebellion, insurrection, invasion, or use of military force to invade sovereign territory with the intent of exerting governing control. Although the definition of war varies considerably depending upon the legal jurisdiction, the fact that war or warlike actions cause severe damage to property is of greatest interest in the present context. Generally, war risk insurance is not available in any standard market. Where war risk is covered by insurance it is most likely to be under a marine insurance policy with war risk added. Land-based property damage by war is rarely covered by any insurance contract, although it is sometimes available through insurance companies that write political risk insurance.

See also **Political risk**

JOHN O'CONNELL

warehouse receipt A warehouse receipt is issued by a warehouser as an inventory of items being stored. Warehouse receipts are often used as proof of existence of goods for the purpose of arranging collateral for a loan. Warehouse receipts may be negotiable or nonnegotiable documents.

JOHN O'CONNELL

warehouse-to-warehouse In ocean marine cargo insurance, warehouse-to-warehouse coverage provides probably the best available continuous coverage for the seller or buyer of goods. In export or import activities the terms of sale are very important in determining the responsibilities of parties with regard to insurance, damage to property, and payment of transit fees. Often buyers or sellers try to save money on insurance premiums by timing the cargo insurance purchase to coincide with transfer of property title as spelled out in the terms of sale. This may cause problems if the insurance is not written correctly or misinterpretations occur as to who has responsibility for insurance during the transportation process. There may also be insurance related problems concerning multiple types of transportation, especially when a policy is written for just the motor truck or the marine portion of the transit.

A cargo policy offering warehouse-to-warehouse coverage protects the financial interests of the insured from the time the goods leave the seller's property until they reach the buyer's warehouse at the final destination. Coverage is provided while in/on truck, ship, warehouse (usually with time limitations for intermediate warehousing) and on to the buyer's warehouse or property.

JOHN O'CONNELL

warehousing In foreign exchange this term refers to the stockpiling of foreign exchange swaps in the hope of profiting by trading them in the future. This is a speculative maneuver which does not always work for the party doing the warehousing.

JOHN O'CONNELL

waybill A waybill is a receipt signifying the sale of an exporter's goods by an agent of the exporter. Exporters often consign goods to agents, who in turn sell the goods to importers or others. This relieves the exporter from having to establish its own international networks of buyers. When an agent sells the exporter's goods a receipt for the sale is provided. That receipt is often referred to as a "waybill" or "consignment note."

JOHN O'CONNELL

West African Economic Community (WAEC) This organization has acted on behalf of member countries to establish freedom of movement and freedom of trade in the region since 1973. Members of WAEC are Cote d'Ivoire, Mali, Mauritania, Niger, and Senegal. The activities of the WAEC include one of the first common customs systems between all members, along with a standardized tax on commodities. The WAEC is also largely responsible for establishing freedom of movement of citizens of member countries throughout the Western African Economic Community. Although the importance of the WAEC has been supplanted by the newer and larger Economic Community of Western African States (ECOWAS), its importance as a pioneer in freedom of international trade and movement of member citizens still stands.

JOHN O'CONNELL

wharfage   When a ship loads or unloads goods or is tied to a dock or pier, a charge is made for the use of the dock or pier. This charge is known as "wharfage."

JOHN O'CONNELL

wholesaler/distributor   Wholesalers/distributors purchase large quantities of goods from suppliers and resell them on international markets. Often individual importers do not have the ability to secure certain products from overseas suppliers or they find that suppliers will sell only in container lots or other large bulk quantities. The inability to secure small amounts of goods at fair prices has led to the development of wholesale international traders and distributors. Wholesale international traders purchase large quantities of goods from suppliers, break them into smaller lots, and resell the goods to

others. By working through the international wholesaler/distributor the smaller business may have access to a larger number of goods than would otherwise be (economically) available.

JOHN O'CONNELL

wholly owned subsidiary   This form of market entry provides a company full control over its foreign operations. This method of market entry requires large capital investment, commitment of time and effort, and normally a willingness of some employees/management to travel to and live in a foreign country. Owned subsidiaries may be existing businesses which are acquired by the company. If this is so the investment in management and expatriate time and effort may not be as significant as a start-up operation.

See also **Market entry strategies**

Bibliography

Cateora, P. R. (1993). *International marketing*. 5th edn, Homewood, IL: Irwin.

JOHN O'CONNELL

WIPO   *see* WORLD INTELLECTUAL PROPERTY ORGANISATION

with particular average   A clause on marine insurance policies that allows the payment of partial losses to covered property.

See also **Free of particular average**

JOHN O'CONNELL

withholding tax   Part of the cost of sending a person overseas on an assignment are the taxes that must be paid in the foreign country. Often taxes are withheld both in the home country and in the foreign country. At other times taxes are withheld in one or the other countries depending upon tax law in the host country. The problem is that if taxes are withheld twice or if withheld by the wrong government, someone is still responsible for paying them. Many countries require an employee of a foreign firm to file a special certification showing that all applicable taxes have been paid "before" the employee is allowed to return to his/her home country. Not only is this inconvenient, but if taxes have not been properly withheld and paid the employee will have to pay them before exiting many countries. It is very important for the employer to become familiar with (or consult with those who are) the tax laws in their own country and in the host country. There may be tax agreements between the countries which will simplify the problem or special forms or other papers that will have to be supplied to assure the proper tax treatment of employee wages and benefits. This is a consideration which must be handled before the employee is sent overseas!

Bibliography

Nexia International Staff (1994). *International handbook of corporate and personal taxes.* New York: Chapman & Hall.

                                    JOHN O'CONNELL

without reserve   When authority to act on behalf of a company is unrestricted it is "without reserve." When an organization uses an intermediary to negotiate or ratify contracts in a foreign country it is very important to specify carefully that intermediary's authority. If authority is given "without reserve," it means that the intermediary has full authority to alter the contract or the terms of the transaction. This type of authority should not be taken lightly, for if the principal (the party hiring the intermediary) does not spell out the details of authority, contracts may be entered into which are not in the best interests of the principal.

                                    JOHN O'CONNELL

workforce diversity   When an organization hires employees from different countries, or even different parts of the same country, workforce diversity occurs. As organizations grow, their workforce normally is comprised of persons of all races, religions, political beliefs, economic status, and geographic regions.

Understanding and developing plans to deal with workforce diversity are essential steps to promoting goodwill among employees and fostering productivity in the workplace. Many of management's most difficult challenges arise because of diversity in the workplace. The major challenge is to motivate all employees toward organizational goals while at the same time allowing diversity to exist.

See also **Cultural diversity**

                                    JOHN O'CONNELL

work permit   Persons who are not citizens of a country normally must receive permission from the government to become employed. Upon granting permission, the government issues a work permit. The person may then be legally employed within the borders of that country.

                                    JOHN O'CONNELL

World Bank   *see* INTERNATIONAL BANK FOR RECONSTRUCTION AND DEVELOPMENT

World Intellectual Property Organization (WIPO)   The World Intellectual Property Organization was created in an attempt to coordinate and enforce intellectual property rights agreements between countries. WIPO has been charged with coordination of the following international agreements concerning intellectual property rights: The Berne Convention for the Protection of Literary and Artistic Works of 1866; the Patent Cooperation Treaty of 1970; and the Paris Convention for the Protection of Industrial Property of 1883. WIPO has also coordination authority for almost twenty other programs or multilateral agreements associated with intellectual property rights protection. WIPO is a special agency of the United Nations.

See also **Berne Convention for the Protection of Literary and Artistic Works; Intel-**

lectual Property; Patent Cooperation Treaty; Piracy

JOHN O'CONNELL

World Trade Center *see* TRADE CENTERS

World Trade Organization (WTO) The World Trade Organization is the successor to the General Agreement on Tariffs and Trade (GATT). On 15 April 1994 the Uruguay Round ended with a resolution which created the World Trade Organization. The WTO is expected to take on the same role with respect to trade negotiations and enforcement of agreements as the International Monetary Fund and the World Bank have with respect to international financial issues. The WTO improves GATT in several ways: (1) the WTO requires a more firm resolution on the part of members to enter into agreements and strictly abide by those agreements; (2) the set of obligations and commitments for each member has been standardized; (3) the organization's dispute resolution program will be given more power; and (4) trade will be treated as an additional topic of international economic negotiations. Under the WTO trade negotiations should proceed at greater speed and with greater adherence to existing agreements.

The WTO will continue in GATT's place as the leading international effort to increase free trade throughout the world.

JOHN O'CONNELL

wrongful calling of guarantees The unfair collection of a letter of credit, on-demand bond, or other guarantee of performance established by a company on behalf of a government. Companies are often required to put up a good faith guarantee of their performance before being allowed to begin work on a contract for a foreign government. For example, a road contractor may be required to provide 10% of the bid amount to a government before the government will allow construction to begin. The guarantee is supposed to provide the government with leverage to force the contract to be accomplished on time and in a workman-like manner. Wrongful calling occurs when the government causes non-performance to occur. Cancellation of the contractor's permit to work in a country or restrictions on working hours could result in non-performance, thereby making the guarantee collectible by the government. Such collection is an example of a wrongful calling of a guarantee.

See also **Political risk; Political risk insurance**

JOHN O'CONNELL

 Y

Yankee bonds Bonds which are issued outside of the United States but are denominated in US dollars. This type of bond must be listed with the United States Securities and Exchange Commission even though it is issued outside the United States.

JOHN O'CONNELL

Yen bond A yen bond is one which is denominated in yen.

JOHN O'CONNELL

— **Z** —

zero haven *see* TAX HAVEN

zero inventory *see* JUST-IN-TIME

INDEX

Note: Headwords are in bold type

A/B *see* airbill
ABEDA *see* Arab Bank for Economic
    Development in Africa
acceptance 1
  banker's 21, 206
  see also bill of exchange;
    documents, against acceptance;
    draft
acceptance financing 1, 108
  see also bill of lading; warehouse
    receipt
account, blocked 28
accountability 1
accounting
  inflation 164
  standardization 2, 9, 165, 168,
    173, 278
accounting differences 1–2
accounting exposure 2
  see also translation exposure
accounting, international 170–2
  and cultural values 170
  and diversity 71, 170
  foreign currency accounting
    114, 123–8
  and harmonization 2, 9, 173, 278
  and individualism/
    collectivism 170, 172
  and International Accounting
    Standards Committee 2, 168
  and lack of consensus 170–1
  and masculinity/femininity 170,
    172
  and power distance 170, 171
  and uncertainty avoidance 172
  see also American Accounting
    Association; foreign currency
    accounting; International
    Congress of Accountants;
    International Federation of
    Accountants; United Nations
    Center on Transnational
    Corporations

accounting system *see* accounting
    differences
accounts receivables 109, 113, 114,
    134
acculturation 2
across-the-board tariff
    reductions 2–3
ad valorem duty 3, 50, 83
  see also duty
adaptability screening 3, 255
ADB *see* Asian Development Bank
address commission 35, 104
  see also cargo broker
Adler, N. 221
admiralty court 3, 202
  see also maritime law
admiralty law *see* maritime law
ADR *see* advanced determination
    ruling; alternative dispute
    resolution
aduana 3
advance against documents 3
  see also bill of lading; letter of
    credit
advance import deposits 3
  and import license 3
advanced determination ruling
    (ADR) 4
  see also reinvoicing; transfer price
advertising, advocacy 4–5
  see also human rights policies
advised letter of credit 4, 4, 193
  see also advising bank; letter of
    credit
advising bank 4
  see also advised letter of credit;
    issuing bank
advisory capacity 4, 33
advocacy advertising 4–5
  see also human rights policies
aesthetics 5
AFDB *see* African Development
    Bank
affective approach to training *see*
    expatriate training

affiliate *see* foreign affiliate
affirmative action 5
  see also equal opportunity; pay
    equity
affirmative dumping
    determination 5
  see also dumping
affreightment *see* contract, of
    affreightment
AFIDA *see* Agricultural Foreign
    Investment Disclosure
    Act 1978
African Development Bank
    (AfDB) 5–6, 244
  see also regional development
    banks
AG 6
against all risks 6, 6
age, and discrimination 112
Age Discrimination in Employment
    Act (US) 112
agencies, supranational 85, 95,
    234, **264**
Agency for International
    Development (AID) 6
agent *see* buying agent; exclusive
    agent; export agent; Lloyd's
    agent; resident buying agents;
    resident selling agents;
    shippers agent
agreement corporation 6
  see also edge corporation
Agreement on Customs
    Valuation 6–7, 281
  see also General Agreement of
    Tariffs and Trade
Agricultural Foreign
    Investment Disclosure Act
    of 1978 (US; AFIDA) 7
agriculture
  and appropriate technology 11
  capital intensity 188
  and exports 45
  and reference price 243

Compiled by Meg Davies (Registered Indexer)